MODERN LAW ENFORCEMENT
WEAPONS & TACTICS

2nd Edition

By Tom Ferguson

Edited by Jack Lewis

DBI BOOKS, INC.

About Our Cover

For the beat cop, there's not much need for a concealable sidearm, but for those who must rely on stealth, the handgun must be kept out of sight as much as possible. And that's the focus of this edition's covers.

On the left is one of the newest auto pistols from Smith & Wesson, the Model 3954. Called the counterpart of the famous Chief's Special revolver, this 9mm Parabellum is only an inch thick through the grip. It's comfortable to carry and easy to shoot, even for those with small hands. With a double-action-only trigger system, the Model 3954 is extremely simple to operate, like a double-action revolver. And with no decocking levers of any kind, the gun has a snag-resistant profile that allows close carry and a smooth draw.

The DA-only system has the slick, consistent trigger pull characteristic of all S&W Third Generation pistols, with slightly shorter travel.

Interested in hard data? The Model 3954 has a 3½-inch barrel, alloy frame with blued carbon steel slide; the hammer is .260-inch semi-bobbed type, while the trigger is .304-inch smooth. The front sight is a post with white dot, while the rear is the excellent fixed Novak with two white dots. Grips are black, one-piece wraparound with checkered panels for a sure hold. Weight? A very manageable 25.5 ounces in its 7-inch overall length that will carry all day without undue stress.

This could very well be the 21st century Chief's Special.

On the right is the Smith & Wesson Model 640 Centennial revolver. Long a favorite for concealed carry in its blued steel guise as the Model 40, it has been reintroduced in stainless steel. This new edition features the original's highly desirable fully-concealed hammer, and virtually snag-proof smooth edges that made it such a popular police and personal carry gun.

The double-action-only trigger pull is consistently smooth throughout its travel, and grips are round butt, smooth Goncalo Alves. With a light weight of just over 20 ounces and overall length of 6¼ inches, this is a neat, compact five-shot revolver that's rated for Plus-P ammunition. Initially available with a 2-inch barrel (shown), now the gun can also be had with a 3-inch tube.

Gone for nearly two decades, the Smith & Wesson Centennial Model is a modern classic made even more modern for the '90s . . . and beyond.

If concealability is what you need for security, Smith & Wesson has it in spades.

Photo by John Hanusin.

Editorial Director
Jack Lewis

Production Director
Sonya Kaiser

Art Director
Rueselle Gilbert

Copy Editor
Kathy Coulter

Production Coordinator
Nadine Symons

Photo Services
Lori Morrison

Lithographic Services
Gallant Graphics

Publisher
Sheldon L. Factor

Produced by

GALLANT CHARGER

OUTDOOR GROUP

ISBN:0-87349-116-5

Library of Congress Catalog Card Number: 86-72618

CONTENTS

INTRODUCTION

Today, in law enforcement, we tend to take many of the technological innovations for granted. It now is possible to communicate voluminous amounts of information in a variety of forms over long distances within seconds.

But in the early Sixties, when I joined the San Antonio Police Department, much of the electronic gadgetry was unheard of. I think this Texas city is typical of what has been taking place throughout the nation, so I asked William O. Gibson, the chief of police, for some recollections.

"In 1964, when I joined the San Antonio Police Department, we had 623 police officers and the city's population was 665,406; there were 213 vehicles, including two river patrol boats. Today, SAPD has 1583 police officers and 389 vehicles — including helicopters — while the city population has increased to 936,000," Chief Gibson reports.

As our cities have grown, so has violent crime, and law enforcement agencies have had to change with the times. In 1983, such agencies were entering the so-called Information Age. In accordance with what was called a "scientific approach," SAPD redeployed its officers to put more officers on the street during peak crime periods. Other cities were doing the same.

In the late Eighties, the nation saw Americans becoming more conscious of the violence that surrounded them. More changes were instituted, including downtown daylight foot patrols, which has a significant impact on crime. Other U.S. cities also returned to what amounted to the old "cop on the beat" system, the presence of a man in uniform proving to be a definite deterrent to crime.

During 1990 and 1991, as we find more and more families breaking up, juvenile crimes and juvenile problems have come to the forefront with gangs and drugs. "Many large police departments are taking another look at their curfew ordinances — other cities are adopting or considering curfew laws," Chief Gibson reports, adding, "We all are exploring new ways of dealing with our juvenile populations."

I think what all this comes down to is that, as law enforcement techniques and equipment have become more complex, the areas and directions for crime have changed. Thus, there is a continuing race for the good guys to stay ahead of the bad...and some techniques that had been all but forgotten have been brought back into play.

Hopefully, this volume will give the reader an idea of law enforcement requirements in the current social atmosphere, as well as what is being done to ensure the safety of our citizens.

Tom Ferguson
San Antonio, Texas

CHAPTER ONE

POLICE REVOLVERS

Down Through Law Enforcement History, The Wheelgun Has Earned Its Still Respectable Reputation

THE TENACITY of the revolver in law enforcement continues to baffle not only arms experts, but the public, and sometimes cops themselves. Brought to near perfection nearly a hundred years ago, the double-action wheelgun serves on without regard to the passage of time. Theoretically, the autoloading pistol should have replaced it in police holsters long ago, and, in Europe, it did indeed topple the old sixshooter from first place. Although the autos are gaining in popularity each day, the revolver is still the mainstay of most law enforcement agencies in North America. The trend is so strong, we're even accused of having an emotional attachment to the gun. Is it true, or is there a good reason for retaining the elderly revolver?

Not long ago, I was in a large western city on business, and chanced to see an acquaintance whose name is well known to the shooting public. This man is a police officer, a gun writer, and a nationally recognized authority on handguns. He's also a longtime competitor in shooting sports, and has won important matches, ranging from IPSC to NRA target competition.

Smith & Wesson was still trying to figure how they might compete with Sam Colt's patents in 1854. This old S&W ad shows the S&W repeating pistol marketed in that era. Nonetheless, it was a step forward in handgun design.

MAKERS OF HISTORY . . . ARMS AND THE MAN

1854

Commodore M. C. Perry arrives in Japan with the first fleet of steamboats in Asiatic waters; diplomatic negotiations open Land of Rising Sun to trade after 200 years of commercial isolation . . . and Smith & Wesson introduces a revolutionary new pistol, a repeater using a self-contained cartridge, a hollow based bullet filled with a propelling charge and detonated with a cap. Crude as this gun seems today, it was then a great forward step, indicative of Smith & Wesson's constant pioneering toward maximum accuracy and safety.

We would be glad to send full details of our various models on request

SMITH & **WESSON**
Springfield   Massachusetts
SINCE   1854

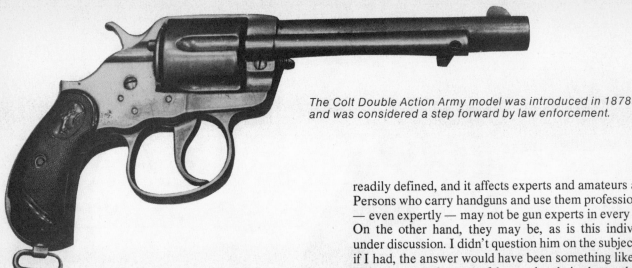

The Colt Double Action Army model was introduced in 1878 and was considered a step forward by law enforcement.

With such credentials, his opinion on handguns, verbal or otherwise, must be respected. In this instance, his actions spoke louder than words. Certainly, he could carry any defense gun he wanted, but the one he wore was a Smith & Wesson M66 .357 revolver.

Good though it is for a uniform holster, the .357 revolver is probably not the best choice for concealed carrying, and is not the gun I'd choose myself. To understand why he preferred the M66, we can theorize logically it may be the gun with which he's most familiar and comfortable. After all, most cops in the United States are armed with a similar medium-frame .38 Special or .357 revolver. This individual's work places him in contact with many police agencies across the country, so there's a compatability factor. It's widely conceded that the .357 magnum with 125-grain JHP bullets has the best street performance of any common cartridge, and this must have influenced his decision.

Still, there's an appeal about the revolver that can't be readily defined, and it affects experts and amateurs alike. Persons who carry handguns and use them professionally — even expertly — may not be gun experts in every case. On the other hand, they may be, as is this individual under discussion. I didn't question him on the subject, but if I had, the answer would have been something like this: "It's not so much a case of the revolver being better than an autoloader. It's more a case of it being entirely adequate, without unnecessary complication!"

It's interesting that the revolver remains good enough to be his first choice, yet critics say it isn't really a state-of-the-art handgun.

Even more harsh, some say — despite modern improvements in sights, rust-resistant alloys, and cosmetic features — it's still the same old revolving-magazine pistol Sam Colt first promoted in 1836. I suspect what they really mean is that it holds only six shots. This limited capacity seems to turn off a lot of otherwise tolerant shooters.

Aside from a barrel and revolving cylinder, Sam Colt's early handguns have little in common with today's police revolver. His first Paterson model guns were five-shooters, not six-shooters. The Paterson was single-action only and had an awkward, delicate mechanism, and poor handling qualities by our standards of today. Even so, the Paterson Colt went right out and built itself a reputation that still lingers on in the minds of those who trust the revolver. They were fighting guns, as were the many improved models that followed in quick succession.

Unlike other innovations of the day, slow to reach the frontier through lack of adequate transportation, the first Colts went where the fighting was almost immediately. The bulk of Paterson model production saw military service in Florida against the Seminoles, then later against the Comanches in Texas. Calibers were light, ranging from the pocket-size .31 to the .40-calbier holster model. Loading was slow with round balls, loose powder and tiny percussion caps. Despite these shortcomings, it was the weapon that defeated the quick-shooting Comanche war bow and made settlement possible.

Some idea of how these primitive revolvers were appreciated can be found in the reminiscences of the men who used them. An early Texas Ranger, Big Foot Wallace, who fought both Indians and Mexican soldiers, stated, "The first Colts we got were small ones, but we used them to good effect. Later we got bigger ones, half as long as your arm!"

In 1856, S&W had developed their first breech-loading revolver loading metallic ammunition. The revolver had a seven-chambered cylinder surrounded by a brass frame!

The L-frame used in building Model 686 S&W is considered a step up from the old K-frame, but some will argue. Stainless steel gun is .357 magnum.

S&W's Model 10 was the source of the maker's K-frame, still in use. It was introduced in 1902 and has been called the most widely accepted police duty revolver ever made anywhere in world.

Hardly a profound statement, but one that indicates the type of revolver preferred on the frontier — one of large caliber taking a heavy powder charge and capable of dropping a horse or man at extended ranges.

The heavy Dragoon and Army model .44s served well and evolved into the Colt Single Action Army of 1873, which fired .45 caliber metallic cartridges. This was the most famous Colt of all, and it continued in popularity long after the frontier had vanished. We seldom think of these Colts as police guns, but in reality they were. The Texas Rangers was a duly constituted law enforcement body, and the U.S. cavalry, aside from Indian warfare, often did as much frontier police work as any civil authority. This long Western experience did a lot to establish the revolver as the preferred weapon in the American imagination.

In spite of the legends the single-action revolver created in the era of westward expansion, there's plenty of evidence improvements were needed even then. Unlike a Texas Ranger, big-city cops always get in trouble up close, and it's always fast and dirty.

As early as the 1850s, San Francisco police patrolling the rowdy Gold Rush tenderloin districts were crying for double-action revolvers to replace their Colt single-actions. As a measure of how serious the need was, we're told they were armed with two percussion Colts and a large Bowie knife, carried in a special pocket in the uniform, to cope with close encounters.

More than likely, the usual revolvers were Colt .36 caliber Navy models, which were relatively common at the time. By and large, it was a wonderful sidearm, but city cops found the single-action mechanism too slow for typical street encounters, the caliber a bit light for certain stopping power.

No doubt they were familiar with the Allen & Thurber or other pepperbox pistols often seen in California's gold fields. Instead of a revolving cylinder behind a single barrel, the pepperbox design consisted of a group of five or six barrels which rotated under the hammer to fire. An early

Colt rival, it was a clumsy revolver design, deficient in many ways. Most lacked sights, and the usual caliber was .31 or .36, no more powerful than the Colt six-guns.

However, the pepperbox had two important advantages: The long barrel cluster, like a miniature Gatling gun, practically eliminated "flashover" ignition of adjoining chambers so prevalent in the Colt. Most of all, it had a double-action trigger mechanism, so useful in close-range defense.

In 1869, Smith & Wesson introduced the .44 American and had it endorsed by Russia's Grand Duke Alexis, who was hunting with Buffalo Bill when he tried this revolver.

MAKERS OF HISTORY . . . ARMS AND THE MAN

1869

Climaxing years of struggle against hostile redmen and the immense natural obstacles of the West, the Golden Spike is driven into a railroad tie at Promontory Point, Utah, joining the oceans with 3,322-mile ribbons of steel . . . Russian Grand Duke Alexis hunts game with Buffalo Bill Cody and finds the new Smith & Wesson .44 American much to his liking. This long, powerful revolver, embodying several entirely new features for enduring accuracy, laid the ground-work for the unbelievably close-shooting Smith & Wesson arms of today.

We would be glad to send full details of our various models on request.

SMITH & WESSON
Springfield TRADE MARK Massachusetts
SINCE 1854

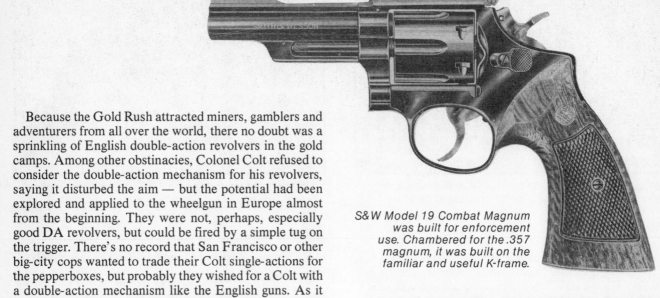

S&W Model 19 Combat Magnum was built for enforcement use. Chambered for the .357 magnum, it was built on the familiar and useful K-frame.

Because the Gold Rush attracted miners, gamblers and adventurers from all over the world, there no doubt was a sprinkling of English double-action revolvers in the gold camps. Among other obstinacies, Colonel Colt refused to consider the double-action mechanism for his revolvers, saying it disturbed the aim — but the potential had been explored and applied to the wheelgun in Europe almost from the beginning. They were not, perhaps, especially good DA revolvers, but could be fired by a simple tug on the trigger. There's no record that San Francisco or other big-city cops wanted to trade their Colt single-actions for the pepperboxes, but probably they wished for a Colt with a double-action mechanism like the English guns. As it happened, they didn't get one while Sam Colt was still alive, or for a long time after his death in 1862.

Few mechanisms or inventions in history have been as misunderstood as the double-action, or trigger-cocking, revolver. For the time, it constituted a controversy as great as ours today over the merits of revolver versus autoloader. Which was "better," the thumb-cocked single-action or the trigger-cocking double-action? Sam Colt was right. Yanking or pulling on a none-too-smooth and primitive DA trigger did disturb the aim. Finer, more accurate shooting was possible with the light SA pull of a thumb-cocked revolver.

One year later, S&W filled an order for 250,000 .44 Russian revolvers. This was a modification of the .44 American. Note the slimmed-down appearance of the gun.

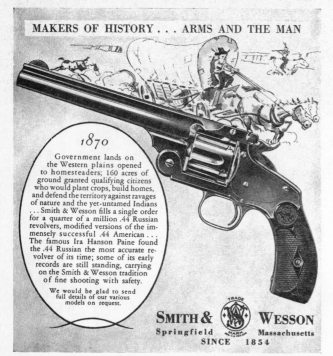

MAKERS OF HISTORY . . . ARMS AND THE MAN

1870

Government lands on the Western plains opened to homesteaders; 160 acres of ground granted qualifying citizens who would plant crops, build homes, and defend the territory against ravages of nature and the yet-untamed Indians . . . Smith & Wesson fills a single order for a quarter of a million .44 Russian revolvers, modified versions of the immensely successful .44 American . . . The famous Ira Hanson Paine found the .44 Russian the most accurate revolver of its time; some of its early records are still standing, carrying on the Smith & Wesson tradition of fine shooting with safety.

We would be glad to send full details of our various models on request.

SMITH & WESSON
Springfield   Massachusetts
SINCE 1854

These embryonic double-actions also tended to be fragile and broke down frequently under use. The DA advocates contended, however, that such a revolver was quicker into action, and, at grappling distance, accuracy wasn't that important. It's significant that, even in later years, the DA feature was considered for emergency use only, and then at close range.

When time permitted, the revolver was thumb-cocked, just as with the single-action. Oddly, neither side seemed to consider that the DA trigger could be utilized to do some pretty fine shooting in the DA mode, as we do today. In fact, this reminds us of the controversy over a cocked and locked SA auto and the newer DA autos, which still continues. While the DA auto has proved immensely popular, there's a great tendency to consider the DA mechanism for hand-to-hand defense use only. In truth, DA auto triggers are being refined to the stage where they are nearly as smooth and clean as a good DA revolver...but not quite.

During the Civil War, a handful of double-action revolvers appeared, including the Starr .36 and .44 caliber percussion models, and a pocket Remington. By the scant accounts that exist, they were well received, but how often they actually were used in DA fashion is a matter of conjecture. The post-war years were dominated by the bigger single-action cartridge guns: the S&W .44 American top-break and, a few years later, the Colt SAA .45 of Wild West fame.

The novelty and convenience of loading with self-contained metallic cartridges made them popular service guns, and advanced features — particularly in the S&W American model — obscured the fact that they weren't double-actions. Frontier conditions still existed, and the two guns were most popular there, not in a big-city policeman's coat pocket. When possible, he chose a smaller handgun, easier to conceal — but few were double-actions.

There was a brief heyday of SA "police revolvers" from Colt and others, notably the Colt New Line model in .38 short and long centerfire, or .41 short and long caliber. Other than convenient size, they had little to recommend them, and were as slow to get into action as the bigger single-actions.

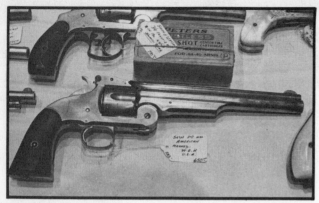

By today's standards, the touted .44 American Model was rather crude looking, but it functioned quite well.

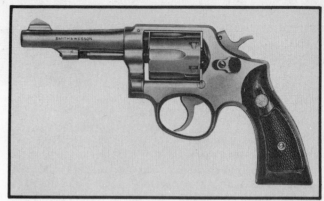

S&W Model 64, introduced in 1981, follows the familiar Military & Police design, chambered for .38 Special.

Although a huge market existed and competition was keen among dozens of handgun manufacturers, there was a surprising amount of trouble experienced in developing a really good, durable double-action revolver. How such a simple camming system eluded good engineers for so long is a mystery.

On January 1, 1877, Colt at last introduced a .38 caliber centerfire DA revolver with birdshead grip, later to be nicknamed the "Lightning" model. The gun was intricate, complicated, and certainly one of the most wretched revolvers ever to bear the Colt name — but it worked well for the times.

For a time, the Lightning was hugely popular among law enforcement people and the gun-toting shadier element alike. Both demanded more power and got it in a .41 caliber version dubbed the "Thunderer." In either bore size, the new self-cocker, as they then were called, figured in more than one legendary shooting affray.

In an era when everyone knew that only single-actions were reliable, frontier cardsharp Luke Short proved the new double-action Colt's worth by using one to kill Big Jim Courtwright, town marshal in Fort Worth, Texas. Both men went for their guns simultaneously, but the speed of bringing the DA .41 Thunderer into action — a virtue predicted by experts all along — was too much for Courtwright's Colt .45 single-action. Short drove a couple of 200-grain .41 slugs into Big Jim's chest, and a third amputated his thumb in the act of cocking his pistol. Courtwright gamely tossed the gun into his left hand to continue the battle, but it was too late. This incident did more than any other to popularize the DA revolver, and we're told Thunderer sales were brisk for some time afterward.

In a later incident, lawman Pat Garrett caught up with the legendary outlaw, William "Billy the Kid" Bonney, in a dusty New Mexico village. Bonney entered a darkened room with a Colt .38 Lightning in hand — Garrett called it a "self-cocker" — but failed to prevail against a well aimed slug from Garrett's own Colt SAA .44-40.

Given the nature and character of a man like Pat Garrett, it's doubtful any gun — even a shotgun — would have done Billy any good that night. Like all successful gunfighters, past and present, Garrett was adept at making it appear to be an even break, when, in fact, he had Billy cold. Against a man like that, no opponent really has any chance

at all. On the other hand, one could have said that about Big Jim Courtwright.

The point is that the Colt Model 1877 just missed, by the slimmest of margins, being the classic police and defense DA revolver from which all others are descended. The size was right, the calibers were adequate — but the mechanism was fragile. After a bit of use and wear, the gun tended to malfunction. Gunsmiths say the tiny, intricate parts were engineered with no tolerance for wear, and the gun just quit working. In addition, it was a gunsmith's nightmare to fix, and gradually developed an exceedingly bad reputation.

During the same period, Smith & Wesson was not idle, and in 1880 marketed their own DA design. The first guns were pocket models, top-break .38s chambered for the .38 S&W cartridge still produced. The firm had been busy fill-

As time marched to 1877, S&W introduced a .38 double-action, favored by many Western sheriffs, according to legend, who carried it as a hide-out or emergency gun.

MAKERS OF HISTORY . . . ARMS AND THE MAN

1877

Union Troops withdrawn at long last from the shattered South . . . re-united nation expands in earnest . . . cattlemen rule the West . . . Eastern railroad men stage the first general strike in labor history . . . and Smith & Wesson introduces the new .38 Double Action, the favorite of many Western sheriffs, who used it as a hide-out or emergency gun, concealed inside their clothes. Small and remarkably fast, this gun was a tremendous aid in preserving Western law and order. Smith & Wesson bases much of its present day supremacy on this arm.

New catalog of modern S & W revolvers now ready. Write for free copy today.

SMITH & WESSON
Springfield   Massachusetts
SINCE   1854

The author considers the SIG-Sauer P220 an excellent vehicle for the .45 ACP cartridge in police use.

.32 ACP as the standard European police cartridge for decades to come. It also put revolvers in such disrepute they never recovered their former status on the Continent.

This story is probably true. The Browning auto was adopted by many police agencies, and the .32 ACP was the most popular police cartridge in Europe. The incident illustrates perfectly why some people prefer the autoloader over the revolver for firepower.

Interestingly, the first autoloading pistols began to appear just as the modern double-action revolver was perfected, about the last decade of the Nineteenth Century. There had been much earlier experiments. In Spain, during the 1860s, one inventor had modified a revolver so it cycled by gas operation, but no really practical autos emerged until thirty years later.

A successful auto design is totally dependent on smokeless gunpowder, and this came into common use about the same time. Generally speaking, the first pistols worked pretty well from the start, and, in the normal course of things, should have made the revolver obsolete overnight, but it didn't happen. The newer DA revolver designs were still new and still too good to discard for a chancy thing like the automatic pistol.

mic neutrino whizzing through a whale. A good jacketed soft- or hollow-point improves any of these small-caliber, high-velocity rounds tremendously, but they weren't common. Full metal jacket bullets functioned better in the early autos, and were first thought to be quite sufficient.

Europe especially was then undergoing a wave of humanitarianism, and expanding bullets were thought to be fiendish. In the Twenties and Thirties, some expanding bullet ammo was loaded here in .30 Mauser, .380 ACP and 9mmP, but discontinued when gangsters began shooting one another with it during the Prohibition era. If this reminds you of anything, it may be the drug wars currently being

In 1956, Smith & Wesson introduced the Model 39 in 9mm, but it received little notice from the law enforcement people.

In addition, handgun designers seemingly felt obligated to create smallbore, high-velocity cartridges for the new pistols, in the same way rifles had been improved.

For example, the first automatic pistol cartridge, the .30 Borchardt, carried an 85-grain FMJ bullet at some 1280 fps, with 312 foot-pounds of energy — almost twice the velocity of the average revolver cartridge. Even so, persons who used the cartridge observed it had minimal stopping power, certainly far less than the slower .44 or .45 caliber revolver rounds.

Velocity alone was not the answer. A felon might be aware that something had passed violently through his body at terrific velocity, but the effect was about like a cos-

fought over our turf. American citizens are about to lose more of their Second Amendment rights and a whole class of perfectly acceptable rifles because these coke-snorting outlaws won't be made to obey the law.

The ungainly Borchardt .30 caliber pistol evolved into the sleek Luger, in time — a better pistol than many think. Some other designs ignored common sense and failed to survive for long.

For instance, some Peiper, Steyr, and Bergmann-Bayard pistols used fixed magazines that loaded from the top with cartridges in stripper clips. This ignored the tactical advantage of detachable spare magazines for a quick reload. Reloading these guns with stripper clips is not that much faster than reloading a revolver to be important.

While Europeans went whole-heartedly for the auto-loading concept, America remained revolver country. Cops and citizens alike considered the auto untrustworthy and prone to malfunction, and, for most of its early career, it was restricted to inefficient FMJ bullets. Police chiefs and patrolmen alike believed they had an ideal police sidearm in the .38 Special DA revolver. The .38 Special, with the round-nosed 158-grain bullet, always had been a bit under-powered, of course, but hardly anyone noticed.

Between the end of Prohibition in the 1930s and the decade of the 1960s, police shooting incidents were relatively rare and peace reigned. Under such conditions, no autoloader — whatever its virtues — stood any chance at all of upsetting the status quo. As late as 1956, when Smith & Wesson introduced their M39 9mm double-action auto, few police agencies showed any interest. The M39 was the first American 9mmP, and had few faults, but the need simply wasn't there.

All that began to change in the 1960s.

With cities burning around them, it's small wonder the cops began to feel the need for improved weapons, if only for self-protection.

The most available autoloader of the times was the Colt .45 ACP M1911, in military or civilian configuration. Because it had an excellent military record as the U.S. service pistol, a number of police departments adopted it, mostly on the West Coast.

The .45 had legendary stopping power, but the police

Ferguson contends the S&W Model 59 did more to break the barrier for the double-action auto in the law enforcement community than any other.

also were aware of the quicker loading ability with spare magazines. Where it was adopted, the .45 auto has usually remained in service, with improved JHP ammunition.

From today's vantage point, we can see that the .45 auto is a better military pistol than a police sidearm. To meet street cop standards of readiness, it must be carried cocked and locked in the holster. This is safe enough in expert hands, but police training isn't always what it should be, and the practice invites accidental discharges. It's also an affront to the public, and public relations are important.

A far better vehicle for the .45 ACP is the SIG-Sauer P220, a state-of-the-art autoloader. The pistol is DA, of course, and can be carried hammer down on a loaded chamber in absolute safety. There is no safety, only a unique hammer drop, which actually lowers the hammer gently. The DA trigger rivals that of the revolver, and the P220 has a well deserved reputation for reliability. Glowing tritium night sights are a sensible option. Not too common in police holsters yet, I predict we'll see more SIG-Sauers, as cops begin to realize their advantages.

No single gun did more than the Smith & Wesson M59 to break barriers and legitimize the DA auto in law enforcement. When introduced in 1971, this high-capacity auto met instant acceptance, and made the 9mmP cartridge

The Browning Hi-Power 9mmP has a large-capacity magazine, but it never has had a big police following.

what it is today: the frontrunner in the caliber race.

The huge initial success of the M59 took even S&W by surprise, for they were backlogged for months. Strangely, cops had routinely ignored the 9mmP for years.

The Browning 9mmP Hi-Power had long been available; it too has a large-capacity magazine, yet few were found in law enforcement.

The reason lay in the ammo, for only the FMJ hardball was available until the late 1960s. When good JSP and JHP 9mmP ammo began to be marketed, interest picked up. Then, like the cavalry riding to the rescue, S&W threw the M59 into the ring. The early guns had a few mechanical bugs, and the model underwent modifications, largely minor in nature.

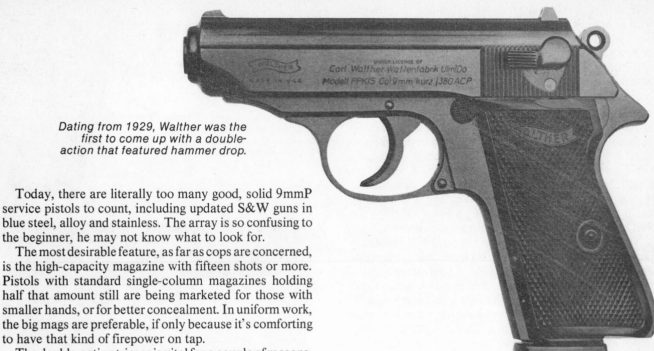

Dating from 1929, Walther was the first to come up with a double-action that featured hammer drop.

Today, there are literally too many good, solid 9mmP service pistols to count, including updated S&W guns in blue steel, alloy and stainless. The array is so confusing to the beginner, he may not know what to look for.

The most desirable feature, as far as cops are concerned, is the high-capacity magazine with fifteen shots or more. Pistols with standard single-column magazines holding half that amount still are being marketed for those with smaller hands, or for better concealment. In uniform work, the big mags are preferable, if only because it's comforting to have that kind of firepower on tap.

The double-action trigger is vital for a couple of reasons. It not only allows quick action in typical snatch-and-shoot incidents at close range, but also permits the pistol to be carried safely with the hammer down.

A third feature, which should be mandatory in every police department, is the hammer drop or decocking lever. This device not only contributes to safety, but is needed for one-hand operation of the pistol, if that becomes necessary. No DA auto lacking this decocking lever should get serious consideration as a service pistol, but there are still quite a few around.

During the Sixties and Seventies, the Colt M1911 .45 auto had a tremendous influence on the shooting public and combat shooting, in general. What developed was a tradition of carrying the pistol cocked and locked, so it was instantly ready when drawn.

In contrast, the first DA autos were equipped with a hammer drop — the Walther PP and PPK dating from

1929 and, later, the Smith & Wesson M39. The "cocked and locked" influence was so strong, however, that this desirable feature was dropped by some manufacturers. Instead, they substituted a DA mechanism that actually could be carried cocked and locked if the owner desired.

This was a giant step backward, in my opinion, yet, for a time, pistols with hammer drops were openly sneered at. At the present time, our most up-to-date pistols have returned to the hammer drop, and the cocked-and-locked DA auto is pretty much relegated to the IPSC circuit. There, many events require a shooter to begin with a cocked-and-locked gun in his holster. We can look for these rules to change in time.

Persons who advocate a cocked-and-locked pistol may not know how frequently accidents occur among large groups of armed individuals. Not all of us are experts, and there's always the danger of a defective gun. I've had many combat veterans from WWII to Vietnam tell me they've seen more comrades shot accidentally with the old .45 auto than the enemy. Much of the time, this occurs when chambering the first round, or in lowering the hammer manually. Careless pointing contributes when the gun fires. We lost a man in Grenada recently in just this manner, so it still happens. After chambering a round, it's much simpler to press a decocking lever to render the pistol safe.

Gunfights involving policemen are quick, nasty little affairs at close range, with few exceptions. Seldom do they last long enough for the pistol to be shot empty, so reloading usually is not required.

In the aftermath of such a traumatic and nerve-wracking event, a cop can be forgiven if his hands shake a little. In a case like this, he'll find a decocking lever most convenient for returning his pistol to a safe condition from the fully cocked mode.

SIG-Sauer's P226 is constructed so that the firing pin remains locked until the instant the gun is fired.

If carrying an older gun without the feature, but provided with a magazine safety, he can drop the magazine a fraction of an inch before lowering the hammer by hand. This, of course, is gilding the lily, for Ruger, Smith & Wesson and others already have pistols that fire in the double-action-only mode, making the decocking lever unnecessary.

Like the decocking lever, the magazine safety was once controversial and the arguments still are heard. During the heyday of the single-column autos, when only seven or eight shots were available, it made more sense, somehow, if the gun could be kept in action with a chambered round while switching magazines. Just how much action one round could provide was rarely discussed, although covering a suspect was considered an advantage. The argument against magazine safeties is losing a lot of validity, now that high-capacity fifteen-shot pistols are common.

There's no question that a cop's service pistol should be provided with a magazine safety. By removing the magazine, he can make the gun instantly safe, not only from accidental firing, but from hands other than his own. All commercially available S&W pistols are equipped with magazine safeties, but the maker will remove it for law enforcement agencies that request they do so. This proves the argument is still alive, if not kicking as hard as it once was.

Ideally, then, a 9mmP service pistol would feature a large-capacity, fourteen- or fifteen-shot magazine; a smooth DA trigger; a hammer drop or decocking lever; and a magazine safety. There's no need for a manual safety, if the mechanism is constructed so the firing pin remains locked until the instant of firing, as with SIG-Sauer's P226 and the Colt Double Eagle pistols, among others. Carrying an older model DA pistol, with the hammer down on a loaded cartridge and without the firing pin lock feature, is risky business. The unrestrained inertia firing pin still can fly forward and fire the gun if it's dropped, even with the hammer down. The firing pin lock is a must.

A relatively minor, but important consideration is the ejection port, and the rule is: the bigger, the better. Even good pistols will trap an ejected case now and then, which inevitably halts the proceedings until cleared.

Beretta M92 slides are without an ejection port, as such. Instead, the slide is fully cut away from the breech face to the front sight, neatly avoiding any ejection problems. Probably next best are the SIG-Sauer pistols, which have an enormous ejection port that takes a huge bite out of the slide. Fortunately, almost every manufacturer recognizes the problem and provides an enlarged ejection port.

The most common cause of a trapped empty case is a weak or insecure hold on the pistol, followed by defective cartridges. A good rule of thumb is that the smaller the cartridge, the greater the chance of feeding or ejection problems.

Unfortunately, the 9mmP has its share of problems. Cartridges with a marginal powder charge fail to provide enough recoil impulse to operate the slide. Sometimes, one will find a cartridge or two out of the box with bullets loose in the case, capable of being turned with the fingers. Such a round will have incomplete, weak powder ignition, and usually will fail to cycle the gun. The only answer is to check each round before loading it into the magazine or chamber. These precautions apply to pistols of any caliber, of course, not just nines.

With up to fifteen or sixteen rounds available in the

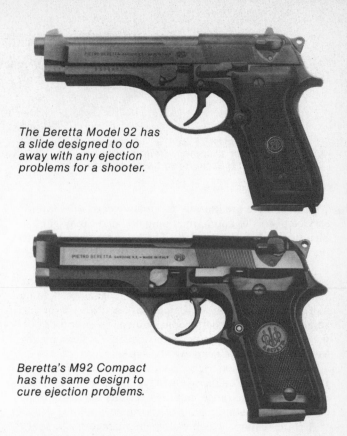

The Beretta Model 92 has a slide designed to do away with any ejection problems for a shooter.

Beretta's M92 Compact has the same design to cure ejection problems.

magazine, there's a great temptation to stagger different loads inside to handle every emergency. This can be a good practice or a bad one, depending on the cartridges. For example, an officer may top off with a pre-fragmented MagSafe or Glaser anti-personnel round for close encounters.

Several of these cartridges may seem like a good idea, followed by half a dozen JHPs. The bottom of the magazine might contain a handful of FMJ slugs, in case of a barricaded suspect or one in an automobile. There's nothing wrong with this theory, as long as it's an established fact that all the cartridges will function the gun. Try them first in actual firing tests. Some 9mms work best with heavier bullets; lighter bullets may not provide sufficient recoil impulse to eject the case and feed the next one from the magazine. The problem can occur in .45 autos — or any other caliber.

Given a large-capacity magazine, there's great temptation to overload it with just one more round. To do so invites feeding problems and stoppages. The magazine spring is over-compressed and can lose strength, break, or take a set. Even if this is avoided, the spring will exert such pressure on the follower it can spread the feed lips slightly, creating another malfunction. If this isn't bad enough, the top cartridge can be under such unrelenting pressure, it may actually freeze to the feed lips and fail to strip properly from the magazine as the slide returns to battery.

Never exceed the recommended load capacity. It's better to have thirteen or fourteen shots you can count on, than seventeen that won't feed in the hopper.

We often hear that magazines should be rotated frequently so the springs can "rest" between tours of duty. With good quality magazines, this is probably unnecessary — and springs don't rest like human muscles.

Much the same relief can be provided by unloading the

The Bren Ten, with its 10mm Auto round, opened up an entirely new field of law enforcement thinking. This auto didn't last long, but others now have appeared.

magazine and waiting a day or so, until the spring resumes normal dimensions and avoids kinks or sets. Wipe it thoroughly with a silicone cloth, including the feed lips, to clear any dirt or corrosion from the brass case. Then it can be reloaded for another extended period.

These big 9mms are getting most of the law enforcement business at present, but there's a trend toward larger calibers. SIG-Sauer's P220 in .45 ACP is available for those who remain loyal to the old service cartridge, along with Colt's Double Eagle. Either of these new DA autos will serve better on patrol than the M1911. The .45 ACP is a fine police cartridge, especially with modern JHP ammunition. It's seen surprisingly little use in law enforcement over the years, and there's no strong movement toward it today. The real momentum is toward a new cartridge: the 10mm Auto.

The original 10mm was a mild little wildcat cartridge of the Sixties, dimensioned to chamber and fire in the converted Browning Hi-Power P-35 pistol. A decade later, it had been lengthened for more powder capacity and factory-loaded to near magnum velocity levels. Along with it came the Bren Ten, an entirely new DA autoloading pistol.

The Bren Ten met with many difficulties in marketing, quality control, and procurement of magazines from outside contractors; in short, everything that usually accompanies a new firearms business. After a couple of halting years, the company folded, and the Bren Ten was no more. It lasted long enough for a few ammunition makers to tool up for the 10mm cartridge, however, including Super Vel and Norma. The Bren Ten was a stout design, and the existing ammo was loaded to high velocity and pressure levels.

Peregrine Industries has brought the Bren Ten out of its ashes, however, with a new name — the Falcon. The name is new; the design is not.

In a surprise move, Colt filled the void with a 10mm version of their Series '80 Government Model 1911 pistol, and called it the Delta Elite. The gun proved popular among individual police officers, but no single-action auto is likely to capture a large segment of the law enforcement market.

Like all other M1911s, the Delta Elite must be carried cocked and locked. In addition, there is now a definite suggestion that the M1911 recoil system is marginal for the full-power 10mm, which leads to gun battering. Installation of a better recoil system, with stronger springs and steel guide, renders the gun satisfactory, but this is a job for a custom pistolsmith.

Although there is no real industry standard thus far, the 10mm Auto began to earn a reputation as an "expert's cartridge" — unnecessarily powerful for police or combat use.

A typical factory 10mm load with a 175- to 180-grain bullet gives 1100 to 1300 feet per second velocity, with attendant heavy recoil. The 200-grain FMJ bullet reaches 1100 fps and kicks even worse; probably more than the average police officer will tolerate gladly.

After extensive ballistic tests, the Federal Bureau of Investigation concluded that the 10mm bore diameter might be ideal for combat use, provided recoil could be reduced to tolerable levels. Their data concluded that a 180-grain JHP bullet at 950 fps velocity would give the desired result, including enhanced penetration and stopping power, over the 9mmP pistols in service. Federal Cartridge Company produced this reduced load, and Smith & Wesson introduced a DA autoloader to accompany it.

Smith & Wesson, under new and dynamic management, is capable of doing some tests of their own. Realizing the basic problems of excess power and heavy recoil, S&W developed the .40 S&W cartridge, a shortened 10mm with reduced powder capacity. The bullet weight is 180 grains and delivers 950 fps in the standard loading. The new round is dimensioned to suit 9mm-size pistols, and is housed in a compact gun called the M1006; it's of stainless steel, of course. Gun capacity is twelve rounds — enough to stay in the running with other high-capacity autos. Still too new to have much of a record, this new .40 S&W may be the gun/cartridge combination of the future.

Do the police really need these fast-shooting lotsa-shots autoloaders to accomplish their basic job of enforcing the law? Or has technology simply surpassed true need with another trendy gadget?

There's little question that, in some circumstances, the need is there. Confrontations with armed militant groups in the Sixties pointed the way. More recently, the infamous Miami shootout in 1986, involving the FBI and rifle-armed felons, showed that the high-capacity autoloader has a definite place in law enforcement.

The double-action auto is as capable as the revolver for close-range reactive shooting, and the big magazine allows sustained fire, if needed. Following the first shot, the subsequent shots are single-action, easy to trigger. Recruit training is faster, as there is no difficult double-action skill to teach.

There never has been a case in firearms history in which a technologically superior firearm failed to supplant an older, less efficient one. We can expect the revolver to remain in cop's holsters for a long time, but gradually we'll see them give way to the big autos.

Smith & Wesson's Model 4006 And Model 4046 — Both In .40 S&W — May Answer The Lawmen's Dream!

The Model 1066 automatic was Smith & Wesson's first 10mm; it was no answer to a compact handgun in that caliber.

WHEN SMITH & Wesson introduced their new Model 4006 pistol in January, 1990, it met with instant approval. In all probability, few — if any — of the S&W staff had any advance conception of the enthusiasm and the rapidity of acceptance in law enforcement circles this pistol and its .40 caliber cartridge generated.

In fact, one gets the impression that this old-line handgun company is pleasantly surprised every generation or so by its own efforts. The handy Model 4006 and the mid-velocity .40 S&W cartridge have been adopted by many law enforcement agencies in its one-year lifespan, including the prestigious California Highway Patrol. Many other departments and agencies are reported to be testing the pistol, but in reality, most of this "testing" is a formality. In many cases, the troops know what they want and it is the S&W Model 4006. Hoping to cash in on the popularity of the mild-shooting but hard hitting .40, most other handgun

manufacturers have models chambered for this round. No doubt some will be accepted.

It would be easy to conclude that the popularity of a given gun/cartridge combination is a matter of sheer luck and good timing.

For example, the last time a Smith & Wesson handgun met with such wild demand was in 1971, with the introduction of the Model 59 9mm double-action auto. The M59 was not the first DA auto by this firm; the single-column eight-shot M39 in 9mm preceded it by years with only mild success.

The M59 wasn't the first large-capacity fifteen-shot 9mm either; other lotsashots 9mms had been around for a long time, including the excellent Browning Hi-Power.

At the risk of being repetitive, the M59 wasn't even the first 9mm double-action big-magazine pistol, but it had one thing going for it: Introduction of the M59 coincided with the marketing of the first really good expanding-bullet

The author rightfully feels that the Model 4006 is a much handier gun (below) than the S&W Model 1006. The former is considerably shorter and more compact and weighs only thirty-nine ounces. Most female officers can handle it.

9mm JHP ammunition.

There had been a few desultory attempts during the 1960s to create a better 9mm round for police and defense work, but these early JHPs were crude and ineffective. By 1971 there was a great improvement and LO! Here was a DA 9mm auto with a large-capacity magazine from a prestigious American handgun manufacturer, to shoot the new ammo. If not for the improved 9mm JHPs which really expanded, the M59 would have been ignored in law enforcement work, just as the Browning Hi-Power had been since 1935.

The Model 4006 chambers a cartridge which meets a pre-existing need and like the hugely popular Model 10 .38 revolver before it, is a happy size for police officers. Sidearms which weigh more than thirty-six ounces are too heavy for packing around all day. The M4006 is still in the ballgame at thirty-nine ounces.

Overall length of the gun with a four-inch barrel is a handy, easily manipulated 7½ inches, important in the toe-to-toe confrontations common to police work. No dainty toy, the pistol is nonetheless of a size most female officers can handle.

The straight backstrap, double-action first shot and no need to switch off a safety make the gun comparable to the best police revolvers for speed into action. Shooting qual-

ities? The recoil from the 180-grain JHP bullet leaving the muzzle at 950 fps can only be described as soft and the resulting 361 foot pounds of energy puts it in the major category, equalling the .45 ACP.

The popularity of the .40 S&W cartridge and the M4006 pistol is the result of fortunate timing. The actual ballistics are old, dating back to the .38-40 WCF cartridge of the 1880s. That heavily tapered revolver round was chambered in Winchester rifles and Colt revolvers so interchangeable ammo could be used out on the frontier where ammunition of any kind was scarce.

The misnamed .38-40 actually used a flat-tipped lead bullet weighing 180 grains and measuring some .401- to .403-inch in diameter. In the case was 40 grains of smoky black powder, which drove the plain lead bullet at about 1300 fps in rifles and 950 fps in shorter revolver barrels. Why it came to have a .38 caliber bullet designation is a mystery.

The heavily tapered case gave easier extraction than the slightly bigger .44-40 in lever-action rifles, with most of the same performance.

Long after frontier lawmen adopted better rifles, such as the Winchester M94 .30-30, the .30-40 Krag M95 Winchester and even the .30/06, the elderly .38-40 remained a favored revolver round. The reasons were exactly the

The AMT Skipper is a single-action auto that now is being chambered in .40 S&W with an eye to law enforcement sales.

same as for the .40 S&W of today, with identical ballistics: recoil was mild and power was ample.

Policemen and defense-minded citizens wanted the .40 S&W all along, but no one offered it to them. Instead, they got the Remington .41 magnum of 1964, housed initially in the heavy N-frame S&W Models 57 and 58. Although a few police departments adopted the fixed sight M58 as late as 1974, the big gun never really found favor with most officers. There were many strikes against the .41 and it didn't survive.

The M58 weighs forty-one ounces empty, which is a lot of weight to pack around on a ten or twelve-hour tour of duty. Female officers found it too big to handle and virtually everyone complained of the recoil. During this period — from 1964 through 1974 — American shooters, in general, were going through a period of magnumania. Probably, for this reason, the heavier .41 hunting load was first on the market. With a 210-grain JSP traveling at 1250 fps, it was entirely unsuitable for police work and created a bad impression with police chiefs and administrators. When the much softer police loading came along, using a lead SWC at a mild 950 fps, it was too late; the damage had been done.

Today the .41 magnum is dead in law enforcement, although it was and still is an excellent police round.

Calibers in the medium .400-inch range keep wanting to happen, but are plagued by incredibly bad luck and/or poor marketing procedures. For a time, there was the .41 Action Express cartridge, invented by Evan Whildin, former vice-president of Action Arms. The cartridge took .410-inch bullets of 170 or 200 grains, but had a rebated rim with 9mm head dimensions. The velocities were good and the cartridge itself is a fine one.

Unfortunately, the Action Arms pistols meant to take it were slow in arriving, then only trickled in. For several years, ammo was fairly plentiful; the problem was in obtaining a pistol for it. Today, only a few guns in .41 AE are marketed and the cartridge isn't threatening to take over the world, as is the .40 S&W.

Simply speaking, the .40 S&W arrived just as shooters were getting tired of fooling with the 10mm Auto and cops were about to give up hope. The 10mm Auto cartridge evolved from a mild, little wildcat round dreamed up by experimental ballistician Whit Collins in the 1960s.

Collins utilized several parent cases for his 10mm wildcat and housed it in converted Browning Hi-Power 9mm pistols. It was meant to offer stopping power superior to the 9mm Parabellum, but with less kick and easier handling qualities than the .45 Auto. It succeeded in this and finally was made legit by Norma and issued as a factory load, but

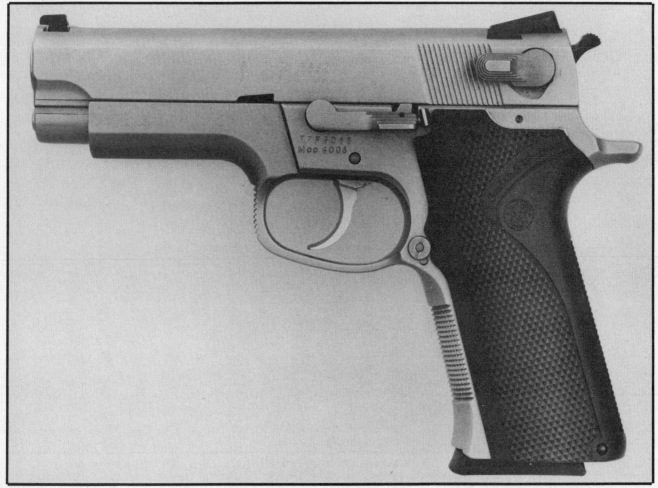

The author feels the S&W Model 4006 is a light, handy double-action automatic that is suited to police work.

much hotter than the original Collins wildcat.

On the West Coast, the firm of Dornaus & Dixon tooled up to produce an advanced automatic pistol for the 10mm, calling it the Bren Ten. The gun had good handling qualities and workmanship, but like the .41 AE autos, it was plagued with troubles. There were magazine shortages — the fault of an outside supplier — and there were quality control problems that resulted in less than perfect guns. Toward the end, there also were indications that the hot Norma 10mm loads were battering and shaking the Bren Ten's teeth out. The company went under, leaving many thousands of Norma and, later, Super Vel rounds lying on dealers' shelves.

Cannily, about 1987, Colt took advantage of the situation and chambered a series '80 M1911 for the 10mm Auto, calling it the Delta Elite. Partly because it was housed in the old reliable M1911 frame, the gun was an instant success at first.

In a short while, though, the Delta Elite also showed signs of abuse from the hot 10mm round. The Norma 170-grain JHP gave 1350 fps in the five-inch barrel, while the 200-grain FMJ bullet reached 1150 fps. What we had was a 10mm Auto magnum, for all practical purposes — along with magnum recoil.

Shooters disliked the sharp, unpleasant kick and the resulting gun damage that usually occurred after some 3000 rounds. The M1911 design will hold the high pressures of the 10mm, but needs a twenty-four-pound recoil spring. The recoil spring guide in the Delta Elite is plastic

Models 4006, 4046 Specifications

Caliber: .40 S&W
Capacity: eleven rounds, plus one in chamber
Barrel Length: four inches
Hammer: (M4046 DA-Only) .260-inch semi-bobbed
Trigger: .304-inch width, smooth faced
Rear Sight: Novak Lo-Mount carry with two white dots
Front Sight: post with white dot
Grips: checkered Xenoy synthetic, one-piece wrap-around; straight backstrap
Construction: stainless steel throughout
Finish: non-reflective
Overall length: 7½ inches
Weight: thirty-nine ounces

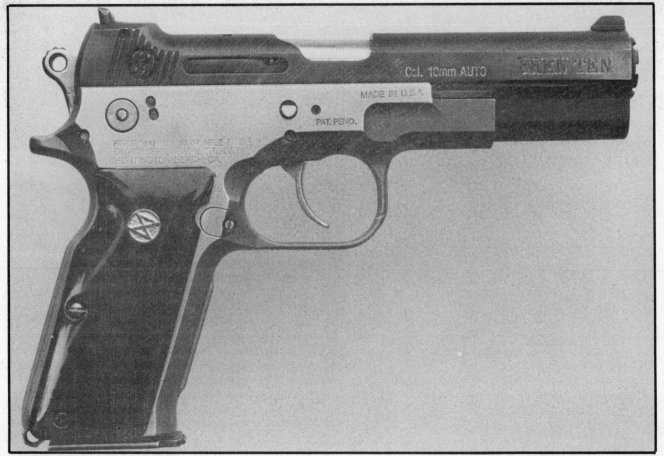

The Bren Ten, no longer made, was the original vehicle for the 10mm Auto round. This particular pistol is being reintroduced in the marketplace as the Falcon 10mm Auto. Whether it has a place in law enforcement is a question.

and should be replaced with one made of steel to take the battering.

Even at this late date, I don't know what the SAAMI pressure specs are for the 10mm Auto, or even if the cartridge has been standardized. It's now being manufactured by Norma, Federal, Remington, Winchester, PMC, Hornady and perhaps others. All use JHP bullets in the 170- to 180-grain range. Norma and Remington are the hottest at some 1350 fps. The Winchester Silvertip is milder to shoot, leaving the muzzle at about 1220 fps. Most of these companies also have the 200-grain FMJ at some 1100 fps, give or take.

In 1986, the FBI got into a bad shootout with two armed felons in Miami, Florida. Before he was slain, one of the agents put a 9mm Silvertip bullet into the chest of one of the gunmen. The 9mm bullet failed by a scant amount of penetration to reach the heart. The felon continued his shooting spree for several minutes afterward. In the subsequent debriefing, it was felt the 9mm JHP had insufficient penetration for combat use. Actually, the Silvertip 115-grain bullet tore through the felon's arm first, then showed normal, even good penetration in the body for this type bullet.

Even so, the FBI experts decided the bureau would be better off with a larger caliber offering better penetration. In the end, they chose the S&W Model 1076 auto, along with a downloaded 10mm cartridge using a 180-grain JHP

at a subsonic 950 fps. The Minus-P load, as some call it, does penetrate well and is pleasant to fire. The M1076 retains the capability of firing full charge 10mm ammo.

The single problem to date with the subsonic 10mm, aside from uncertain bullet expansion, is it doesn't seem to be a particularly accurate cartridge. Where the full-house 10mm 170-grain JHPs such as the Norma load often gives one-inch, twenty-five-yard groups in accurized Delta Elite pistols, the subsonic loads print four- to five-inch groups at best. This is sufficient combat accuracy, but civilian shooters doubt it's an optimum choice.

Someone at S&W reasoned that, if police and civilians alike preferred the mild-shooting characteristics of the 950 fps load, you really don't need that much case capacity to achieve it. The 10mm case was shortened from .992-inch to a mere .850-inch, given a small pistol primer instead of the larger size utilized in the 10mm — and the .40 S&W was a reality.

The smaller pistol was used to avoid striking the primer against the ejector when extracting a live round from the chamber, which could cause an accidental discharge. When the 10mm Auto was reduced in length to .40 S&W, it then was suitable to use in double-column, high-capacity magazines, which in turn could be fitted into smaller, 9mm-frame pistols. It was a happy circumstance.

As for timing, the .40 S&W cartridge and Model 4006 appeared just as the many 9mm pistol owners, mostly

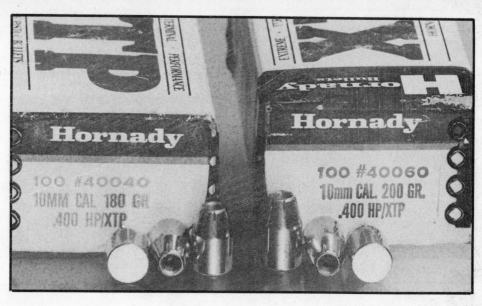

The .40 S&W cartridge takes the same .400-inch bullet as the 10mm Auto cartridge.

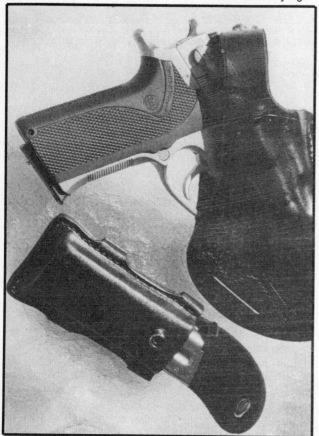

During his tests, Ferguson found the S&W Model 4006 to be small enough for comfortable concealed carrying.

cops, discovered a bit more stopping power was desirable, regardless of the hotter 9mm loads available.

Many departments and many individual officers will keep their 9s, of course, and probably will use the superior Remington and Federal 9mm +P loads at 1250 fps with good expanding 115-grain JHPs. This is the best bet for good street performance in the 9mm autos. Others, however, will switch to the M4006 .40 caliber, which seems to offer more certain fight-stopping ability.

Like all third generation Smiths, the M4006 is a more accurate, dependable pistol than any that have gone before. The M4006 commonly gives two- to three-inch groups at twenty-five yards, equal to the usual .357 magnum service revolver. The old Smith accuracy problems seem to be licked and the .40 S&W, with its lessened case capacity, may be a more inherently accurate round than the subsonic 10mm Auto with identical ballistics.

Smith & Wesson has conducted comprehensive studies on pistol magazines and what happens with them during the feeding cycle. As a result, magazine malfunctions are virtually a thing of the past and the new guns are totally reliable.

In 1991, S&W announced that henceforth all their auto-loaders will be also available in double-action-only configuration, with no external safety controls whatsoever, except the double-action trigger. In operation, they are exactly like the double-action revolver, but can't be cocked. The new double-action-only .40 caliber is designated the Model 4046 and closely resembles the Model 4006.

The various brands of double-action-only lack the sheer firepower of the usual double-action/single-action auto, but are much safer. One can spray the contents of a magazine quicker with a DA/SA pistol, if that means anything in police work. You'll hit more with the deliberate DA trigger squeeze of the DA-only pistol. They may become the norm in law enforcement.

Controllable power in a light, handy sidearm has been the street cop's fervent wish for many years. It looks like we have it in the new S&W Models 4006 and 4046. There already are a lot of them on duty now — and there will be a lot more!

Choice Of A New Handgun For The FBI Isn't Really Settled Yet!

Chuck Karwan uses a convenient boulder as rest as he checks out the Smith & Wesson Model 1076 10mm auto.

IN A SISTER publication, our colleague, Frank James, reported on a 10,000-round torture test of the S&W Model 1006 10mm auto. That particular pistol made an excellent showing for itself and clearly demonstrated that Smith & Wesson had been successful in fielding a normal-size 10mm auto that could hold up to extensive shooting with hot 10mm ammunition. Unfortunately, 10mms from some other makers have not held up nearly so well.

James reported, at the time, that S&W had been awarded a contract by the Federal Bureau of Investigation to supply that agency with some 9500 10mm pistols.

Since then, S&W has delivered most of their contract, and the FBI has been training with and using its new handgun for nearly a year. The basic model adopted by the FBI is the S&W Model 1076NS. The S&W model numbers actually describe the pistol, if you know the code. The first two digits designate the model/caliber, in this case 10mm. The next digit means it has a frame-mounted decocking lever and a "non-standard" mid-length slide and barrel. The final digit in the model designates the pistol's construction material, with 6 meaning all stainless steel.

For a key to all the S&W Third Generation pistol model numbers, you can write to S&W and ask for one of their free, clever, little whiz-wheel model decoders. The NS after the numbers means "night sights" that consist of tritium glow-in-the-dark dot-type inserts with one in the front blade and two in the rear on a Novak Lo Mount sight set. The idea is that, in the dark, the front dot is placed directly between the two rear dots and the sights are aligned.

Chuck Karwan, a longtime student of military and law enforcement tactics and armaments, had been a close observer of the FBI's decision-making progress in regard to obtaining a new handgun for agents. I asked him to tell us what he had learned through his investigations:

The exact pistol supplied to the FBI also is available to civilians except for one feature. The FBI Model 1076NS has no magazine safety; the civilian model does have that feature. Personally, I prefer my combat pistols without that particular feature, because without it, the pistol still may fire the round in the chamber when the magazine is out of the gun as may be the case during a reload. With a magazine safety, once the magazine is unseated, even just slightly, the round in the chamber cannot be fired.

There is no question that the presence of a magazine

In this view of the left side of the pistol, note there is no slide-mounted safety; instead, just below the slide release is the new gun's decocking lever.

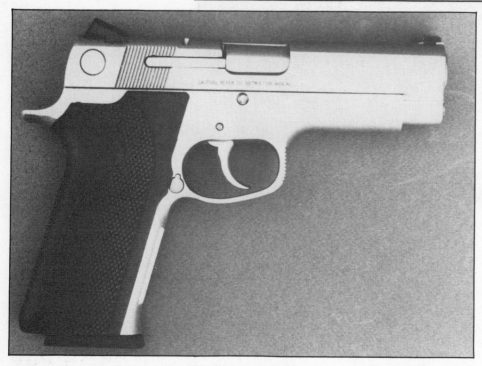

The right side of the auto is relatively smooth; this makes it ideal for hidden carry in civilian clothes.

safety can prevent accidents that may result from improper gun handling. Actually, any advantages of having no magazine safety are more theoretical than actual. The one instance when the presence of a magazine safety really shines is in the home where children or even safety-ignorant adults may have access to the pistol. The pistol can be left safely with a round in the chamber and the magazine removed to a safe place or on one's person. If the pistol is needed, it takes but a second to insert a loaded magazine and bring the pistol to fully operational, loaded condition.

Our test and evaluation S&W 1076 had the magazine safety, but did not have the night sights. Otherwise it is

identical to the FBI-issued version. The biggest departure for this pistol from what we think of as the regular S&W autos is that it does not have a slide-mounted hammer-dropping safety as has been standard on all previous S&W autos.

The Model 1076 pioneers for S&W the use of a frame-mounted decocking lever. The FBI specified this type of operating mechanism for its proposed handgun procurement and S&W complied. Now S&W offers this feature on many other of its models.

The main advantage of a frame-mounted decocking lever is simplicity. There is but one reasonable way to

The Model 1076 has no spur on the hammer. Grips are of one-piece wraparound type many officers favor.

carry the pistol, fully loaded with the hammer down. If you pull the trigger, it will go *bang*. There is no safety to release or to be engaged accidently.

Frankly, I like this simple approach, because I have seen individuals forget to take off their manual safety in the stress of combat. The down side is that, in a snatch situation where the pistol is taken away from its owner, there have been many occurrences when an engaged safety delayed the bad guy from shooting long enough for the good guy to save his own bacon. With the decocking lever system, there is no safety and this advantage is lost.

However, it is important to realize that snatched gun situations apply primarily — though admittedly not exclusively — to uniformed police wearing their sidearm externally.

Since FBI agents carry their handguns concealed the vast majority of the time, I concur with their decision to go with the simpler system.

With the Model 1076, once a round is chambered, the decocking lever is pressed. This automatically lowers the hammer to the carrying position. Interestingly, the carrying position of the hammer is not fully forward, but in a partially cocked position, approximately a quarter-inch back. This has the added advantage of shortening the double-action trigger pull and effectively shortening the trigger reach slightly. This would be of considerable help for those with small hands and/or short fingers.

Since the Model 1076 is designed primarily for concealed carry, it has a spurless hammer to minimize snagging when being drawn. However, manual cocking still can be accomplished easily, because the top of the hammer is serrated.

In size, the Model 1076 is almost precisely to the parent Model 1006 what the Colt Commander is to the Government Model. Both S&Ws have the same size grip frames but the 1076 slide and barrel are .75-inch shorter.

The weight of 36.5 ounces for the M1076 is only two ounces lighter than its M1006 big brother. Depending on the actual load used, this gives the M1076 a full-up loaded weight of about forty-two ounces. That's nearly half a pound heavier than the fully loaded round-butt S&W Model 13 three-inch .357 that was the previous standard-issue FBI handgun. However, these statistics reflect a ten-round capacity versus six for the revolver.

The story behind the FBI selection of the 10mm S&W 1076NS is somewhat controversial. With other law enforcement agencies across the country turning to semi-automatic pistols, the FBI also had been considering a move in that direction. Indeed, by 1986, the FBI Hostage Rescue Team (HRT) was using customized Browning Hi-Power 9mm pistols and FBI SWAT team members were allowed to use S&W Model 59 series 9mm autos. The catalyst that brought the move away from the revolver to a 10mm auto was the blackest day in FBI history.

From top are; S&W's 4506; the Model 1076 ordered by the FBI and the compact Smith & Wesson Model 4516.

In the spring of 1986, eight FBI agents became engaged in a gun battle with two heavily armed and determined bank robbery and murder suspects. The incident has become known as the "Miami Massacre" because of the results.

Of the eight agents involved, two were killed, two were wounded so badly they were permanently disabled, three others were wounded seriously. Both murderers were killed in the exchange, but that is small consolation for the damage they inflicted to the agents.

The incident was examined in microscopic detail to establish what exactly happened — and why. Most subjective observers attribute the poor results to inadequate preparation and equipment, poor tactics and procedures, poor marksmanship — and just plain bad luck.

With regard to inadequate preparation and equipment, most agents involved were without ballistic vests and long guns such as shotguns, submachine guns, rifles or carbines. The shotguns on hand were plain-Jane pump shotguns that are difficult to operate with one hand, slow to reload, sans good sights for accurate shooting of slugs and they were loaded only with ordinary buckshot.

Most of the damage done by the bad guys was inflicted by a .223 Ruger Mini-14 loaded with high-capacity magazines. None of the agents had a comparable weapon. A handgun is rarely the best choice for any combat situation. It is best regarded as an emergency weapon for use when nothing better is available. Even though these particular bad guys were known to be heavily armed, most of the FBI agents went out with only their handguns as armament.

The incident saw eight FBI agents in five separate vehicles attempting a felony car stop, facing off against two heavily armed and extremely dangerous criminals. The poor tactics and procedures became evident by the almost bizarre set of occurrences that resulted. The car stop was accomplished by the questionable procedure of having several vehicles ram the suspect's vehicle.

Prior to the ramming, two agents in separate cars had removed their revolvers from their holsters and put them on their car seats for easy access. When these vehicles made contact with the suspect's vehicle, the revolvers went flying, leaving one agent totally unarmed and the other armed solely with his two-inch .38 backup gun. In another FBI car, impact caused the agent driving to loose his glasses. This agent — probably the best shot on the team — was armed with a high-capacity S&W 9mm, but was rendered nearly totally ineffective by his poor eyesight.

In the post-shooting investigations, it came to light that both bad guys had received multiple buckshot and pistol

From left: Jacketed hollow-points in .45 ACP, .40 S&W and 10mm Auto. All fire 180-185-grain bullets at 950 to 980 feet per second. However, the .45 ACP +P and full-power 10mm, with 180-grain bullets, will travel at 1200 fps.

wounds that had failed to incapacitate them. The Mini-14 wielder who inflicted most of the terrible carnage had received one solid torso hit from a 9mm hollow-point as well as multiple peripheral hits. The 9mm bullet entered from the side — after passing through his arm — inflicting what was determined to be an ultimately unsurvivable wound to the major blood vessels reaching the heart. The tragic consequence was that the killer still was able to murder two of the FBI agents after receiving the 9mm wound to his torso.

John Hall, former chief of the FBI Firearms Training Units (FTU), has been quoted as saying, "All other things aside, Miami was an ammunition failure." I hardly think that is a true or even fair statement. With even less adequate ammunition, but with superior marksmanship, the incident could have had happier results.

Regardless, the FBI conducted a workshop attended by several authorities on handgun effectiveness. As a result, they seem to have adopted the theories, approach, and procedures of Colonel Martin Fackler, M.D., director of the U.S. Army Wound Ballistics Laboratory.

Fackler's simplistic and highly questionable system for predicting the effectiveness of handgun cartridges considers only two ballistic factors. These are distance of penetration and volume of permanent wound cavity as measured in shots fired in ten percent ballistic gelatin. Fackler's theories for predicting effectiveness are considered highly questionable by some, because they do not correlate well with actual field shooting data which is, after all, the ultimate check on the validity of such a theory.

The FBI version of Fackler's theory demands a minimum of twelve inches of penetration to be considered adequate. The magical twelve-inch number allegedly was arrived at by looking at the 9mm performance in the Miami shooting and how much penetration was needed to hit the killer's heart with a shot from the side through his arm!

Using the above criteria, the FBI tested all the handgun rounds available and found the 10mm auto in its full load was the best performer, followed closely by certain high-performance .45 ACP loads.

In investigating further, it was found that recoil and muzzle blast of the full 10mm load was too much for many FBI agents to handle. They then experimented with 10mm loads that were loaded down to about 950 fps with a 180-grain bullet. Using *their criteria,* this version did nearly as well as the full 10mm loads.

It also was decided to adopt a new semi-automatic handgun in 10mm using a standard load that would deliver a 180-grain JHP at 950 fps. Specifications for the new 10mm pistol called for no magazine safety, no manual safety, a frame-mounted decocking lever, stainless construction and twelve-round magazine capacity.

The S&W 1076NS came the closest to fulfilling the specifications, being right on for everything except magazine capacity; it holds only nine rounds. I am told that extension magazines holding twelve rounds are issued to agents to be carried as spares or for use when entering a high-risk situation. Thus, the S&W 1076NS was adopted by the FBI as its standard handgun.

There has been a great deal of criticism of this choice

From left: The old .38-40 — also called the .38 WCF — the 10mm FBI load, the .40 S&W and the venerable .45 ACP. All have roughly the same ballistics, Karwan's research reveals. All will hit about 950 fps with 180-grainer.

based on both the gun and the ammunition. First, there are those who say that, if the FBI wanted .45 ACP-type ballistics — 180-grain bullet at 950 fps — they should have just procurred .45 ACPs and be done with it. Indeed the same exact pistol can be had in .45 ACP — the S&W 4576NS — but with the loss of one round from the magazine.

FBI officials countered with statements to the effect that the 10mm round had more potential for ammunition improvements than the .45 ACP, and that the 10mm has the ability to use higher energy ammunition if desired.

In my own testing, I found that the Model 1076 would handle either FBI-level loads or full-pressure 10mm loads with equal alacrity, though obviously with more recoil with the latter.

Another criticism was that if the FBI wanted sub-10mm ballistics, they should have settled on the new .40 S&W which offers virtually equal ballistics. S&W catalogs a Model 4026 that has all the features of the 1076, except that it is chambered in .40 S&W with a staggered magazine holding eleven rounds. The two pistols are virutally the same in size and weight. The obvious advantage of the .40 S&W is the two more rounds in the magzine. The obvious disadvantage is loss of the capability to use higher performance ammunition like the full 10mm loads.

The full 10mm loads have tremendous potential as carbine or submachine gun ammo. Rumor has it that the FBI is interested in just such a 10mm carbine capable of using high-pressure ammunition. Heckler & Koch has developed a 10mm version of its MP5 submachine gun that has tremendous promise; Glock is known to be working on a 10mm semi-automatic carbine; and D Max Industries has an extremely accurate 10mm semi-auto carbine in production now.

For my money, I would rather keep the high ballistic potential of the 10mm Model 1076 rather than trade it for only two extra rounds in .40 S&W. However, there are other makers of .40 S&W pistols that hold more rounds and some that are smaller and/or lighter in weight.

The original FBI duty ammunition was developed to give 950 feet per second in a five-inch barreled auto. Fired in the S&W Model 1076 with its 4.25-inch barrel, this same ammunition registers about 920 fps. Extensive testing by the FBI revealed the fact that a velocity of 980 fps with the 180-grain JHP bullet resulted in optimal performance. As a result, the current-issue 10mm ammunition is designed to give 980 fps out of the issue S&W Model 1076. Thus, it is a little bit hotter load than the original FBI 10mm specifications required.

The sample Model 1076 was tested thoroughly with full-power 10mm loads and with commercial ammunition that approximated the ballistics of the lighter FBI load. Accuracy was quite good with the better loads doing under 2.25 inches at twenty-five yards from a hand-held, supported position.

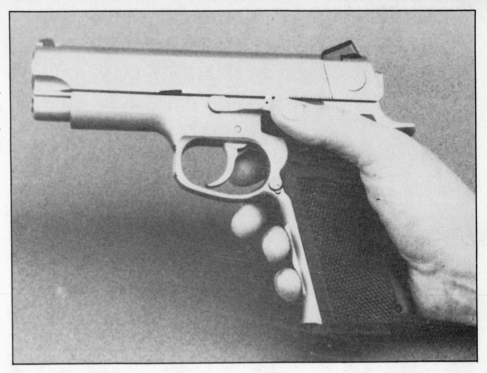

Operating decocking lever of the Model 1076 allows the hammer to rest in its carrying position, slightly to the rear. Hammer does not go all the way forward.

The M1076 grip (left) is thinner than that of the M4006 .40 S&W. Latter is somewhat fatter, but is comfortable in the hand. Thinner grip has the edge for concealability.

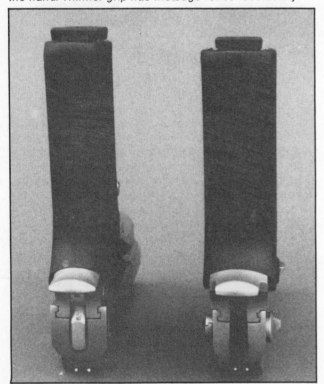

Recoil sensation with the FBI-level loads was quite mild, even less than one would expect from a Colt Government Model .45. With full-power 10mm loads, the recoil was noticeably heavier, but still far more comfortable than the same loads in a Colt Delta Elite 10mm. The full-power loads were flat shooting, and hits on one-foot-square gongs at one hundred yards were easy to achieve just by aiming at the top part of the gong.

All in all, I think the FBI has a hell of a versatile gun in the S&W Model 1076. After working with two different specimens for several months, it has become one of my favorite combat pistols, although a bit big and heavy for many people to carry concealed. Also, there is no compact or lightweight version of the Model 1076 as there is in the S&W Third Generation 9mm, .40 S&W or .45 ACP families — nor is there likely ever to be because of the high pressures of the full 10mm load.

As this chapter is going to press, the FBI has announced that all S&W Model 1076NS 10mm pistols in service are being recalled. Allegedly there have been persistent problems with malfunctions, durability and quality control. I have no idea why this should be, because S&W has spent millions of dollars on manufacturing, testing and monitoring equipment to ensure all pistols produced meet the highest standard. Certainly the basic design of the pistol has been proven.

When the FBI announced that all its S&W Model 1076 10mm pistols in service were being recalled, rumor ran rampant. Conjecture was that they were abandoning either the Model 1076 or the 10mm cartridge altogether. A recent telephone interview with James Pledger, the chief of the FBI's Firearms Training Unit (FTU), revealed that all these rumors should be put to bed.

The primary reason for the recall had to do with the triggers of the M1076s. It seems the FBI approached S&W about reducing the take-up slack in the pistol's trigger when the pistol is in the cocked mode. In an effort to be obliging, S&W developed a trigger for the FBI that accomplished what they wanted. Unfortunately, a problem developed with a few pistols where there was a tolerance stack-up situation; no part was out of specification, but several parts were on the high margin of such specs.

While bugs are worked out of the recalled Model 1076 pistols, the FBI has procurred 1000 SIG-Sauer 226 9mms.

This created a situation in certain circumstances where the pistol, so inflicted, could lock up and refuse to fire. In fact, the pistol cannot be cocked or the slide retracted when this problem is present. This problem was so bizarre that neither the FBI nor S&W had any reason to expect or look for it. Indeed, until a couple of occurrences of this malfunction came to the FBI's attention, there was no inkling of the problem. Once S&W was brought in, their capable engineering staff quickly identified the cause of the problem.

Once the problem was identified, the next question was what to do about it. With about a thousand M1076 10mms in the field and another thousand on hand, it was decided to pull all these guns in for inspection and modification, if necessary.

Jim Pledger said he has complete confidence S&W would be able to totally correct this problem. He further stated that the FBI's contract with S&W for M1076 10mms — a total of 9500 — still is in effect and not in danger of being cancelled. He further stated that the FBI is pleased with the 10mm cartridge and has no plans to abandon it. In fact, he revealed that the FBI is looking at procurring a 10mm carbine for special use and possible future procurement of an even more compact 10mm pistol for those agents who might need one.

Pledger said that since all these pistols were being withdrawn from service temporarily, something was needed to replace them in the interim. Reissuing the S&W revolvers

on hand was rejected for several reasons. First, it was considered a step backward. Also, quite a few of the recent graduates of the FBI Academy had been trained only on the S&W auto and had received no revolver training at all. It was felt that any money saved by issuing revolvers on hand would be lost in retraining those agents on revolvers. Consequently, it was decided to procure a thousand SIG-Sauer P226 9mm pistols to fill the gap until the S&W M1076s were available for issue again.

The SIG-Sauer P226 was a logical choice for several reasons. First, it is a model with which the FBI has had considerable favorable experience, since it was procured several years back for use by FBI SWAT teams. Also, the manual of arms is identical to that of the S&W M1076, both having frame-mounted decocking levers. Thus, little or no retraining is necessary for those agents that had their M1076 replaced with a P226.

Pledger also stated that, with the proper ammunition, they considered the 9mm round to be extremely effective.

The FBI has a personally owned firearms policy that allows agents a wide discretion on the guns they may carry, as long as they are among one of the many makes and models approved, are chambered for one of the approved cartridges and issue ammunition is used. Many agents prefer to carry 9mms for their larger magazine capacity, lighter recoil and, in some cases, lighter weight than the 10mm, .45 ACP or other options.

The FBI's Search For A New Holster To Match A New Pistol Rang Bells At Safariland!

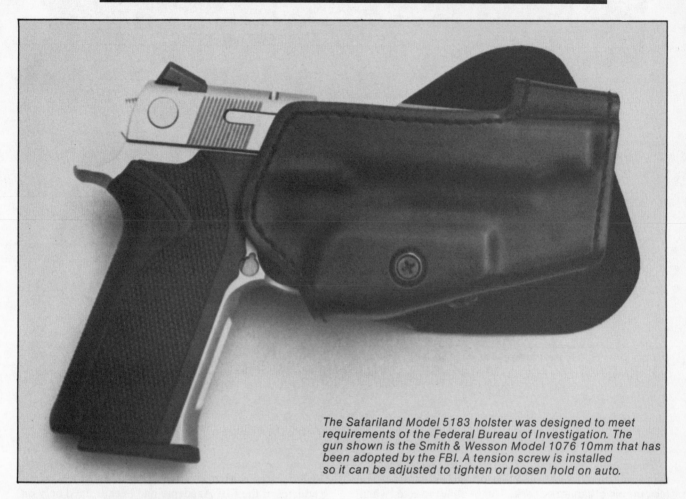

The Safariland Model 5183 holster was designed to meet requirements of the Federal Bureau of Investigation. The gun shown is the Smith & Wesson Model 1076 10mm that has been adopted by the FBI. A tension screw is installed so it can be adjusted to tighten or loosen hold on auto.

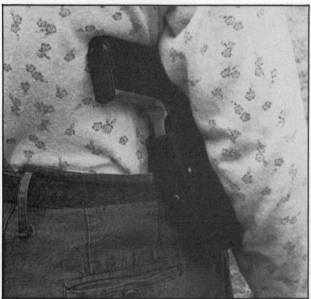

The holster rides high and is held close to the back just behind the right hip. To some, this seems awkward.

WHEN THE FBI adopted a new handgun, it was only natural that they would also have to adopt one or more new holsters as well. Among the companies that answered the FBI's Request for Proposal was Safariland, one of this country's largest and most innovative holster manufacturers. Indeed, their work in thermoplastics, synthetic laminates and other ultra-modern materials is the most extensive of any manufacturer of which I am aware.

Chuck Karwan is one of those who has kept a weather eye on this situation, so I asked him to let us know what is happening. The report that follows is what he has been able to glean through numerous sources:

The folks at Safariland assigned their resident holster genius, Bill Rogers, to the task of designing a holster to meet the FBI's specifications. The results were impressive, to say the least. Rogers turned to the technology used in the latest high-tech competition holsters to invent a new combat holster that represents, in my opinion, a genuine breakthrough in combat holster design and function.

The feature of this new holster — designated the Model 5183 — that separates it from other holsters currently on dealers' shelves and racks is its incredible speed in use,

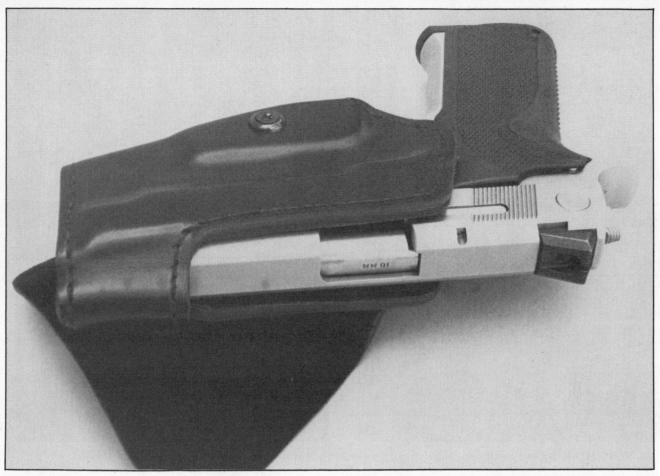

The cutaway section in the front of the holster allows the pistol to be drawn from the front, although a bit of an upward motion is required first. The tension screw assures that the automatic will be held securely in place.

without loss of security. The speed is achieved by having the holster front cut down to just a short distance above the muzzle of the pistol. This allows the pistol to be drawn upward only a short distance, then punched forward into a shooting position with an extreme economy of motion.

The Model 5183 is of the high-ride, strong-side belt type. It would normally be carried just behind the right hip of a right-handed person. By having the front of the holster cut away, the person making the draw does not have to raise his or her arm to anywhere near the degree necessary with a conventional holster. This is especially important to a fast draw when you realize that the gun and holster normally will be carried under a jacket that can restrict movement of the shooter's arms to a significant degree. This is particularly true for those of us that are of "stocky" build.

If the holster is cut away to such a significant degree, how can it be secure? By secure I mean it holds the pistol in such a manner that the gun is unlikely to fall out of the holster, even with vigorous movement.

Actually, security of this holster is brought about in several ways. First is its construction, using Safari-Laminate, a multi-layered laminate created by thermally bonding four different layers of material together. The outer layer is a microporous polyurethane with the feel and appearance of fine leather, but with a far higher resistance to scuffing and much easier maintenance than leather. The middle two

If wearing a sweater or coat, one need only swing back garment and the pistol can be grasped, ready to draw.

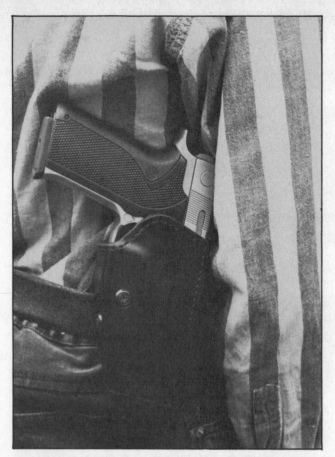

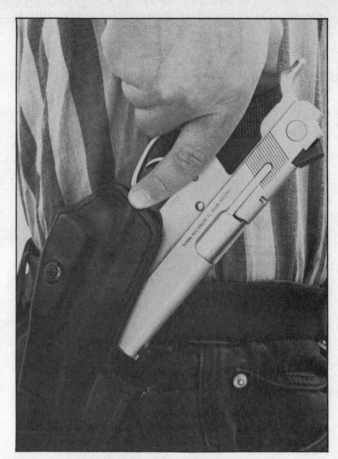

In a normal stance, the arm tends to conceal the outline of the pistol. If a coat is worn, the pistol is concealed.

Looking down into the holster, this is the mechanism to lock the pistol securely when the gun is inserted.

layers are a tough polyvinylchloride that supplies structural strength, shape and stiffness to the holster. The inner layer is a special vegetable-tanned suede that protects the finish of the handgun being carried.

The Safari-Laminate is moulded thermally to the exact shape of the pistol to be carried in the holster. In this way, the pistol is held firmly by the shape of the holster. Best of all, it never will lose its shape as leather is prone to do. To further enhance security, the holster is supplied with an adjustable tension screw that controls how firmly the holster grips the pistol. So far, all the features described are true for most Safariland holsters. The thing that sets the Model 5183 aside from other combat holsters is its use of a patented trigger guard locking mechanism invented by Bill Rogers that grips the bottom side of the pistol's trigger guard in such a way as to prevent the pistol from rotating or moving forward.

There are two spring-loaded cams located in the holster, so the front of the pistol's trigger guard pushes them in as the pistol is inserted into the holster. This, in turn, cams out two arms that fit inside the bottom of the pistol's trigger guard.

The beauty of this system is that the pistol is perfectly secure against movement in any direction, except straight up out of the holster. In addition, it only takes a small movement in that direction — less than one inch — and the pistol is free of the trigger guard lock. The pistol then can be drawn out the front of the holster through the cutaway section. The net result is an extremely smooth draw with a

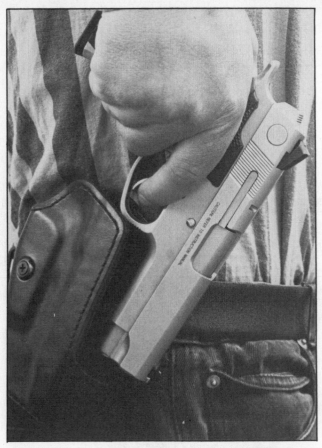
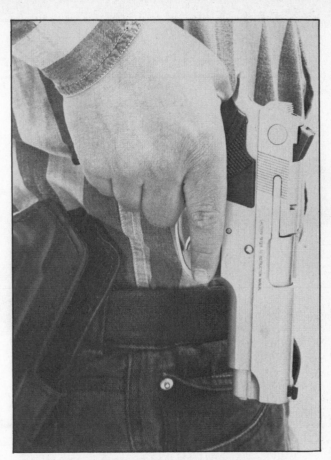

In the next step in drawing from the Safariland holster, the gun is pushed forward through the cutaway front. As seen in the photo at upper right, the handgun then is free to put into action. Practice brings a rapid draw.

minimum of motion. I believe that this is the fastest belt-type combat holster with which I have ever worked.

You also will note that this holster is of the paddle type, which allows quick mounting without undoing one's belt or trousers. In fact, you do not need a belt at all, if your waistband is stiff enough. I suspect that this feature was requested because it is common practice for FBI agents to carry their handguns in their briefcase until actually going into the field. The paddle-type holster is extrememly convenient for such use.

It was found that the Model 5183 carries the Smith & Wesson M1076 close to the body and in a reasonably concealable mode when placed under a jacket. I also found that paddle was reasonably comfortable, but not as comfortable as a similar holster mounted on the belt in the usual manner. Undoubtedly, there will be variations of this holster in the future that will have other mounting systems besides the paddle.

Unfortunately, as this is written, the Safariland Model 5183 holster is available only for the Smith & Wesson Third Generation autos with the same size slide and trigger guard as the M1076. This includes the Models 1076, 1066, 1086, 4566, 4576 and 4586. Other models of pistols will be accommodated later, according to Neal Perkins, president of Safariland.

I firmly believe this holster represents a genuine breakthrough in combat holster technology that will find a ready market among police and gun-carrying civilians. As this is being written, a new and improved version of the holster

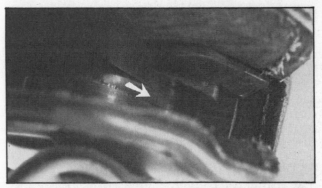

As the front of the trigger guard cams down the lever in the holster (arrow), the other end bobs up to hold the bottom of the trigger guard against inside of unit.

discussed here is being evaluated by the FBI, along with a variety of types from other manufacturers.

An FBI spokesman told me that they would probably adopt several different holsters to suit the needs of different agents, since they come in all sizes, shapes and both sexes. Obviously, what might be perfect for one agent may not work well at all for another.

It still is not known if the Safariland Model 5183 will be one of the holsters adopted by the FBI, but, fortunately, it now is available through commercial channels from Safariland.

Selection Of A New Handgun For Law Enforcement Can Be A Trying Situation For Weapon And Test Staff

When the California Highway Patrol called for firearms companies to submit samples as possible replacement for current revolvers, Colt offered the Delta Elite 10mm.

JIM ANDREWS, now retired, spent most of his law enforcement career with the California Highway Patrol, thus is familiar with the organization and its needs. When it comes to discussing the testing that a handgun — or any other weapon — undergoes in the hands of this agency, we figured he could dig out the facts. Here's what Andrews has to report:

THE CALIFORNIA Highway Patrol was formed in the late 1920s to insure that traffice laws were enforced uniformly throughout the state. Over the years other duties have been assigned to this department, so that today its duties are not exclusively those relating to traffic. With 96,000 miles of highway to patrol, including cities, mountains and locations below sea level, the traffic role alone is formidable. This mileage requires a fleet of close to 2500 class A patrol vehicles, twenty-four aircraft and almost 6300 uniformed sworn officers in over one hundred command locations. They are assisted by over 1000 civilian employees.

During the sixty-odd years of its existence, the CHP has developed a reputation as being a leader in matters of traffic enforcement. This reputation has been built on its ability to change with the times, and not only adopt measures successful in other places, but in being an innovator of practices and procedures.

There is one area, however, in which this agency has been slower than others to make changes. This is in the adoption of a semi-automatic pistol as a primary defensive weapon for its members. For over sixty years, the sidearm of the CHP has been the revolver in .38 Special or .357 magnum chambering.

In the latter part of 1989, the CHP Academy's weapons training staff started an extensive testing program of semi-automatic pistols chambered for the 10mm cartridge and its variants.

While it is unstated in the report, I am sure this caliber was chosen because of the FBI testing program which resulted in that agency adopting a down-loaded 10mm as its cartridge of issue. As with any test program, fault can be found with the methods used by the FBI. However, one

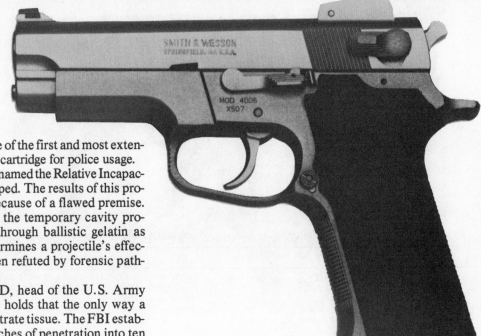

Only three armsmakers submitted samples to the CHP for evaluation. This Smith & Wesson Model 4006 was chosen. It fires the .40 S&W cartridge, a shortened 10mm type.

should not forget that it was one of the first and most extensive of any program to select a cartridge for police usage.

During the 1970s, a program named the Relative Incapacitation Index (RII) was developed. The results of this program have fallen into doubt because of a flawed premise. That premise was to consider the temporary cavity produced by a bullet's passage through ballistic gelatin as being the standard which determines a projectile's effectiveness. This premise has been refuted by forensic pathologists.

Colonel Martin Fackler, MD, head of the U.S. Army Wound Ballistics Laboratory, holds that the only way a bullet can have effect is to penetrate tissue. The FBI established a minimum of twelve inches of penetration into ten percent ballistic gelatin as a standard for judgment of effectiveness.

Concern about over-penetration may well be unfounded. Studies have indicated that almost eighty percent of shots fired by police in times of hazard fail to hit the target, therefore, concern should be about hitting the target rather than the possibility of over-penetration.

Prior to testing of the 10mms, the CHP had conducted a field evaluation of 9mmP semi-automatic pistols. This was more of a study on the carrying of a semi-automatic pistol than a test of pistols and calibers, however. A survey was conducted of the 406 police and sheriff's departments in California, and it was found that the 9mmP was the most common of the semi-atuomatic pistols authorized. Three CHP command areas were selected to participate and several different manufacturers' high-capacity 9mmP pistols were rotated among the officers within these areas. In addition, some of the plainclothes units evaluated the standard capacity 9mmPs. These pistols are more easily concealed.

For CHP testing, Smith & Wesson submitted four automatic pistols. Among them was the Model 1006, a double-action-only configuration that fires the 10mm Auto cartridge.

This evaluation allowed the CHP to determine and solve many of the problems that arise when a policing agency makes a major change in firearms. The problems included types of holsters, magazine pouches, clearing stations and the retraining of officers accustomed to revolvers. This evaluation also allowed the department's gunsmiths and armorers to become familiar with the potential problems that may arise with semi-automatics and prepare themselves.

The 10mm testing program included both objective and subjective factors in the selection process Objectively, the staff members were interested in the problems that might develop during a 5000-round test, the ability of an officer to field strip, clean and reassemble a pistol without tools, availability of spare parts, armorers' classes and any special tools or equipment necessary to service the pistol. Subjectively, they were interested in felt recoil, rapidity of second and subsequent shots, and how easy the pistol was to operate by those with small hands or stature.

To insure that they had all of the information necessary, the staff reviewed records of all members of the CHP who have had their grip strength measured. In addition, critical hand measurements were made of a representative number of the uniformed force. This information allowed the firearms staff to have data to compare with the dimensions obtained from the pistols submitted for test.

Letters were sent to vendors who normally submit bids to the State Office of Procurement, asking them to submit weapons for testing. The only manufacturers to respond were Colt, Glock and Smith & Wesson. Other manufacturers either did not respond or stated that they were not sending weapons.

Glock submitted three models, all of them basically the same pistol. This Glock 22 is virtually the same gun as the original, the Glock 17, but fires the .40 S&W round.

Pistols submitted were:

Colt Double Eagle	10mm
Glock Model 20	10mm
Glock Model 22	.40 S&W
Glock Model 23	.40 S&W
S&W Model 1006	10mm, double-action only
S&W Model 1076	10mm
S&W Model 4006	.40 S&W, frame decocker
S&W Model 4006	.40 S&W, standard safety

When the pistols were received at the academy, they were inspected by the academy gunsmiths to insure they complied with the manufacturers' specifications. After this, the handguns were weighed and measured to determine dimensions, including trigger reach and grip size.

After the initial inspections, the pistols were extensively tested for performance. Accuracy, safety, durability and ease of magazine changes were among the things considered during the firing tests. Subjective evaluations such as recoil were tested, not only by staff, but by members of the cadet class then undergoing training. This was a clever thing to do, since all too often selections are made by recoil-hardened instructors without regard for the people who will carry and use the equipment.

Five thousand rounds of ammunition were to be fired through each pistol, and a malfunction rate established, based on the number of malfunctions. This rate was to be calculated even if the pistol did not complete the entire test.

Parts breakage also was considered and criteria established to consider this. After the initial disassembly for inspection, the firing test was to continue without cleaning or other maintenance. If a pistol failed to function because of a buildup of residue or debris, that was not considered a failure, if it could be resolved by a simple cleaning. Some of the weapons could not complete the 5000-round test program because of parts breakage which rendered the pistol unuseable.

After the firing test was complete, a drop test was conducted to insure that the pistol would not fire accidentally if dropped or tossed a given distance. Another function of this test was to determine whether the pistol would still function after being dropped.

The last evaluation was to determine if the pistol could be field stripped and cleaned by an officer in the field without use of tools. This is an important consideration with the CHP. With offices spread throughout the state, it is possible a user of the equipment could be several hundred miles from the state headquarters and even several hours from his own command location. Also considered was the availability of armorer classes and tools for the armorers.

During endurance testing, note was made on the ease of second and subsequent shots, rapidity of magazine changes and ease of reloading the magazines. All of the standard 10mms were noted as having too much recoil for quick, accurate second shots, even by experienced shooters. The malfunction rate varied from one in eighteen rounds to one in 2545 rounds. The latter was the rate of malfunction for the pistol selected.

In reading the report, one must keep in mind that all of the pistols were pre-production models and that the malfunction rate may not reflect that of the production pistols. One does, however, wonder why there were such problems with

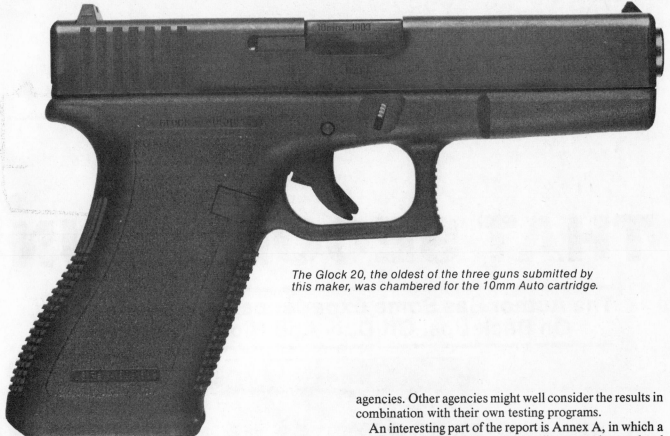

The Glock 20, the oldest of the three guns submitted by this maker, was chambered for the 10mm Auto cartridge.

weapons sent for test by one large agency. There also were more parts breakage in some of the pistols than one would anticipate. I know the CHP testing program is not gentle, but one would think manufacturers would ensure that even pre-production pistols would be fairly well tested before submission. It also appears plastic magazines do not hold up too well when subjected to rough usage.

Included within the CHP report is a disclaimer stating that the tests were conducted to evaluate the pistols only with the unique needs of the CHP in mind and that the procedures and methods may differ from those of other testing

The Glock 23, although chambered for the .40 S&W, has virtually the same specifications as the 9mm Glock 19 Compact. It, in turn, had been cut down from Glock 17.

agencies. Other agencies might well consider the results in combination with their own testing programs.

An interesting part of the report is Annex A, in which a comparison is made between the various rounds tested and those in use presently by the CHP. This chart includes tested velocities, penetration in ten-percent ballistic gelatin and expansion. It is noted that the .40 S&W had the second deepest penetration into the ballistic gelatin — and the largest expansion of any of the bullets that stayed together. Ammunition tested included .45 ACP Winchester Silvertips, the Federal 10mm FBI load and the 125-grain .357 made by Remington for the CHP. The ammunition used to test the 10mm was Winchester's 175-grain Silvertip and the ammunition used in the .40 S&Ws was Winchester's cartridge.

This is a report prepared by people who have the interest of the end user in mind. While it is certainly not the only valid testing program that has ever been conducted, it is a report that should be read and considered by any department interested in a change of pistols. Sergeant Ed Fincel and the academy weapons training staff should be commended for a job well done.

On May 19, 1990, CHP Commissioner Maurice J. Hannigan signed an order adopting the recommendation of the weapons training staff which had selected the semi-automatic pistol as best meeting the needs of the CHP.

At the conclusion of their extensive testing program, the Smith & Wesson Model 4006 chambered in the .40 S&W was the pistol selected. The version selected is the standard model with the slide-mounted safety/decocker, with some modifications deemed necessary by the weapons staff. These modifications include a spurless hammer, rounding of edges in areas which could hurt the shooter's hand and a slight change to the base pad of the magazine. Seven thousand of these pistols have been ordered.

CHAPTER THREE

THAT SECOND GUN

The Author Has Some Experience-Based Opinions On Back-Ups, Off-Duty And Hideout Needs

The Iver Johnson Pony is a small .380 that Ferguson feels is perfect for duty as a backup gun. This one is engraved, personalized.

THERE'S NO doubt some people believe they can ride along on their good luck forever. I recall a conversation I had a few years ago with two veteran police officers, one a patrol sergeant, the other a deputy chief.

We'd known each other for quite a long time and were exchanging opinions on various subjects, including other officers. Some of these cops under discussion, according to the deputy chief, were either so timid or gung-ho they habitually carried an extra gun or hideout piece.

He was contemptuous of this practice and stated, in his opinion, it was over-dramatizing the hazards encountered on patrol duty. In his long career, he never had found the need for a hideout gun and doubted any real need existed. It should be added that although of high rank and therefore

exempt from street work, this deputy chief had proven himself on many occasions and his courage is unquestioned.

The patrol sergeant agreed with this opinion and likewise stated he doubted — though no stranger to trouble — that a need for a concealed weapon, in addition to the service sidearm, could be demonstrated.

This talk left me with the impression both were like small boys scoffing at dangers in the night to prove they weren't afraid.

My respect for them wasn't diminished, but I felt they had short memories. I knew both were aware of a tragic double murder that had occurred in the downtown area only a short distance from police headquarters.

At a nearby motel, an armed robber entered the office late at night, probably with just the thought of making a quick withdrawal from the cash drawer. As he held the night clerk at gunpoint, one of the motel's uniformed security guards strolled unaware into the scenario. Caught by surprise, he was disarmed and handcuffed by the holdup man.

The guard then was forced to reveal the whereabouts of the motel's second security guard. In a couple of minutes, the robber had them disarmed and cuffed. He bound and gagged the clerk with tape, then led both guards into the basement. There he made them kneel and shot both in the back of their heads as they pleaded for their lives. The story came out in his statement after he was captured. Incidentally, the robber didn't receive the death penalty for this double murder.

Would a hideout gun on the person of either guard have prevented their deaths? Or is that the real question? Maybe the question involves whether it would have prevented them from being shot on their knees, begging for mercy. The answer to the latter question is: Yes!

The guards had limited options when first encountering the robber. Perhaps they had seen too many movies in which a man's arms always fly up in surrender when a gun is pointed at him. Then, once disarmed, they had nothing to fall back on. Suppose both or even one of the guards had a hideout gun. The usual line of faulty reasoning goes, "Well, I couldn't go for my hideout piece because he had me covered!"

This is nonsense, of course. You can always go for your hidden gun, as long as your arms are free. Yes, you'll probably get shot. A good thing to remember is that the biggest percentage of handgun wounds are not fatal, even if an incompetent robber manages to hit you.

Another thing to consider is the pipsqueak calibers usually carried by such criminals. Most robbers' guns are intended to intimidate unarmed victims, not win a gunfight. If he's holding a .44 magnum just an arm's length away, you might want to reconsider the choices available. But surrender a .357 six-gun to a .22 or .25 auto? It's a lousy trade.

Suppose you do decide to surrender and suppose the bad guy has a real gun. Consider that even then you'll be putting yourself at the complete mercy and disposal of a person who can't be normal. It gets scary.

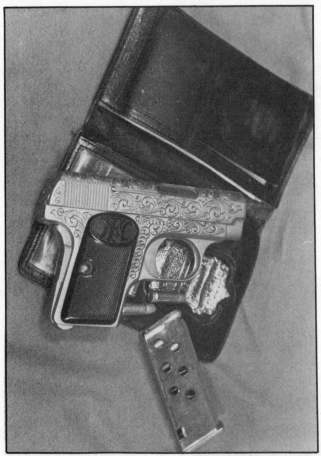

Above: Browning hammerless .25 auto still is on duty in many officers' pockets.

Author considers Walther PP as Cadillac of all .380s. This one served as an off-duty and backup for him, loaded with MagSafe ammo.

S&W Model 6944 9mm is one of author's choices for a hideout gun. This particular model is double-action only.

People who rob motels or even banks just can't cut it doing anything else. Usually they have an I.Q. like the mid-winter temperature figures in Helena, Montana. They probably grew up in a slum without benefit of parents, stole their first bike at age 6 and set fire to a dozen dogs before they hit puberty. Along the way, they picked up a nasty aversion to uniformed authority figures. Still want to surrender your gun to this person? Or if you have a hideout gun, will you go for it?

I'd rather give up to Attila the Hun. It doesn't bother my manhood, policehood or macho image to carry a hideout and I've always done it, sometimes more than one. What's more, I've used them on occasion. Aside from the obvious purpose, they are useful in other situations. Restaurants are a good example.

While I was eating a late supper one night, the restaurant manager alerted me to a nearby table where a would-be outlaw sat eating with a gun under his coat. It was a bit crowded that night and a shoot-out with all those bystanders and witnesses held no appeal. Fetching a .38 Chiefs Special from a boot top, I rose in pretense of paying my bill. Walking instead to the bad guy's table, I let him see the .38's snout from behind my hat, just like John Wayne in the cowboy movies.

I know it sounds ridiculous, but guess what? He stood up and I walked him out and no one noticed a thing. I took a Walther .380 out of his pants, which might have been stiff competition had gunfire erupted.

I could go on with this. I pulled the same trick on two burglars one rainy night. They had been jumped and then had hidden inside a crowded diner. Approaching them with both hands in my raincoat pockets, I opened the coat and showed them the .38 Special. It was only a little two-inch Chief, but again we walked out with no disturbance. Why is this so important? Well, have you ever jerked out your service gun inside such a place? The patrons run and scream, trampling one another, smashing the crockery and forgetting to pay their tab on the way out. The scene

becomes pandemonium. I've been there and prefer the calm scenario.

By far the most popular hideout gun among police officers is some sort of tiny .25 automatic. They are easy to conceal in a uniform and no burden to carry. Let's put the shoe on the other foot and say you are disarmed, but see your chance to go for the little .25. Will your opponent shoot it out with you? If so you may be in trouble, facing your own .357-or-bigger holster gun.

I've already said the .25 auto isn't much in the hands of a robber, yet here you stand holding one on him. Is the situation equal? Not by any means.

The usual opponent probably knows little about guns. He knows guns are deadly and likely thinks any gunshot wound is fatal — most of the time, anyway. Also, you are a police officer and the criminal thinks, therefore, an expert shot who never misses. In addition to these burdens on his fighting spirit, he fears all cops and knows of the public disapproval of shooting one. Then, too, he may simply be a coward. He knows none of the things we discussed in relation to the officer, especially the fact that it's shameful to surrender a .357 to a .25 auto. It seems unlikely he'll carry on the fight, unless it erupts so quickly he fires before he thinks. That could happen, too.

Any officer caught in that situation should fight back the normal instinct to run. The odds are pretty good you can't get far enough way quickly enough to keep from getting hit. If cover is nearby, get to it. You must be close enough to fall down immediately or it's no good. When possible, dump the whole clip in him, not just a trial shot or two.

In most winter uniforms with coats or jackets, there's little problem in hiding just about any handgun that suits you. In summer dress, however, the hideout gun must be small in size and usually in caliber, too. If the gun is too big, a cop simply won't carry it, thinking it not worth the bother. For this reason, the tiny .25 autos are popular and better than no extra gun at all.

A number of small .22 autos are available, but the center-

Author considers the Colt Officer's Model .45 ACP a reliable hideout weapon. A pistol larger than this one is difficult to conceal.

fire .25 ACP is virtually immune to damage from perspiration, unlike the .22 rimfires which carry a flimsy sort of cartridge for this application. In the short barrels of these autos, the .22 rimfire has no advantage in velocity or striking power.

Late one night, I received a call for a street shooting and after arrival discovered the following facts. Two gentlemen of the night were competing for territory in which to display their girls and one had shot the other with a cheap .22 rimfire revolver. He'd been carrying the gun for weeks under his shirt and it got the full benefit of body moisture. The .22 rounds admitted some of the sweat at the case neck where the heeled bullet failed to make a tight seal. The rounds were seriously weakened and of five shots, four of the bullets actually bounced off the victim's chest and stomach. The single .22 slug that entered penetrated only an inch or so, causing a flesh wound.

The lesson is that the .22s make an inferior hideout gun and the waterproof .25 ACP is better in every way. If you must carry a .22 auto, change the cartridges often.

Another gun to avoid, in my opinion, is the derringer. Most are lacking in safety features now considered mandatory, although in careful hands they can and have served. Once, when I owned nothing better, I carried a derringer in my boot. It's a poor hideout, as I learned from packing it around. None have trigger guards and an opponent can wrest one easily away in close encounters. All the modern derringers I'm aware of are about as bulky as a Chiefs Special .38 revolver and thus offer no advantage.

No doubt the next most popular hideout is the little S&W Chief .38, which also serves many officers as an off-duty gun. A round-butt, two-inch Chief is hard to fault as a hideout. For an off-duty gun only, the three-inch barrel version is easier to hit with and milder to shoot. The extra inch of barrel offers a slight ballistic advantage over the two-inch. The only thing to warn of on the Chiefs Special is that all revolvers have many openings and require frequent inspection for the intrusion of lint or pocket debris.

This warning applies to small autos, also. If the slide rails become packed with lint or dirt, you'll get just one shot. Keep any hideout gun clean.

There is the .32 ACP which an officer may prefer, as in the Walther PPK or Seecamp DA auto. Still better is the Walther .380 ACP, a surprisingly serious package. Over the years, I came to prefer the flatness of such autos over the .38 Chiefs Special. Any of the several Colt Mustangs in .380 should be good, particularly the alloy-frame airweight model. The main thing I have to say about any concealable small auto is that it should be of top-notch quality to begin with, then checked out thoroughly in a functioning test. After all, you must be certain the thing will fire if called on. A cheap, bargain-basement gun that fires only once in awhile or breaks down frequently is no bargain.

I had a cute little .25 auto once, made to look like the Baby Browning. It fit neatly in a handcuff case and I carried it for months after a thorough check-out. Functioning was perfect.

I had an offer to buy the gun from another officer who demanded a firing test. To my surprise, the gun malfunctioned with every shot and I lost my customer. The cause is worth mentioning, I think.

In more than thirty years of gun handling, this gun suffered the only genuine magazine spring failure I've seen. This .25 auto had been left loaded so long it took the push out of the dainty spring and it wouldn't feed the cartridges.

Magazines of good quality for bigger guns such as the 9mmP or .45 auto can be left loaded for long periods — some times. All parts in a small pistol are potentially weaker and the smaller the gun, the greater the chance of breakage or failure. Check all hideouts regularly, but check the tiny ones more often.

Where to carry a hideout is a problem and a matter of personal choice. An ankle rig is the slowest, but also the most undetectable and secure. The waistband is usually an uncomfortable place; also slow and not too secure. I once despaired of finding an acceptable carry position and in-

The author confirms that the Grendel P-10 .380 pistol is not much in the looks department, but he insists it can serve an officer admirably as a hideout or extra police weapon. The design of gun is simple and uncomplicated.

vented my own. It was a cheap rig, incorporating two elastic bands from a Second Chance vest, both with pressure fasteners.

I wrapped the bands around my chest up high and put in an old breaktop .38 S&W revolver in a makeshift shoulder holster. The gun rode under my left armpit and once my thin uniform shirt went on, it was virtually unnoticeable and also secure. It was fast, too, for I had merely to slip a hand inside the shirt to get the gun. Many guns will be too heavy for a rig like mine, but a .25 auto will ride.

When a coat or jacket is worn, the problem is over. I used the slash pockets of my jacket to hold either the Walther .380 or a pair of Colt .25s — but I didn't leave the jacket on the restaurant coat rack when I broke for lunch. It went where I went.

Don't bother carrying a spare magazine, speed loader or extra, different caliber rounds for a hideout. If disarmed and frisked by a stout-hearted outlaw, this is a dead giveaway you have another gun somewhere. As another precaution, I tape an extra handcuff key to my boot top or other handy location. The less you leave to chance, the less chancy it gets. I took some ribbing by those few who knew, but I'm still doing business at the same old stand.

Winter uniforms are a good excuse to carry a full-size extra gun. Your coat hides it and you may be glad you had it. It doesn't have to be a mated pair, nor do they need to be the same caliber. A revolver man can tuck away a .45 auto or Browning 9mmP, remembering how each works, if necessary.

There are good reasons for carrying two guns, even if you feel like Wyatt Earp. At times, service sidearms do break or malfunction. In the well known FBI shootout in Miami in 1986, one of the slain agents took a .223 rifle bullet through the slide of his S&W automatic. Even if he'd lived, he still would have been effectively disarmed.

More and more law enforcement departments are switching to the one-gun idea for on duty and off. I don't buy it, but if you must, then you have to. A handgun big enough for duty doesn't really conceal all that well. Then, too, it presupposes the officer is so dumb he can recall only how one gun operates. There is some argument for total familiarity with just a single piece, but it has to be a busy cop who can't find time to learn another.

I like a small off-duty gun and a big on-duty gun. Smaller will do off-duty simply, because the pistol is worn concealed. You can pick your time and place to use it to a large extent.

On duty, in uniform, you must greet each situation as it arises and it may well take all the gun you can get.

Like many others, I carried a Chiefs Special .38 for a long time and it'll do. I like a round butt with grip adapter to fill the hand. It's much better than a set of custom stocks

Browning Baby Model 25 was imported from 1954 to 1968. Importation was dropped because it did not conform to new laws. The Colt Junior Model (left) was made from 1968 until 1973, chambered for .22 short and .25 ACP. Although neither are currently in production, both are sought by officers for use as backup or hideout gun.

that are too big. And I preferred the three-inch-barreled Chiefs.

Gradually, I became unhappy with cylinder bulk and just five shots in the system and switched over to the flat-sided Walther .380 PP. You can conduct plenty of business with those eight shots.

As a sidenote, the Walther PPK model is shorter and just about as good. However, under the grips, it has no back strap. Lint or debris can enter the works over time and I prefer the PP model with back strap.

Not so long ago, penetration to a vital spot was about all you had going for you with these weak hideout and off-duty calibers. The situation is improved with JHP ammo, but we also have the newer "exotic" combat ammo.

I'll say right off that this is an area where the buyer should use caution. Much of this exotic, highly lethal ammo doesn't work as advertised and if it fails, so do you. Better a solid FMJ bullet than fast expanders that offer only shallow flesh wounds — or don't expand at all. The rule is to verify all claims before carrying it as defense loads.

The pre-fragmented Glaser has a good reputation. It has a copper jacket filled with tiny shot that practically detonates on contact due to high velocity. It comes in just about every handgun caliber used in law enforcement. I'm told it does well up close.

The latest advance is the super-hot MagSafe ammo which comes in virtually every handgun caliber. It's not a pre-fragmented bullet, but properly a frangible bullet. The copper jacket has an epoxy core laden with large-size birdshot driven to extremely high velocities. On impact, the jacket ruptures, creating a severe and permanent wound. The jacket fragments, disintegrated epoxy core and the birdshot are flung ahead to make a nasty, deep wound channel.

MagSafe rounds in any caliber from .380 ACP on up make chest wounds practically non-survivable. I have used a lot of MagSafe ammunition — though never on a human opponent — and prefer it to all other exotics. Dealers have it or you can order it from MagSafe Ammo (2725 Friendly Grove Road NE, Olympia, WA 98506).

Finally, I know some individuals who believe in shooting the daylights out of a small hideout gun for the sake of familiarity. I don't agree with this practice and never do it. The more you shoot any gun, the closer it is to breakage or being worn out, just like your automobile.

It brings a smile to read where some budding gunfighter puts five hundred rounds of .44 Specials through his Charter Arms Bulldog in an afternoon. Sure you can do it, but it's wise to have two identical guns. Then you can carry the newer one with the lesser mileage.

Remember, all it has to do is fire when asked — and hit a man at six or seven feet. After that, any other virtue is a bonus.

CHAPTER FOUR

A TREATISE ON SCATTERGUNS

The 12-Gauge Is Much Touted For Law Enforcement Purposes — But Just How Effective Is It?

Shotgun-equipped patrol cars still make sense. A shotgun can be brought into action quickly and it will provide superior firepower in fast-breaking situations. Author also feels there are situations where it's a problem.

Uniformed officers check equipment preparatory to a drug raid. The shotgun is usually included in gear.

FOR MANY years, the police recipe for serious trouble has been the pump-action 12-gauge shotgun and 00 buckshot. Thousands are carried daily in patrol vehicles, mostly unused and being unracked only when it appears that the service handgun won't suffice.

In most cases, the police pump is nothing more than a bird hunter's model with the barrel cut back to a more handy length and eliminating the choke. Few are shorter than eighteen inches, the federally mandated minimum, and none longer than twenty inches.

Longer barreled shotguns do shoot a bit harder, offering a little more velocity, but the convenient shorter length wrings most of the ballistic potential from the shotshell.

Such shotguns are available from most manufacturers: Winchester, Remington and Mossberg, along with numerous less well known names. Increasingly, their police models are being dolled up with warlike appendages, including rifle sights and ventilated metal handguards. You wouldn't mistake one for a sporting shotgun, but essentially it is, with the same handling characteristics and dropped buttstock complete with recoil pad.

This configuration used to be a good idea, but is becoming less so every day, according to armchair theorists and bowling pin combat authorities.

Not so long ago, virtually all police recruits had previous experience with firearms, either in the military or in the hunting fields. The conventional sporter-stocked police shotgun was thoroughly familiar to them, which not only simplified training, but also made these officers deadly effective in combat situations. Handling reflexes were swift and sure, especially among officers with hunting experience. Such an officer armed with a shotgun, even if taken by surprise, might easily down several opponents in the blink of an eye.

Today's police recruit or cadet is more likely to be an urban youth, too young to have military experience and with little or no interest in hunting. The sporter-stocked

police pump holds no advantages for these people, who could mount and aim a ski pole about as readily as a conventional shotgun. In short, they are not accustomed to any type of firearm and training must start from Day One. The usual police shotgun frightens them with recoil and muzzle blast. They flinch involuntarily, pulling the trigger with eyes closed. After a shot, they forget to actuate the pump handle to chamber another cartridge, losing valuable time, or they'll short-stroke it only to hear the firing pin click on an empty chamber. They often confuse the slide release with the safety, punching one when they should have punched the other. Without some fairly intensive training, raw recruits are hopelessly inept with the shotgun.

The shotgun has turned from a superb combat weapon in skilled hands to a liability for the often ill-trained police officer.

To counter the disadvantages of the sporter-type police shotgun, there have been a number of attempts to introduce a more suitable combat configuration. Over twenty years ago, the now-defunct High Standard company built their abbreviated Model 10, a short semi-automatic bullpup design complete with a flashlight mounted on the suitcase-type carrying handle. By all accounts, it was a thoroughly good shotgun, but the unconventional appearance left most cops cold.

A more recent attempt is Mossberg's Bullpup 12, based on the M500 pump action, but likewise of bizarre shape. Mossberg's M500 action is an exceedingly good one, but it remains to be seen if the Bullpup design will catch on. Odds are it will, since younger officers have no bias against military-like shoulder weapons and little special preference for traditional designs.

This is unfortunate, for if military-style, generic-fitting shotguns become the norm, law enforcement will be the loser. A shotgun with a sporting stock such as those now in common use — Remington's 870, the Winchester 1200, the Ithaca M37 — is designed specifically to be lethally

Shotguns carried in patrol cars should be checked on a regular basis by the officers who may need to use them.

Hogan's Alley doorways and windows, firing blank 12-gauge training cartridges at paper opponents.

After the first training exercise with live buckshot, all of the officers had face lacerations, pinched fingers and a bad attitude toward folding metal buttstocks. Scores plummeted and more than one SWAT member discovered he couldn't hit a thing, if firing from the hip with the stock folded.

The place to saw off a shotgun is the barrel, not the stock, which is a vital component that aids in shouldering and aiming the gun. Any close-quarter shotgun ought to have a standard buttstock, but a barrel only twelve to fourteen inches long. Such a gun handles as easily indoors as one with a folding stock and it is far more capable of placing slugs or buckshot where you need them.

Unfortunately, federal law makes these short barrels illegal. To comply with the law, the barrel must be eighteen inches long at minimum. The statute was passed over a half-century ago in a frenzy of anti-gangster legislation during the Prohibition Era. It certainly makes no sense today, when even juvenile gang members have access to submachine guns with ten-inch or shorter barrels.

Why not give the good guys a break and repeal this nonsensical barrel-length restriction? Write your congressman, but don't hold your breath. This is definitely not the Age of Breaks for Good Guys.

I've said the shotgun for police work should have a standard buttstock, but that isn't quite true. In fact, it should be an inch shorter than ordinary to enhance speed in aiming.

What we're talking about is "length of pull," the distance from the butt to the trigger. Hunters measure the length of pull by placing the butt of the gun in the crook of their elbow and reaching to the trigger. If they can place the forefinger on the trigger easily, then the stock fits — or so the saying goes.

Actually, both hunters and police officers would benefit from shorter stocks. The usual way of measuring doesn't take heavy clothing into account, so when the duck hunter mounts his shotgun on a cold rainy day, he finds it awkward and too long. A SWAT officer wearing protective body armor will find the same thing to be the case.

Buttstocks on shoulder weapons have a peculiar characteristic. One that appears or feels too short still can be mounted and fired quickly with great accuracy, but one that is too long by the same amount is hopelessly awkward.

It may seem useless to discuss shotgun fit, for no law enforcement agency issues personalized shotguns and the officer must use what's available. However, many officers do buy their own shotguns when regulations permit. This freedom can be abused unless good judgment is used. One undercover cop I know purchased a Winchester Model 101 over/under and sawed the barrels back to eighteen inches! He overlooked the fact that a good combat shotgun should be cheap as well as reliable.

Good, reliable pump shotguns can be had for relatively low prices. Despite the fact that police shotguns are fired infrequently in anger, they take incredible abuse in other ways.

Partially because of this abuse, the less the shotgun has on it in the way of trickery, the better. Rifle sights are good and reasonably sturdy as well as useful. A box magazine, if introduced by some enterprising manufacturer, would sim-

effective on fleeing, flying game animals. What designers and innovators overlook is that these handling qualities are exactly what are needed for combat use.

Too many modern shotgun designs — both civilian and military styling — have poor handling qualities, in spite of other advantages such as extended magazines and less recoil due to straight-line stocks.

My own rule of thumb is never to take any shotgun into a combat situation that I wouldn't take quail hunting. It's comforting to have an extended magazine holding eight rounds, but it makes the gun muzzle heavy and slow to get into action. A recoil pad is nice, but the soft rubber tends to catch on the shirt when mounting the gun and this could well cost you your life in fast, close action. Under those conditions a sore shoulder is the least of your worries.

A semi-automatic action is fast and relieves one of the burden of actuating a pump handle — until it jams unexpectedly and at the worst possible time. Folding metal buttstocks make a combat shotgun easy to carry and manuever in close quarters, thus are popular with SWAT teams — right up to the time the SWAT member fires his first round and experiences the savage recoil. If the stock is extended, he'll find it awkward to get to his shoulder and even then, the flimsy contraption may collapse when the gun is fired.

A SWAT team in my native Texas raised hell, until the police chief bought them short shotguns with folding metal buttstocks. These scatterguns performed wonderfully in all their training exercises, as they dodged in and out of

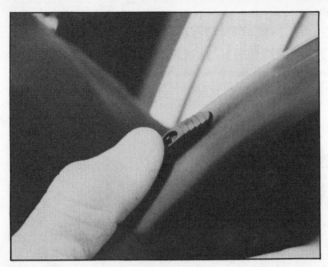

The Mossberg Model 500 police shotgun features a top tang-mounted safety that is fast and ambidextrous.

A Williams 5-D aperture sight is excellent for slug use. This one is mounted on a single-shot 12-gauge raid gun. Author says it's excellent indoors, out or "in between."

plify and speed up loading and unloading drills. Every police shotgun should have a tang-mounted thumb safety like that of the Mossberg M500 series and a firing pin safety.

Normally, the shotgun has an inertia firing pin that is held away from the cartridge primer by light spring pressure. If dropped, thrown or mishandled, the gun can fire a chambered round, even when the trigger-block safety is engaged. Trigger-block safeties are fine for gentlemen hunters, but not so good for rough-and-tumble police duty.

Police shotguns are simple because they better accomplish their intended purpose that way. Police combat is not like military combat in which rapid, sustained fire is necessary. It's true that cops, at times, must face multiple opponents. In such cases, they had better be armed with submachine guns and other automatic weapons, just as the bad guys are. However, superior tactics will be of more benefit to the officer than any increased firepower. It's a matter of using one's head.

More commonly, the officer faces one or, at most, two felons who lack sophisticated weaponry. When that happens, the battle takes on the nature of a personal duel, not an assault on an entrenched enemy position.

The idea is to get at least one shot on target as quickly as possible. Rifle sights, extended magazines, soft rubber recoil pads and recoil-reducing straight-line stocks are absolutely meaningless under these conditions. On the other hand, a shotgun which mounts and aims quickly can be vital and those with awkward weapons will be the losers.

At one point in my career, I deliberately armed myself with a double-barreled 12-gauge for a three-day bodyguard assignment. I took a lot of kidding about my "farmer's gun" from others, less experienced than myself, who couldn't understand why I chose it. After all, anyone knows you have to pack a multi-shot, mean-looking piece of hardware to be effective.

Rather than deliver a lecture, I agreed the old double required a lot of reloading in a fight.

"On the other side of the coin," I added, "I don't miss much with it either." In truth, the double-barrel is still in use with some elite police units in big-city departments.

Currently, a lot of horror stories are floating around about how incredibly tough felons have taken numerous shotgun blasts of buckshot, and even slugs, without going down.

I acknowledge these incidents and won't insult the officers involved by saying they wrote a false report. Someone, however, should throw a few grains of salt at these stories by reminding us that these cases are worth the telling because they are the exception, not the rule. Policemen are supposed to have common sense and common sense tells us anyone taking a full charge of buckshot at close range is not going to be in good physical or mental condition afterward. If an officer can deliver a torso shot at close range, I'll practically guarantee he can handle whatever tricks his opponent pulls later — if any.

Most shotgun arrests are simple, uncontested affairs where no shooting is required. An officer working alone, sometimes even with backup help, may find the shotgun he's holding a distinct liability. What does one do with the thing while handcuffing a prisoner? The main thing is to avoid placing it where others at the scene can get their hands on it. If at all practical, it should be placed in the vehicle with an empty chamber — a best-case scenario. When that isn't possible, the gun can be slipped under the pistol belt at the rear. It's an awkward position, but sometimes the only immediate alterative when you need both hands.

Police shotguns have some disadvantages in spite of their awesome reputation. The shot cloud is a bit too comprehensive in today's crowded cities and effective range is less than that of the handgun.

Much of the work that the shotgun does now could easily be handled by a short, light carbine of semi-automatic persuasion. The carbine could be of pistol caliber or something in .223 (5.56mm) and offer great precision in shot placement and lower recoil. Proper bullet selection — soft or hollow points — would reduce the ricochet factor to less than our buckshot loads.

The police shotgun is a tradition, though, and traditions die hard. We'll probably have shotguns around for quite a while.

The Mossberg Model 500 Intimidator Brings A New Dimension To Combat Shotguns!

Ferguson has long been a proponent of Mossberg's Model 500 for any law enforcement chore. This test didn't change author's mind in any respect.

VIRTUALLY ALL of our nation's major shotgun manufacturers have carried — or still carry in their product line — what they consider a law enforcement shotgun. Most of these makers have had their periods of popularity, their gun — or guns — being adopted by enough police departments to make the project profitable.

But a few seasons later, another maker has come up with an improvement — or at least a change — that struck the fancy of the agency purchasers — or maybe the price was better. The cost component has had a lot to do with police armament sales over the years, you know.

One company that has kept pace with the law enforcement market — both in innovative thinking and sales — has been O.F. Mossberg & Sons (7 Grasse Avenue, North Haven, CT 06473). For several decades, little was said about their law enforcement line. There was no need. It was there and a respectable number of agencies and departments bought Mossberg guns. All of the variations were based upon the maker's familiar Model 500 pump-action that gained initial prominence as the reasonably priced shotgun that farmers kept behind the kitchen door.

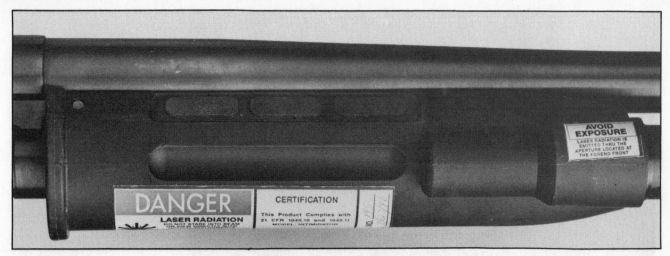

Appropriate warnings are published on the laser unit. This is a serious law enforcement tool and not a toy.

Currently, Mossberg has the shotgun contract for the Department of Defense. This has given the law enforcement line added importance in the eyes of law enforcement purchasing agents, of course. Some of the military thinking also is being integrated into the law enforcement shotguns.

For example, laser sights have been around for several years but only now are becoming popular for use on defense guns. The laser takes all the guesswork out of aiming and once you put the projected red dot on the target, a hit is virtually assured. When this potential is combined with a

With plenty of ammo in his belt, a plastic jug for the target and the laser-sighted shotgun, Ferguson is off to an appropriate river bank for a bit of plain and fancy long-range plinking to check potential of unit.

first-class fighting shotgun like Mossberg's Model 500 12-gauge pump, the result is formidable.

I've been a fan of the Mossberg for more decades than I care to admit. I was attracted initially by the ambidextrous top tang-mounted safety and the rugged action. When my police department decided to sell off our motley collection of shotguns, I campaigned for adoption of the M500 as the standard police shotgun. Today, more than 150 are in use in that department. It's a reliable piece without noticeable flaws.

The laser-sighted Mossberg I've been shooting is cataloged as the #50521, the standard blue police model.

Mossberg's catalog shows five versions of the Model 500 and 590 Special Purpose shotguns, including the military Intimidator model with perforated metal heat shield, bayonet lug and full-length magazine. The laser carries the Intimidator label, also, and is available as an accessory forearm that may be attached to any M500 or M590 shotgun. This is an accurate bit of nomenclature, for any felon on whom that red dot comes to rest isn't likely to be cocky about the situation.

Mossberg may refer to these as Special Purpose shotguns, but they are fighting or combat shotguns; no doubt about it! The M500 deserves a lot more praise than it usually gets. This is the gun that outperformed all competitors in the tough endurance tests set by the U.S. military. All branches of the Armed Forces are equipped with Mossbergs and the ruggedness makes it a favorite of sportsmen and competition shooters.

In addition, Mossberg's M500 also proves a shotgun doesn't have to be ugly to be efficient. The clean, sleek lines tend to remind me of my venerable old Model 12 Winchester that set pump gun standards of beauty.

The M500 action is a great improvement, however. Older pump models had a tilting breech-block that tended to wear and give functioning problems after long use. When operating the Mossberg, you'll notice the breech block rides straight back; there's not much there to get out of order.

The M500 and M590 shotguns have twin everything: two actions bars, double shell extractors, even dual shell

The laser unit beneath the magazine tube is innocent in appearance, but author found it works as claimed.

latches. The receiver is of aluminum alloy to reduce weight, but barrel lock-up inside is steel-to-steel. Thanks to the incorporation of twin parts, the gun still will function if one part is damaged or broken. This is comforting when you realize it isn't uncommon for your weapon to take a hit in a hot firefight.

The laser rides in a neat contoured housing on the right side of the black synthetic forearm and is activated by a finger-pressure switch. It's a Class 111A unit and has a 5 MW max output, according to the label.

The beam may be adjusted with an Allen wrench (not supplied) to approximate the point of aim, using the sights. It's only approximate, because like all pump shotguns, the forearm necessarily has some play and the movement precludes any precise alignment. It's good enough to place a charge of buckshot accurately, but not for slugs at long ranges.

This laser sight is manufactured by Mossberg and they even included the batteries for my testing: three of the 1/3N lithium type. There's no information on how long they last or the effective range of the beam. However, in talking with another laser sight maker, I learned such batteries usually are good for four hundred to five hundred hours and the beam can be seen quite easily out to several hundred yards at dusk or at night.

The ruby-red dot covers about a half-inch at twenty-five yards and is highly noticeable. Mossberg literature says it's designed to prevent confrontation before they start. I understand how it would tend to do that.

But herein lies a problem and a potential danger. It doesn't mean you should bluff or threaten an antagonist. If shooting is required, shoot. I see the laser as a sighting aid rather than a scare device. Under no circumstances would I throw this red dot on a felon's chest, then wait with an arrogant smile for him to give up. The delay of a split second can cost you the battle. If anyone is going to surrender to me in a shooting situation, he had better do it quick!

Speed is, in fact, the key to success with a combat shotgun. Unfortunately, many shooters don't understand this as well as they should. Some designs, especially military experimental models, tend to be awkward and difficult to mount. I've said it before, but quick handling qualities never should be sacrificed for magazine capacity — or for any other reason!

This Mossberg police model gives up nothing in speed of action. The length of pull is correct for me and the cylinder bore barrel is a handy 18½ inches long. This length is plenty to get the most ballistics per bang from heavy buckshot loads.

Magazine capacity is six rounds of 2¾-inch shells and the magazine tube doesn't go all the way to the muzzle. I prefer a tube of this length, for when you stash a full-length tube with buckshot, it gets a bit muzzle heavy. The weight of a combat shotgun should be between the hands, just as with a sporting model birdgun.

Because of a long hunting background, I'm accustomed to mounting the gun fast for running or flying game and, in the past, I have always preferred aimed shoulder fire. I've had little use for hip shooting or shotguns with a pistol grip stock instead of a conventional one. This laser-equipped Mossberg could possibly change my mind.

The gun comes with a pistol grip kit to reduce overall length for use at close quarters. The synthetic buttstock can be detached and replaced with the large finger-grooved pistol grip. So equipped, such shotguns must be fired practically from hip level. For that reason alone, they never have appealed to me.

With the Intimidator laser sight, we have a different situation entirely. Even from the hip, all the shooter need do is put the dot on target and start pulling the trigger. The slug or shot cloud will go to wherever the dot is held. The shortened gun and laser sight makes sense and it's a good entry weapon for SWAT teams. Could a shotgun man pick up the small dot fast enough indoors? You bet he can, even in daylight. It sticks out well.

The accuracy of a laser beam sight is hard to believe. In the early 1970s, I test fired for the San Antonio Police Department one of the first commercially available lasers.

That one was a bulky unit attached rather bulbously to the butt of a Colt .38 New Service revolver. The big gun probably was chosen so the laser sight and its necessary battery wouldn't appear so huge.

Shooting .38 wadcutters from the hip at twenty-five yards on the indoor range, I cut a one-inch ragged hole in the target with five shots. These older lasers were awkward and expensive, costing up to $3000. The Mossberg unit is infinitely more compact and lacks exposed wiring or other encumbrances. Also, it costs about $500 for the entire laser forearm.

After reading the owner's manual, I began a functioning check of the Mossberg and was surprised when the magazine refused to accept more than two shells. Obviously it was plugged. Why anyone would want to hunt game with a police shotgun is beyond me, but I did know a cop once who shot ducks with his patrol car scattergun.

On short-barreled Special Purpose models, it seems that plugging the magazine is a waste of time and money. Anyway, I removed the magazine cap and shook out the small wooden dowel as the manual directs.

I expected no malfunctions and performance matched that expectation. The magazine feeds either 2¾- or three-inch shells interchangeably. Positioned on the anti-jam elevator, the bolt drives them home. With three-inch shells, the magazine capacity is reduced by one round. The action of the test gun was new and therefore not really slick, but if worked smartly, there was no problem. No doubt it would smooth out with use.

This seems a good time to say that pampering a pump shotgun and treating it gently is a mistake. The result is a short-stroke that may fail to chamber a round. It won't hurt it, so always rack the heck out of a pump. This is especially true of pistol-gripped guns.

Shooting slugs and buckshot loads from a light shotgun isn't that much fun. The kick is approximately the same as a .375 H&H magnum rifle and neither gun is a plinker.

On the rear of the Mossberg stock is a ventilated black rubber recoil pad which helps prevent gun headaches during practice. I'm on record as opposing recoil pads, because they can snag on shirts and prevent shouldering the gun properly.

After some amount of shooting with the Model 500 Intimidator, I decided to try some three-inch shells and their heavy payloads of buckshot. After that experience, I figure I now can live with the recoil pad.

Firing inside the parameters usual combat shotgun distance — more than twenty-one feet, but less than seventy-five feet — the Intimidator threw all sizes of buckshot into tight patterns, but all some four inches high. So were the Winchester and Brenneke slugs.

Stamping verifies that the Mossberg is made in USA and that this Model 500A is chambered for 12-gauge shells.

I'd like it if the point of impact was dead on, but this isn't a serious problem. The combat shotgun is no tricky elitist's weapon; it's more like Paul Bunyan's axe. If you do what you're supposed to and shoot at the middle of an opponent, you'll hit him somewhere every time.

The Intimidator laser sight wasn't much help in the bright Texas sunshine. It disappeared completely past ten feet, so all this aimed fire was done with the simple brass bead on the muzzle. The red laser dot is useful only in indoor and in low-light situations, but almost all deviltry occurs in the dark hours, inside or out!

Mossberg — or the end-user — could cure the elevation problem simply by installing a larger, taller brass bead. The bead on the M500 sits atop a hex-sided, tiny brass platform and screws out easily for replacement.

There is no rear sight, but I proved the efficiency of the rudimentary brass bead by exploding plastic gallon milk jugs filled with colored water at a hundred yards, using both Winchester and Brenneke slugs. I had to hold eighteen inches low, but I squeezed carefully and missed few. Recoil was cruel, but the power and accuracy were there. A felon or other enemy caught in the open at this range wouldn't have much of a chance.

The Mossberg Intimidator performed sturdily and well throughout the shooting sessions, with no malfunctions. The laser makes this shotgun a formidable defense proposition for a cop or private citizen who wants the ultimate in protection. The Intimidator sight is compact and affordable; a worthwhile addition to an already superb combat shotgun. The pistol grip is included in the package and, like all Mossbergs, it has a cable and lock system to render the gun inoperable by unauthorized personnel.

SPECIFICATIONS

Action:	pump, twin action bars, anti-jam elevator
Barrel:	18½ inches, cylinder bore, three-inch chamber
Stock:	black synthetic, swivels for detachable sling
Finish:	blue or parkerized
Sights:	brass bead front, special laser forearm
Magazine:	tubular, six round standard length capacity, five rounds of three-inch
Accessories:	detachable pistol grip, cable lock safety for securing and storage
Suggested retail:	shotgun only , $311. Intimidator laser forearm, $500

Mossberg stocks and barrels are interchangeable within gauge.

Update Of An Aging Shotgun Model Gives It New Life For Law Enforcement Purposes!

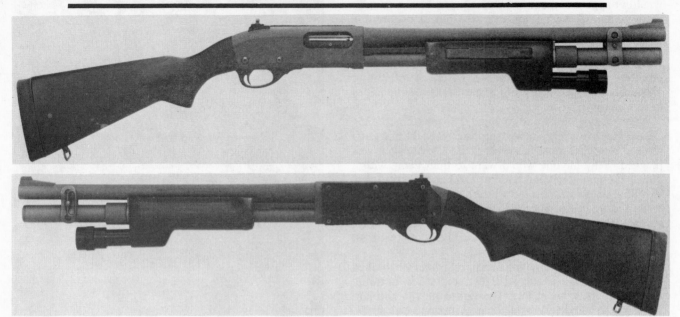

In either left or right profile, the Tactical Response 870 bears little resemblance to the venerable Remington 870. The basic shotgun has undergone major rework by Automatic Weaponry in Tennessee to improve its law enforcement use.

DOWN TENNESSEE way, a batch of folks are working hard to make life easier for working lawmen. This outfit is run by one Roger Small and is called Automatic Weaponry (Box 1124, Brentwood, TN 37024).

These folks have been aware that a lot of police departments have been armed, over the years, with the Remington Model 870 pump-action shotgun. A lot of police officers like this old corn sheller and have come to depend upon it.

In that regard, since it first became available nearly a hundred years ago, the 12-gauge pump-action shotgun has been the overwhelming choice across the nation for serious law enforcing chores.

However, even today the usual police shotgun amounts to nothing more than the cheapest field-grade bird gun equipped with a short cylinder-bored barrel, meaning it has no choke.

Normally, it lacks other refinements as well, including adequate sights. Because of this unsophisticated configuration, two schools of thought have developed within recent years. The negative camp holds that the usual issue pump-gun is far too old and simple to be effective and is not a technologically acceptable tool for modern times. These people want drastic changes in shotgun configuration and ammunition performance. The U.S. armed services have made great progress along these lines, but many of their experimental designs are clumsy and miss the entire point of the fighting shotgun. Suited, perhaps, to a warfare role few are ideal for urban law enforcement.

The other side believes there's not much wrong with the basic shotgun chassis, and a few simple improvements could make it more combat worthy.

I think the sort of fighting shotgun this latter group has been talking about is mirrored in the Tactical Response 870 — the TR870, for short — that is being turned out by Roger Small's Tennessee works.

As suggested earlier, the Remington Model 870 12-gauge in three-inch chambering is designed to take the most powerful buckshot loads — and nobody in the world would mistake it for a bird gun. Modified for law enforcement use by the Tennessee firm, the TR870 retains the quick and lively handling qualities of the sporting M870, so vital in an actual combat role.

Roger Small is a dealer and collector of impressive background and experience. His Tennessee-based company specializes in machine guns, suppressors and short-barreled firearms. His company also offers a number of cut-down smoothbores based on the Remington 870P magnum with Parkerized receiver.

One of these is the famed Witness Protection model favored by the U.S. Marshal's Service, and used in their witness protection program. The little sawed-off is pistol-gripped and has a mere 12½-inch barrel, enabling it to be concealed beneath a coat. Such guns offer better hitting potential at close range and more power than any handgun. The contention is that the nearer the opponent, the faster you must stop him. The short shotgun is ideal for this purpose. I've built or altered a couple of similar shotguns for myself during my years of active enforcement work.

Despite their utility, the useful range of such guns is only a few yards, making them extremely specialized. I was more interested in the TR870 with conventional stock and barrel and requested a test gun from the cooperative Roger Small.

The TR870 fighting shotgun exudes a kind of chunky

One looks through, not at, "ghost ring" aperture sight for precise slug shooting. Ferguson discovered that such sighting systems are becoming common with cops.

reassuring competence. It has a barrel length of eighteen inches and an overall length of thirty-eight inches, measured on my tape. Length of pull is 13½ inches, and the trigger is surprisingly light, crisp and clean. Finish is Parkerizing or dull gray phosphate.

The full-length extended magazine takes a cargo of six standard-length shotshells or five of the three-inch type. There is a black nylon webbed sling attached in such a way that it can't tangle itself around the gun. Permanently attached to the left side of the receiver is a web holder for six extra cartridges. Mounted at the rear of the receiver topside is an adjustable Williams "ghost ring" peep sight for precise placement of slugs.

At the muzzle is a ramped blade carrying a glowing green dot for night shooting. Both buttstock and forend are of tough black synthetic, so solid it can't be considered flimsy in any way. I'm certain the shotgun could be used, if necessary, to deliver a devastating butt stroke and remain intact. My only complaint is the one-inch-thick black rubber recoil pad on the rear.

Recoil pads on fighting shotguns are a dangerous, amateurish nuisance. Real-life firefights don't last for dozens of shots like an afternoon of bird hunting, and there's no place for a recoil pad on a shotgun meant for combat.

Practice? Sure, they're fine for practice. I keep one on my practice shotgun to prevent gun headaches, but my two combat shotguns lack recoil pads. The pliant rubber is almost certain to catch on your shirt when mounting the gun, stopping it halfway to your shoulder. If you're lucky, only a high shot will result. Slick steel or plastic won't hang on anything. While we're on the subject, keep all pens, pencils, cigarettes and other objects out of your shirt pockets when expecting trouble.

The forend of the TR870 is moulded in a bulbous shape in front to accept a high-intensity flashlight. The actuating switch is a long bar on the right side of the forearm. This is no weak, pale and unfocused Mickey Mouse rig. It is a powerful, blinding and truly effective light that would blind an enemy temporarily in dark or indoor situations. SWAT teams and raiding narcotics officers will love it for throwing more light on normally bleak circumstances. To a felon unlucky enough to see both light and muzzle flash, it probably looks like the end of the world has come in demoralizing fashion.

With no intention of re-opening an old controversy, a legitimate question is, "Why a pump combat shotgun from a company named Automatic Weaponry?" After all, there is a trend toward semi-auto shotguns, at least among the competition crowd and combat elite. A friend of mine may have said it best: "Autoloading shotguns (in practice) are just fine and often go through a case or two of shells with no malfunctions. Then, just when you want the damned thing to work, it won't." This pretty well sums up my own feelings — and it's noteworthy that there are no autoloaders in Automatic Weaponry's brochure.

As I was about to test fire the TR870, a unique opportunity arose to put it in the hands of real-life narcotics officers. The men were six agents from the 216th Judicial District Task Force who use similar shotguns in their everyday work. I felt their comments would be more valid than mine — and more up-to-date, as well. I've been through a door or two, but through great good luck, have now reached the age where I prefer to open them first.

To get the opinions of working officers, I placed the TR870 in their care, along with a variety of shotgun ammu-

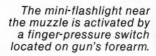

The mini-flashlight near the muzzle is activated by a finger-pressure switch located on gun's forearm.

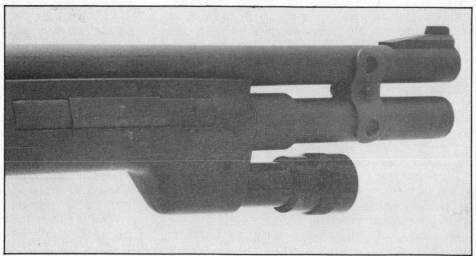

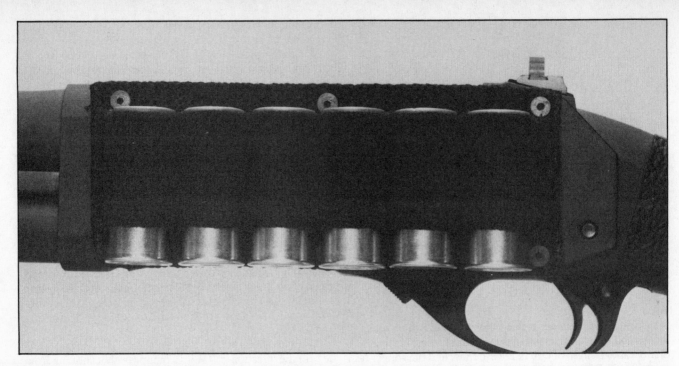

The side-mounted web shell-holder will carry six additional rounds in upside-down position for fast removal and loading. This brings the total number of rounds within easy reach to fifteen, including those loaded in TR870 extended magazine.

nition. Included were Winchester's one-ounce hollow-point rifled slugs, as well as some 1⅛-ounce Brenneke slugs supplied by Roger Small. According to Small, these show the best accuracy. The buckshot was a mixture of both three-inch and 2¾-inch Federals carrying 00 pellets.

Among them was the new Federal H132-00 Tactical Load which uses nine copper-plated 00-size pellets of which not enough good has been said. The velocity has been lowered to some 1150 fps, retaining good effect on close-range human adversaries, but reducing recoil to more tolerable levels. Practically all buckshot available consists of hunting loads traveling some two hundred feet per second faster. It batters veterans and cadets in training, and the extra power simply isn't needed in room-size encounters common to police work. Federal deserves congratulations for recognizing the problem and offering a lethal, but reduced loading. It's a pussycat to shoot, especially in the TR870.

Balancing these were the three-inch Roman candles from the same firm. Designated Premium buckshot, they hurl a fierce broadside of fifteen 00 pellets, and will move your feet in the sand when fired. Heaven only knows what the velocity is, but the striking effect is almost nuclear in character and impact on target. So is recoil, which can only be described as bad. A few such rounds go a long way to satisfy many shooting appetites, and I threw them in to save on ammo expenditure. When you need max power this is a good choice, and no doubt will stop the hairiest Huzzunkus in mid-charge.

The overworked narcs liked the TR870 a lot. They approved of the three-inch chambering, which adds versatility. They were fascinated by the built-in flashlight and agreed it was a first-class setup.

They thought the trigger pull unusually good, and the smoothed action with twin action bars gave no malfunctions.

This appealed to me, also; I may be one of the few police officers who ever broke an action bar just when I needed it most. This occurred during a fall and left me with a single shot and one round in the chamber. Will a shotgun with twin bars function when one is broken? Indeed it will and that extra action bar is good insurance. A shotgun with no extra bar will not function when the single bar is broken, of course. No feed; no extraction.

The narcs also liked the Federal Tactical Loads with reduced recoil. This indicated they would be useful in cadet training, where new recruits often have little hunting or firearms experience and are intimidated by muzzle blast and recoil. Many actually shut their eyes when pulling the trigger, making the shotgun almost useless to the individual who fears it — to say nothing of misdirected lead. The Tactical Load could restore confidence and make the police shotgun a deadly tool in their hands. The patterns are about average for the nine-pellet 00 buck load, running eight to twelve inches at twenty yards.

When it came to slug shooting, a curious but all too familiar situation developed. Several of the agents complained that the rear sight aperture was much too large, and they had trouble centering the front bead in it.

Clearly, they were not familiar with the so-called "ghost ring" sight or principle involved in its use. Such a sight is the best and by far the fastest of all metallic sights, yet here were men accustomed to firearms who didn't know how to use it. Not an encouraging situation, I thought. In their defense, it must be said that aperture sights are not that common nowadays on either shotgun or rifle. It's a custom touch that few appreciate.

When the agents made this criticism, I wasn't present to explain the sight's function to them. Perhaps the worst thing that ever happened in regard to these sights was when

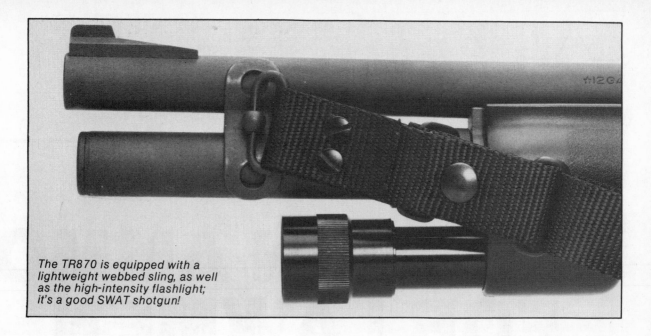

The TR870 is equipped with a lightweight webbed sling, as well as the high-intensity flashlight; it's a good SWAT shotgun!

someone nicknamed them "peep sights." Many shooters believe one must actually "peep" through a tiny aperture, if accurate shooting is to be accomplished. In reality, the shooter simply focuses on the front sight, and allows the hole in the rear to fade away in blurred, hazy obscurity. The human eye is such a wonderful mechanism that it will center itself on the incoming light automatically, and the shot will go where the front sight is. One never should attempt to center the front sight, and if you see the rear aperture in clear focus, you're doing it wrong. The "ghost ring" name comes from the blurred image of the rear sight ring which should be big.

My test squad of narcs didn't know this, but this lack of understanding didn't keep them from placing all slugs in the head of the silhouette target at twenty-five yards. We're talking of groups no larger than four to six inches; not great shooting, but obviously adequate. The Winchester slugs, at this close range, did as well as the imported Brenneke brand.

SPECIFICATIONS

Action:	Remington 870P magnum; Parkerized finish.
Barrel:	Length eighteen inches, Cylinder bore.
Buttstock:	Fiberglass filled polypropylene with recoil pad.
Forend:	High-impact nylon by Laser Products.
Magazine:	Extended length, five- or six-shot capacity for standard or three-inch shotshells. Choate non-binding follower.
Sights:	Aperture rear by Williams, adjustable for windage and elevation. Ramped front post with luminous Trijicon Tritium insert.
Sling:	Three-way adjustable action sling by S-N-S, black nylon, width one and a quarter inches. Choate swivels.
Safety:	Crossbolt at rear of trigger guard, Uncle Mike's Jumbo Head button.
Flashlight:	Forend-mounted high-intensity 11,000 candle-power. Pressure sensitive tape switch on right of forend.
Weight:	Eight pounds, 14.50 ounces, empty.
Price:	$695.

The men were either centering the front bead carefully or unconsciously using the ghost ring sight as it should be used. No shooting was done at greater yardage simply because the agents lacked confidence in the sight due to unfamiliarity. Typically, however, the slugs — any kind — will stay in the chest area of the silhouette at ranges up to one hundred yards.

My view of the TR870 is that it's exactly what the name indicates, a tactical response shotgun offering heavy firepower when the situation calls for it. It isn't an entry weapon per se and one of Automatic Weaponry's pistol-gripped models might serve better in that role.

The TR870 is not a shotgun for general issue for patrol, yet. It's too expensive for that. Anyway, the cops would steal the flashlights out of them to give to girl friends, or put them to other uses. Instead, the TR870 is an ideal shotgun for SWAT teams or an officer who expects trouble. Although it lacks range and should be used at thirty yards maximum, it has more actual projectile throw weight than any submachine gun — and it will place those projectiles more accurately than a submachine gun burst. Every gadget on the TR870 is functional, and if you dreamed of your own fighting shotgun, it would look like this.

With the extended magazine fully loaded, the tonnage of the TR870 goes up and you pay the price for the extra firepower. Officers of small stature will not find it manipulated as easily as the usual police pump, but stout individuals will have no problems.

In shotgun fights, the action is so instantaneous the gun needs to be mounted and fired quickly, almost by instinct. When the opponent is armed equally well, old quail hunters stand the best chance of survival. The TR870 appears to be a good compromise: Ideal for SWAT work and useful for any number of other police emergencies.

As an added bonus, the gun comes in a padded black Cordura nylon case with a zipper closure. Inside are six deep pockets for ammo and other gear, along with one outside pocket with a hook and loop closure. The case offers good protection and has a sling so you can grab it and take it with you.

CHAPTER FIVE

SHOTGUN AMMO FOR LAWMEN

Like The Shotgun Itself, Certain Ammo Has Specific Uses In Enforcement

Cubic shot was developed for hunting use. It's a good load for SWAT entry shotguns, offering great shock, decreased penetration. Some departments use it as a standard load in densely populated areas. Its short range is a real plus!

THE PRINCIPAL advantage of the shotgun in law enforcement is its versatility — and that means ammunition. Without question, today's ammo is more of everything — more powerful, more diverse and more effective. Traditionally, the police load has been the nine-pellet loading of 00 buckshot and was the only one in common use for many years. The .33-inch pellets give reasonably good penetration on "hard" targets, but is at its best on non-barricaded personnel caught in the open. The load was used by the U.S. Army as early as World War I and gained an almost legendary reputation for effectiveness, no doubt accounting for the immediate acceptance in law enforcement.

In the 1960s, many police departments began a switch to smaller buckshot, which allowed more pellets in the case. The increased payload was thought to have a number of advantages, including greater hit probability at unknown but longer ranges and decreased penetration in building materials — important in urban areas. Usually, number 4 buckshot was the choice. Each standard length 2¾-inch shell contains twenty-seven pellets of .24-inch buckshot. A later magnum loading held thirty-four pellets.

Generally speaking, number 4 lived up to what was expected of it and is still in use by numerous police departments. The swarm of small pellets often shows great stopping power at close range; under ten yards.

Number 4 will even put more shot on target at the longer distances than does the rapidly spreading 00 buck. The problem is penetration — or the lack of it. Because of poor sectional density (light weight for its size) number 4 buck loses velocity rapidly; on the positive side, this means an errant pellet won't penetrate a house wall and injure the occupants.

Unfortunately, the negative side is that it also lacks penetration on human opponents, except at close range. While it may be possible to hit an adversary at somewhat longer distances than with 00 buck, the wounds made by number 4 are likely to be superficial and ineffective.

Larger, heavier buckshot with greater sectional density

Federal's 2¾-inch Tactical Load carries nine #00 buckshot. The copper-plated shot is made in 12 gauge.

per pellet such as the 00 size offers enough penetration to damage skeletal structure at close range. At long ranges — thirty to fifty yards — the effect is diminished, but the wounds made are still serious and likely to be incapacitating. The problem is in getting hits with the thin patterns and fewer pellets per load.

As a rule of thumb, number 4 buck pellets are finished at about twenty-five yards, regardless of how many hit the target. The big 00 shot is effective as far as you can hit with them, but due to fewer pellets and rapidly expanding patterns, this means about fifty yards. Past that distance, the average police shotgun won't print enough pellets on target, regardless of shot size.

Police use of shotguns increased dramatically during the 1960s.

Since the end of the turbulent Prohibition Era in the 1930s, the shotgun had been only a minor part of police equipment. As the civil rights movement deteriorated into

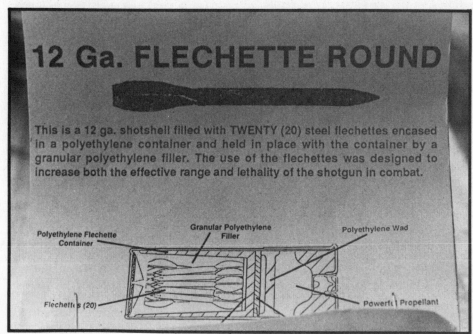

12 Ga. FLECHETTE ROUND

This is a 12 ga. shotshell filled with TWENTY (20) steel flechettes encased in a polyethylene container and held in place with the container by a granular polyethylene filler. The use of the flechettes was designed to increase both the effective range and lethality of the shotgun in combat.

Polyethylene Flechette Container

Granular Polyethylene Filler

Polyethylene Wad

Flechettes (20)

Powerful Propellant

Flechette rounds extend range, lethality of the shotgun. The tiny finned steel darts were developed for use by the military.

rioting and unabashed looting for profit in some areas, police officers came to realize they might actually have to use the "riot gun" for its intended purpose. Many more shotguns were purchased and the older standard load of 00 buck came under closer scrutiny.

It became clear that while 00 buck was as good as it ever was, more effective loads were possible, along with the technology to make them. A good beginning was the plastic shotshell case which began replacing paper cases in 1959. Externally, the plastic case was more weatherproof, abuse-proof and improved functioning in both pump and autoloading shotguns. Internally, the older, more bulky wadding was replaced by cushioned plastic shot sleeves that permitted more internal capacity for the pellets, allowing more of them to be loaded into each shell. The shot itself often was buffered by plastic sawdust to reduce deformation in the bore and increase pattern density at longer ranges. To get the same effect, the shot was made harder than pure lead, and could be had in either copper or nickel-plated. All these, with other continuing improvements by the manufacturers, add ten to fifteen yards to the effective range of the combat shotgun.

By the mid-1970s new police shotguns were being chambered for the three-inch shotshell with its larger payload.

Federal introduced its premium buckshot with fifteen copper-plated 00 buckshot in each case. Other manufacturers followed suit, although not always with plated shot. Remington went the competition one better by increasing the size of the buckshot. Number 00 buck at .33-inch had been the largest available. The new three-inch Remington offering carries ten pellets of .36-inch diameter shot for increased penetration and added power at extended ranges.

The benefit of the larger buckshot should be obvious. Out where patterns are thin and velocity is lower, it may require five to seven 00 buck to neutralize an opponent. With the larger 000 .36-inch buck, as few as two or three hits may suffice. Inside thirty yards, however, there would be little to choose between the two sizes. Both double-0 and triple-0 have the power and penetration to do the job.

Recognizing that a great many police shotguns still in service have the shorter, standard 2¾-inch chamber, most manufacturers offer a "magnum" loading in this length. We've already mentioned the magnum number 4 loading for which pellet count was increased from twenty-seven to thirty-four. Remington did the same for 00 buck, increasing the pellet count from nine to twelve. Generally speaking, these heavier loadings always should be chosen for serious combat work. The object is not to punch that many more holes in a felon, but to increase pattern density. Buckshot flying free is haphazard at best, and the more pellets you have in your shot cloud, the better your chances of multiple hits.

There is another way of going about achieving the same results. In the United States, we manufacture five standard sizes of buckshot in factory loadings. The smallest is number 4, which we've discussed. The next largest is number 3 buck at .25-inch; normally, it is loaded only in the 20-gauge shell. To my knowledge there are no 12-gauge number 3 buckshot shells.

Going up the size ladder we come to number 1 buck, which is .30-inch. Number 0 buckshot is next at .32-inch.

The steel fletchettes packed in a single 12-gauge case are displayed. Coins are for comparison of the sizes.

Number 00 buck is .33-inch, and the big 000 size is .36-inch.

Aside from slightly better sectional density for the larger shot, I can't see why such small differences in diameter make any difference on target. The fact is that .30-inch number 1 buck works about as well as the .33-inch 00 buck, except for a slight decrease in penetration. Moreover, there is roughly a fifty-percent increase in pellet count for number 1 buck. The officer or department now using the nine- or twelve-pellet loading of 00 buckshot would do well to take a look at factory offerings in this slightly smaller size.

These heavy loadings in 2¾- and three-inch lengths offer maximum efficiency, but the shooter pays the price in muzzle blast and heavy recoil. Neither is too important in actual combat, since the usual encounter won't consume many shells. Who notices anyway?

Where it matters is in routine shotgun qualification and cadet practice while training. The loud uproar and vicious kick can — and does — intimidate officers unaccustomed to firearms. A thing to remember is that virtually all buckshot is loaded by the factories to deer-hunting specifications, which translates to cramming in as much raw power as possible. Typical loads smack the shoulder with thirty-five to fifty foot-pounds of free-recoil energy; much more than that of the average big-game rifle.

To counter this, most police shotguns are equipped with recoil pads which really don't belong on a combat shotgun. The pad is prone to catch or snag on clothing while the gun is being mounted, causing a missed shot. This might well be fatal, if that's the only shot you'll get. However, due to the terrific recoil, a rubber recoil pad is practically mandatory in order to endure practice and training sessions.

To counter this objectionable characteristic, the Federal Cartridge Company has introduced what they call the *Tac-*

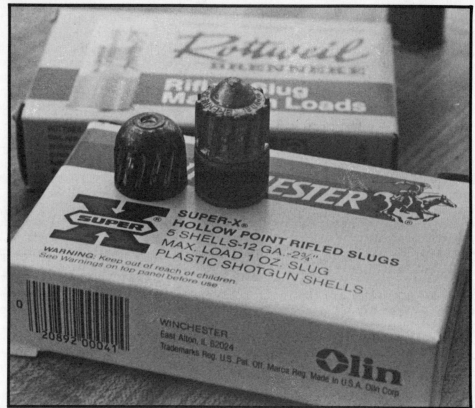

American-made Foster slug is on left, with Brenneke type made in Europe. The shotgun slug is useful in police work and replaces buckshot in some instances.

tical Load. Designed specifically for police use, the standard length 2¾-inch case carries nine copper-plated 00 buckshot with a reduced velocity of 1150 fps. The people at Federal no doubt reasoned that most police encounters are at close range, so the usual 1300+ fps of deer hunting loads is neither necessary nor desirable. Nine pellets, when you are virtually certain all will strike the target, are enough. No doubt, Federal ballisticians reflected on the fact that the police shotgun is not used to extend the range over the service handgun, but to insure greater hit probability — and more power.

Given these facts, the reduced-power Tactical Load makes a lot of sense. The ballistics are virtually a return to the days of black powder, but if history is correct, a lot of law enforcement was done with just such a load.

The Tactical Load is a pure pleasure to shoot. Recoil is mild, but the power is there for combat purposes. This new Federal 12-gauge round could be issued for patrol duty, as well as for qualification and practice.

As a rule, the size and type of buckshot loading will be decided by the chief, the range instructor or the training bureau, and no other will be issued. If regulations permit, however, the individual officer can choose from a multitude of projectiles for use in special circumstances.

For example, it's logical to carry a few rounds of small birdshot in the briefcase for rabid or sick animals that must be destroyed. One of the best of these is the 12-gauge *Brush Load* offered by the Cubic Shot Shell Company, P.O. Box 118, Youngstown, OH 44501. The shell contains an ounce of cubic or "square" shot, said to be number 7 in size. The purpose of such cubic shot is to maximize pattern spread for hunting birds or small game in heavy cover.

In police work, the large pattern insures hitting with the first shot, thereby reducing the disturbance level. Because of increased air resistance, the squared shot pellets won't fly far in congested areas. I'm told at least one department in New England has adopted the Brush Load for patrol duty. At close range, it would be lethal, of course.

For increased penetration on the larger small-animal species, a few rounds of duck loads carrying ordinary round pellets of number 2 or 4 birdshot will handle a lot of problems.

Although he probably won't be issued any, a good officer will have a handful of shotgun slugs on hand for his patrol shotgun. Ideally, he will have fired a few through the gun to determine point of impact, but all too often, this is not practical. Many times, unfortunately, the individual cop will have a different shotgun every day due to vehicle changes or when patrolling different sectors.

The shotgun is departmental equipment, not personal armament. At a range of twenty-five yards or so, the point of impact should be close enough for large targets, even from a strange shotgun.

A great deal has been said and written about the relative inaccuracy of shotgun slugs. Much of it is unfair, coming from riflemen who tend to compare smoothbore accuracy with that of their pet rifles. The truth is that the so-called rifled slug is accurate enough for most police work out to a hundred yards. True, a five- or six-inch group is not pinpoint accuracy at this distance, but the slug retains minute-of-malefactor capability. Practically any police shotgun — crude bead sight regardless — will keep a magazine full of the heavy projectiles in the chest area of a silhouette easily.

The one area where the shotgun slug might prove inadequate in police work is in SWAT-style sniping. This job is best left to the riflemen.

When it comes to slugs, a curious situation exists. The United States leads the world in quality of ammunition, but for some reason, American-made shotgun slugs have a poor reputation for accuracy. Of course, given the variability of individual shotgun barrels, this charge might be hard to prove.

The usual slug is the Foster-type with a rounded, bluff ogive and a hollow base. Around the circumference is a series of angled ribs moulded into the lead. The ribs and grooves between are supposed to impart a spin to the slug in flight to increase accuracy much like a rifle bullet. Recent studies have shown that these ribs have little or no effect — and the slug doesn't spin. However, the nose-heavy projectile flies more or less true due to the weight up front.

Prior to the introduction of the American-made Foster slug, round balls were the most common single projectile. The archaic old round ball was wildly erratic beyond fifty yards, and the current rifled slug is far superior. In recent years, it has become popular to increase the weight slightly from one ounce to 1¼ ounces, and to add a hollow-point or dimple in the nose to aid in expansion. No doubt these improvements are worthwhile.

One readily available shotgun slug with a reputation for accuracy is the German-made Brenneke. This ribbed, cylindrical projectile has a rounded point and weighs 1⅛ ounces.

Muzzle velocity for the Brenneke is some 1600 fps, and muzzle energy amounts to over 2700 foot-pounds. The Brenneke often shows improved accuracy in individual shotguns. Whether it would do so as an item of general issue for hundreds of guns is another matter. Because it's more expensive than domestic slugs, not many police departments have adopted it, and the Brenneke is seldom seen in police work.

The now-famous BRI sabot slug is referred to more correctly as a bullet. The 443-grain projectile is a full .50-caliber aerodynamically improved bullet contained in a two-piece plastic sabot. When fired, the two halves of the sabot are peeled away by air resistance, leaving the spool-shaped bullet flying accurately toward the target. The BRI has been around since 1968. Olin/Winchester bought the ammo part of BRI! To date, it is the most advanced of all shotgun solid projectiles, offering great accuracy, flat trajectory and extreme penetration. The BRI is so good one wishes it was better distributed. As things stand, it's difficult to find, and not often seen in police service, even on SWAT teams.

Due to bad experiences with buckshot, a number of SWAT teams and stakeout units have adopted slugs exclusively, and prefer them to buckshot of any size. There are recorded incidents wherein felons received one buckshot blast after another without going down or ceasing hostile action.

It may seem foolish to question official police reports supported by many witnesses. However, something is odd about these reports, and they sound more like a ballistic error than a case of Superfelons being immune to buckshot.

It could be true that a drug-numbed, physically powerful human being is able to sustain severe wounding without going down. This usually occurs with flesh wounds which often look more serious than they are, or when organs not absolutely vital to supporting life temporarily are hit.

For example, a felon hit with a charge or two of light number 4 buckshot possibly would have such wounds. Even so, the toughest of human beings must be supported by the skeleton in order to stand, and the skeletal structure is not anesthetized by drugs. When heavy buckshot such as 00 or 000 is used, the large heavy pellets penetrate deeply, and will break and shatter every bone they hit. When this happens your opponent is going down, no matter how drugged or charged with adrenalin.

Common sense should tell the officer not to keep shooting at the midsection when no effect can be seen. If your load won't drive through to break the spine, what's wrong with breaking both legs? The point is that buckshot of the right size, used properly, will take any man off his feet. Once he's off his feet he is finished, for all practical purposes. I tend to take all horror tales of felons absorbing dozens of buckshot and pistol bullets with a large dose of salt. If nothing else, you could simply blow his fool head off.

The primitive, round-ball buckshot is not the only multi-projectile load for the shotgun. Over the last few decades, the U.S. armed services, principally the Army, has been experimenting with dart-like missiles called flechettes.

The flechette is a short metal arrow resembling a nail, with fins at one end. Up to twenty of these projectiles are loaded into each shotgun shell. When fired, they fly point-forward to the target. Because of their light weight and small diameter, the nail-like flechettes probably lack the smash of a handful of buckshot at close range, but this is not their purpose. The intent is to increase the range of the combat shotgun. A side benefit is increased penetration over that of round buckshot. Whether police need either of these virtues is open to question.

In this instance, the military requirement is opposed diametrically to that of the police. Flechette rounds extend the wounding power of the shotgun at battlefield ranges, and the military can be content with lesser wounds than the police officer. Bluntly put, almost any wound that bleeds can take a reluctant soldier out of action and reduce him to a casualty. Chances are good he lacks enthusiasm and doesn't particularly want to be there anyway. Heroic soldiers are the exception to the rule, which is why they are awarded the Medal of Honor.

In contrast, the dangerously combative felon fights because he wants and chooses to do so.

Such a person knows he has the option of surrender at any time in complete safety, yet makes a conscious decision to fight. Such an individual is harder to stop than ten reluctant individuals. No superficial wound is likely to change his mind; he must be smashed into impotence with overwhelming force. At close range — the usual police circumstance — time permits no other course of action. Flechette rounds may do it, but the track record is sketchy on this. Heavy buckshot or a rifled slug through the brain or spine are known to achieve the desired result.

There is a source for flechette rounds outside the military establishment. Officers or police departments that believe flechettes meet their requirements can order them from Rhino Replacement Parts Company, P.O. Box 669, Seneca, SC 29679.

The Rhino cartridge is loaded into white plastic, low-brass 12-gauge cases. Each round carries twenty flechettes inside an internal shot sleeve that protects the bore from abrasion. To make a symmetric payload, ten of the flechettes are loaded point forward while the other ten are loaded backward, with the fins up. In flight, the reversed flechettes are supposed to flip over to a point-forward attitude; apparently they do.

Recoil is mild, and ballistically they are presumed to be the approximate equal of the military round. Just how much they extend shotgun range is a moot point. My guess is, what you can hit with 27-pellet number 4 buck loads also can be hit with a flechette round.

The Rhino Replacement Parts Company has an interesting array of unusual shotgun ammunition not found anywhere else. Like the hold of the space shuttle, the 12-gauge hull will accommodate nearly anything you want to put in it, and some of the Rhino offerings are rather fiendish as well as unique.

For example, they offer a shotshell packed with magnesium or similar flammable material which burns at high temperatures. The shell apparently emits an intensely hot ball of flame some twenty feet in diameter which burns for three seconds.

Other Rhino offerings include shotshells filled with non-lethal but painfully impacting rubber bullets and exploding air bombs. All these rounds are expensive, but could be worth every penny in the right circumstances.

Standard tear gas shells also are available. Suppose you had an unruly, violent mob of protestors. You could meet them with several squads of shotgun-armed officers provided with a variety of ammunition. Simultaneously, with no attempt at escalation, one squad fires tear gas to stir them around a little. The next squad pelts them with air bombs bursting at ear level. Still another squad chews their ankles with rubber bullets. This combined assault, delivered all at once, would be guaranteed to disperse any mob.

Though police officers may not be noted for compassion toward rioters, they are concerned with public safety. Specifically, this involves non-involved parties that may be injured by stray bullets, buckshot or slugs. As a police

Web buttstock shell holders that fit over the stock are a common way of carrying extra ammo on shotguns.

cadet many years ago, I was surprised that no mention was made in training of the maximum ranges of firearms projectiles. It seems to me this is a legitimate subject for concern.

Later, as a patrol officer, I had occasion to hold my fire several times simply because I couldn't be sure where the bullet would strike if it missed the target. A lifetime of shooting safety was too difficult to break, for I like to know where my bullets go. This isn't always possible in police work, but it's better to cancel a shot at a distant felon than to injure, even slightly, a distant citizen minding his own business. The real issue is moral responsibility.

Remington has thoughtfully provided the danger ranges of both slugs and buckshot in their catalog. The data represents the calculated maximum range, with a ten percent safety margin, of 2¾-inch loads fired at a twenty-five degree angle of elevation. Maximum range at sea level is listed, as well as a hypothetical 12,000-foot altitude. The 00 buckshot — with a muzzle velocity of 1325 fps — will travel 1895 feet in the thicker air of sea level. At 1325 fps, 000 buck goes a bit farther: some 1980 feet. Number 4 buckshot travels 1520 feet.

Rifled slugs at 1550 fps fly to a range of 3780 feet and arrive with a terminal velocity of 187 fps. The speed necessary for a projectile to give a disabling wound is 170 feet per second. Of the shotgun projectiles listed, only the rifled slug arrives at a dangerous velocity.

Some lawmen criticize the shotgun as outdated and inefficient. What they really mean is they wish it was a rifle or carbine. We'll take a look at that opinion in another chapter.

Meantime, the variety and versatility of shotgun ammo should keep the smoothbore in front-line service for a long time to come.

Federal now has a three-inch 00 buckshot load that is said to offer maximum effectiveness in shotguns that are chambered properly. A 2¾-inch load shows comparison.

CHAPTER SIX

A HARD LOOK AT RIFLES

SWAT Has Made A Name For High-Priced Rifles; The Author Doesn't Necessarily Agree With This Approach

The type of sniper rifle favored by SWAT teams is the same as that used by the military forces, complete to the camouflage finish, heavy barrel, expensive optics and a bipod. Author feels that is overdoing what is required.

SPECIAL WEAPONS and Tactics units — or SWAT teams in the popular vernacular — take a lot of kidding from other cops because of their elite status. It is always friendly kidding, because many officers like myself remember how it used to

be without SWAT. Until you've been there, it's impossible to know how badly a situation can deteriorate in police work, and I believe my tale is the best possible illustration. I hardly believe it myself, and I was there.

One afternoon in 1975, a citizen-taxpayer with a good

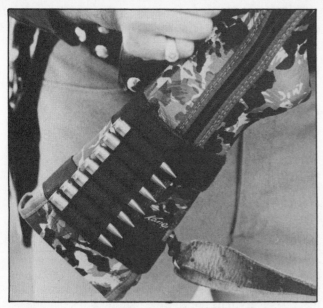

The web cartridge holder that attaches to rifle stock gives rifleman access to more ammunition immediately.

Camouflage cover for the rifle is of form-fitted nylon that is held in place by zippers and is removed easily.

job came home from work and began arguing with his two teenage sons. The big problem was that the citizen was an alcoholic, and had been for years with no outward manifestations.

At some point in the argument, his mood turned murderous. He loaded a scoped .243 bolt-action rifle and fired at one of his sons, wounding him slightly in the arm. Both boys fled the house to summon help, and in no time at all a lone police officer arrived in a patrol car. As he approached the house, he too received an arm wound from the .243 deer rifle. Realizing the talking was over, he radioed for reinforcements and got them in abundance.

A dozen officers from the area surrounded the house and endured sporadic sniping from the deranged drunk. They returned his shots with revolver and shotgun fire, but it was futile. The home was well built of limestone and shed bullets like a fort.

A theft detective cruising nearby heard the radio traffic and gunfire, and quite naturally went to investigate and help if he could. Upon arrival, he dismounted from his vehicle and was killed instantly by a .243 bullet to the head. One cop wounded, and another dead, in addition to the wounded teenager. For a drunk, the guy didn't miss much.

I was off-duty that day, but also kept tabs on the situation by radio. The afternoon wore on in gunfire. This was pre-SWAT, remember? By seven o'clock that evening, it wasn't looking any better and the idea occurred to me that a good rifleman might pick the killer off with a lucky window shot. I stuck two .45 automatics in my belt, loaded a .270 Winchester and drove over to do it if I could. After all, my badge was as good as anyone's. In those days, that's the way we did it.

It was ludicrous. Police cars were parked willy-nilly around the house, cops crouched behind them. Neighborhood citizens stood upright behind as if somehow immune to gunfire.

There was no perimeter, no crowd control and apparently no one in charge. The killer's home was ringed by dozens of officers firing independently. Their pistols flashed in a large circle, and their bullets came through the house windows to endanger those of us on the other side. You could hear these bullets chunking into the circled patrol cars and smashing glass. I placed myself behind a motor block and put my fingers in my ears. It was insane.

I heard a voice roar on a bullhorn and the gunfire slackened a bit. In quick conference, several of us decided to use the opportunity to rush the front door sixty feet away and put an end to the matter. I laid the rifle aside, cocked both .45s and ran toward the house. Suddenly, the gunfire resumed in all its fury, and I fell on my face in the short grass of the front yard, twenty feet from the door. It wasn't the killer and his .243; it was a hail of lead from my fellow officers. I lay like paint on the grass, yet bullets plucked at my clothing, dug divots in the dirt in front of my nose, and a pistol slug dinged the clip in my right-hand .45 auto.

I was there a long time, and it just got worse. Behind me, an officer armed with an M14 and a Starlight scope kept shouting for me to get out of his way, firing over my head occasionally to emphasize the point.

Later, because of the scandal, he denied being there to my face, but I know it was he. By now, I was getting lead backsplash from the stone walls, and was starting to lose my reasoning ability. Thoughts of digging through to China entered my head, and I wept a time or two. Over head, police helicopters ferried rifles, ammo and supplies to the crowd of cops. Concerned neighbors fetched deer rifles and boxes of shells and loaned them to individual officers so the fire could continue without interruption. In a couple of hours, I was so tired from hunkering it was impossible to flee. My shirt cuffs were shot off, and once I felt the back of my head to see if any hair still inhabited that planet.

In the smoky gloom, I saw the figure of a well known police captain emerge holding the booming bullhorn. He sent a brave group of three officers toward the door, one holding a shotgun. For the benefit of the thronging citizenry he shouted into the bullhorn, "Take him alive if you can, boys!" Twenty feet away, I raised the .45s and shouted, "Like hell you will!" But it was all over and I wept again at the futility and wasted ammo. An hour earlier, the killer had put the .243 barrel in his mouth and took his own life.

A bad end to an even worse situation, which is not exaggerated here in the slightest.

And did we ever get in trouble for that festive fiasco! It was a miracle no citizens were killed or even hit by the wild gunfire. In the neighborhood for a mile around, not a house window that faced the fight was without a bullet hole.

Today, these situations are handled by a carefully picked SWAT outfit which handles everything. The shooter uses a rifle that can splatter a quarter or nick a dime at a hundred yards. For the most part, these are domestically produced bolt-actions, with the Remington Model 700 playing a conspicuous role. I'm aware there are technologically superior sniper rifles, based largely on military semi-auto actions. They are expensive, and you can pay about what you want to for a rifle and advanced sighting systems.

Frankly, I'm not qualified to discuss these specialized rifles, but I can have an opinion. I approve of a semi-auto SWAT rifle, but to me, most of the other features are window dressing. For a great deal of money, you can equip your SWAT shooter with an expensive, gadgetized rifle that does everything but give the latitude and longitude — and perhaps even that. The name of the game, however, is to put a free-flight bullet into a distant target exactly where you want it, and the bolt-actions will do that. Were I a police chief, I'd turn thumbs down on a request for a megabucks sniper rifle.

The only reason I can think of for these expensive rifles is civil liability suits. You want to be able to say in court

Cowboy Carbines In The City Of Angels?

At Downey station of the Los Angeles Sheriff's Department, in 1923, deputy seated in center had two Model 94 rifles.

that your SWAT team had the best available modern equipment.

While not qualified to discuss these rifles, I am qualified to talk about rifle shooting. I grew up with a rifle in my hand, and learned to be pretty deft with one. In 1983, I had an opportunity to go to a city in the northern part of Texas to witness a regional SWAT team match. To be blunt, I was not impressed, and I hope by now the five departments represented have cleaned up their act.

We were on a broad plain next to a lake, with targets set at 100, 200 and 300 yards. There was a strong wind blowing from the port side, but the day was bright and clear. The men fired five at a time, and every rifle in the line was a bolt-action, the Remington M700 predominating. Calibers were about equally divided between the .308 (7.62mm) and the 6mm Remington. There were a few .243s, but there is a belief among expert riflemen that the 6mm Remington has a slight edge in accuracy. Some of the .308 shooters had military match ammo, but the remainder used mostly Remington 6mm and .308 hunting cartridges.

The shooters were young men in their early twenties, clear of eye and obviously in top physical condition. Apparently, they had little rifle experience and poor coaching — or none at all. I saw them shoot at fifty yards on a sighting-in range, and most of them cut one ragged hole. When they switched over to the longer ranges, the shooting went to pieces fast. The left-hand wind drifted their groups completely off the ringed targets at two hundred and three

hundred yards. This was especially noticeable with the .243s and 6mms.

It seems no one ever told them wind will move a bullet and change the point of impact. The groups were all to the right, and not too tight at that.

Throughout the afternoon, I watched them handle their rifles. I saw none that used the edge of their palm in the proper way, and there was a good deal of short-stroking the bolts and consequent failure to feed the next cartridge. It was an amateur performance from beginning to end.

It would be easy to equip such shooters with expensive semi-autos, if you had the money, but were I their chief, I'd make them learn to operate the bolt-actions as a cheaper alternative.

One other thing I noticed was a lot of dropped cartridges during reloading. It's too bad we don't have some sort of clip-like device to load the magazines on bolt-actions. I'm not mechanically inclined, and don't know what such a loader would look like, but it would have to shove the cartridges into the port of a scoped rifle.

One of the better shooters in this regional match was a sergeant in his early thirties. I fell into a caliber discussion with him and he stated his preference. His rifle was in .308, and he believed it to be as accurate as the 6mm Remington. He felt it got through obstacles better than the 6mm. For instance, he told me it was sometimes necessary to shoot through a plate-glass store front window where the glass is nearly an inch thick. I don't know if this is approved pro-

"I COULDN'T believe it!" the sheriff's deputy said. "We're in the middle of the 1965 Watts riots, buildings are burning all around us and you can hear automatic weapons going off on Central Avenue. The Sarge puts me on the roof, tells me to guard Firestone station — and all he gives me to do it with is a damn cowboy gun!"

The deputy's so-called cowboy gun was one of ninety-one Winchester saddle ring carbines that the Los Angeles County Sheriff's Department had owned since 1921. The guns were purchased when Eugene Biscailuz was still an undersheriff. He had just been appointed to the position and wouldn't become the most famous sheriff in the West for another ten years.

"In that era, the Sheriff's Department had only 650 men to staff a jail and police nearly 4000 square miles of unincorporated area — sheriff's territory — that took in the rich movie world of the Sunset Strip, the mountains of Newhall and Castaic, and crossed the desert to Lancaster," says Dick Love, a long-retired deputy.

From the saddle scabbard of a Newhall-based deputy in the early Twenties to the Watts riots, the Winchester Model 94s saw active service with the Los Angeles County Sheriff's Department for over fifty years. Even as late as 1972, every cadet going through the sheriff's academy was trained on the old .30-30 Winchester.

"For my money, it's the nicest weapon we had," recalls range officer Don Kalberloah. "They're accurate, dependable and easy to learn."

The Model 94 Winchester is based on a Browning patent of 1894 and is the first sporting repeating rifle made with a receiver designed to handle the new high-velocity smokeless powder. The early 94s were chambered for black powder loads, and it wasn't until 1895 that Winchester developed a nickel-steel barrel strong enough for the new .30-30 cartridge. Barrels on the Los Angeles County carbines are stamped "nickel-steel barrel — especially for smokeless powder," an indication of the period when they were manufactured.

The cartridge, originally with a 170-grain .30 caliber bullet over 30 grains of smokeless powder, is still widely used today as a sporting load for medium-size game. The .30-30 Winchester has been called the most popular deer rifle of all time.

In 1973, Los Angeles County sold these Winchesters under sealed bid to John Barkley, a gun dealer in Van Nuys, California. Along with the Winchesters, Barkley also purchased the county's surplus .35 caliber Remington rifles and .45 caliber Reising submachine guns.

"Los Angeles wanted to purchase the Colt AR-15 for the Sheriff's Department and use these old guns as part payment. Colt was on strike at the time, but I finally found a dealer back East who had enough AR-15s on hand. I sold the AR-15s to the county at cost and unloaded the Reisings for just eighty-five cents apiece more than I paid. Anything I make is going to be from resale on the Winchesters and Remingtons," Barkley stated at the time.

"I'd heard the sheriff had a few of these carbines that

SWAT members Jesse Hester (left) and Gerald Tyler, suited up for operation, discuss merits of Ruger's Mini-14 and Colt's AR-15. Both are in .223 caliber.

cedure on all SWAT teams, but he says the .308 seldom deviates from course. In addition, there is a wide variety of .308 ammo available, ranging from military hardball and match ammo to commercial hunting loads. The 6mm lacks this advantage, of course.

The wind problem over long distances is probably not too important. Although these are long-range rifles, SWAT snipers seldom have to shoot at these extended yardages.

In fact, at the close ranges usually prevalent when SWAT takes a shot, a good set of open sights and young eyes could handle the situation. Then too, if the first patrolman arriving at the scene had such a rifle available to him, SWAT might never be needed. This would require some shifting in

responsiblilites and perhaps some legal juggling, but it might save time and lives.

There is a growing amount of dissatisfaction with the shotgun in law enforcement. It is a chancy weapon at best, even with the heaviest buckshot and the most accurate slugs. Many officers would prefer a light, handy carbine, maybe one firing pistol cartridges for greater precision. My department had a few Winchester M94 .30-30s, but they were never issued or used to my knowledge. The .30-30 is probably too powerful to be ideal, and I know that some police agencies in the past used Winchester Model 92 lever-guns in .25-20 caliber.

Such a light rifle still could cut through most problems,

were in almost-new condition, but I sure haven't seen them," he added. "Some of the guns are less used than others, but there's not a one of them in what you would call really nice shape. They've all seen pretty rough service."

The old Winchesters are stamped *LACO* on the stock and most of the carbines have the unit of assignment painted on the stock in one-inch white letters, such as *Range* or *Norwalk.* Each carbine has a saddle ring on the left side of the receiver, a factory accessory intended for use on horseback.

Are they rare? "Well, I don't know," John Barkley said in 1973. "They're old. According to the serial numbers, they were built around 1918, but a county purchasing man named Krieger told me his records show that Los Angeles bought them in 1921.

"I run a lot of guns through my shop," John Barkley added at the time. "In the last few years, I've only seen two saddle ring 94 Winchesters and neither of those was a .30-30. Yes, I guess they're pretty rare."

John Barkley died several years ago and his shop on Woodley Avenue, a landmark for gun fanciers for over twenty-five years, has long since closed. The range staff

who used to teach the old 94 Winchester have all retired and new sheriff's recruits are instructed on Colt's AR-15.

A lot has changed since the department first used the old carbine. The Los Angeles County Sheriff's Department now has more than 8000 deputies and, with Sheriff Sherman Block, has pioneered such innovations as the contract city concept and police helicopter patrol.

Trained special weapons teams, equipped with individual radios and assisted by a hostage negotiator and a psychiatrist, now handle the hot calls that used to be assigned to two patrol units and the field sergeant. It's a different world and things are done safer and a lot smarter. Equipment now is state of the art and there is no question that the Winchesters have long since outlived their usefulness as a police weapon. Still...

Back in 1973, an old range master summed up the feeling. "Those carbines have been here for over fifty years," Sergeant Bill Burns said then. "I don't know for sure when we used them against a man. Lots of coyotes, maybe." He paused and smiled kind of wistfully. "Some of the guys are kind of sad to see them go."

The Ruger Mini-14 in .223 is a popular rifle with modern law enforcement personnel. Some have folding butt stock.

Latest variation of Colt's AR-15 is the M16A2 Commando. Some SWAT teams have adopted this latest configuration.

Ferguson feels that the Marlin Camp Carbine in 9mmP or .45 ACP would make a good law enforcement longarm. The price is considerably less than some rifles favored.

but it probably is too backward in technology to be accepted. We are far past the lever-gun stage now, and a similar caliber in a semi-automatic carbine seems more appropriate.

I have to be careful on this subject, lest I recommend something not suited to younger generations. All my rifle experience has been with conventionally contoured rifles, not military models.

Also, I'm presupposing that anyone can shoot a rifle, or shoot better with one. That's true only if you have some experience. If you're starting from Day One, it could be a different story.

I can hit fast with any rifle that has some drop to the stock, but the army's M16 with a straight-line stock is an abomination to me. Even the Ruger Mini-14 is too straight, and is awkward and clumsy in my hands. An officer accustomed to either of these guns might do okay. I'd do better with a Marlin Camp Carbine in 9mmP or .45 ACP, due to the conventional stock. It looks like a grown-up .22 plinker, and it feels like one.

In Europe, carbines in police work are an old story. Spain's Guardia Civil used locally manufactured copies of the Winchester M92 in .44-40 caliber. They also issued bolt-action carbines chambered in 9mm Bergmann-Bayard, not too different from the 9mmP. The carbines were ideal for the Spanish cops on foot, for they had no side-arms.

American police officers have handguns for quick response to danger, and the carbine could replace the shotgun in the patrol car.

However desirable that might be, I wouldn't look for it to happen overnight. It represents an added training problem, and there undoubtedly will be some legal opposition.

For most officers, though, the carbine using pistol ammo is a better deal than the shotgun.

CHAPTER SEVEN

CARBINES FOR COPS

A Survey Of What's Available And What's Preferred

David E. Steele demonstrates the Heckler & Koch MP5A3 with the Wilson Arms sound suppressor properly attached.

The Heckler & Koch HK93 in 5.56mm is an excellent semi-automatic rifle for SWAT use. The author, however, feels it may be slightly bulky for routine carrying in the modern-day patrol car that already is crowded with gear.

THE CURRENT wave of drug-related crimes has demonstrated a need for more efficient back-up weapons in patrol cars. While military police have the M16A2 assault rifle and its specialized variations available, most civilian departments plug along with the 12-gauge shotgun, partly out of tradition and habit, partly out of public relations — and mostly because of limited training budgets.

David E. Steele has a lengthy career in law enforcement and has made a study of the armament available to the street cops and special units. Here are some of his thoughts:

The 12-gauge pump shotgun has a number of drawbacks. It has about the same recoil as a .375 H&H magnum big-game rifle without the accuracy, range or power. Also, most patrol car riot guns are equipped with only a "sporting" bead front sight; if the gun does have rifle sights — usually of the buckhorn variety — there is no guarantee it will shoot to point of aim. And, patrol car guns such as the Remington 870 usually are loaded with four rounds total of #00 buckshot. The tubular shotgun magazine is slow to load and unload, and at urban combat distance — often less than twenty feet — the pattern is so small it must be aimed as carefully as a single-projectile weapon.

Buckshot, incidentally, is a poor choice for barricade situations or any circumstance where accurate head shots may be required. Shotgun shells may be deformed by heat or abuse such as ejecting live rounds from the chamber or letting them hit the floor, setting up the possibility of failure to feed.

Also a negative, patrol car guns are not assigned to specific individuals who are responsible for their maintenance; in fact, in some departments the guns stay in the cars from one shift to the next. A riot gun with an eighteen- or twenty-inch barrel is bulky, requiring two hands to maneuver.

Buckshot does not penetrate car bodies well. In terms of stopping power, the most effective shotgun round is the slug, but this round is no different from a rifle round except for its lesser range and accuracy. Also, the pump-action shotgun must be cycled by hand for each round, requiring two hands and more time than a semi-automatic action.

The disadvantages of the shotgun are not just theoretical. A few years ago, in Norco, California, a half-dozen bank robbers, armed with semi-automatic assault rifles, killed one policeman, wounded others and disabled thirty-two police vehicles — including a helicopter — during a wild chase in which no pursuing policemen had anything heavier than a shotgun.

In 1986, the FBI in Miami lost two killed and five wounded

Heckler & Koch-made HK91A2 7.62mm semi-auto rifle is another that would serve SWAT teams.

to a pair of bank robbers, one of whom had a .223 Ruger Mini-14. The FBI agents had shotguns, some of which had become unavailable, because they had slipped off the back seat where they were kept. A gent Mireles, who finally prevailed, had to cock and fire his shotgun with one hand, his other arm having been wounded, a trick that he had to invent on the spot, since FBI training did not foresee this possibility.

In 1969, Los Angeles Police Department SWAT officers were pinned down behind a curb — the only cover available — when intense fire was directed at them from the Black Panther headquarters where they were trying to serve a warrant. In this low position, they were unable to cock their Ithaca shotguns, a fact that later led to SWAT's adopting the Remington 1100 semi-auto.

In European police departments, shotguns are practically unheard of, being considered inhumane. History-oriented readers will recall that in World War I Germany filed a complaint in Geneva against American troops using Winchester 1897 "trench guns," declaring it a violation of the rules of war. Americans, on the other hand, had used shotguns in virtually all of their wars, most recently against Moros in the Philippines and guerrillas in Mexico. Whether multiple-projectile weapons like the shotgun can be construed like the hollow-point "dum-dum" ammunition invented by the British at their arsenal in India, then forbidden among "civilized nations" prior to World War I, is open to question.

Instead, European police departments prefer the submachine gun for backup, as anyone who tried to run a French roadblock would soon discover. For example, the last time I took an El Al flight, during a stopover at Orly airport, the plane was guarded by a gendarme with a MAT-49 submachine gun. This 9mm weapon was made famous by the Foreign Legion in Indochina, and in police service it replaced the 7.65mm MAS-38, an anemic submachine gun developed before the Second World War.

British police now use the German Heckler & Koch MP5 submachine gun, set on semi-automatic, for guarding Heathrow Airport, as well as other sensitive targets, against terrorism.

The idea of using submachine guns exclusively on semi-automatic is not a new idea. When British troops in Northern Ireland carried bulky FN rifles, noncommissioned officers usually carried Sterling L2A3 submachine guns, always set on semi-auto, so as to avoid making unnecessary civilian Irish martyrs. British service marksmanship competition with the submachine gun also is done on semi-auto. In Kenya, during the Mau-Mau uprising of the 1950s, British farmers were issued semi-automatic versions of the Sterling submachine gun.

A semi-auto version of the Heckler & Koch MP5 has

Deputy Sheriff Pete Fosselman checks out the M-1 carbine. Some feel that this World War II weapon has been badly underestimated when it comes to law enforcement work.

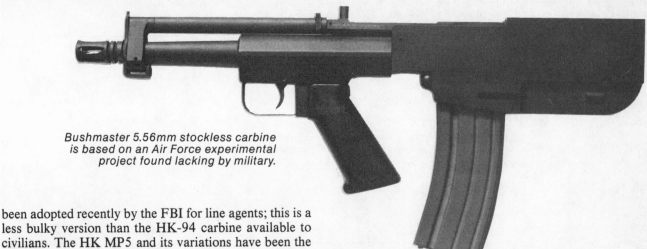

Bushmaster 5.56mm stockless carbine is based on an Air Force experimental project found lacking by military.

been adopted recently by the FBI for line agents; this is a less bulky version than the HK-94 carbine available to civilians. The HK MP5 and its variations have been the standard for counterterrorist forces since the British Special Air Service used it at the Princess Gate Iranian Embassy in 1980 to rescue hostages. It had been pioneered by the GSG-9 counterterrorist Border Police in Germany, but the British incident put it on the map for Americans. Of course, it also has been used by the terrorists themselves, particularly the German Red Army faction.

I saw the first MP5s imported here when I worked in Washington in 1970, prior to Heckler & Koch setting up a regular operation here. At that time, they were brought in by a company called Security Arms Corporation. I could see its potential right away for police work, mainly because of its closed-bolt operation and excellent sights, providing extremely fine semi-auto accuracy. I believe I was the first to demonstrate it for the Secret Service, but they were not impressed because the "Canadian" (actually CIA) ammunition they were using in their Uzis would not function in the MP5 due to its rim size. Fortunately, I had brought along seventy-five rounds of Finnish Lapua ammo, so they did see it perform — and HK immediately corrected later batches of MP5s for the peculiarities of American ammo. Now, of course, the MP5 is the clear front-runner among U.S. law enforcement users, such as the Los Angeles County sheriff's special weapons team.

Drug Enforcement Agency field men now are issued the 9mm version of the Colt Commando submachine gun, again usually blocked for semi-automatic fire only. This brings us to why firepower has become more important to U.S. law enforcement generally: drugs. Thanks to the incredible profits from drugs — crack cocaine, in particular — dealers can buy whatever level of firepower they need to protect themselves against other dealers and sometimes against police. In Colombia, they have had both the firepower and political strength to assassinate supreme court judges, top police officials and a presidential candidate. While I was in Customs, I heard that our man in Colombia had just been shipped an armored Ford Bronco; his family had been returned to the U.S. because of death threats.

Meanwhile, in the United States, gangs have competed for street sales of rock cocaine, their "competition" having doubled the murder rate in Washington, D.C. These drug sales also have provided the cash to allow Los Angeles gangs to move sales outlets all the way to Omaha and Kansas City. Legitimate gunowners are paying the price in "assault weapon" legislation, because some gang mem-

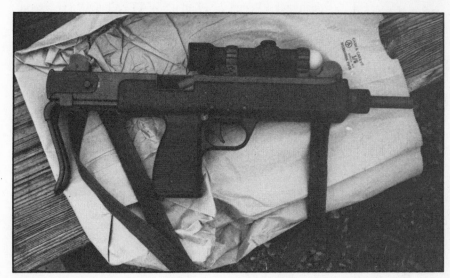

David Steele feels the Steyr 9mm submachine gun with the Singlepoint sight can be used by lawmen in some highly specialized enforcement work.

Police in Bangkok advance on dissident students during a 1975 riot. Note the hodgepodge of weaponry that includes M-1 carbines, Thompson submachine gun, M-16 rifles and a MAC-10 submachine gun. Standardization was needed.

bers have discovered semi-automatic technology that has been around since 1896. In the 1950s, you could be a "badass" or a "cool dude" with a straight razor or a .32 in your shoe, but now it takes "an oozie or ay-kay."

Back in 1970, I toured Chicago's Cabrini-Green Project buildings from which two policemen had been assassinated as a type of celebration when three gangs established a coalition.

One of the outfits was the Black P-Stone Nation, a notorious black gang which later gave itself a Muslim name and entered into a conspiracy with Khadaffi of Libya to perform terrorist acts in the United States for cash.

David Steele contends that in a stakeout situation such as this bedroom scene, H&K MP5A3 is a natural choice.

Obviously, this increase in criminal sophistication did not occur overnight.

According to the Chicago police in 1970, to the gang members every rifle was a ".30-30," and they often got the wrong ammo for the military surplus rifles they bought. Still, with their simple bolt and lever-action rifles, they managed to kill these two officers walking across a field. They also killed a nun in her convent a few blocks away, as well as other victims, in the course of their almost daily sniping attacks.

At that time, Chicago patrol cars carried backup weapons — shotguns usually — in the trunk, because these areas were so dangerous that a dozen shotguns were stolen out of cars in a two-week period when they experimented with dash racks. When they had a SWAT call, the "war wagon" would arrive with a truckload of M-1 carbines for the street officers. Also, a station wagon load of police dogs was dispatched just to protect the war wagon from hostile crowds.

With the increase in gang firepower, some departments, such as those of Los Angeles and Miami, have started issuing high-capacity 9mm semi-automatic pistols, including the Beretta M92 or Glock 17, to their street officers.

This may or may not be the way to go. Some officers are tempted to "spray and pray" with this much ammunition. One report made positive note of the fact that an LAPD officer got off ten rounds from his 9mm before he was cut down by a drive-by gangster with an AR-15. First, the gang member would have been more dissuaded by even one or two rounds that hit. Second, no 9mm pistol has the power or accuracy of an AR-15 semi-automatic rifle, which can put its rounds easily through the windshield or side of a patrol car.

One step up from the pistol are the machine pistols,

including the HK VP70, the Beretta M93R, the Czech Skorpion or the MAC-11, all of which are capable of fully automatic fire. However, these are not appropriate to police work, having been designed for special military operations. Most are designed for suppressive fire at close range, keeping the enemy's head down to allow contact or disengagement from sudden combat. A less common use is with a "snuffer can" suppressor on the barrel for assassination missions.

The submachine gun, usually in 9mmP or .45 ACP, is capable both of suppressive fire and accurate aimed fire out to two hundred meters. These usually were carried in military operations by officers, NCOs, tankers, et cetera, when conventional battle rifles, such as the M-1 Garand or FAL, were too bulky.

The ammunition invariably was compatible with the service pistol. For example, in World War II, the United States issued the M1A1 Thompson and the M3A1 "greasegun" in .45 ACP, while the Germans issued the MP38 and MP40 submachine guns in 9mmP. Today, with the introduction of more portable, lightweight, "subcaliber" assault rifles like the M16A2, Galil, and AKS-74, most modern armies have dropped the submachine gun from frontline use. However, in its modernized, sometimes semi-automatic-only versions, the submachine gun can be highly useful in police work and limited urban combat (e.g., Northern Ireland) where standard assault rifle ammo can present a problem of overpenetration.

Somewhat larger and more conventional in appearance than the modern submachine gun is the carbine. Developed hundreds of years ago as a short-barreled rifle for cavalry, the carbine is seen most often with a conventional wood stock. It may be found in pistol calibers, such as the Marlin Camp Carbines in 9mm and .45 ACP or the Ruger carbine in .44 magnum. It may be in a unique, intermediate caliber of its own, such as the .30 M-1 carbine, or it may be in a full-power rifle cartridge, such as the Ruger Mini-14 in 5.56mm. Incidentally, all of the carbines mentioned would make excellent "low profile" backup arms for patrol cars, since their conventional wood stocks do not present a "menacing" military appearance like those that have folding stocks or pistol grips.

Finally, at the high end of efficiency and power are the semi-automatic versions of current military assault rifles,

such as the Heckler & Koch HK91 and HK93, the Steyr AUG, the AR-15, the Valmet, Galil and others.

Given the "assault weapons" furor, these may have to be reserved for the SWAT team or carried in the trunk of the patrol car. Still, from the viewpoint of firepower, ruggedness, and efficiency, these are the weapons to have when a drug dealing gang-banger opens up with his Uzi, TEC-9 or Chinese AK. It is foolish to think gangsters are going to turn in their guns because of some politicized "assault weapon ban." Although these firearms are used by them mainly to intimidate their own neighborhoods and rival drug dealers, policemen cannot expect such characters to go peacefully when submitting to arrest, which means the loss of their dope-selling territory as well as the confiscation of their favorite consumer goods, including cars and houses.

If I were asked to recommend just one all-around backup weapon for patrol cars, I couldn't think of any better than the World War II M-1 carbine, loaded with soft-point ammunition.

There is one potential problem that must be considered, however. The M-1 carbine was not designed for soft-point ammo, thus there can be a feeding problem unless the chamber has been properly throated. The wise carbine carrier takes care of this problem before it comes about, even if it means spending private funds for a bit of gunsmithing.

This carbine has over forty years of history and public acceptance behind it. Its reputation as a "poor stopper" in military combat was due to its Geneva Accord hardball ammunition.

When Jim Cirillo served with the NYPD Stakeout Unit, 1967-71, he found that the M-1 carbine loaded with hunting ammunition was the best stopper available to the teams which usually were armed with Ithaca 37 shotguns, M-1 carbines, .38 revolvers, and, occasionally, Thompsons. The .30 carbine round has much greater velocity than a .357 magnum pistol round, for example, and with proper ammunition, it will expend its energy inside the body instead of penetrating through it like military hardball. The gun could be carried chamber-empty in a special rack constructed below window level, attached at the front of the driver's seat.

While not ideal, the carbine combines firepower, stopping power and light recoil with public acceptance.

Not many departments need equipment like the Colt Commando with night vision device and sound suppressor.

CHAPTER EIGHT

GUNS FOR MAKING ENTRY

Here's A Special Job That Requires Special Tactics — And Weaponry

Jim Cirillo, veteran officer with the New York City stakeout unit, demonstrates the Wilson Arms Witness Protection version of the venerable Remington M870.

IN HIS classic, *The Tactical Edge,* Charles Remsburg says, "Entry weapons assigned (for SWAT) should be as short as possible, to increase maneuverability and flexibility. Increasingly, special weapons teams are making entry armed *only* with semi-automatic handguns. Or they are supplementing shotguns with semi-automatic rifles or sound-suppressed machine pistols. If one or more...members do carry a shotgun, it should be sawed off — twelve inches is a favored length, if this is legal in your jurisdiction — with a guard near the end of the barrel to keep your hand from slipping off the slide into the line of fire."

David Steele has made an extensive study of the guns and tactics currently being used for making entry, so I asked him to cover this particular segment. His thoughts and observations follow:

Physical entry into a skyjacked airliner or the location of a barricaded suspect is always the last resort, pursued only when all other tactics such as negotiation, dogs, tear gas or sharpshooting have failed. In addition, there must be an immediate threat to the hostages, and the physical conditions are known to allow a high probability of complete success.

Success in a civilian police context means that no policemen and no hostages are killed. The military accepts a certain ratio of friendly force and civilian casualties in order to accomplish the mission. That is not acceptable in the civilian context. If anyone is killed unnecessarily, it should be the criminal — at least, from a civil liability point of view. In only one recent case, the McDonald's Massacre in San Diego, was there media outcry that the police should have acted sooner to neutralize the suspect; usually

The Heckler & Koch VP70 fires three-round bursts when the holster/shoulder stock are attached to the pistol.

temporarily deafening noise and blinding light) to disorient the suspect just before entry. These often are used in pairs, just in case the first grenade does not operate properly or a terrorist suspect has equipped himself with ear plugs and dark glasses.

An alternative to flash-bangs in certain situations is the halogen spotlight. The objective is the same: to disorient the suspect and to take his attention away from the hostages long enough for the team to enter and neutralize him — which usually means two rounds to the chest and one to the head.

The rapid assualt technique was developed by the British SAS, the German GSG-9 and Israeli counter-terrorist teams. It should be used only by those SWAT teams with first rate equipment and long-term team training. When entry is made, the team should have a mental picture of the suspect (preferably from an actual photograph), a pre-planned route and a specific destination in mind.

A great deal has been written about SWAT entry team equipment. Generally, the team will wear military fatigues or coveralls, with body armor, gas mask, ski mask or SAS-style hood and flexible boots or tennis shoes. For the close confines of an apartment or aircraft interior, the handgun seems to be the most versatile weapon. Whatever handgun is chosen must be practiced with constantly.

Large-capacity, double-action 9mmP automatics are the most fashionable now, but it is good to keep in mind that the British Special Air Service teams use the traditional Browning Hi-Power designed in 1935. In one practice session, an SAS team member was videotaped during a fast session of judgment pistol shooting. He had one stoppage during the exercise which he cleared between targets. However, when the action was freeze-framed, it was found he had actually field-stripped the gun to clear a serious jam. His reaction time was so unbelievably fast that it had appeared to be a simple failure to feed.

The advantages of the modern 9mm Parabellum auto are low recoil impulse, fast reaction time, large magazine capacity and a straighter recoil action with quicker recovery than a revolver. Obvious disadvantages are less stopping power than with a large-caliber revolver or a shotgun, plus its slightly greater tendency to stoppages.

Some of the more popular semi-automatic SWAT pistols are the Browning Hi-Power and Double Action, the

the opposite is true, with the commentators accusing police departments of "premature," "precipitious," or even "Ramboesque" assault tactics.

According to Remsburg, assaults can be divided into the "tactical entry," with its slow, cautious approach, and the "rapid assault," used to rescue hostages. Without thorough intelligence and rehearsal, the latter is quite likely to fail, especially against trained terrorists or well armed survivalists.

Usually the assault is preceded by a diversion, such as lights and sirens, that draws the suspect away from the entry point. This is followed by a distraction such as a "flash-bang" (flash powder stun grenade that produces

The Heckler & Koch MP5A3 submachine gun is widely used by counter-terrorist units, including British SAS, German GSG-9 and the Los Angeles Co. Sheriff.

Author demonstrates Wilson Arms Executive Protection shotgun based on Mossberg 500 without shoulder stock.

Beretta Model 92, the SIG-Sauer P226, the Heckler & Koch P9S and P7 and the Colt Government Model .45. All are effective, given sufficient practice and training.

There is some overlap between semi-auto pistols and modern machine pistols. For example, the Beretta Model 93R machine pistol, which fires single rounds or three-round bursts, is in short supply due to a constant demand by European counter-terrorist teams. This is barely larger than the 92S pistol, but it has substantially greater firepower, not to mention the advantage of an attachable shoulder stock.

In spite of the high level of combat pistol development in Europe, some members of German and French teams have shown a preference for the revolver. Perhaps this is a case of "the grass is always greener," but there are some real advantages to the revolver. The first is reliability, the second is stopping power. Since revolver feeding is accomplished by an external source of power — the trigger finger — it always will have a theoretical advantage in reliability over weapons that depend on the cartridge for cycling (blowback, semi-blowback, etc.). Also, the revolver can easily accept cartridges of great power or unusual design.

For counter-terrorist use, the best revolver is a .357 magnum, which is capable of accurate fire with a variety of .357 and .38 Special +P+ police loads. While the .357 cartridges produce the greatest shock and stopping power, some of the .38 loads produce less flash and blast and have shorter recovery time, especially when used in heavier .357 guns. The .38 Special +P+ 110-grain, hollow-point "Treasury load" used by several agencies of the federal government is an example of this type of load.

In this country, the most popular guns of this type are medium-frame revolvers such as the Colt Python and King Cobra, the S&W Models 65, 66 and 686, and the Ruger

GP-100. All have four-inch barrels, except the Smith 65, which is the stainless version of the three-inch Model 13 issued by the FBI.

Submachine guns used by modern entry teams include the Heckler & Koch MP5 (especially the MP5 SD suppressed version and the MP5K shortened version), Walther MPK, Beretta Model 12, the Uzi and the Mini-Uzi. The MP5A3 (folding stock model), MP5SD and MP5K have been widely used by SAS and GSG-9 counter-terrorist teams.

The most recent major action was the 1980 SAS operation at the Iranian Embassy in London. The MP5 also is used by the Los Angeles Sheriff's SEB team.

The MP5 has a number of advantages: closed bolt action (more accurate than an open bolt slamming forward when the trigger is pulled), adjustable rotary sights, etc. The Beretta Model 12 is widely used by Italian teams, although the ones I have tested seemed to be ammunition sensitive. The Uzi is used by Israeli commando teams as well as the United States Secret Service. The Mini-Uzi is just now coming into its own; I was impressed by the one example I tested.

The Ingram MAC-10 (9mmP and .45 ACP) and MAC-11 (.380 ACP) submachine guns also have been used on occasion, usually with a MAC suppressor attached. Various SMGs, made here or in Europe or Israel, have been threaded and equipped with other suppressors such as those made by Wilson Arms of Brunswick, Georgia.

The suppressor not only makes these small guns easier to hold on to, but minimize flash as well as noise, giving them a substantial advantage indoors. Most of these guns are issued in 9mmP; subsonic ammunition is necessary for optimum suppressor use to avoid the supersonic crack of the standard load as it passes through the air. Such loads are now more widely available.

Occasionally, semi-automatic or full-automatic rifles are used by entry teams. Among the best are the M16, the Steyr AUG, the Galil and the HK series. Usually these

The Mini-Uzi, shown with threaded barrel and a Wilson suppressor, has both firepower and maneuverability. It's favored for use in airliners and inside houses.

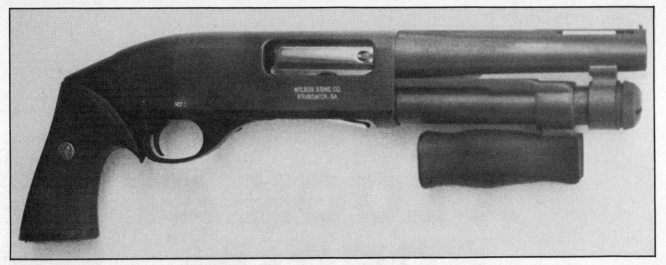

The Miami Vice *version of the Executive Protection shotgun in 12 gauge was made for the television show, but it also has found use among real special agents who have the need for a short, foolproof scattergun.*

arms are chambered for the 5.56mm (.223 caliber) now standard in NATO and quite effective for urban warfare.

In spite of its Space Age appearance, the AUG has some substantial advantages beginning with its short, bullpup-style overall length. It also is extremely rugged, immersion-proof, and has an excellent sighting system. Adopted by the Austrian military, this weapon has become popular with a number of other agencies, including special narcotic interdiction teams in U.S. Customs. I like the semi-auto version best, since full-automatic fire depends on a pull-through two-stage trigger which I find difficult to get used to.

Most police riot guns are oversized for entry team use. The eighteen- or twenty-inch barrel and the full-size wood

In spite of the fact that the shoulder stock has been removed, ejection is quick and positive with Executive Protector. The slide-action is relatively foolproof.

stock tend to bump on furniture and against doorways. One of the most popular solutions is to trim the ever-reliable pump-action shotgun at both barrel and stock, producing a much more maneuverable gun that is still accurate in close quarters. For example, NYPD Stakeout Unit teams used an Ithaca Model 37 12 gauge with shortened stock and a foot-long barrel. A strap was attached to the forend to speed up cycling and to keep the officer's left hand from slipping in front of the stubby barrel.

Although "whipit guns" have been around since the Nineteenth Century, some of the recent improvements have been impressive. One of the leaders in this conversion trade is Jim Wilson of Brunswick, Georgia, whose first model was called the "Witness Protection" after the U.S. Marshals' protection teams who often use this sort of gun.

The WP was a shortened Remington 870 12 gauge equipped with a handguard in front of the slide, even with the chopped barrel and a stock reduced to its pistol grip.

Wilson recommends an eye-level shooting stance, with the left hand pushing forward on the slide while the right pulls to the rear on the pistol grip, giving an isometric hold which minimizes recoil. In fact, the web of the hand is better constructed to accept recoil than the shoulder.

The successor to the Witness Protection is the Wilson Executive Protection shotgun based on the Mossberg 500. He has two versions, one cut just in front of the standard slide handle and to the rear of the pistol grip. The other is a super-short version with replacement pistol grip and fold-ing vertical foregrip. This is the model he made for the *Miami Vice* television series, so it is sometimes called the "MV" model.

This version is quite fast and controllable, although magazine capacity is reduced to two rounds. With one in the chamber and in-action reload capability, it is still more effective than a traditional double-barrel shotgun.

In sum, tactics count for more than weapons during high-risk entry, but there is still a need for the highest-tech, most reliable weapons available. Stopping power, accuracy, firepower, reliability and short overall length are the main criteria for adoption.

CHAPTER NINE

A LOOK AT SPECIAL EQUIPMENT

There's Something For Almost Every Law Enforcement Need These Days!

The ASP tactical baton is extended for use and can be used as an intermediate force weapon. Some feel that the greatest value is as a psychological deterrent weapon.

DURING THE past two decades there have been literally hundreds, perhaps thousands, of tools and devices developed for the law enforcement officer; some good, some not so good. One of the most valued innovations is without question soft body armor (SBA).

Bill McLennan is a twenty-five-year veteran of the San Antonio, Texas, police department. He joined the department after a tour of duty with the U.S. Marine Corps, serving first as a patrolman. Later, thanks to a natural talent for training and handling police dogs, he served several years on the K-9 corps with his German shepherd, Sam. After being promoted to detective-investigator, he worked first as a crime-scene detective in uniform, then as a plainclothes forgery and robbery detective. McLennan is now chief firearms instructor for the SAPD, and has been a certified firearms instructor since the early 1970s.

In 1974, he was appointed to the selection committee charged with the responsibility of choosing a new sidearm for the SAPD. Thanks to his efforts, the department began issuing the .41 magnum revolver and discarded the ineffec-

With a simple flick of the wrist, the ASP tactical baton can be extended from only nine inches to twenty-six.

This metal stock plate adds ballistic protection and will reduce blunt trauma. It is covered with neoprene which reduces some effect of low velocity flat-point bullets.

tive .38 Special. His knowledge of guns and ballistics has benefitted the department on many other occasions.

With his background, Bill McLennan has an opportunity to review a lot of new law enforcement equipment, so he's a natural to write this chapter. Here's what he has to say:

SBA gained a foothold in law enforcement during its initial introduction in 1972, but it is still not used on an habitual basis. No one disputes its value, but only about twenty percent of the nation's cops regularly wear it.

My own introduction to SBA came in February, 1973, while competing in the First International Police Combat Matches at Las Vegas, Nevada. There I saw Richard Davis, the founder of Second Chance Armor, realistically demonstrate his vest. Davis turned a .38 caliber revolver toward his abdomen and fired point blank into the vest he was wearing. That wasn't his first time to shoot himself, nor his last. He alone has probably done more than any individual to promote SBA to the law enforcement community.

I've had a strong interest in SBA ever since that introduction. Unfortunately, I cannot say that all of my experiences with the armor industry have been pleasant. I have encountered some pretty unsavory people in the business.

During the past four years, I have conducted a stringent and on-going evaluation of SBA for my department. Dur-

ing this time I have encountered and uncovered a multitude of "dirty tricks." The most incredible occurred while testing bid samples from a major manufacturer; let's call this Brand X. The bid invitiation specified that a sample vest and a twelve-by-twelve-inch swatch of identical construction be submitted for testing. Even though the test was closed to the public, the sales representative from Brand X showed up. Right off the bat he refused to let us test the sample vest his company had submitted. He alleged there had been some construction problems with the sample vest. He stated that the test swatch submitted by Brand X would pass our test, but the vest would not. The bid invitation had stated clearly that the sample vest would be tested, and if accepted, would become a quality control model for the duration of the contract.

The rep from Brand X assured me the problems inherent in that specific vest would not be present in later models. In fact, he swore the faults had been resolved overnight and he would have another sample shipped in air express. The bid deadline had passed, so I refused to give him additional time — but I was overruled by my superior.

The following day, we received an express package containing another sample from Brand X. The third sample was quite dissimilar from the original two. The original vest sample had several layers of Kevlar coated with a tar-like substance. The test swatch contained quite another

The Chapman search position is ostensibly the most versatile system for handling a handgun and flashlight. It avails itself of "third-eye" technique told in text.

substance and in addition was diamond-stitched; this type of stitching enhances the ballistic integrity of Kevlar. Diamond-stitching was not listed in the bid specs. The third sample contained what appeared to be a Kevlar stabilizer patented by American Body Armor and sold by that company under the trade name, *Black Magic.* Brand X is not American Body Armor and is not associated with that company.

To make a long story short, our laboratory testing revealed the third sample was indeed American Body Armor's patented Black Magic Kevlar. The rep from Brand X denied it. He assured us his company could and would provide ballistic panels just like that in the third test sample, if they won the bid. Since Brand X's third submission passed all tests with flying colors and Brand X came in low bid, by all rights they should have won the bid. However, the rep from Brand X denied his employer had submitted another company's patented product. Having discovered his deception, we did not award Brand X the bid.

The armor industry is a cutthroat business, and there is no stopping the dregs of this trade. The rep from Brand X was hurried out of state before criminal charges could be filed. Just weeks later, another scoundrel — as crooked as the first — was at our door. This rogue was not as stupid as the first. He spread adverse rumors about his competitors, not wanting us to collect physical evidence against him, as we had done his predecessor.

Fortunately, not all of the armor industry is so dubious. I state without reservations that I have not discovered any deception from the folks at American Body Armor, nor any of its distributors. In fairness, I must also say that I have not dealt with every manufacturer in that trade.

What's just as frustrating as those unscrupulous merchants is the role of the National Institute of Justice (NIJ) in its certification of SBA. NIJ tests all SBA that the manufacturers submit to them. Testing is voluntary. NIJ has no enforcement power. As this is written, the NIJ is a malevolence to the armor industry and law enforcement. Thomas E. (Ed) Bachner, Jr., Du Pont's ballistics account manager, has aptly labeled the issue "The Great Body Armor Controversy."

Bachner will furnish a report — available from Du Pont Company, Fibers Department, Chestnut Run Plaza, Wilmington, DE 19880-0705 — that puts NIJ's attitude in perspective. In a nutshell, the report says that NIJ's current standard (NIJ STD-0101.03) does not provide reliable nor realistic testing of SBA. *Oh-three* as it is known in the trade, neglects ballistic testing of SBA against .22 rimfire rifles and 12-gauge buckshot. In hard armor, .03 neglects the testing of 5.56mm M855 FMJ.

It should be noted that a vest designed to defeat the .44 magnum may not defeat high-velocity .22 rimfire rounds. The ballistic integrity of a vest panel is dependent on the

Streamlight's AC/DC rechargeable flashlight system will thrive on hard use and save dollars over the long haul.

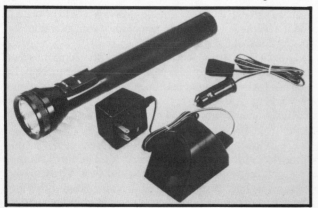

Mag Instruments' Mini-MagLight is a handy little lamp — in or out of uniform — that tucks out of the way well.

DEF TEC's 12-gauge TKO carries a load of compressed zinc for knocking out dead-bolt locks, steel hasps and hinges. Zinc disintegrates on impact without ricochets.

number of threads in the Kevlar's weave configuration, i.e. the number of threads per square inch. The tighter the weave, the more effective the Kevlar material will be in defeating small-diameter bullets and vice versa. At least one manufacturer skirts this fact in his advertisements. One model of his vest will stop the mighty .44, but not the lowly rimfire rifle. NIJ regulates the labeling of armor, but not the sales literature.

The .03 standard does not specify that a vest panel be strapped to the test medium in a particular manner. The standard disallows straightening of the panels between shots. Both requirements are unrealistic, because the vest panel is not attached to the backface medium with its original straps, and more complications evolve because the medium does not even remotely resemble a human torso. At each point of impact, the vest panel puffs and bunches up. Eventually, air pockets form between the panel and backface medium and a projectile penetrates the

DEF TEC's F16 is a non-burning teargas grenade that is designed to eliminate all risk of fire when it is used.

vest. The puffing and bunching effect that occurs on a static test dummy does not occur on the dynamic human torso.

The .03 is further flawed in that conventional handguns are not used in the laboratory tests. NIJ uses closed-breech test barrels. They do this to try and meet a narrow velocity

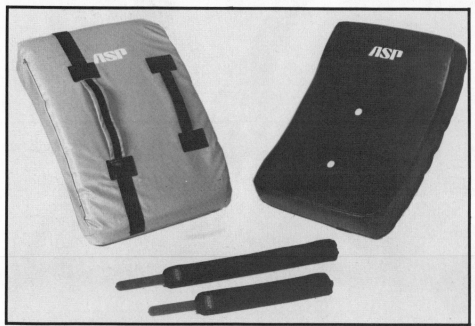

Supreme Court decisions have mandated that police training be realistic. As a result, training batons and bags allow contact during the training of officers.

requirement. For instance, .03 mandates that Threat Level II SBA must defeat six .357, 158-grain JSPs at 1395 fps (+50fps). That's 1395 to 1445 fps, period!

In the reports I've examined the laboratory cannot consistently hold its test rounds within that 50 fps span, even with test barrels. The 50 fps interval is simply too small for all the variables involved.

I would suggest that, if any one of the first six test rounds dropped below the minimum 1395 fps, the test should be started over. That, however, is not what happens. My test data reveals that the lab simply fires another round when there have been substandard velocities and they keep on firing until six of the rounds fired reach or exceed 1395 fps. In some tests, samples were shot up to twenty times before six rounds fell within the 1395-1445 fps interval. Needless to say, many vests fail because of excessive hits. Under the circumstances, it's not surprising that a particular vest passes .03 one day and fails the next.

When Kevlar fabric is struck by a bullet, each thread that this bullet impacts suffers trauma, not just at the point of impact, but all along its length. Obviously, there is a limit to the amount of projectiles a panel will resist. Five or six rounds is realistic.

There is no case history that even remotely suggests SBA has been subjected to more than three or four hits on the street. A six-round test is valid, but the +50 fps is not. It would be more realistic to increase the acceptable velocity to 1395 fps plus or minus 50 fps.

At this writing, SBA never has failed in actual use. It is tough and reliable. Today's Kevlar 129 is lighter and ballistically stronger than its counterpart of only a year ago, but it doesn't fare any better than its predecessor, Kevlar 29, in NIJ testing because .03 is too inconsistent.

Bianchi Speed Strips are convenient reloading devices for the civilian-attired cops with .38/.357 revolvers.

Although bureaucrats ignore NIJ's certification on handguns, handcuffs and many other products, they do not ignore NIJ certification of SBA. There are no handguns and few handcuffs that presently meet NIJ standards, so why should SBA be any different?

In order to comply with .03, vest makers are going to be forced to add twenty-five to thirty percent more Kevlar to each panel, front and back. That means more weight and more weight means more discomfort. Discomfort unequivocally translates to less wear, the one thing NIJ should be striving to overcome.

ASP cases are constructed from premium leather, stitched at the corners with nylon cord. These scabbards feature a recessed, one-direction snap and are available in black or cordovan, plain or basketweave, high-luster.

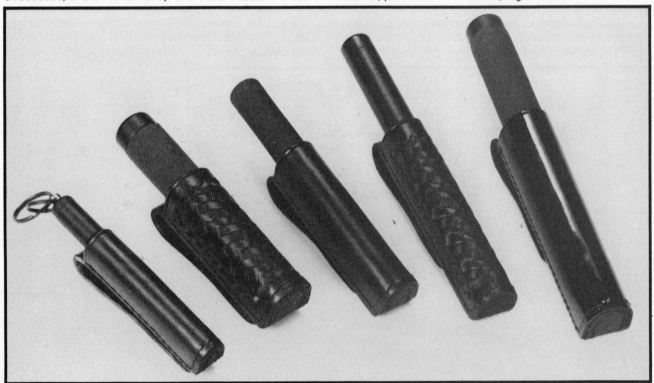

The body armor manufacturers are so put out with NIJ that they have established their own standard. Dubbed Personal Protective Armor Association (PPAA) STD-1989-05, this document is more realistic and practical than NIJ's .03. The PPAA was formed out of necessity when the makers of modern armor realized a watch dog was needed to clean up the deceptive practices of the industry. It was also through necessity that PPAA established a practical certification process that an individual officer or agency could conduct on the common firing range — PPAA .05 does just that. Conventional handguns are used and any ammunition that is suspect can be tested. A copy of PPAA-STD-1989-05 is available from Du Pont's Ballistic Account Manager, Ed Bachner, Jr. Until the .03 inconsistencies are resolved, Kevlar SBA will hang in limbo, passing NIJ certification one day and failing it the next.

A recent innovation in the armor industry — Spectra, made by Allied-Signal, Incorporated, P.O. Box 31, Petersburg, VA 23804 — may prove to be superior to Kevlar as a ballistic fabric. Armor made of Spectra products is available from Progressive Apparel, Incorporated, 2807-A Merrilee Drive, Fairfax, VA 22031. Progressive Apparel uses two Spectra configurations in their bullet resistant vests: Specta Fabric and Spectra Shield. Vest panels may be constructed exclusively of either the fabric, the shield or a material combination of both.

Spectra Fabric looks much like any woven and scoured cloth, while Spectra Shield is a non-woven material. The latter is made by placing two layers of unidirectional fibers at right angles and laminating them at zero degrees Fahrenheit in thermoplastic resin.

Ballistic panels made with Spectra Shield provide several advantages over comparable levels of Kevlar: Spectra is more resistant to water, lighter in weight — it floats — more resistant to multiple hits and angled shots, more slash, stab and cut resistant and faster at wicking away body heat.

Spectra Shield is resistant to abrasion, mildew and common chemical agents; in fact, it is chemically inert. Being twenty-five percent lighter than Kevlar, Spectra also is softer and more pliable. All considered, it is an impressive fabric. Allied-Signal says that, "pound for pound, Spectra is ten times stronger than steel."

In addition to SBA, Spectra Fibers are used in armored vehicles, ballistic helmets, radomes and cut-resistant gloves. Spectra is also used in the manufacture of bicycle frames, tennis rackets, hockey sticks, skis, canoes, sailcloth and rope.

Unlike Kevlar, Spectra has a low melt point: three hundred degrees Fahrenheit. This is the only adversity that opponents to Spectra seem to harp on, but it is not a great disadvantage in body armor. Cops do not fight fires!

Spectra Shield seems to fare better than Kevlar when tested under the flawed .03. Its thermoplastic unidirectional construction maximizes ballistic integrity against multiple hits and efficiently disperses blunt trauma over a wider area of the backface medium.

Using Spectra Shield, Progressive Apparel makes specialty armor that readily defeats high-powered rifle bullets without the addition of hardened strike face materials such as steel or ceramics. Spectra Shield plates reduce the

Straight design or side-handle batons still are favored in some law-enforcement jurisdictions. The front-break carrier is practical and quick to use in releasing the baton, which will not fall out even when one is running.

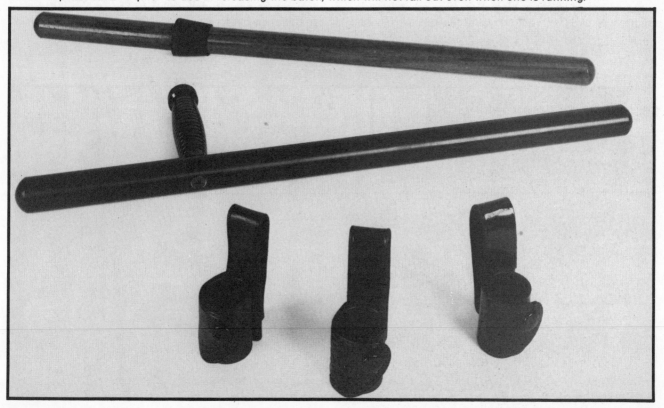

weight of tactical vests by fifty percent over comparable models of Kevlar that require ceramic or steel inserts.

Spectra is more expensive than Kevlar. An average piece of soft armor will cost about $30 to $50 more per unit; a paltry sum when your life is at stake. Spectra sounds like a revolution in police armor, but only time will tell if it will meet our needs.

Regardless of brand, style or composition, any armor that is worn regularly is superior to that left at home or in the trunk of the cruiser. Whether the officer is performing a mundane task or a high stress crisis situtation, the use of body armor cannot be devalued.

In a barricade situation, the law enforcement officer has three choices: talk him out, force him out — or take him out. The most undesirable choice is going in after him. Every time a tactical entry must be made, there is high probability an officer will be injured or killed. In most cases, barricade suspects are talked out. When communications break down, it is far safer to force him out than to go in after him — especially if the suspect is without hostages. Chemical agents give lawmen a superior advantage over any dynamic entry ever devised.

The use of chemical agents seems to have fallen from vogue in modern law enforcement. This disuse stems from the improper use of military munitions which has resulted in the burning of homes and, in several instances, entire neighborhoods. Military munitions are commonly pyrotechnic and not appropriate for use in civilian law enforcement.

There is no perfect chemical agent for resolving a barricade situation, but tear gas — CN (chloraceteophenone) and CS (orthochlorobenzalmalononitrile) — comes close. Both are available from the DEF-TEC Corporation, 2399 Forman Road, Rock Creek, OH 44084-0208, a leader in the field of chemical munitions. DEF-TEC markets aerosol chemical mace; multiple blast dispersion grenades containing CN and CS; continuous-discharge CN, CS and smoke grenades; colored smoke grenades; triple charger CN, CS and smoke grenades; rubber ball CN, CS and smoke grenades; and 12-gauge and 37mm projectiles charged with CN, CS and smoke. DEF-TEC munitions are labled specifically for indoor or outdoor use. Those designed for indoor use are made of liquid or mist agents rather than thermally ignited compounds that could cause a fire.

DEF-TEC's F16 flameless expulsion grenade is a revolutionary new concept in non-burning CS. It is a spoon-activated, rubber ball-type grenade with a one-second delay fuse, that disperses its micro-pulverized agent by means of a CO_2 cartridge.

DEF-TEC also markets grenade launchers for handguns, shotguns and 37mm gas guns. Pepper foggers, for laying down clouds of dispersement gas and/or smoke, are also available. For forced entry, DEF-TEC engineers a frangible 12-gauge Avon round. It is listed in their current catalogue as the No. 22 Tactical Knock Out Round (T.K.O.).

Properly applied, the T.K.O. will defeat door locks, hinges, door knobs and dead bolt locks on either solid or hollow-core wooden doors as well as hollow metal doors. The T.K.O. also will punch out automobile door and trunk locks.

The T.K.O. is made of compressed zinc that disintegrates into a fine powder upon impact. Fragmentation of the T.K.O. payload is complete. However, secondary projectiles may be generated from the debris of a disintegrating target.

The T.K.O. can be used with any standard law enforcement shotgun equipped with DEF-TEC's stand-off/launcher. The stand-off/launcher insures that the proper distance is kept when using the T.K.O. to blow away locks, hinges, et cetera. It does not interfere in any way with the firing of standard 12-gauge ammunition. The stand-off/launcher also can be used to deliver DEF-TEC's No. 90 tactical grenade, an outdoor pyrotechnic device containing CN,

The officer who wore this windbreaker was struck in his chest by a charge of 12-gauge #00 buckshot. He says it was like a sledge hammer blow. Body armor beneath this jacket saved his life. His adversary was not so lucky.

CS or smoke. The No. 90 tactical grenade is a continuous-discharge device that generates an abundance of irritating agents.

Chemicals are rather easy to use, but in this time of lawsuit-happy attitudes only a fool would not seek certification and training in their application. The DEF-TEC Training Academy provides training and instructor certification programs in the use of distraction devices, chemical munitions, chemical mace, anti-sniping and the tactical shotgun.

The so-called *impact weapon* has been in vogue for some time now. Nightstick has virtually slipped from our vocabulary. One of the most popular impact weapons in current use, the side-handle baton, is really not a modern invention. It is a facsimile of the Seventeenth Century Okinawan *tonfa*. The tonfa, originally a grain-grinding instrument, became a combative weapon after the Japanese overran the Ryukyu Island in the 1600s. After Japanese occupation, the island natives were disarmed. From that time on their weapons were disguised as tools.

The tonfa was one such tool. Although crude in appearance, it proved effective. Today, the tonfa is just as effectively used — as the PR24 police baton — by lawmen all over the world.

The PR24 baton or side-handle baton, as it is sometimes called, was invented around 1971-72 by Iowa conservation officer Lon Anderson. Anderson was assaulted while attempting to quell a disturbance at a neighborhood tavern. Even though armed with a conventional baton, Anderson was severly injured. While recovering from his injuries, Anderson began thinking about a better baton. A martial artist, he was familiar with the tonfa and surmised it would be suitable as a police impact weapon.

When Anderson got out of the hospital, he began experimenting with the tonfa. He eventually settled on a simple design — the PR24 police baton. He then convinced his chief that it was more court defensible and effective in use than the straight baton, and obtained the chief's permission to carry it on duty. Ironically, while investigating another dispute at the same bar, he was again assaulted. The outcome was quite different this time. Anderson engaged his adversaries with the newly designed baton and neutralized them in short order.

Anderson later offered his invention to Monadnock Lifetime Products, P.O. Box B, Fitzwilliam, NH 03447, who undertook its patent and production. Today it is marketed as the Monadnock PR24 Police Defensive Baton.

The PR24 baton has many advantages over a straight baton. The PR24 generates two to three times the velocity of a straight baton which translates to more impact on target. The PR24 is easy to learn to use; perhaps easier, than the straight baton. With a little practice, one quickly perfects the spinning, punching and blocking techniques in the PR24 baton's manual of arms.

Because of its peculiar spinning and punching techniques rather than the lurching and swinging motions used with a conventional baton, the PR24 does not appear sinister and bludgeon-like when used. In execution, the techniques appear artful, as well as composed and more humane in the eyes of by-standers.

Monadnock's latest addition is an extendable baton, the PR24X. The PR24X is ideal for the officer who must carry his baton on his person at all times. While the PR24 baton is a fixed twenty-four inches long, the PR24X collapses from twenty-four to fourteen inches. To extend it to full length, all it takes is two flicks of the wrist. It is retracted to its stored length by pressing a pin and pushing the tailshaft back into the main housing. The PR24X is a clever design, and like all Monadnock products, is made of quality material.

The officer shot with the buckshot load was wearing this Level II American vest beneath. The load of #00 buck, fired at point-blank range, tore a gaping hole in the outer fabric, but failed to penetrate the first layer.

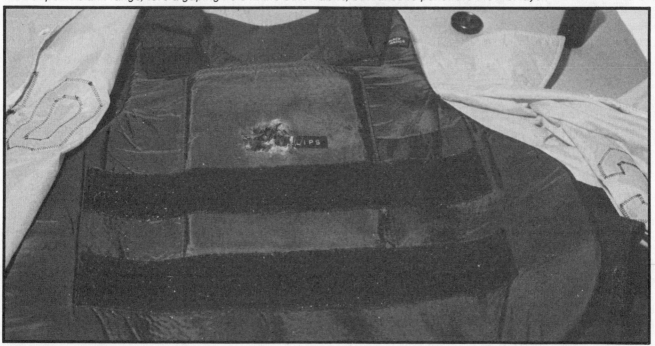

Officers contend that body armor should offer adequate protection from the side as with this wrap-around model. This particular style is made by American Body Armor.

Monadnock also offers extendable straight batons, the SX24 and MX18, and a mini-baton, the Persuader.

One of the most ingenious and convenient impact weapons developed to date is the ASP tactical baton by Armament Systems and Procedures, Box 1794 Appleton, WI 54913. The ASP is a collapsible baton that is available in several lengths: 6 to 16, 7 to 16, 8 to 21 and 9 to 26 inches. It is available in chrome or black finish and easily carried in a leather scabbard on the belt.

The ASP tactical baton is an excellent impact weapon for the plainclothes officer. In its collapsed state, it is easily concealed. It is not likely to be detected even by a trained eye, hence it is practical for undercover assignments. Bailiffs and court officials who prefer to convey a passive appearance also will find the ASP suitable.

The ASP is brought to the ready by a sharp flick of the wrist and its mere appearance has proven to be a deterrent. The resounding "clack" of the ASP baton locking into battery has proved to be as psychologically effective as racking the action of a pump shotgun. The ASP baton is that heretofore missing step in our continuum of force. It nearly fills that gap between hand-to-hand combat and deadly force.

The ASP baton is made of high strength steel with a Rockwell hardness of 55C, yet is light enough that it will not crush bone. It will generate shock waves that reach bone deep.

Regardless of what type baton an officer chooses, he must use it properly. Engagement should be made only with appropriate strikes. Strikes should be short and snappy and delivered to vulnerable areas that will incapacitate an adversary temporarily, yet not cause serious bodily injury. Such vulnerable areas are the instep, ankle, shin, knee, thigh, hip, floating ribs, xyphoid process, manubrium of the sternum, collar bone, scapula, biceps, elbow, forearm, wrist and hand.

Mini-batons or Kubotans neatly fit that step in the ladder of force between hand-to-hand combat and major impact weapons. The Kubotan is a formidable pain compliance device. First introduced by Takayuki Kubota in 1979.

The Kubotan (Reliapon, P.O. Box 14872, Station G., NE, Albuquerque, NM 87111) is a 5½-inch plastic wand with a key ring at one end. It is highly concealable, yet awesomely effective when used to apply wrist and thumb locks. A Kubotan wrist lock will bring the biggest and baddest adversary to his knees.

Kubotan training with either the official Kubotan or with a mini-flashlight like the Legend is available from Defensive Tactics Institute, Incorporated, P.O. Box 14872, Station G., NE, Albuquerque, NM 87111. Training seminars can be arranged by writing to the attention of John G. Peters, Jr. Peters also offers VCR correspondence courses, an excellent mode of training for those who can't afford his personal classes.

Flashlight/handgun shooting techniques are a necessity in law enforcement. Lawmen spend a considerable part of their careers in low-light environments. Probably the most widely taught flashlight/shooting technique is that known as the FBI position. In theory the technique sounds valid, but in actuality, it does not prove true. The shooter holds a flashlight in the non-shooting hand at arm's length to the side of his body. The handgun, held in the other hand, is extended toward the target. It is assumed that, by holding the flashlight at arm's length, it will draw incoming fire away from the shooter's body. It supposedly masks the shooter's position, providing him with concealment, but the hypothesis is invalid. When one looks at the FBI position from an adversary's viewpoint, he sees it exactly for what it is: an officer holding a flashlight and handgun at arms' length. Additionally, it is nearly impossible to synchronize the flashlight and handgun on target. The widely spaced hand positions are not conducive to eye-hand coordination, let alone practical for moving about during a search. To assume such a position after being fired upon is an act of futility.

There are two techniques which simultaneously put the flashlight and handgun on target: the Harries and Chapman Positions. They are search techniques and both work quite effectively, depending on the shooting stance one has learned.

The Harries lends itself to the Weaver shooting systems while the more versatile Chapman obliges either the Weaver or Isosceles techniques. In the Harries Position, the flashlight is held backhand to backhand. The control button is switched on and off by the ring or little finger. The barrel of the flashlight may or may not rest on the opposing forearm.

In the Chapman Position, the flashlight is held forehand to forehand and the control button is depressed by the thumb. The middle, ring and little fingers of the flashlight hand encircle the same fingers of the gun hand.

During actual use, the *third eye* technique is employed. Simply put, the flashlight/handgun combination points everywhere the eyes look. While searching, the flashlight is turned on for three to five second intervals, ideally from behind cover or while on the move, with movement continuing for several steps after the light has been extinguished.

Today's high-intensity flashlights are superb tools. I routinely encourage each new police cadet to invest in a good high-intensity flashlight instead of an off-duty sidearm, if they can't afford both. Their money is better spent on a good flashlight, considering that the issue revolver can suffice for off-duty carry. The flashlight certainly sees more actual use than the off-duty handgun.

Streamlight, 1030 Germantown Pike, Norristown, PA 19403, and Mag Instruments, P.O. Box 1840, Ontario, CA 91762, both make ideal high-intensity and mini-flashlights.

Another mini-light, the Legend, by Keller Company, P.O. Box 80-9003, Dallas, TX 75380, is also an excellent tool. I like its end cap switch. Mini-flashlights are ideal for the officer who wants a backup lamp or those who work the day shift and have the foresight to know they inevitably will find themselves in a poorly lighted building. The mini-lights can also double as a Kubotan.

Speedloaders have been around for nearly three decades. The HKS from HKS Products, 7841 Foundation Drive, Florence, KY 41042, is unequivocally the best speedloader on the market. It is reliable and simple to operate. With a few hours of practice, one can reload the revolver in less than four seconds.

HKS also markets belt pouches. They are made of Du Pont's Hytrel, a leather look-alike material that is extremely durable and inexpensive. The pouches are available in plain or basketweave finish and are black, brown or tan colors.

For uniform wear, speedloaders should be worn on the Sam Browne belt near the center of the body, accessible to either hand, but more so to the strong side.

In addition to speedloaders, an officer must carry a few cartridges in belt loops. It is not tactically sound to rely solely on speedloaders. Every defensive tactics instructor I know advocates, "Reload at every opportunity, whether one, two or more rounds have been fired!" and, "Never venture into unexplored territory with a partially loaded weapon!"

One of my students recently became involved in a heated gun battle. Her partner emptied his service revolver, then

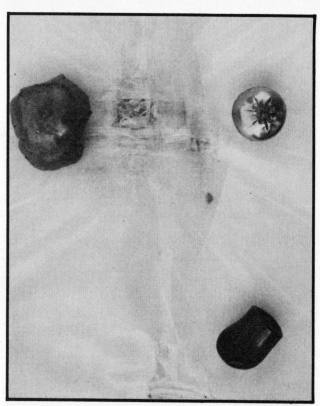

This test swatch of Spectra Shield 1000, revolutionary new fabric for the body armor industry, defeated .357 magnum and 9mmP jacketed hollow-point ammo.

reloaded and fired six more rounds. During a second reload, he dropped his speedloader. It rolled beneath the vehicle they were crouching behind. Neither officer could reach it. It contained the officer's last six rounds. Fortunately for both officers the incident soon ended. Having dodged more than two dozen bullets, their adversary surrendered! Both officers now carry a brace of speedloaders — and an additional twelve rounds in loops on their belts.

As a plainclothes detective, I carried Bianchi Speed Strips (Bianchi International, 100 Calle Cortez, Temecula, CA 92390) for more than seventeen years. Speed Strips are not as fast as speedloaders, but they are easier to conceal and more convenient to carry. I preferred to carry them in the side pocket of my suit coat, but they will tuck nicely into a belt pouch, too.

Half-moon clips were the predecessor to speedloaders. Clips of one configuration or another have been around for the better part of this century. They work marvelously in revolvers chambered for rimless pistol cartridges like the 9mm, 10mm and .45 ACP. Today, there is a full array of moon clips — full, half, third and quarter — all of which are more concealable than any speedloader. Two full-moon clips of .45 ACP take up less space than a single speedloader of .357 JHPs. Moon clips are aviailable from Ranch Products Company, Box 145, Malinta, OH 43535.

Only time will tell what innovations are on tap for the future. Without question, we will see more high-tech equipment, but some tools and devices like soft body armor will remain simple, unsophisticated and practical. Some will be good, some not so good. Regardless of what comes, you can bet that only the good will survive.

Chapter Ten

POLICE SERVICE AMMUNITION

Today's Defensive Handgun Rounds Give Law Enforcement A Wide Range Of Options

The .41 magnum enjoyed a brief, limited popularity among police officers during the Sixties and Seventies. This is the author's Smith & Wesson Model 58 with the 210-grain lead police load and Winchester 175-grain Silvertips.

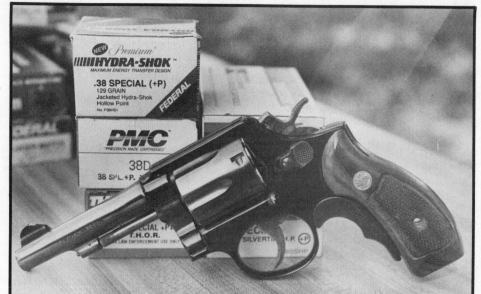

For decades, S&W's K-frame .38 Special was a standard for most police agencies. Plus-P ammunition has made it a far better performer.

STONISHING IS the only way to describe what has happened in the last few years in regard to handguns and ammunition in law enforcement. Always before, things have moved with such glacial slowness that few of us thought we'd see the day when these dramatic changes took place. Now there are new and vastly improved handguns and better cartridges, even entirely new calibers, designed expressly for police officers.

The swiftness with which these events have taken place leaves cynical old-timers gasping in disbelief. Instead of making do, improvising and wishing for better things, real attention is being paid to law enforcement and morale is at an all-time high.

A few years ago, it looked as though the bulk of the half-million-plus police officers in the United States would enter the next century with the old .38 Special revolver in their holsters. There are still a lot of them out there, but times are changing fast. Now it looks like even traditionally conservative police administrators are committed to the semi-automatic pistol when replacements are purchased.

Until that happens, we need the best, most effective defense ammo we can find. If anything, it's more important for the revolver than the new breed of semi-automatic pistols. Worsening social conditions (read drug wars) have made bigger fire-fights inevitable. A cop with speedloaders and lots of practice can get by, but the first cylinderful is still the most important. Each enemy you take out with a single shot leaves you one more bean in the wheel to deal with others. Yes, it's that bad.

If sidearms are changing for the better, so is the ammunition. Even after Lee Jurras and his Super Vel ammo of the Sixties showed us the way, really good jacketed hollow-point ammo was a long time coming. When the switch was made from the older lead projectiles to the JHPs, the velocity was sometimes increased, but too often, not enough.

The goal of the major ammo makers was to stay inside established pressure figures for a given cartridge, mostly to prevent excessive gun wear and avoid case failure. Standard working pressure for the .38 Special is 18,900 CUP (copper units of pressure), regardless of bullet type. Reluctantly, pressure was increased to some 22,400 CUP for the first .38 Special Plus-P loads. The guns held up to this modest increase and the JHP bullets worked much better. They began to really expand and offer more of what we call stopping power.

Today, the .38 Special is no slouch with these rounds, and is even better with Plus-P-Plus cartridges that operate at still higher pressures and velocities.

The Plus-P .38 Specials inevitably led to the same treatment for other cartridges used in law enforcement. The track record of the 9mm Parabellum almost duplicated the poor one of standard .38s, so it got Plus-P upgrading. Velocity went from the 1100 fps range to some 1200+ and even this slight increase greatly improved performance.

The .357 was another beneficiary, and with the favored 125-grain JHP from Remington and Federal, went to nearly 1500 fps in four-inch barreled .357 service revolvers. These loads proved highly lethal in street use and still are favorites in many departments.

The .45 ACP was brought up to date at last, with a Plus-P load. In a rather bold move, Remington introduced their new version using the 185-grain JHP at about 1150 fps, a two hundred feet per second advantage over most .45 JHPs — even faster than the .45 auto Super Vel load of the Sixties.

Remington has shown before that the company can be innovative. Back in 1964, Remington collaborated with Smith & Wesson to introduce the .41 magnum, then considered the ideal police cartridge by several noted gun writers. At the time, the few JHP loads available were showing poor performance even in the .357 magnum. The larger diameter .41 semi-wadcutter bullet wouldn't need expansion for good stopping power.

Gunwriters Elmer Keith, Bill Jordan and Skeeter Skelton were absolutely correct on that point. The .41 magnum "police load" used a 210-grain SWC bullet at 950 fps from four-inch barrels, and it proved to be a good stopper.

The .41 could have been the major police cartridge of the

next two decades, but marketing strategy and execution were so poor they verged on incompetence. Remington felt it was wise to cover all the angles and produced a hotter .41 magnum cartridge for hunters, using a 210-grain JHP at 1250 fps. Inevitably the hotter rounds made their way into the .41 M58 S&Ws used by police, who found recoil objectionable. The hunting round is totally unsuited for combat or police use.

To make matters worse, the lower velocity police load leaded bores badly and accuracy suffered. The .41 revolver was adopted by a few departments, but there was no stampede. It languished until the mid-1970s, when female officers began entering law enforcement in large numbers. They found the big N-frame .41 too much to handle, literally. Already enfeebled, it died completely for law enforcement use. The demise of the .41 magnum was due primarily to these factors, but it's also true it coincided exactly with the advent of really good .357 ammunition in JHP persuasion.

Those few officers who still prefer the .41 can be assured it works as well as ever.

As a medium or intermediate caliber, there always has been a good deal of interest in the .40 or .41 bore size. What you want in a combat cartridge is just enough — but not too much — in the way of overkill. Excess power

A couple of decades ago, the 210-grain lead SWC was the issued .41 magnum police load (left). Velocity was 950 fps in 4-inch barrel. The Winchester Silvertip came later, with a 175-grain JHP that travels at 1130 fps.

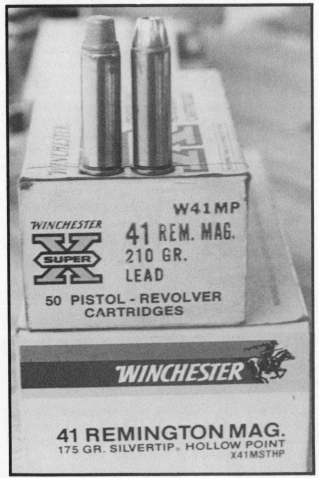

Author contends modern American handgun ammo is the best in the world in any caliber choice. These are the top police loads, offering a wide variety of capability.

means too much recoil, which prevents fast recovery time when follow-up shots are needed, or when facing multiple adversaries. The requirements seemed to be misunderstood completely by ammo makers right up until recent years.

The 10mm Auto cartridge appeared as the decade of the 1980s opened. The 10mm had existed as an exotic wildcat round for twenty years, usually used by experts in custom-converted Browning 9mm P-35 pistols. The West Coast firm of Dornaus & Dixon legitimized it with their Bren Ten, an advanced autoloader with many desirable features. The reorganized Super Vel ammo company produced a 10mm auto cartridge, but it died with the company in just a couple of years.

Taken up by Norma short months later, the previously mild little wildcat in 10mm now showed its teeth. The Norma 10mm used a 170-grain JHP at a hot and sizzling 1350 fps. Norma's military load was a 200-grain FMJ flat-point traveling at a resounding 1150-1200 fps. Many cops and shooters considered velocity — and resulting recoil — a bit on the high side for best results.

The new 10mm was *not* on its way to capture the hearts and minds of law enforcement people at that point. To worsen matters, the single pistol model available for the cartridge, the Bren Ten, disappeared when the parent company folded.

These setbacks clearly implied that the 10mm was finished after a shorter life than even the luckless .41 magnum. It stayed in limbo until 1987, when Colt, for reasons never made public, chambered the 10mm in the Series 80 Colt Delta Elite. There was still plenty of Norma ammo on dealer's shelves, hot ammo though it was, and the cartridge was still in full production. Colt's Delta Elite rescued the 10mm from oblivion, and the caliber has continued to grow in popularity, especially among civilian shooters.

Because it's a single-action pistol — a modernized M1911 — the Delta Elite never had a chance in police work. Such guns must be carried cocked-and-locked for instant readiness, and this dangerous looking practice scares all police chiefs and most civilians. Double-action service-type autos from S&W weren't long in coming. They can be carried with the hammer down for safety.

There still remained the excess recoil and velocity of the standard 10mm load. As a result of the 1986 shoot-out in

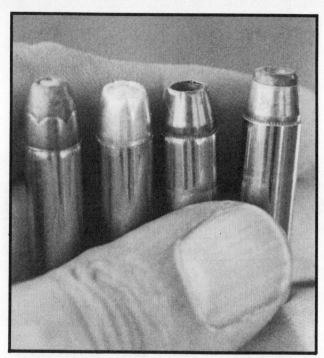

In the .38 Special only the best +P ammo should be used on duty. From left: Remington 125-grain scalloped jacket, PMC 125-grain JHP, Federal's Hydra-Shok 125-grain and 110-grain Silvertip cartridge from the Winchester factory.

Florida in which several FBI agents were slain, a study of bullet performance was undertaken by the bureau.

One conclusion was that excess velocity inhibited penetration; the faster a JHP is driven, the more it expands. And the more it expands, the less it penetrates. This characteristic was cited for the failure of a 9mmP Silver Tip to penetrate the heart of an armed felon during the shootout. What a reversal of thought! At first, we had difficulty in getting any expansion at all from handgun bullets. Now they expand too well! In the first edition of this book, I warned of the danger myself. I said, "Whatever else you get from a handgun bullet, you must get penetration to vital organs."

Even so, there is an aura of scapegoatism concerning the FBI investigation. In reality, the 9mmP Silver Tip performed well and as expected. It penetrated the felon's arm, then drove several inches into the chest cavity before stopping barely short of the heart. The solution is to get more and better hits, not blame the bullet. Nevertheless, the FBI incident sparked a trend toward lowered velocity, and thus enhanced penetration from handgun bullets.

When the FBI adopted the S&W M1076 auto in 10mm, the agency demanded — and got — a reduced loading of the 10mm cartridge. The load consists of a 180-grain JHP bullet at some 950 fps. It penetrates well; whether it will expand is open to question.

The FBI position is that penetration is the main goal and expansion, if it occurs, is just a side benefit. This is an extreme attitude, and there should be a happy medium somewhere. If one hundred feet per second velocity was added to the 10mm FBI load, the extra recoil could be tolerated and expansion of the bullet made more likely. There is such a thing as expansion and adequate penetration, too.

In 1989, Remington introduced a .357 magnum load designed for snub-barreled .357 defense revolvers. It uses the excellent scalloped jacket 125-grain JHP at a claimed velocity of just 1220 fps, instead of the usual 1400 fps. In this case, the velocity is still enough that expansion should be good, but recoil and muzzle blast are reduced to more tolerable levels. There's no reason it shouldn't be a good defense load in longer, four-inch barreled revolvers, as well.

In 1990, Smith & Wesson surprised the shooting world with the announcement of the new .40 S&W cartridge to be chambered in the S&W M4006 autoloader. Essentially, it's a shorter-cased 10mm with subsonic ballistics — a 180-grain JHP bullet at 950 fps muzzle velocity. There's no doubt it made a good impression with law enforcement. Several large agencies have adopted this gun/cartridge combination.

"Sub-sonic" — velocity below the speed of sound — is definitely in. Most ammo manufacturers also have a subsonic, heavy-bullet 9mmP load, as well. Thanks to mild shooting characteristics, it should do much to improve hitting potential for less than expert markspersons. That category includes most police officers.

Sub-sonic jacketed hollow-points that may or may not expand seems more a fad than sound ballistic theory. High velocity kills better; it's as simple as that. If you achieve it with standard weight bullets, recoil and muzzle blast make accurate shot placement difficult. Fortunately, there is a way to attain high handgun velocity and excellent stopping power with low recoil. The answer is the frangible bullet, extremely light in weight, but highly lethal in terminal effect.

Hornady has been a leader in developing new loads for law enforcement needs. Their 180-grain JHP XTP load has found great favor with some police departments.

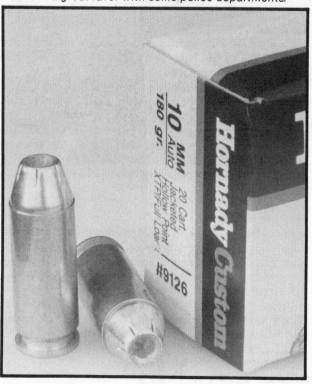

A few years ago, inventor Joe Zambone began offering his frangible-bullet MagSafe ammunition which is now available in all handgun calibers. The bullet consists of an annealed copper jacket filled with carefully layered #2 birdshot fixed in an epoxy core.

In .38 Special, the MagSafe .38 KD Agent +P+ load uses a 56-grain frangible bullet with an astonishing velocity of 2020 fps. Energy is 507 foot-pounds. On impact, the soft copper jacket ruptures, making a large permanent entry wound. Like a shaped-charge projectile, the epoxy resin core and #2 pellets are flung forward through the target for deep penetration to vital organs. A MagSafe bullet wound looks much like a shotgun wound.

The lightweight MagSafe's massive tissue destruction and effectiveness tend to discredit the long-held heavy bullet "momentum" theory of stopping power. This frangible bullet eliminates most of the faults of previous bullets, as it lacks severe recoil, and disintegrates on contact with hard materials, thus reducing the danger of ricochets.

This type of bullet may never replace the jacketed hollow-point in police work completely. At present, MagSafes are made by hand and therefore are expensive, but it's making a strong showing. In the meantime, we have some good choices available in less exotic persuasion:

THE .25 ACP

The .25 ACP is carried by many officers as a back-up gun. With the usual standard load of the 50-grain FMJ bullet, it's definitely on the puny side, but penetration is better than many shooters think. Winchester's X25AXP uses a 45-grain expanding-point bullet with a lead ball in the hollow nose; this should be slightly better than the FMJ slug. There is a MagSafe round available with a 30-grain bullet at 1250 fps, and this turns the little .25 auto into a more serious proposition for defense.

THE .380 ACP

It's often used for backup, also. Standard factory loads use a 95-grain FMJ bullet at a nominal 955 fps, but true velocity often is much less.

PMC's .380 loads include an excellent JHP and a FMJ round-nose. They seem especially hot and the latter chronographs at 1040 fps with the 95-grain bullet.

Winchester's 85-grain Silver Tip gives about 1000 fps in Walther PPs, somewhat less in shorter barrels, and has established a good street record. MagSafe's .380 +P+ carries a 52-grain frangible bullet at 1720 fps; a deadly load, indeed.

THE .38 SPECIAL

Thousands of .38 Specials are still on duty and both cartridge and revolver may never disappear from police work completely. Dozens of good factory loadings are available — too many to list individually.

As a rule of thumb, however, anything you put in your .38 Special, regardless of barrel length, should be of the Plus-P variety of JHP ammo. The best of them hover around the 1000 feet per second mark with bullet weights of 125 grains. It's a good idea to stick with this weight and choose nothing lighter in JHP design.

Federal's 129-grain Hydra-Shok JHP #P38HS1 is a

It was the Bren Ten that started the 10mm Auto craze, if it can be called that. The original gun no longer is made, but an all new version is to be called the Falcon.

hard act to follow in .38 Special. There are three MagSafe loads available. The hottest is the .38KD Agent which drives the 56-grain frangible bullet to 2020 fps. Despite the light bullet weight, it is wickedly destructive for close range defense use.

THE 9mm PARABELLUM

This round once was routinely ignored by police, because no good expanding bullets were available, and stopping power with the FMJ round-nose military bullet was poor.

The rush to 9mmP began in 1971 when S&W introduced the double-action high-capacity magazine M59 pistol. By that time, really good 9mmP JHP ammo was beginning to appear, and this helped popularize the round. So many agencies went to the 9mmP, it threatened the .38 Special's place as the principal police cartridge.

Like the .38 Special, the 9mmP has a poor record for stopping power, unless ammo is carefully chosen. There are, once again, dozens of good JHP cartridges available. Virtually all use a JHP weighing 115 to 124 grains at a moderate velocity of 1100 fps or so, depending on barrel length. Listing these individually is futile, as they have been rendered obsolete by newer 9mm ammo in Plus-P persuasion. Remington's 9mmP Plus-P is a good choice, with a 115-grain JHP at 1250 fps.

There is a trend in the opposite direction with the heavy-bullet subsonic 9mmP JHPs. Typically, these use a 147-grain JHP at only 950 fps. The intent here is to give the 9mmP more penetration, which it does, but at the expense of bullet expansion.

These subsonic rounds have only moderate street success. The way to go with the 9mmP is the Remington Plus-P 115-grain JHP at 1250 fps. A good alternative is the MagSafe 9 +P Police load. It uses a 68-grain frangible bullet at 1850 fps.

THE .357 MAGNUM

Next to the .38 Special, the .357 is still the most popular police round. Thanks to higher velocity which gives good bullet expansion, it's difficult to find a poor choice of ammo. Almost anything works well. The most effective seem to be the Remington or Federal 125-grain JHP at

1400 fps or so in four-inch barrels. These have good street reputations but recoil and muzzle blast make them rather unpleasant to shoot.

In 1989, Remington introduced a milder .357 load intended for use in snub-barreled defense revolvers. It utilizes the excellent scalloped-jacket 125-grain bullet at only 1220 fps. This is still enough velocity to expand the bullet, and there's no reason it wouldn't be a good defense cartridge in longer barreled .357s, too. The MagSafe 357D Defender cartridge gets 1860 fps with a 70-grain slug in four-inch barrels.

THE 10mm AUTO

This excellent pistol cartridge had to wait for modern double-action autos to appear before it became popular in law enforcement.

One of the first — and still the hottest — JHP rounds is the Norma, now marketed by Dynamit Nobel RWS. It carries a 170-grain bullet traveling at 1350 fps in the five-inch barrel of a Colt Delta Elite; somewhat less in shorter tubes. A close runner-up is the 155-grain Hornady, offering similar velocity.

Both are good choices, but recoil may be a bit sharp for some officers. Winchester's 175-grain Silver Tip is milder to shoot at 1220 fps. The FBI chose a subsonic loading of the 10mm using a 180-grain bullet at 950 fps.

Winchester, Federal and others manufacture subsonic 10mms. In general, they show less accuracy than the hotter loads, but are lower in recoil and muzzle blast. The 10mm is a somewhat temperamental cartridge, with best accuracy and stopping power tied closely to high velocity. The faster you drive the 10mm bullet, the better it performs.

THE .40 S&W

The .40 S&W is a shortened version of the 10mm Auto cartridge, with a case length of only .850-inch and utilizing the small pistol primer, instead of the large one of the 10mm. Original ballistics showed a 180-grain JHP at 950 fps in Winchester-made ammo. This practically duplicates the old .38-40 revolver cartridge, which had a reasonably good reputation as a manstopper. The .40 S&W is intrinsically more accurate than subsonic 10mm loads due to lesser case capacity.

Thanks to mild recoil and muzzle blast, the .40 S&W became instantly popular in law enforcement. If any round can do it, the .40 S&W may replace the 9mmP as the autoloading pistol cartridge of choice. MagSafe's 40D Defender load uses an 84-grain bullet at 1800 fps for greatest stopping effect.

THE .45 ACP

It took modern double-action pistols to popularize this old round in law enforcement. Despite an awesome reputation for stopping power, the older 230-grain hardball military round often did poorly on the street, and didn't bring out the full potential of the cartridge.

The 185-grain JHPs work much better. For years, the top choices were the Winchester 185-grain Silver Tip at 950 fps, the Remington 185-grain at 975 fps and the Speer

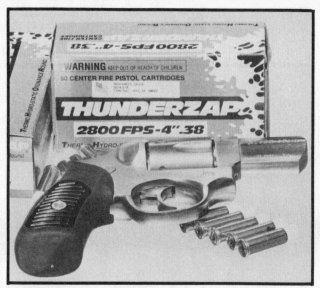

The Thunderzap cartridge in .38 Special is a +P+ load designed specifically for law enforcement work. In a four-inch barrel, the round hits 2800 fps muzzle velocity.

Lawman 200-grain JHP at 978 fps.

These will still do what they used to and are good choices. However, Remington now manufactures a Plus-P loading of the .45 ACP which drives the 185-grain JHP to 1150 fps in the five-inch barrel of Colt M1911 pistols. This is a good choice in shorter barreled pistols when you need all the velocity you can get. In pistols such as the Colt Officer's Model, and others with 3½-inch tubes, you need the speed.

MagSafe is a natural for these snubbies. The 45D +P Defender uses a 96-grain frangible bullet at 1660 fps in the Officer's Model and at 1760 in five-inch barrels.

These are the major calibers used in law enforcement today. There are others, of course, which may be popular locally on a smaller scale. For example the .41 magnum, .44 Special, .44 magnum and .45 Colt are missing from this list. Their big bullets hit hard and good JHP ammo is available for them. MagSafes and Glaser ammo are available also.

Also deliberately ignored are energy figures for these rounds. Energy is expressed in foot-pounds; the more the better, of course. Energy figures don't necessarily relate to effectiveness, and my personal feeling is that they can be misleading. As an example, a certain high velocity 9mmP FMJ round-nose bullet may give four hundred foot-pounds of energy. However, it would be a mistake to choose it on the basis of energy figures alone, for such bullets perform poorly as manstoppers.

What you're after is bullet performance, not a high energy rating. For purposes of judging street-worthiness, energy figures are virtually meaningless.

In the last few years, there has been a great explosion of "exotic" defense cartridges using various forms of trick bullets. Some, like the older Glaser and MagSafe, have built good reputations. As a rule, exotic ammo relies on high velocity for effectiveness. When buying any of it, use caution and verify claims before carryng it as defense ammo.

Is Subsonic Ammunition The Magic Answer For Law Enforcement?

Because of heavier weight and lower velocity, a subsonic bullet's point of impact will be different from that of a supersonic bullet's. This isn't of particular import in close-range encounters of usual type for the police.

SUBSONIC LOADS are the most recent trend in law enforcement handgun ammunition. The new 10mm FBI load, and the recently introduced .40 Smith & Wesson are two examples. The 9mm caliber has seen the introduction of 147-grain "heavy bullet" subsonic loads by every major manufacturer. The .45 ACP, which has always been subsonic, has seen adoption by a few agencies in recent years.

Most experienced shooters acknowledge that handguns are only marginal stoppers. Police officers, needing to stop suspects quickly and reliably, have often expressed displeasure with issued handguns and ammunition. "Stopping power" theories appear, gain favor and are eventually replaced by other theories. This has lead to many changes in both police handguns and types of ammunition provided for them.

Tony Lesce, who operates out of Arizona, is well known as a law enforcement journalist, tactician and analyst. He never has been a working law enforcement officer, but he has worked closely with police agencies in reporting tactics and in testing and evaluating equipment. Among other things, he is an editor on the staff of *Police Marksman*. With his testing background, I asked him to take a look at the subsonic ammo scene and make some evaluations. Here is what he has to tell us:

"A simple approach to increasing handgun effectiveness in the past was simply to pack more powder into the case. This sometimes resulted in new cartridges, such as the .357 magnum, a development of the standard .38 Special during the 1930s. More recently, Plus-P loads in various calibers provided marginal power increases over standard-pressure .38 Special loads," Lesce explains.

Increasing bullet effectiveness was another approach. Using soft-point and hollow-point bullets produced larger holes upon impact from smaller calibers. This gave the advantage of small-diameter bullets retaining good ballistic coefficients during flight, which mushroomed upon impact.

This is a typical 9mm supersonic cartridge, with recovered bullet from another round. Note that the bullet was fragmented upon impact, thus reducing overall penetration. In current thinking, penetration is gaining importance.

A major problem was that hollow-points needed high velocites to expand properly. During the 1960s, the current wave of lightweight, high-speed hollow-point cartridges began, using light bullets to insure high velocities without excessive pressure.

For many years, the threshold of expansion seemed to be around 1000 feet per second. Below this velocity, hollow-point bullets did not expand reliably. The most popular loads with police and civilians alike were those delivering significantly more than 1000 fps at the muzzle. Soft-point handgun bullets did not appear to expand as well, other things being equal. High-speed bullets also tend to produce a "temporary cavity" from hydraulic shock, as well as the permanent cavity they drill through the target.

One problem that developed with lightweight bullets was premature expansion in some cases. This led to the currently fashionable "penetration" theory of stopping power, which states that a handgun bullet should penetrate far enough to insure reaching vulnerable organs, even with the subject wearing heavy clothing or hiding behind light cover. According to this theory, the bullet's temporary cavity — and its diameter — are less important than bullet penetration. Other things being equal, the heavier bullet penetrates farther, because of greater sectional density.

The main problem with this theory is that, although many people have given it lip service, practically nobody appears to believe it, judging by their actions. Today, we see law enforcement agencies ordering an array of heavy-bullet versions of various calibers, almost all with hollow-point bullets for maximum expansion. Manufacturers and customers alike appear to be hedging their bets, accepting heavier bullets, but retaining the hollow-point design.

Several decades' experience in hollow-point bullet design have produced some remarkable bullets such as the Federal Hydra-Shok, using a center post to help expansion at low velocities. The .45 ACP version of this bullet expands reliably in water at slightly over eight hundred feet per second. Hydra-Shoks are available in most common handgun calibers.

One of the first manufacturers to respond to the demand for heavy bullets was Winchester, with its 9mm 147-grain JHP. To keep pressure to a safe level, this cartridge is loaded to deliver about 950 fps from a handgun. Other manufacturers followed, including Federal, with a 147-grain version of its Hydra-Shok.

Three-D, a Nebraska manufacturer, produced a 147-grain JHP load with the same point of impact as the Winchester load, to make it perfectly compatible with duty ammo for training and qualification.

All of the newly introduced loads are hollow-point, as soft-points have fallen from favor. Variations in hollow-point designs have produced a crop of bullets that I have found expand reliably at subsonic speeds.

Another early entry was the Federal Nylok 158-grain

These recovered 9mm subsonic bullets have split jackets, but they are intact. This results in better penetration.

.38 Special cartridge. This used a bullet of the original weight specification, but with a hollow-point for expansion and a nylon jacket to reduce airborne lead contamination. Street experience quickly showed that this ammunition justified its existence.

The .357 magnum did not undergo any changes, mainly because few doubted its effectiveness. The main problems with the magnum were that few police officers, especially those of small stature, could shoot it effectively, and that it's a revolver cartridge.

After many decades of resistance to auto pistols, American police are switching away from revolvers. One important reason is the increasing use of high-capacity automatics by felons, such as those who killed New Jersey State Trooper Philip Lamonaco during what began as a routine traffic stop in December, 1981. Another is the advent of modern double-action autos, such as the Smith & Wesson, Beretta and SIG-Sauer models, in police calibers. Yet another is the adoption of the 9mm auto round by the U.S. military, which gave a tremendous boost to the acceptance of the "nine" in this country.

Although the .45 ACP has been the official U.S. military handgun cartridge since early in the century, American police officers had largely ignored it, much to the frustration of its advocates. The reason was that the pistol chambered for it, the Colt Government Model, could not be loaded without taking off the safety. This led to many accidental discharges. The single-action design meant that a police officer could not fire it simply by pulling the trigger, as on a revolver. For safety, it was necessary to keep the mechanical safety engaged, or keep the hammer down, until time to fire. This dictated a two-step operation that was unattractive to police officers.

The double-action SIG-Sauer P220, with its decocking lever, led to a resurgence of the .45 ACP. One of the first significant agencies to authorize it was the Arizona Department of Public Safety, in 1986. The DPS allowed its officers to choose either the .45 caliber P220, or the large-capacity, double-column 9mm P226.

Most law enforcement ammunition for the .45 uses a 185-grain JHP bullet driven at about 950 fps. The CCI Lawman and Blazer cartridges use the 200-grain large-cavity JHP, which fire from a P220 at about 900 fps. Federal 235-grain Hydra-Shok bullets fire at slighty over 800 fps.

Another special case is the Remington 185-grain Plus-P JHP. Remington recognized that a major problem with the .45 ACP from its inception has been its anemic velocity. Using a slower powder, Remington was able to increase muzzle velocity to over 1100 feet per second, with a maximum pressure of 23,000 psi, measured by transducer.

The 10mm Auto cartridge was stillborn for several years, having been tied to the commercially unsuccessful Bren Ten pistol. More recently, the FBI developed a medium-power version of this cartridge, with a 180-grain Sierra JHP firing at 950 fps. This is close to the performance of most .45 ACP ammunition. A new model 10mm Smith & Wesson double-action auto pistol will, according to FBI sources, be the issue sidearm for the agency.

Major ammunition manufacturers have picked up on this trend. Federal Cartridge Company, for example, has introduced the 10mm "950" load, with a 180-grain JHP, in addition to its Hydra-Shok load. The most powerful 10mm load at the moment appears to be the Winchester Silvertip, which sends a 175-grain JHP bullet downrange at 1276 fps.

Of these two subsonic cartridges, the Uzi 9mm 158-grain low-velocity FMJ fires at about 900 fps from a SIG-Sauer P226 with four-inch barrel. The Winchester 147-grain 9mm JHP subsonic cartridge hits 950 fps in the same handgun.

TEST-FIRING

Test-firing several types of subsonic ammunition was from a Ransom Rest with the target at twenty-five yards to check accuracy. The bullet path was over the screens of a PACT timer-chronograph, which yielded velocity and spread, the difference between the highest and lowest velocities.

AMMUNITION	VELOCITY	SPREAD	25-YD. GROUP SIZE
9mm: Federal 147-grain JHP Hydra-Shok	994 fps	35 fps	3⅜ inches
Winchester 147-grain JHP Subsonic	956 fps	25 fps	3 inches
UZI 158-grain FMJ Low Velocity	907 fps	26 fps	4⅝ inches
10mm Auto: Federal "950" 180-grain JHP	946 fps	43 fps	1 7/16 inches
Federal 180-grain Hydra-Shok	967 fps	52 fps	1¼ inches
Hornady XTP 200-grain JHP	1050 fps	68 fps	1½ inches
.40 S&W: Winchester 180-grain JHP	989 fps	8 fps	2¾ inches
.45 ACP: Federal 230-grain Hydra-Shok	807 fps	14 fps	2⅛ inches

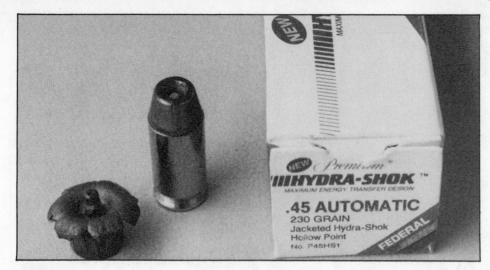

In .45 ACP, the 230-grain Federal Hydra-Shok will expand well with a muzzle velocity of about 807 fps.

The problem with the 10mm subsonic load is the same one that made the .41 magnum impractical for police use almost three decades ago. A down-loaded .41 magnum developed only 950 fps with its 210-grain lead bullet, but never became popular with police. The long cartridge requires a large pistol, despite its moderate power, and the S&W Model 1006 is adapted from the .45 Auto frame.

In practice, firing such a handgun requires a large hand and carrying a three-pound pistol during an entire shift can be uncomfortable. Recognizing these drawbacks, Winchester and S&W collaborated to produce the .40 S&W cartridge, a modified 10mm with a shorter case, small primer and the ability to chamber in a 9mm-size pistol.

Nominal ballistics for the .40 S&W are 980 fps with a 180-grain JHP bullet. This is slightly more powerful than

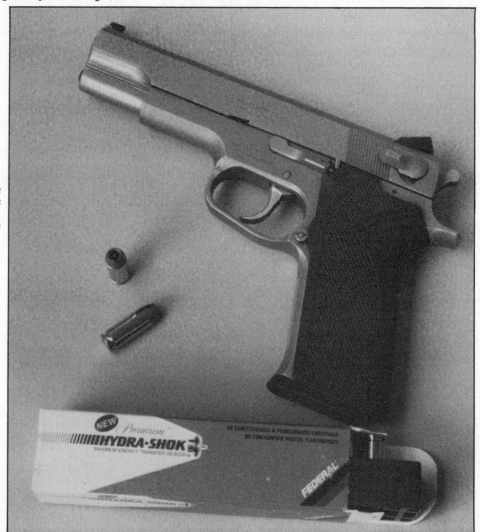

Federal's 10mm subsonic Hydra-Shok ammunition has a handgun made to fire it, the S&W Model 1006. This combo develops 957 fps.

The Glock Model 23 is a compact handgun that has been developed specifically to fire the .40 Smith & Wesson.

the down-loaded 10mm; maximum pressure is 35,000 psi, according to Winchester. The 1.135-inch maximum overall length allows fitting these cartridges in a double-column 9mm magazine, with a suitable magazine follower.

The Glock 22, built on a 9mm frame and chambered for the .40 S&W, holds fifteen cartridges in its magazine. Its smaller brother, the Glock 23, holds thirteen in its double-column magazine. This is in sharp contrast to the large-frame 10mm Smith & Wesson Model 1006, which holds only nine cartridges in the magazine.

The net effect is that the .40 S&W appears to have stolen the show from the 10mm. Although it's unlikely that police agencies already equipped with modern auto pistols are going to scrap them in favor of the new cartridge, there are many which haven't yet converted. The .40 caliber offers a compromise between power and bulk which can appear attractive to police firearms instructors evaluating the 9mm, .45 ACP and the new cartridge. A pistol chambered for the .40 S&W holds almost as many cartridges as the nine, while delivering about as many foot-pounds of energy as the .45 ACP.

With all that, there is a place for the full-power 10mm. The Smith & Wesson Model 1006 is a comfortable pistol to shoot, even with full-power loads, and is worth considering for special units of elite marksmen. The 10mm can be an excellent premium-power cartridge for SWAT teams, stake-out teams and other special-duty units. The Winchester Silvertip leads by a slim margin, with the Norma 170-grain JHP coming in second, with 1267 fps. The Hornady 170-grain XTP takes third place, firing at 1251 fps. All magnum-power 10mms make good choices for those who can handle them.

Hornady Manufacturing has announced the release of their new Extreme Terminal Penetration bullets or XTP, offered both as components and as loaded cartridges for law enforcement use. In caliber .40 S&W, these will have a nominal velocity of about 950 fps.

Subsonic loads appear to offer adequate power and accuracy, with low velocities designed to enhance penetration. Higher velocities would cause the JHP bullets to expand more, reducing penetration. Still, manufacturers are retaining hollow-point bullets, because law enforcement agencies expect them, despite the new theory regarding penetration being paramount.

The clearest evidence of this is the new FBI 10mm load, which the FBI devised according to their studies on penetration and bullet effectiveness. This uses the Sierra 180-grain jacketed hollow-point bullet. The brand-new .40 Smith & Wesson likewise uses a 180-grain JHP as standard load, as does the forthcoming Federal .40 caliber load.

At the moment, most low-velocity loads lack track records. A few years' experience will provide this, allowing a new evaluation of their effectiveness.

CHAPTER ELEVEN

COMMENT ON CALIBERS

This Subject Has More Facets Than The Hope Diamond!

COPS NEVER seem to tire of talking guns and calibers, so I didn't feel justified in denying them a look from Joe Zambone's point of view. Zambone is a professional writer turned ammomaker who has authored hundreds of articles on shooting and firearms.

I've followed the Zambone search for the perfect defense bullet since his earliest attempts in the 1970s. When his MagSafe ammo came on the market a few years ago, I began using it as my personal choice for my defense guns. It is the most awesomely destructive round I've seen. Some of the comments made here repeat statements already made on calibers, but Joe Zambone has his own style of investigation and explanation. I doubt if there's a punch pulled in this whole essay.

OVER THE past years, about two zillion "ballistic experts" have crawled out from under a mushroom and begun flooding gun magazines with their pet theories on stopping power.

Readers have heard opinions based upon shooting such test media as modeling clay, phone books (wet or dry),

Through long, often bitter experience, officers have found there's a big difference between paper-punching and that real world of take-'em-out law enforcement!

melons (ballistic melons, maybe?), pine boards, DuctSeal, Georgia red-clay mud and so on. Everyone with a chronograph and a chunk of something to blast is now an "expert" on which handgun slug will stop an attacker faster.

And a whole bunch of 'em don't know their fannies from a wheelbarrow. Even some experts, who test by shooting ordnance gelatin and examining the resultant wound, often go astray in their conclusions.

At the Army's Wound Ballistics Laboratory, Dr. Martin Fackler shoots into naked refrigerator-size blocks of 250A ordnance gelatin. Fackler is off-base on two accounts: People are not a solid four-feet-thick mass; and most felons wear clothing, which drastically alters the performance of whiz-bang jacketed hollow-point (JHP) slugs like the Hydra-Shok and Silvertip.

To further confuse the issue, we have cosmic-level experts shooting cows in the forehead to test .45 ACP stopping power. Since slaughterhouses routinely use .22 rimfire bullets to slay cows, it doesn't take a rocket scientist to figure out that nearly anything shot into a cow's brain will cause it to drop. A more realistic test would be to shoot the critter in the ribs or chest, since these areas are where most humans get shot.

The hullaballoo over stopping power was launched when the FBI got involved with a Keystone Kops episode in Miami. The FBI's inability to stop bad guys with a Mini-14 was blamed on a 9mm Silvertip which didn't penetrate deeply enough. Sure, it was a lethal wound, but during the time it took the felon to notice it, he shot half a dozen agents, killing two.

Enter Fackler, whose tests in blocks of naked gelatin proved that 9mm Silvertips expanded too fast and thus didn't go deep enough to damage vital organs. It wasn't long before the FBI switched to Winchester's controlled-expansion 147-grain subsonic 9mm round, which will shoot through the average buffalo without mushrooming.

They wanted penetration, they got it — but at the expense of anything resembling a nasty wound channel. My own tests in *clothed* gelatin show this slug reaches twenty-five inches without a hint of expansion, making a wound channel which looks like a piece of dental floss stretched tight — maybe .20 caliber in diameter after the first few inches.

Before continuing, it's best to note that I'm the inventor and manufacturer of MagSafe Ammo, a frangible (pre-fragmented) round which does unusual things to whatever it hits.

The salient point here is that I've spent several years now shooting every type of bullet available into six-inch cubes of *clothed* 250A ordnance gelatin (ten percent mixture at thirty-nine degrees). Rather than rely on memory, I videotape each shot in slow-motion, so I can replay bullet impacts one frame at a time to see precisely what takes place.

While I don't classify myself an expert, preferring to leave that dubious label to a slew of others, I do know what I'm talking about when it comes to terminal ballistic tests done realistically.

Although the raging controversy nowadays is 9mm versus .45, with a sprinkling of 10mm and .40 Smith & Wesson caliber tossed in for flavor and confusion, let's begin with the wimpiest calibers and work upward to real Rambo stuff which will unscramble a moose with one shot. We'll first cover conventional ammo, then look at exotic stuff.

The .22 Rimfire

The .22 rimfire brings up a logical question: Why? In short barrels the .22 is often just an annoyance to the six-foot junkie coming at you with a meat cleaver. Sure, it's deadly in trained hands and is a favorite tool of professional hit men because of low noise signature, but you pretty much have to stuff the slug into an ear or eye socket to stop an attacker fast — as in before the next Ice Age.

It helps to understand that .22 rimfire factory cartridges are loaded for rifle use, and snubby barrels don't begin to generate the velocities you think you're getting, even with hyper-velocity loads. In short, the .22 is normally valid only against a target which is asleep or unsuspecting, not some clown with a nose full of powder or gallons of adrenaline pumping through his system.

The .25 ACP

Again, the real question is why? It's a wimp. I always try to talk customers out of this as a primary weapon, because it's like bringing Reeboks to a butt-kicking contest when everyone else has on steel-toed boots.

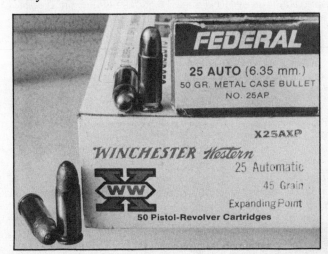

In the typical pocket pistol, there is *no* standard factory slug which will expand in flesh. They won't even deform slightly, so your only hope is an eyeball shot or slipping one between the ribs and into the spinal column. This is easy, of course, if you're a legend like Jeff Cooper, but it's a lot harder for us average folks.

Normal muzzle energy for standard factory ammo in my Raven .25 is about fifty foot-pounds. I have an air rifle which comes close to this. The MagSafe load puts out 106 foot-pounds in a Raven and mushrooms well, because of its design. But I'd still use it only as a last-ditch weapon.

The .32 ACP

This is another caliber I'd carry only as a last resort or as a second backup gun. There just isn't enough energy or velocity for any factory slug to expand in flesh.

Many of my customers carry a Seecamp .32, because it's so small and light. They didn't mind the year-long wait it takes to get one. I carried one for a time, as my #2 backup gun, but it dawned on me that if I couldn't solve a problem with my Glock 19's sixteen rounds, then my Grendel .380's eleven rounds, I was probably gonna be dead by then anyway.

The .32 H&R Magnum

Only Federal makes standard factory ammo in this caliber, and the stuff is so slow in a snubby wheelgun that you can almost watch it go downrange. Their JHP round

may expand, if it hits bone or a rhino, but their other load, a solid round-nose (RN) lead slug, doesn't have a prayer of making a wound channel larger than about .15 caliber.

The .32 Smith & Wesson Long

In a short revolver, it's no better than a .22 long rifle and will not expand in flesh, even if you're plinking at dinosaurs.

Granted, it's a favorite in South America, where such high-powered cartridges as the .38 are hard to come by. But only those with a sincere death wish will bet their lives on this bitty caliber with standard factory ammo.

The .380 ACP

Now we're getting into something which — with a bit of luck — can make a dent in an attacker's plans.

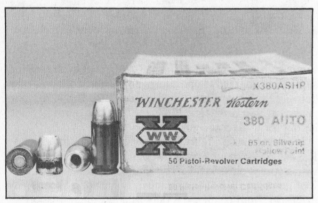

In short pistols like the Grendel or Colt Mustang, the sad news is that no standard factory JHP — Fiocchi, Silvertip, Hydra-Shok, et cetera — will expand in flesh after first going through layered clothing. Unless your beat is a local nudist camp or the beach, don't bet on stopping an attacker fast unless you connect with the head or spinal cord.

In longer pistols like the Walther or Beretta, my tests show that *some* JHP slugs wil expand slightly after going through clothing — but not reliably. Wound channels made by .380s are way less than .30 caliber in tissue, which has "memory" — the ability to spring back to its former shape.

Once a sheriff buddy of mine proudly showed me his shiny new Taurus .380. After we compared it to the Glock 19 I carry, another of those pesky logical questions arose: Why lug around a gun with marginal firepower which weighs more than a Glock 19, is slightly larger to boot, yet has fewer rounds in the magazine? That's like taking a Peterbilt to the drag strip.

Although gun scribes talk about .380 Silvertip slugs expanding well — again, in clay tests — and Evan Marshall has a number of shooting reports saying this caliber may get the job done, I have my own opinion: It ain't worth much without exotic ammo. The .380's only saving grace is that it's easier to conceal than a baseball bat or a frying pan, either of which is just about as deadly up close.

The .38 Special

No standard factory load I've fired from my Model 60 two-inch will expand in ten percent gelatin after going through clothing first. The hottest load I've tried is Silvertip's 95-grain +P. It bored through fifteen inches of gel and was recovered in new condition, with not even a hint of expansion. The wound channel wasn't any wider than that made by a slow-moving .380 slug.

On the other hand, this same load fired into the same block of gel, without clothing, expands fairly well. However, it flip-flops at about five inches and spends the rest of its twelve-inch journey going backwards.

Federal's +P Hydra-Shok offering does even worse. If you can get one of these to expand in a clothed human, I'll pay $20 for the recovered slug.

That ol' trick of handloading a 148-grain hollow-base wadcutter backwards to expose a mouth the size of a manhole cover, doesn't get you much, if any, expansion in snub-nosed guns. There simply isn't enough velocity.

In four-inch guns — the usual duty carry weapon — some ammo, like the hot Silvertip, will expand. But let's not forget the police desk-jockeys, who prescribe use of some wondrously effective bullets like the 158-grain +P semi-wadcutter (SWC) lead slug. I've spoken to cops who've filled felons with these things, only to have the riddled clown turn around and run.

Yes, I realize there are case files wherein this slug comes up #1 in stopping ability, but keep in mind that one helluva lot of folks get shot with these and it's logical that a large data base is available.

In virtually every incidence I've reviewed, the big, lumbering slug won't anchor a drugged attacker instantly — unless the shot bores right through the brain or spinal cord. Peripheral hits often are just an annoyance to attackers, say the cops with whom I've spoken.

The biggest factor is that available data is almost always derived from shootings with four- or six-inch revolvers, where there is often some expansion. In a snubby gun, .38 Special standard ammo is a bad joke which gets cops wasted.

The .357 Magnum

For those who favor wheelguns, there isn't much which will dump someone faster than a 125-grain Remington JHP fired from a four-inch gun. Sure, if it's low light, you'll be seeing spots before your eyes for a week, but it's a fine slug which works well. I haven't yet tested the Hydra-Shok

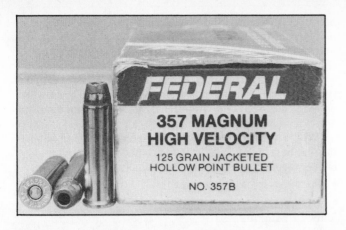

entry, but my gut feeling is that it won't come close to the Remington slug's performance.

Actually, in a four-inch .357 magnum, just about any round will make a decent hole in flesh. Drawbacks are excessive muzzle flash, recoil which some shooters cannot manage, and being limited to six shots without having to speedload.

For civilian shooters, always keep in mind one important fact of life: The word "magnum" suggests you're a very special kind of person, like Dirty Harry or Charles Bronson. A sharp prosecutor, bent on making a name for himself, may nail you to a cross if you shot even Jack the Ripper with a magnum anything.

The 9mm Parabellum (Luger)

Many readers will burn me in effigy for saying I prefer the 9mm to a .45 ACP, but I'd rather carry a Glock 19 instead of an anchorweight Colt Government Model auto. Many of my videotaped tests have been in this caliber and I've learned a lot along the way which refutes much of the trash you read in endless articles about "wondernines."

Most important is the fact that a certain velocity must be reached before 9mm slugs will expand. Heavy, subsonic loads don't cut the mustard. I have a nifty collection of 147-grain Winchester and Hydra-Shok slugs which went through a couple of layers of Levi's denim into gelatin and came out several feet later looking the same way they left the factory — except they had rifling marks!

Subsonic slugs make a tiny wound channel no larger than the 9mm "hardball" or full metal jacket (FMJ) stuff called for by the Geneva Convention. Unless you can stuff one of 'em into a guy's spinal column, throat, head, et cetera, subsonic slugs are a nice way to get wasted.

Lighter yet faster JHPs also have an unreliable track record for expansion, depsite what people like Fackler say. I've talked to a lot of cops who've made solid multiple torso hits on felons, yet the bad guys weren't affected.

A Border Patrol buddy of mine shot an alien six times in the torso with 9mm Silvertips, which passed completely through him, yet the guy got into his car and drove away. He bled out later on down the road and stacked up his car, but had he a mind to attack the agent, there'd be one less guy on Uncle Sam's payroll.

And we've all seen the autopsy report of the doped-up clown who took thirty-three hits from 9mm Silvertips, all over his body, and was still shooting back when a savvy cop clobbered him with a couple of 12-gauge slugs. Even

the first slug didn't slow the guy down, however. The second one severed his spinal column and did the trick.

This points out the whole screwed-up mess with ballistics. On one hand, some expert says Silvertips expand too fast to reach vital organs, while in field use, the darned things shoot clear through felons. Who are you to believe?

Still, there are some pretty good loads in 9mm. Remington's 115-grain 9BP is a stone killer most of the time and Hydra-Shok's +P+ Law Enforcement 124-grain slug actually will expand a bit after going through clothing. Their standard velocity 124-grain slug would be useful on bull moose, however, and their 147-grain subsonic slug will overpenetrate and kill an innocent two blocks away.

The 10mm

Only a silly millimeter wider, the 10 has leapt into fame mainly because the FBI tried to reinvent the wheel. However, since standard factory loads recoiled so much, they began specifying a downloaded version of the 10mm, using a 180-grain JHP slug at about 950 fps. If those figures look familiar, it's because the .45 Silvertip is virtually identical, but it makes a slightly wider hole. It also penetrates a whole lot with a minimal wound channel.

The only benefit I can see in my Delta Elite is that a few more rounds fit the magazine and handloading makes it possible to brew up some really lethal ammo. But then we're back to excessive recoil and the typical agents' inability to control a hard-bucking gun.

The only factory 10mm load I've tested in gel is Winchester's Silvertip and it's pretty mean, because it goes fast enough to expand reliably. Many other JHP loads are available in 10mm and they're all nasty if muzzle velocity is above 1200 fps.

The .40 S&W

To arrive at downloaded 10mm ballistics, yet with a cartridge short enough to fit in 9mm handguns, the .40 S&W was sprung on us in 1990. The idea was to have a low-recoil load which would still have enough penetration to reach vital organs.

My initial tests in a Glock 23 show the only offering so far: Winchester's 180-grain JHP clocks 922 fps. I didn't think it'd expand in gel after first going through a few layers of denim, but it did — to about .65 caliber. Nice mushroom, with penetration to 14.5 inches. That's ideal, according to some experts, but it still equals overpenetration of most humans in a frontal shot.

And let's face it; most shots at a bad guy will be from the front and designing a slug which'll go through his arm first will almost guarantee it will zip entirely through his torso. If the bullet passes through the dude, it hasn't dropped its minuscule 338 foot-pounds of energy in the right place.

My impression? This round will not build an enviable track record until it's hopped up a bit, to perhaps 1100 fps with a lighter slug. That way, the initial entry wound will be permanent and overpenetration will be limited through better expansion.

The .41 Action Express

This is a nice cartridge, capable of stunning performance, yet the only two available factory loads (from IMI) don't have enough velocity to wreak havoc on an attacker. That's why the makers of the new Jericho pistol recommend MagSafe Ammo to their clients. Sadly, I think the .41AE will be eclipsed by the .40 S&W.

The .41 Magnum

Although designed to give cops firepower which should drop a drugged attacker like a stone, this cartridge still hasn't caught on with the law enforcement community.

One problem is that many departments are switching to autoloaders for increased firepower (or the ability to spray more shots around town before having to reload). There's also the social stigma in our liberal nation that says shooting a guy with a magnum is cruel and unusual punishment — no matter that he just raped and strangled a covey of Brownie Scouts.

The .44 Special

I've read a number of glowing reports from writers who say their snub-nosed Charter Bulldog, filled with Silvertips, is all they'll ever need for defense. They obviously don't know that the slug chronographs only about 725 fps, and has about the same muzzle energy as a .38 Special. It will *not* expand in clothed humans when fired from a short gun.

I've fired Silvertips into both flesh and ordnance gel and have yet to see one expand. Wound channels are about .30 caliber; unless you hit vital areas, the .44 Special simply will not shut down an attacker fast.

PMC's tubular "cookie cutter" round isn't a bad bet in this caliber, owing to light recoil, but it will not cut a .44 caliber wound channel and it won't make a big entry hole.

The .44 Magnum

Unless you're a road deputy in some remote rural area, this is just too much gun to carry. With conventional ammo, it'll shoot clear through people and the recoil is tough for some folks to master. Recovery time between shots is thus slower.

The guns are also heavy and harder to carry concealed. But the .44 mag does have its place — out in the sticks, where a cop might come up against a car full of crackheads who're trying to kill him. The .44 will blast right through car doors (unless it hits the lockwork inside the door) and take out anyone in the way.

The .45 Colt

The so-called Long Colt is a nice caliber, but it's limited to slow, heavy slugs which don't make much of a wound channel in flesh. Certainly, many bad guys bit the dust in the old days when clobbered by a few of these, but folks weren't on designer drugs back then. What's needed now is a bullet which makes a large permanent wound channel through a chest wall, then does a Vega-Matic trick to vital organs. The .45 Colt won't do this, no matter how hard the big bore fans scream.

The .45 ACP

"If it was good enough for my daddy to carry in WWII, then it must be good enough today," is what you'll hear a lot of folks say.

Chuck Taylor and Jeff Cooper swear by the .45 auto with hardball ammo. I totally disagree with them, since the only way hardball will stop some druggie fast is if it's placed between his eyes.

No matter what brand of JHP ammo you use in .45 ACP, it won't expand reliably in flesh after going through clothing first. I've talked to a great many cops who've shot felons with this caliber, only to watch them stand there and soak up the hits. But there's a "mystique," or maybe it's a macho thing, that causes many people to carry a .45: "It makes a bigger hole to start with, because it's a wider bullet."

Horsefeathers! A fast, well designed 9mm bullet will make a far nastier hole and stop an attacker much quicker than a lumbering .45 ACP slug. So burn me in effigy!

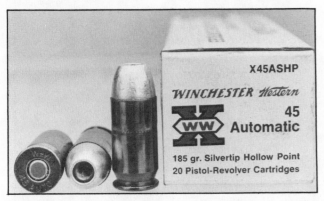

We've all read about Speer's "Flying Ashtray" 200-grain slug and how it makes a monstrous wound. In clothed tests, fired from a five-inch auto, I've never gotten one to open up. Ditto for Silvertips. There simply isn't enough velocity to cause expansion after the nose cavity plugs up with clothing.

One standard round which performs well is Remington's new +P 185-grain JHP. This slug will mushroom after going through many layers of clothing and while recoil is a bit stiff in light guns, it's a good round on which to stake your life.

The Cor-Bon .45 is also pretty fair stuff, but it's simply a 185-grain Sierra JHP slug loaded to +P velocity. I've found that in naked gel shots, it expands too fast and doesn't penetrate reliably, while in clothed shots the clogged nose often won't open up and the slug bores through two feet of gelatin. That equals human overpenetration.

To sum up standard ammunition, not a whole lot of it works as well as many folks believe. Peripheral hits, even with the biggest, slow slugs hardly get an attacker's attention. When the chips are down so far that you've got a millisecond to save your bacon, there just aren't many Death Ray loads available in standard ammo.

Exotic Ammunition

This is the stuff which costs a couple of bucks per round, and some is worth every penny of that. Some isn't worth as much as standard hardball, because it doesn't perform as claimed.

The *Glaser Safety Slug* is the best-known exotic. These are pre-fragmented slugs which allegedly break open fast and spew large numbers of #12 shot throughout the wound channel. My tests and those of many others show that Glasers often fail to open at all, thus becoming expensive hardball rounds.

On the other hand, *if* they open, Glasers will penetrate a

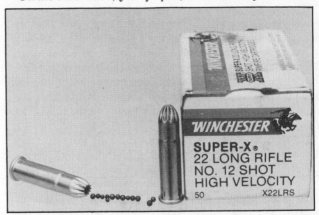

maximum of about five inches in any caliber. The faster they go, the less the penetration. I've never had one come out the back of a six-inch gel block; the shot usually stops before the four-inch mark. The problem is that #12 shot is very small — over 2300 pieces per ounce — and doesn't have enough inertia to reach vital organs.

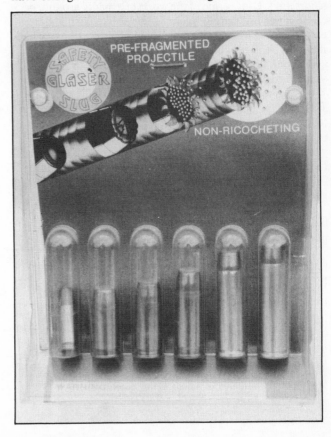

Accuracy can be a problem with Glasers, and that isn't just my finding. Colonel Claude Hamilton tested Glasers a while back and found group sizes ranging up to seventeen inches at twenty-five yards — enough to completely miss an attacker. The reason is that loose shot clumps together when the bullet starts spinning, just like socks in your dryer, and this leads to an unbalanced bullet.

Duplex loads, offered by several bullet makers, are a poor bet for self-defense. Most shootings take place at close range — arm's length in many cases — and a stack of lead wafers doesn't have enough time to separate in that short a distance.

The theory looks nice on paper, but my tests at five to seven yards show that duplex loads are a bad joke. They're heavy and slow. A slow-moving wadcutter takes the path of least resistance and turns sideways for its trip through flesh. That makes a tiny wound channel. At closer than five yards, duplex loads I've tested don't come apart into individual projectiles, leaving you with an overpenetrative slug which will make a wound channel perhaps half its diameter, with luck.

Beehive ammunition is a take-off on the Glaser, using the same tiny #12 shot, but with a JHP slug on top to get around Glaser's patented frangible tip.

Beehive works about the same as Glaser in my tests. It clogs with clothing and fails to expand quite often, or breaks apart so fast in a naked shot that penetration is as little as two inches. That isn't enough to reach vitals and shut a felon down fast.

One parameter you can use when evaluating the worth of exotic ammo is to take a look at what that ammo maker tests his rounds in. Beehive videotapes show huge holes being blown in clay blocks and this should be a signal to smart folks. Clay is one of the worst test media around, because it has no "spring-back memory" like flesh and thus exaggerates a wound channel far out of proportion to what it would be in real life.

Anyone who boasts about test rsults in clay will also sell you a bridge in Brooklyn. *Caveat Emptor.*

Core-Shot is a Beehive copy, again with #12 shot and a JHP slug on top for "better initial penetration," according to the maker. My tests show that a .380 Core-Shot won't expand even in naked gelatin. Ditto for their .45 ACP, which chronographs a lot slower than advertised. However, their 9mm round does break up nicely, reaching almost four inches in gelatin before running out of steam. They show test results in warm clay, if this tells you anything.

GECO BAT (Blitz Action Trauma) ammo is a copper hollow-point slug with a hole completely through it. A plastic nose cap allows reliable feeding going up the feed

ramp; the cap is blown off by powder gases when the BAT round is fired, exposing a gaping cavity which is supposed to gobble flesh.

Unfortunately, the GECO ammo I tested was quite slow — 1261 feet per second average in my Glock 17 — and had a huge variation in velocity from round to round — well over two hundred-feet-per-second in three shots.

The nose hole readily clogs up when shot through a Levi jacket into flesh or gelatin. It usually mushrooms anyway, however, but this leads to a minor drawback which reduces wounding ability. Upon expansion, the GECO round has effectively thrown out a parachute in front of a heavy rear portion. The bullet then flips over and travels backwards from that point on. Wound channels are minimal.

The *Thunderzap* is a plastic, super-velocity bullet in .38 Special, created by Richard Davis of Second Chance body armor fame. The name alone may get you an additional two years in jail after you've shot an attacker with one. Rambo-like bullet names are a favorite of prosecuting attorneys.

My feeling is that Davis used the wrong plastic for this 32-grain slug. On impact with flesh or gelatin, it fragments into tiny pieces of plastic (imagine putting your credit card into a blender on high for several minutes). The resultant wound is wide, yet measures less than two inches deep. Such a wound would make an attacker angry, unless you

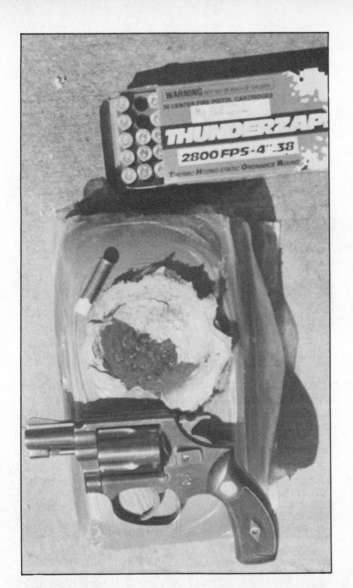

hit him in the head or throat.

Omni-Shok is a cast lead slug with four "petals" formed in the nose. A screw covered with red paint is driven down between the petals. On impact with flesh — in theory — the screw causes the petals to expand and "slice 'n' dice" flesh.

My own tests showed the lead alloy used is too brittle, and as soon as the petals open up, they drop off. What's left is a semi-wadcutter lead slug at low velocity, making a wound channel much less than the bullet's diameter. In many gel tests of the Omni-Shok, we found that none of the petals would open up, in effect making a round-nosed lead bullet which creates a teensy wound channel.

This ammomaker also shoots into warm clay to show the immense wound created by the Omni-Shok.

Turbo-Grabbers sport a wicked appearance, and at first glance you'd expect 'em to tear someone up. They're light, jagged-mouth plastic bullets driven at high velocities; so fast, in fact, that in every test made they came apart in mid-air (except the .45 ACP, which has a copper jacket). At a mere four feet, for example, their .44 magnum load, fired in a six-inch Dan Wesson, printed five separate hits on a gelatin block. Max penetration of the heaviest chunk was half an inch.

Turbo-Grabbers are pressure-swaged from the PVC plastic gallery slugs made by CCI. The forming process induces stress cracks throughout the bullet, which is why you could be the only cop in town with a Dan Wesson .44 mag shotgun. You'll also announce your presence to everyone in the county, thanks to mind-boggling flash.

Personal Protection Systems (PPS) offers light, copper hollow-point bullets with a plastic nose cap to ensure reliable feeding. On impact, the cap is supposed to "ribbon" and expose the wide hollow nose cavity. In practice, this sometimes happens, but usually only when naked gel or flesh are shot.

In .25 ACP, PPS makes a non-expanding 29-grain slug

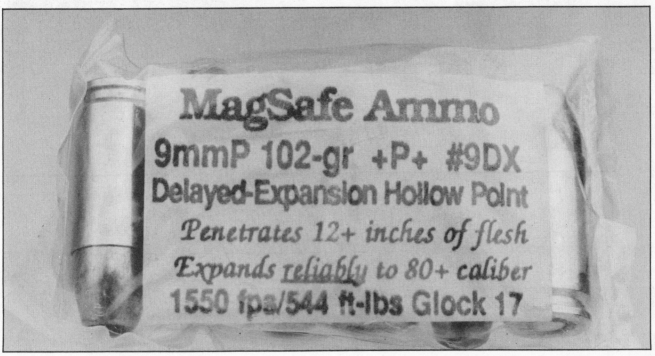

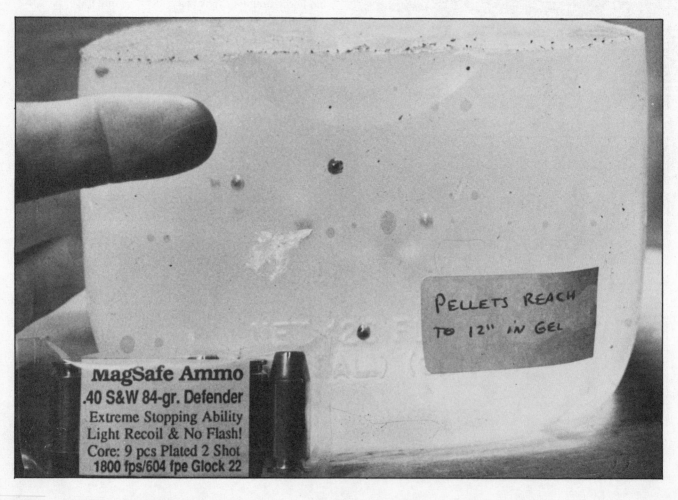

MagSafe Ammo

.45 ACP 103-gr +P Defender #45D

12 pcs #2 Nickel, 5 pcs #4 copper shot
Pellets Penetrate 12" Ballistic Gelatin
S&W 645-1,675 fps/641 fpe; Officers-
1,580/571; Marlin Carbine-1,933/854
85% More Energy than Silvertip!

which won't ricochet off a skull like other .25 loads will. However, at least seven gun dealers around America have reported that some of this was so over-loaded that the case head simply blew off when fired. This would leave you with a single-shot .25 auto with its chamber filled by a non-extractable case.

My gel tests show that when a PPS round in any caliber breaks up, the foremost (hollow) part of the slug peels away as tiny curls of copper which stop within three to four inches. The only object remaining which could inflict a vital organ wound is the base, weighing maybe 30 grains in 9mm. It always travels sideways like a tiny pie plate. The

PELLETS REACH
TO 12" IN GEL

MagSafe Ammo
.40 S&W 84-gr. Defender
Extreme Stopping Ability
Light Recoil & No Flash!
Core: 9 pcs Plated 2 Shot
1800 fps/604 fpe Glock 22

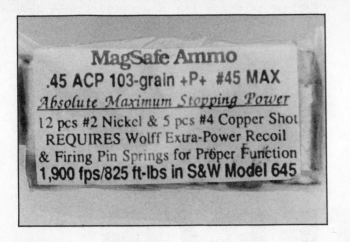

MagSafe Ammo
.45 ACP 103-grain +P+ #45 MAX
Absolute Maximum Stopping Power
12 pcs #2 Nickel & 5 pcs #4 Copper Shot
REQUIRES Wolff Extra-Power Recoil
& Firing Pin Springs for Proper Function
1,900 fps/825 ft-lbs in S&W Model 645

wound channel is quite underwhelming.

Evan Marshall has spent time bragging up the PPS .45 ACP load, a 100-grainer which doesn't go as fast as claimed. It might work well in naked gel, but in gelatin covered with what most folks would wear in winter, the bullet does not expand at at all.

With *MagSafe Ammo* the basic concept is similar to Glaser, except that it uses #2 plated shot pellets (eighty-six per ounce compared to over 2300 per ounce for #12 shot). You don't have to be real sharp to figure out which will penetrate deeper in flesh.

The main difference between MagSafe and other exotics is that the shot core is placed in each jacket in a precise pattern, then bonded together with epoxy resin which fills the projectile.

By varying core design, resin formula, nose design, velocity and several other factors, MagSafe rounds can be made to do nearly anything. For example, the company builds the only ammo in the world which will defeat Kevlar body armor, but won't ricochet intact or shoot thorugh a

can of Coke (or an unvested felon) without breaking apart.

MagSafe offers ammo in many calibers, which other exotic makers don't bother with, including .32 S&W Long, .32 H&R magnum, .41 magnun, .41 Action Express, .45 Winchester magnum and the latest, .40 S&W caliber.

Owing to high velocites but controlled break-up, MagSafe rounds tend to produce wide, permanent wound channels completely through chest walls. Pellets break out in a conical pattern at about five inches, in search of vital organs to disrupt. Pellet penetration is ten to thirteen inches in all MagSafe rounds, two to three times as deep as the other frangible loads, if they break up.

For specialty applications, MagSafe has created the nastiest ammo in the world for such wimpy calibers as .380 ACP and .38 Special. The .38 MAX load, 65 grains at 1670 fps in a two-inch Model 60, was used recently to permanently anchor a drugged felon who was tightening the trigger on a gun aimed at an agent.

As the world's most potent .45 ACP loads, the .45 MAX and the .45 Agent, both use trimmed-down .45 Winchester magnum brass. These things, at 1900 fps and 2020 fps respectively, offer more than eight hundred foot-pounds of energy on target, make three-inch permanent wounds through a chest wall, yet won't overpenetrate.

A .45 Agent load was used recently in a sideways shot. It nearly severed the felon's arm, yet pellets continued into the chest and blew away his heart.

The most important thing with any ammo, is to hit what you're aiming at. An eyeball hit with a Raven .25 is far more deadly than a clean miss with a .44 Magnum. There ain't any magic bullets if you can't put 'em where they belong.

When choosing the ammo your life may depend on, look at the manufacturer's claims, then do some valid testing yourself!

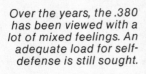

Over the years, the .380 has been viewed with a lot of mixed feelings. An adequate load for self-defense is still sought.

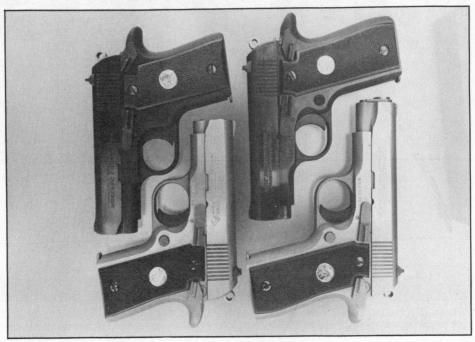

CHAPTER TWELVE

A MATTER OF FIREPOWER

In Law Enforcement, A Curtain Of Lethal Lead Doesn't Replace Accuracy!

Officers use the semi-automatic D Max in both carbine and pistol configuration for entry. While there is no full-auto version, the appearance of the firearm offers a high degree of surrender appeal when a wrong-doer sees it.

Heckler & Koch G3 rifle in 7.62mm NATO caliber (above) and the more recent H&K MP5 probably are more valuable in a military situation than in the average face-off in law enforcement work.

IN EUROPE and many foreign countries, the police are armed regularly with submachine guns and, by U.S. standards, other heavy automatic weaponry.

The American public never has bought that scenario and tends to think a sidearm is all a cop needs. When the chips are down, he may resort to the 12-gauge pump shotgun — it has a more wholesome public impact — but no submachine guns, please.

There was a brief time during the 1920s and 1930s, when Thompson .45 caliber submachine guns were in frequent use on both sides of the law, but when Prohibition died, so did permission to utilize them. The Thompsons gained such a bad reputation for lawlessness the inventor himself, General John T. Thompson, lamented before his death that the gun had come to be such a burden on society. He had only intended it for use in trench warfare during World War I.

Although little used since the days of Al Capone, the Thompsons stayed in police armory inventories for decades afterward. Many still are there and, occasionally, get an overzealous officer in hot water. For example, take an incident I know of from the 1960s.

A residence burglar well known to police had been looting homes for months, unhindered by arrest, much less conviction.

As veteran patrolmen know, daylight house burglars are among the hardest thieves to apprehend. This one enjoyed a long string of good luck, outraging many homeowners and frustrating the cops. At last, the burglary office got a tip where the burglar would hit next and two veteran detectives loaded up to put an end to his career permanently.

Fetching two commercial Thompsons from the armory

— complete with drum magazines holding fifty rounds of .45 ACP — the burglary detectives staked out the home. As I recall, they reported seeing no one enter, but in a little while saw the thief emerge holding the loot. One called a brief surrender demand, then the other sewed the hapless burglar a neat vertical stitch with his Thompson. Hit with three rounds from kneecap to abdomen, he was down for the count, but survived his wounds.

The two detectives almost didn't survive once the story hit the newspapers. COPS MACHINE GUN BURGLAR! the headlines shrieked. It's astonishing how public reaction can be manipulated by the media, too often in a perverse way.

Despite the fact that this outlaw was caught in the act, despite the undeniable truth that the shooting was entirely legal and regardless of the many irreplaceable possessions and family heirlooms this sneak thief had stolen, he emerged as the persecuted underdog. The detectives were made to look like sadistic killers.

Any reasonable person would think this public menace merely got what was coming to him, but nobody ever claimed the man in the street is reasonable.

We can grin now and say, "Well, so the detectives overreacted a little to the situation." The incident does bring two things to the forefront, however. Primarily, it shows how misplaced public sympathy has allowed criminals to get the upper hand in society. Instead of a wounded thief, this burglar was turned into a celebrity and had taxpayers lining up to donate their blood to him — thanks to the media. It also reflects the unique American horror of submachine guns, as if somehow something innately evil lurks in their oiled mechanisms. The point is, had the cop popped

Thumbhole-stocked SR9 rifle has found favor with some SWAT units, replacing the old HK 91, a longer rifle.

(Right) Operation of the M-1 carbine is simple and foolproof. It has potential for use in law enforcement.

the burglar with three slugs from his Colt M1911 .45 auto pistol, the story would have been buried on page five of the local tabloids.

Seemingly, the American public and the American court system can't distinguish between mercy and justice. They're right, however, on one point: full-automatic fire from machine guns belongs on a military battlefield. In a war between governments, the impersonal fight is so fierce and dreadful the side who puts the most lead in the air usually wins. In such battles, a machine gun also is a great morale builder. It feels and sounds like you're fighting, even if you don't hit a thing. No one argues a return to bolt-action service rifles now and there's no question that full-auto, or "rock n' roll" is proper in wartime — but it can be overdone.

Every Vietnam veteran knows most of the U.S. media was hostile to the American war effort in that bitter conflict, some disloyal to the point of treason. Still, there was no opportunity to disguise or propagandize one firefight that hit the TV news hour during the 1970s.

The camera showed a platoon of GIs lying on their stomaches firing their M-16s at a treeline some two hundred yards distant. Most of the rifles were on full auto and there were a couple of light machine guns going, too. After a lengthy period, the fire slackened, giving the reporter a chance to ask what all the ruckus was about. The young lieutenant in charge answered, "A sniper in those trees!" waving an arm toward the shredded jungle.

One sniper is worth a quarter-million rounds? It has been said the U.S. fights rich wars, which amounts to understatement.

There are no such free-fire zones on American streets, regardless of the drug barons and their sophisticated weaponry. Only the shots that hit the felon count to a cop and the others merely jeopardize the non-involved public. In police work, there is no such thing as fire suppression or grazing fire to keep an enemy's head down. Every shot a policeman fires should hit meat. There is another danger involved besides the inevitable bystander, and that is to the officer who relies on a hail of lead to put an enemy down.

Police gunfights are more in the nature of a personal duel rather than a war. Unlike a soldier, the officer usually can see his enemy and his opponent can see the officer. To miss under these circumstances is folly.

The Heckler & Koch MP5/10 is the new 10mm version of the MP5 submachine gun. It has a synthetic magazine, bolt hold-open device. A .40 S&W version is currently in the planning stages for '92.

(Right) The author feels Marlin's Camp Carbine in .45 ACP or 9mmP could be useful in law enforcement.

If we reduce the ballistic equation to the level of fisticuffs, it comes out like this: a person armed with a submachine gun is like a belligerent drunk who shouts and blusters, then windmills into a fight, his fists hitting only thin air. A deadlier opponent is the cool, quiet individual who says nothing, but is full of resolve. The first punch he throws is likely to break your neck. So it is with machine guns and so it is with controlled fire. A good argument can be made that law enforcement should stick to semi-automatic fire, even in prolonged fights. Remember, every shot that doesn't hit is a chance missed to stop a felon.

We've spent a lot of time explaining why promiscuous fire is wrong in police work and it's only fair to include the shotgun in this denouncement.

Once a cop triggers a blast of buckshot, the individual pellets are uncontrolled and become a to-whom-it-may-concern proposition. As the yardage increases, so does pattern size and a high percentage of the pellets will miss the target. The effective range of the shotgun is actually much less than that of the service sidearm, in every case.

Shotgun slugs are an improvement and these have heavy recoil. In fact, the reoil from any 12-gauge load is so

The M-14 military rifle (top) has long been used in sniping situations by law enforcement. (Beneath) The bullpup version of the M-14, utilizing a McMillan stock, is a handy length for utilization by today's teams.

severe it frightens cadets and makes training difficult.

There's a growing trend to replace the traditional racked patrol car shotgun with a light, handy carbine of pistol caliber. The advantages are obvious: controllable fire, the ability to place a single bullet more accurately than a cloud of buckshot pellets, less recoil and greater ease in training.

The carbine enables an officer to single out an individual representing danger in a crowd or a hostage situation. Shotgun or even pistol fire in these scenarios is unthinkable. An ordinary patrol officer arriving first at the scene could, with an accurate semi-automatic carbine, handle tasks which now require rolling an entire SWAT team. Unlike a shotgun, the carbine would be a true extension of the sidearm.

The most promising and the most popular carbine with knowledgeable instructors today is the robust D Max self-loader from D Max Industries, Incorporated (P.O. Box 2324, Auburn, WA 98071). This is a rugged, conventional blowback weapon available in the most favored pistol calibers: 9mm Parabellum, .38 Super, .40 S&W, 10mm Auto and .45 ACP.

On today's high-priced market, the D Max is simply the best dollar value available. There's more gun for the money, in my opinion.

Two models are available. One is an abbreviated assault pistol, while the other is a carbine with conventional wooden buttstock and separate pistol grip.

The D Max is the gun replacing the shotgun in patrol cars today. This is not a semi-automatic version of a full-auto weapon. The D Max was designed from the beginning as a semi-auto only and is not converted easily to full automatic fire.

Both the pistol and carbine versions fire from a closed bolt for maximum accuracy — which is superb, thanks to the premium-grade barrels. The hammer-actuated firing pin is identical to and interchangeable with that of the widely available M1911A1 pistol.

The gun's bolt has spiral grooves which carry away dirt and powder residue in a self-cleaning action. The result is utter reliability under adverse conditions. The extractor is large, giving sure purchase for easy case extraction. The trigger group is a modified Garand-type with an improved, braided stainless steel wire hammer spring. All critical parts are chrome-moly steel, heat-treated for strength.

The safety lever is mounted on the left side of the receiver and is pushed down easily to the fire position when the hand grasps the pistol grip. The gun is quick into action, an absolute necessity for police work.

The most prominent feature of the D Max is the side-mounted magazine which extends from the left side of the receiver like the British Sten gun. The practical advantage, of course, is that it allows the shooter to lie down or otherwise take a low cover position. This is next to impossible with guns having bottom-feed magazines.

The D Max has a large-diameter perforated barrel sleeve which not only adds to the appearance of lethality, but dissipates heat mirage generated in prolonged firing.

Standard sights are a ramped post front and a Williams aperture rear, the latter adjustable for windage and elevation. The aperture or peep sight is the fastest and most accurate of all non-optical metallic sights. This type of sight is only now becoming popular once again, after a long period of neglect.

The peep sight has been around since before the invention of firearms — it was used in medieval crossbows — but fell into disuse, because of ignorance on the part of the

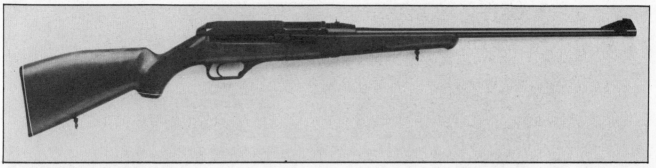

The H&K 770 rifle in .308 Winchester has been dropped by the manufacturer. It was a semi-automatic. For use by police snipers or SWAT personnel, the bolt-action is much more in favor and is considered much more accurate.

shooting public. It's astonishing in this day and age of advanced shooters that so many profess a lack of knowledge about aperture sights. A common belief is that the front sight must be exactly centered in the circular rear aperture for accurate results.

In reality, the proper method is to simply look through the rear aperture and put the front sight on the target. The human eye is constructed in such a way that the front sight centers itself automatically, so that only the front sight is in focus. The rear aperture will be fuzzy, which is the reason such sights are often referred to as "ghost ring" sights.

The advantage is that the aperture sight puts the target and front sight in the same focal plane exactly as would a telescopic sight, but without magnification. The ghost ring works as well with older eyes as it does with young and poses no disadvantage to those with visual impairment due to age.

This type of sight is familiar to veterans who have trained with M1 Garand, M14 or M16 rifles. Another common belief — even among shooters familiar with the aperture sight — is that the opening must be small for good accuracy. Actually, it can be quite large without sacrificing grouping capability.

In addition, the D Max has a base positioned on the receiver for mounting telescopic sights, night vision sights, laser target designators and other optical devices. When fitted with telescopic sights, the D Max makes a viable urban counter-sniper or SWAT rifle due to the high accuracy from the premium barrel. In short, the D Max makes a far more versatile and satisfactory tactical response weapon than the usual police shotgun.

The D Max chosen for test firing is the carbine with a 16.25-inch barrel chambered in 10mm Auto. The gun weighs about 7½ pounds and is 38½ inches long. The

D MAX CARBINE SPECIFICATIONS

System of operation:	blowback, semi-auto
Caliber:	9mmP, .38 Super, .40 S&W, 10mm Auto, .45 ACP
Length:	38.5 inches
Weight:	Approximately 7½ pounds
Barrel length:	16.25 inches
Front sight:	post, fixed
Rear sight:	adjustable open, peep optional, integral optical sight base
Safety:	turn lever trigger block
Magazine:	30-shot; 5, 10 or 15-shot optional
Finish:	black crackle Max Coat
Stock:	walnut, conventional butt with pistol grip

D MAX PISTOL SPECIFICATIONS

System of operation:	blowback, semi-auto
Calibers:	9mmP, .40 S&W, .38 Super, 10mm Auto, .45 ACP
Length:	13.75 inches
Weight:	five pounds
Barrel length:	six inches, standard; eight inches, optional
Front sight:	post, fixed
Rear sight:	adjustable
Safety:	turn lever trigger block
Magazine:	side feed, 30-shot or pistol magazines
Finish:	black crackle rustproof Max Coat
Stock:	walnut, laminated wood optional

It is the author's contention, based upon many years of experience, that the semi-automatic carbine may well be an improvement over shotguns for squad car carry.

magazine I have holds thirty rounds, but ten-shot versions are available. The D Max may be ordered by any law enforcement agency to accept the same magazines used in the issued sidearm. For example, the St. Petersburg, Florida, police department carries the Glock 17 and 19 as primary weapons and ordered D Max guns which take the thirty-two-round Glock magazine. Naturally, the shorter pistol magazine also will fit. The D Max also will be available to take SIG-Sauer and Smith & Wesson magazines.

The D Max in 10mm Auto seemed likely to give the best ballistic performance. It fires the standard 10mm loads using 170-grain JHP bullets. These rounds have a muzzle velocity of 1350 feet per second in five-inch pistol barrels. In the longer D Max barrel, velocity is upped to 1600 fps.

The 200-grain FMJ now available from nearly all ammo

The D Max pistol configuration is ideal for use in close quarters where movement is limited. Going through a door certainly qualifies for this type of action, author says.

The D Max pistol, with its thirty-round magazine, may well give an offender pause to consider quick surrender.

Tom Ferguson tested the D Max carbine. Its accuracy he found a surprising plus.

manufacturers for 1150 fps in pistols will leave the muzzle at approximately 1300 fps in the D Max. This firearm also will function with 10mm subsonic loads that travel at a nominal 950 fps in pistols. The long barrel of the D Max enhances the ballistic performance of other pistol calibers as well.

Contrary to what I first thought, the horizontal magazine of the D Max didn't unbalance the gun or pose any particular problems in handling, even when fully loaded with thirty rounds of 10mm cartridges. It can be fired by grasping the forend in a normal manner or by grasping the magazine housing with the left hand. Unlike purely military designs, the conventionally stocked D Max mounts quickly and easily, making target acquisition time a fast proposition.

The trigger on this test gun was a good one, indeed, for police work. There's a bit of slack to take up, then the release is extremely light. Technically, this is a two-stage trigger, but once the slack is taken up, there is no perceptible click or stop, as it comes up against the sear. The D Max simply fires as you increase the pressure. The trigger slack is intentional and provides a measure of safety in tense situations where trigger fingers tighten instinctively.

To begin the firing tests, we chose Remington's R10mm1 cartridges. This is a full-house 10mm load using a 170-grain JHP bullet which gives 1350 fps in five-inch pistol barrels. The velocity is increased in the D Max barrel, of course. Loading the magazine was made easier by the loader which is provided with each gun.

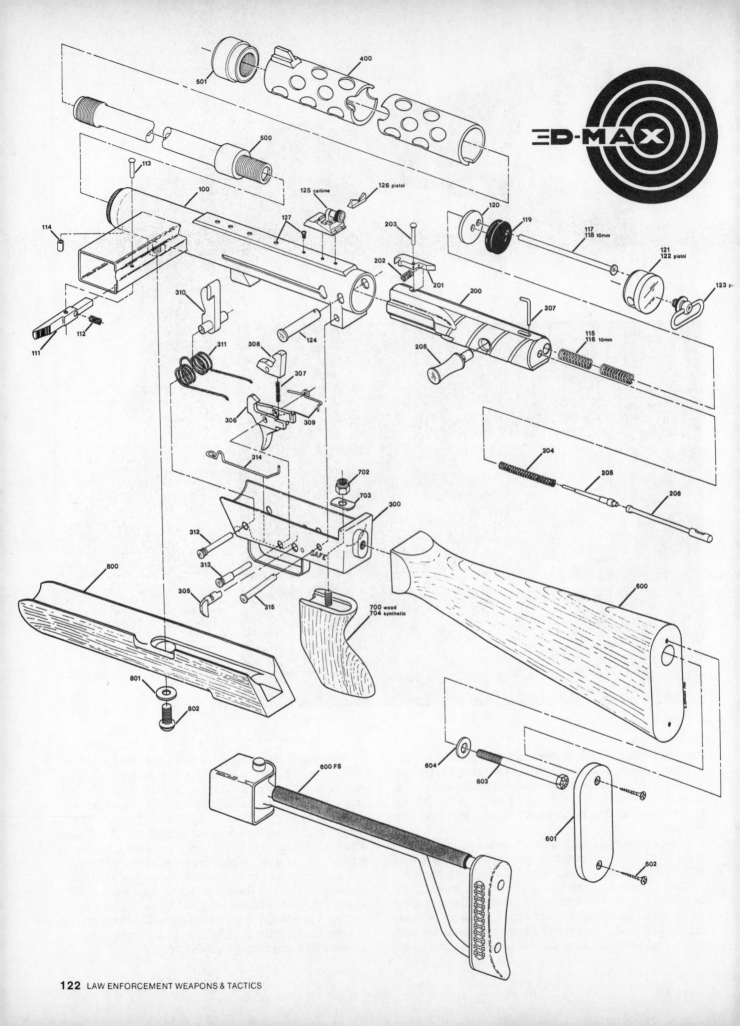

ED-MAX

PART NUMBER	DESCRIPTION		PART NUMBER	DESCRIPTION
100	Receiver		500-9-6	Barrel-9MM-6 inch
111	Magazine Catch		500-9-8	Barrel-9MM-8 inch
112	Magazine Catch Spring		500-9-10	Barrel-9MM-10 inch
113	Magazine Catch Pin		500-9-12	Barrel-9MM-12 inch
114	Shroud Locator Pin		500-9-16	Barrel-9MM-16 inch
115	Recoil Spring		500-10-6	Barrel-10MM-6 inch
116	Recoil Spring -10MM		500-10-8	Barrel-10MM-8 inch
117	Recoil Spring Guide		500-10-10	Barrel-10MM-10 inch
118	Recoil Spring Guide-10MM		500-10-12	Barrel-10MM-12 inch
119	Recoil Buffer- Rubber		500-10-16	Barrel-10MM-16 inch
120	Recoil Buffer- Steel		500-38-6	Barrel-.38 Super-6 inch
121	Receiver End Cap - Carbine (Shown)		500-38-8	Barrel-.38 Super-8 inch
122	Receiver End Cap - Pistol		500-38-10	Barrel-.38 Super-10 inch
123	Pistol Sling Swivel		500-38-12	Barrel-.38 Super-12 inch
124	Receiver End Cap Pin		500-38-16	Barrel-.38 Super-16 inch
125	Rear Sight - Peep		500-40-6	Barrel-.40 S&W-6 inch
126	Rear Sight - Blade		500-40-8	Barrel-.40 S&W-8 inch
127	Filler Screw		500-40-10	Barrel-.40 S&W-10 inch
			500-40-12	Barrel-.40 S&W-12 inch
200-9	Bolt - 9MM		500-40-16	Barrel-.40 S&W-16 inch
200-10	Bolt- 10MM		500-45-6	Barrel-.45 ACP-6 inch
200-45	Bolt- .45 ACP		500-45-8	Barrel-.45 ACP-8 inch
201-9	Extractor - 9MM		500-45-10	Barrel-.45 ACP-10 inch
201-10	Extractor- 10MM		500-45-12	Barrel-.45 ACP-12 inch
201-45	Extractor- .45 ACP		500-45-16	Barrel-.45 ACP-16 inch
202	Extractor Spring			
203	Extractor Spring		501	Barrel End Cap
204	Firing Pin Spring			
205-9	Firing Pin- 9MM		600	Walnut Buttstock
205-10	Firing Pin- 10MM		601	Buttplate
205-45	Firing Pin- .45 ACP		602	Buttplate Screw
206-9	Firing Pin Extension- 9MM		603	Buttstock Bolt
206-10	Firing Pin Extension- 10MM		604	Buttstock Bolt Washers
206-45	Firing Pin Extension- .45 ACP		600FS	Folding Stock
207	Firing Pin Extension Clip			
208	Operating Handle		700	Pistol Grip - Walnut
			701	Pistol Grip Stud
300	Trigger Housing		702	Pistol Grip Nut
305	Safety Lever		703	Pistol Grip Washer
306	Trigger		704	Pistol Grip - Synthetic
307	Disconnector Spring		705	Pistol Grip Bolt
308	Disconnector			
309	Trigger Return Spring		800-6	Forend - Walnut - 6 inch
310	Hammer		800-8	Forend - Walnut - 8 inch
311	Hammer Spring		800-12	Forend - Walnut - 12 inch
312	Hammer Pin		800-10-8	Forend - Walnut - 10MM - 8 inch
313	Trigger Pin		800-10-12	Forend - Walnut - 10MM - 12 inch
314	Safety-Pin Clip			
315	Trigger Housing Pin		801	Forend Washer
			802	Forend Bolt
406	Shroud 6 inch			
408	Shroud 8 inch			
410	Shroud 10 inch			
412	Shroud 12 inch			
416	Shroud 16 inch			

I began on a standard pistol target at twenty-five yards, sighting in. Groups were tight but to the right, so I moved the Williams adjustable rear sight to the left to compensate. To my surprise, the D Max then cut a ragged one-hole group spanning hardly more than an inch. Frankly, I didn't expect this kind of accuracy and realized with a shock that every shot fired would have taken a squirrel's head off at this range! A police carbine — a semi-automatic, at that — which could double as a squirrel rifle is remarkable!

The tight group was fired from a sandbag rest, but after sighting in, I fired offhand at targets of opportunity on the one hundred-yard berm. The first shot fired struck a small soft drink can, flipping it high in the air. The hot 10mm bullets arrive at one hundred yards with considerable authority and remaining energy and velocity still is high.

Recoil wasn't enough to be objectionable, but was more than expected from a pistol cartridge. Muzzle rise, however, was practically nonexistent thanks to the combless straight-line stock. It was easy to keep rapid-fire shots in a six-inch group at a hundred yards.

Like any new design, the D Max requires a certain amount of handling for familiarization. For instance, the charging handle is on the left side of the receiver. The best way to chamber the first round (for a right-hander) is to hold the gun in the left hand, give it a half-turn to the right,

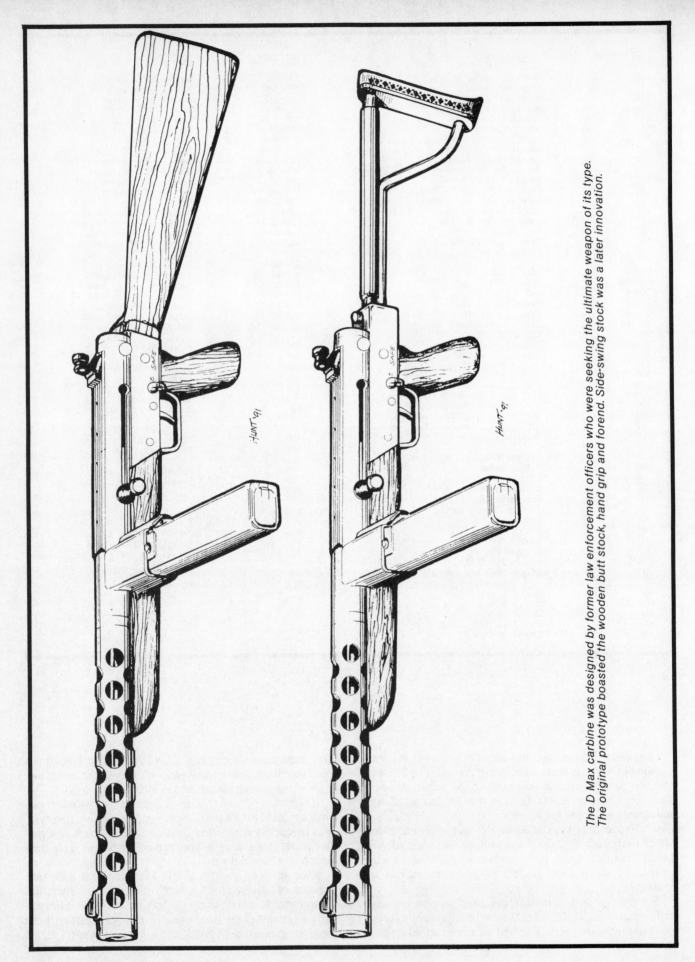

The D Max carbine was designed by former law enforcement officers who were seeking the ultimate weapon of its type. The original prototype boasted the wooden butt stock, hand grip and forend. Side-swing stock was a later innovation.

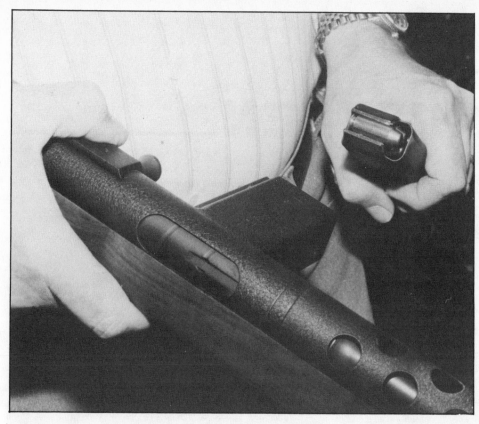

Reason for making D Max a side-loader was so gunner could maintain a lower image if firing from the prone.

then operate the bolt with the strong right hand. The safety should be on during this operation, as it allows both loading and unloading the chamber in the safe mode.

While shooting, I tried holding the forend with the left hand in conventional rifle-shooting style, then holding the magazine housing in an upturned left palm. The latter seemed to work well and I developed a slight preference for this technique.

When shooting any box-fed weapon, it's important not to hold on to the magazine itself. Many of them have some amount of play when seated; grasping or pulling on it could move the upcoming cartridge enough that it doesn't chamber properly. The D Max magazine fits with precision, but from long habit, I kept my supporting hand off it and used the magazine housing for a handhold.

There were no malfunctions of any kind during the firing tests. Ejection was to the right rear, but the cartridge cases weren't thrown with such force they would be a hazard to others in close quarters.

With the thirty-round magazine in place, there could be some problems fitting the D Max into existing shotgun racks in patrol cars. The magazine would extend into the space normally occupied by the radio, siren control and MDT unit. However, any such weapon should be carried in the car with an empty chamber and, in this case, the magazine could be removed and placed in another location. In high-crime areas, this could make the gun useless, even if a thief managed to free it from the rack. With the short pistol magazine installed, there would be no space problem.

In summary, the D Max seems sturdier, simpler and better suited to police work than its competitors. The parts are large and unlikely to break. The action is uncomplicated, with no gas piston or other mechanism to fail or require takedown for cleaning. In fact, the D Max is cleaned just like any sporting rifle. When disassembly is required for any reason, the drill is swift and simple.

Accuracy and reliability are second to none and the trigger pull is fine just as it comes from the factory. So is the standard-issue peep sight, but other sighting options are available.

The D Max comes with a base positioned on the receiver to mount telescope sights, night vision sights and lasers. Other options include a sling and swivels and shorter magazines. In the .45 caliber D Max, the U.S. M3 submachine gun magazines can be used. In 9mm guns, the British Sten and Lancaster mags will function perfectly. All D Max magazines carry the same black crackle, rust-proof finish as the rest of the gun.

Many firearms designs, unfortunately, are those of engineers who have no need of a gun and the end result reflects this lack of experience. Not so with the D Max. The company was founded in 1986 by David M. Dugger, a career law enforcement officer who has worn several badges.

As the administrator of a small police department, he realized the need for a reliable, low-cost police weapon capable of high firepower. Dugger also is a qualified police firearms instructor who specializes in weapons of this type.

The D Max is purposely designed to be relatively inexpensive, durable and easily maintained. The short pistol version is an ideal entry weapon for hazardous building takedowns and room clearing operations. The carbine is far more versatile for tactical response than is the usual shotgun carried in patrol cars. Interested departments or individual officers can contact D Max Industries, P.O. Box 2324, Auburn, WA 98071.

CHAPTER THIRTEEN

A MATTER OF TRAINING

Real-World Thinking Means A Tough Curriculum That Will Save Law Enforcement Lives!

In recent years, law enforcement training has become more realistic, with less competitive-type shooting. Ranges are at combat distances and the targets are the standard silhouette type on which the killing hits can be scored.

MANY YEARS before Andrew Jackson became the seventh president of the United States, he was a frontier magistrate — or county judge.

One morning, as he was holding court in a log-cabin community in Tennessee, the proceedings were disrupted by a raucous disturbance outdoors which consisted of loud swearing and shouting. To continue business amid the din was impossible, so Judge Jackson beckoned for the sheriff to approach the bench.

"Go outdoors and bring a halt to that racket!" Jackson ordered. The sheriff left and was gone but a few minutes when he returned, more than a little crestfallen. The noise continued unabated. To Jackson's quizzical countenance,

On today's ranges, targets are controlled electronically and there is constant communication from the range officer.

the sheriff explained the man responsible for all the cursing and hollering was a well known rough-and-tumble fighter. Moreover, the bully was drunk and armed with pistol and dagger, making it impossible for the sheriff to arrest him. At the least, it didn't appear to be a one-man job.

Judge Jackson was visibly angered. "Go then," he told the sheriff, "and gather a posse of citizens from the street to help you!" Shame-faced, the sheriff went to do Jackson's bidding.

In a short time, a dozen townsmen crowded into the court-room headed by the sheriff, who once again approached the bench.

"Judge," he complained, "the man refuses to be arrested by us, many though we are!" Jackson lost his temper completely.

"Very well, sheriff," he shouted, "then you and your posse can stand from under!"

Snatching up his pair of fine flintlock dueling pistols, Judge Jackson marched swiftly outside to halt the disturbance himself. Stepping into the street, he was confronted by a large, bearded and formidable-looking giant who paced up and down with a cocked pistol while shouting

curses. Every so often he'd wave the gun at the gathered crowd, which fell back in awe. With a cocked dueling pistol in each hand, Jackson stepped in front of the raging drunk and roared, "Throw down your weapons this instant, mister, or I'll shoot you through!"

With a look of surprise the man hesitated for a moment, then let the gun fall into the dirt. Now meek as any lamb, he allowed Judge Jackson to march him to the primitive jail-house to sober up.

Next morning, after paying his fine, the bully was back at the tavern for a hair of the dog to cure his hangover. Several friends hovered nearby, and one asked timidly why he had surrendered to just one man after defying an entire sheriff's posse.

"Well," he muttered darkly, gazing into his glass, "I looked into the sheriff's eye and didn't see 'shoot!' Then, I looked into the posse's eyes and didn't see 'shoot!' there, either.

"But then," he continued, "I looked into Andy Jackson's eye and I saw 'shoot!', so I figured it was time to talk small — and I did!"

This is only one of the folktales told of the raw courage

Those who handle police firearms training invariably are veterans of their profession and know street tactics.

and indomitable character of the man who was the hero of New Orleans in the War of 1812 and later the President of the United States. As tough and inflexible as an axe-handle, he earned the nickname, Old Hickory. It's not only a good story, but a lesson in law enforcement.

To a good cop there is only one way, and that is his way. To be intimidated is out of the question, and even a favorable compromise is accepted grudgingly.

That doesn't mean one has to make a shooting situation out of every encounter with a drunk, but it does mean the law will be enforced.

To be willing to back this premise to the hilt makes the desired impression, even if the original offense is a trivial one. In my early training as a law enforcement officer, this philosophy had been emphasized to the point that I never forgot it, whether the miscreant was a felon or a casual misdemeanant. It is a good way, in spite of modern psychiatrists who counsel otherwise.

For example, police officers often are told it's better to back off from an arrest attempt, if the offense was not great to begin with, lest a death result. In modern society, few crimes are felt to be worth a life, either that of the offender or of the arresting officer.

If one considers only the crime, then this view is indisputably true. Unfortunately, there is much else at stake, and failure to take other factors into consideration has led to the crime-spree and chaos we see around us. If anarchy is to be prevented, the principle of the law has to be upheld. The police officer has a gun belted around his waist, a badge pinned to his chest, and this principle of law. The public entrusts him with these things and says, "Here, take these and do our will; be our protector against the lawless." They pay us money, and we do it — often to the hilt.

But a police officer is only a human being, just as mortal as anyone. We must take the necessary precautions. When I was a young patrol officer and city budgets were much smaller, we had only enough men to assign one to each patrol car. Riding alone, we often were far from help, vulnerable and weak. For self-protection, it was absolutely necessary to cling to an iron-clad policy when dealing with the public — especially, the law-breaking public. The rule, which spread quickly on the street, was this: The police uniform is inviolate, and no one must touch it.

Police officers wear sidearms to back up their authority, if necessary; unfortunately, today they must use those handguns more often than the cops of twenty years ago. Thankfully, training methods are more realistic and effective today.

Once, the firearms program for my own department was really just a series of exercises that taught marksmanship. We began using S&W K-22 revolvers on bullseye targets at twenty-five yards. After learning sight alignment and trigger control in single-action mode, we graduated to the S&W Model 10 .38 Special with wadcutter target loads. Ranges varied up to sixty yards; unrealistically long for a city officer.

The best phase was at seven yards where we were required to fire double-action only. I felt a vague sense of dissatisfaction with this training, but couldn't put my finger on what exactly was wrong. Later I realized the course of fire taught us a lot about hitting with a handgun, but not much about street survival.

Exercises in which one must pick up the handgun with the weak hand and fire qualifying shots are now important.

Although police officers tend to feel the job is interesting and know it sometimes can be dangerous, few consider themselves gunmen. After all, good character is part of the reason they were hired. The thought of being forced to take a life is repugnant to them, often to the point it's difficult to get them on the range for practice and qualification.

However, the bottom line in police work is: "Can you win a gunfight?" Many cannot, and somehow must be taught by events that the ability is vital to them.

In the early 1970s, the U.S. Supreme Court ruled that capital punishment was "cruel and unusual" and specifically prohibited by the Constitution of the United States. The momentous decision had an immediate and horrifying effect on law enforcement.

Formerly, it had been rare for an officer to be killed in the line of duty, but overnight the situation changed. Knowing their lives could not be made forfeit, the criminal element which lives by robbery, theft and murder began shooting down police officers for the most trivial of reasons.

It's a good lesson in reality for those who argue the death penalty is no deterrent. Where once criminals submitted to arrest, many now elect to shoot it out. In the months that followed the Supreme Court decision, my department lost a lot of good men to these killers and the situation was grim. I went to too many police funerals!

Obviously, these officers needed a training program in survival. I'd been acting as a firearms instructor and recognized the problem. The head of our training bureau asked me to revise the firearms course to suit our terrible situation.

The best street survivalist in the department was an aging, modest, little police officer who had worked a tough area of the city for years. I knew he had been involved, along with much other trouble, in five lethal encounters in which his opponents were armed as well as he. He never boasted of this fact, and it was like pulling teeth to get any information from him.

Driven almost to desperation, I asked him if these were fair, upright shootings, or had he relied on something more than luck. His reply was honest and went something like this:

"The Grand Jury has never indicted me for any of these killings in the line of duty, and to the law, all were necessary and fair.

"But in confidence, I can tell you that none of those men ever had the slightest chance of winning at all. The true fact is, I made up my mind to shoot seconds before they did, and I was prepared mentally to shoot them down. No one ever took me by surprise. In a gunfight, you must never give an opponent the slightest edge. If you do the odds are only fifty-fifty you'll survive. It's really true that guns make all men equal."

This officer was not even a particulary good shot, but he knew when the talking should stop and the shooting should begin. It was a matter of reading the proper signals.

To the cadet classes — less so to longtime veterans — I began teaching body language. Most veteran officers knew a lot on the subject due to years of street experience in handling violent people.

The younger officers learned to interpret gestures, voice inflections, even seemingly innocent statements that might give warning that shooting was about to erupt. Years afterward, the New York Police Department did a study on the subject, and the report indicated that, in seventy percent of all such incidents, there was a clear warning of this kind if only the officer knew how to detect it.

Few persons, even hardened criminals, can avoid giving a warning word or gesture, and the officer must be alert to it. At the same time, it shouldn't be forgotten that the other thirty percent of the time there is no warning — and this doesn't always mean an ambush-type situation.

In revising the course of fire, we de-emphasized pure marksmanship by discarding bullseye targets and the .22 revolvers. After awhile, we succeeded in discontinuing the use of wadcutters and substituting a semi-wadcutter .38 Special. It was not only hotter, more closely resembling duty ammo, it was easier to load in the chambers during timed exercises of fire. We began weak-hand training and abolished all single-action fire. The longest course of fire was at twenty-five yards, not the sixty of before.

Few police cadets then — or even today — had any previous handgun experience, and they didn't surprise me by their lack of knowledge. However, I was astonished at what experienced veterans didn't know about the revolvers they had carried every day for years. Many didn't know

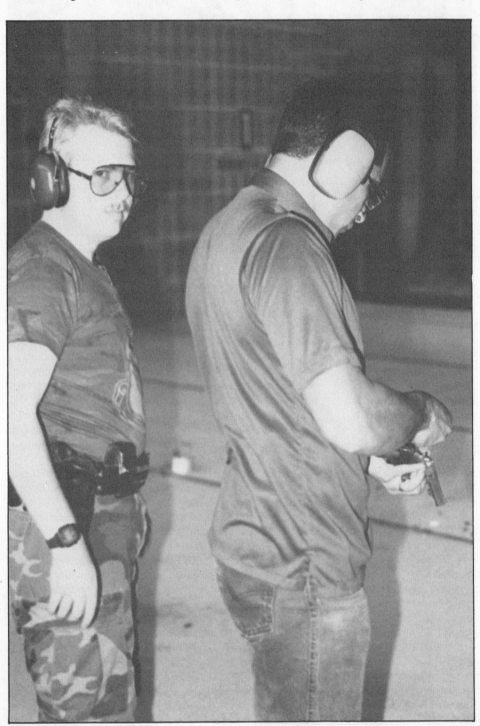

No one needs a police agency that is made up of deaf and blind officers. Today, eye and ear protection are given more importance than has been the case in what some call "the recent past."

which direction the cylinder turned, and a couple didn't realize it turned at all.

In two-shot exercises, they often put one of the cartridges directly under the hammer and were puzzled when it rolled from under without firing. A number of oldtimers felt it wasn't important to learn double-action fire and insisted on cocking their revolvers even when time limits were short. Many remained adamant and shot poor scores, of course, then blamed the instructors.

We had a difficult time retraining these men, but I learned from them, too. A good instructor will watch the shooter and his handgun, not the person's target. If there are hits, they can be judged and recorded later. If you watch for gunhandling mistakes, you can correct all the problems which cause a miss.

In addition, never forget the object is to teach the student to handle his sidearm, not display your own prowess. There is a type of instructor who believes he can bully and shout this information into a student, and he relies on loud, demeaning intimidation. It is usual for this macho leader to snatch up a revolver, give a stunning display of marksmanship, then demand the same of the student with no other information.

Such people are not truly instructors and should never be allowed to remain on the job.

Another bad situation was contributing to the deaths of

There's satisfaction, the trainees discover, when a good score is shot on the silhouette-size targets.

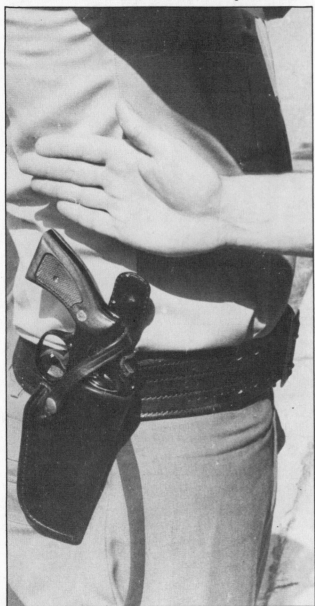

Older thumb-break holsters were dangerous to the officer. A quick hand chop could release the thumb break and a felon could disarm an officer and turn the gun on him.

showed timidity, and I didn't want to see any on their part. I reminded them they were the pick of the community, too good to be shot down in the streets by some socially worthless punk with a cheap pistol. Then I reminded them they had civil rights of their own, and relinquished none by joining the police department.

The criminal element had shown us savagery and no compassion, and we would hand it back to them with interest. In a couple of disgraceful instances, we'd had officers wounded in shoot-outs who had given up the fight. I told the troops that from now on they would fight until they no longer could hold their pistol and give as good as they got.

In short order, my department stopped losing gunfights. During a traffic stop, one young officer was shotgunned to

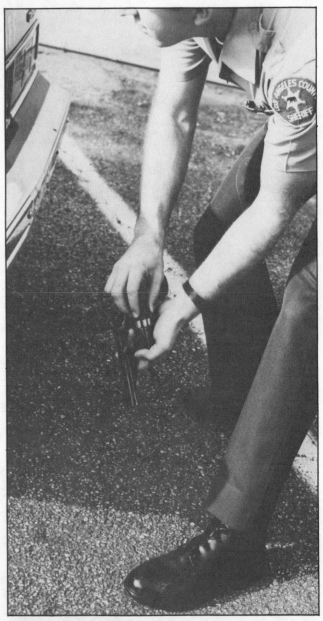

If recruits pay attention in their continuing course of training, hopefully they will react with coolness in any shoot-out or other situation of a dangerous nature.

our officers at the hands of criminals, and it had nothing to do with firearms training. Ironically, it was the other training bureau instructors. They were specialists in the state penal code, Constitutional law and the code of criminal procedure. As experts, they kept current on case law and court decisions such as the ill-considered Supreme Court view that capital punishment was "cruel and unusual."

By excess zeal in cautioning police cadets they shouldn't abuse their authority, the effect was to frighten the young lawmen out of their wits with tales of civil rights lawsuits which might be filed against them. The information was true, and good to know, but it didn't instill a lot of confidence. The result was predictable — the academy was graduating timid police officers.

To counter these unwise instructors, I put the shoe on the other foot. I told the cadets it was time the criminals

Plainclothes narcs Pete Carllson and Jim Barbe plan the strategy for a drug raid with uniformed officers who will take part. A great deal of serious training is required before an officer is qualified for this type of duty.

the ground, but he drew his revolver and killed the man who shot him.

In another incident, one of my former cadets was shot in the back, but chased his assailant on foot, firing at him. When finally he bled out from his wound, he crawled to the residence and was met by the owner, who heard the shots.

The citizen said, "Lie still, you're bleeding badly. I'll call for an ambulance!"

The young officer said, "Forget the ambulance, help me reload my revolver!" He fully intended to continue the chase. He lived and is an outstanding police officer today.

My inflexible stand made me unpopular with the chief and the other instructors, but it turned the killings around. Evidently, the public agreed with me on criminal-coddling, and a couple of years later, the Supreme Court reinstated the death penalty for capital crime.

In the meantime we had killed more than forty scofflaw hoods who thought we were pushovers. It is well to rehabilitate a criminal if you can, but if you ask the dead ones their opinion they sayeth not; neither do they complain in court of brutality.

Now we are entering the 1990s and have a similar situation as that which existed in the 1970s. There are more criminals and whole groups of people who believe that the law is what you can get away with, no more and no less. They seem to display even less humanity or fewer ethics than before and are told constantly by their peers and leaders that nothing is their fault and self-responsibility is an outmoded joke. They have better weapons and are more

Belt loops or dump pouches are obsolete for carrying any extra ammo. For cops armed with revolvers, speedloaders like these from Safariland are the present-day favorites.

willing to use them, even against police officers. To counter them, the law enforcement community has been forced to adopt high-capacity autoloaders and reject the older revolver with its six-shot capacity. This is no doubt a good move, and I approve.

What shouldn't be forgotten, though, is the willingness to go the limit and do the best you can with what you've got. As Andrew Jackson knew and taught his opponent, the fight is in the man — not the pistol.

The California Highway Patrol Puts Emphasis On Serious Weapons Training — And It Pays Off!

The California Highway Patrol Academy is responsible for training all new officers and updating veterans.

AFTER INITIAL indoctrination, firearms training is all too often a function neglected by policing agencies. A new officer receives training in firearms during the initial training period, then is required to "qualify" a certain number of times each year thereafter.

Range officers frequently are selected on the basis of their interest in shooting and may receive no additional instruction for that function. Generally, this works much better than it should, because most agencies are in a small geographical location and it is possible for administrators to have reasonably close control over this activity.

That degree of control may not be possible in a policing agency which has a large geographic area to cover and becomes even more difficult when there are many command locations within that department. One of the largest such agencies, both in terms of uniformed personnel and in area to cover, is the California Highway Patrol. This department has over 6200 uniformed officers and is responsible for traffic control on 96,000 miles of highway. This mileage includes the freeways in Los Angeles as well as the road net in Death Valley.

Being responsible for traffic in all unincorporated areas within the state requires that the officers be trained in tactics that apply to urban areas as well as to the most rural. Potential problems are compounded by the need to have over one hundred command locations. Any equipment used must work equally well at 120 degrees as it does at 20 degrees below zero. In addition to its traffic responsibilities, the CHP has several other policing functions. A few examples are auto theft, insurance fraud, dignitary protection, mutual aid and narcotic task forces.

If the governor deems it necessary, the patrol can be used in any police activity within the state. When one considers that in September, 1990, the population of California passed the 30 million mark, almost twice the population of the next most populous state, New York, the task facing the CHP and other policing agencies in California staggers the imagination. Therefore, any training program must consider not only that which is, but also that which may be.

Jim Andrews spent several decades with the CHP, serving as a training officer during part of that career. I asked Andrews to give us a rundown on the type of training that the California agency gives its officers. Here's what he has to report:

TO SEE how the CHP handles this task, I contacted Sergeant Greg Manuel, Commander of the Office of Public Affairs at CHP Headquarters, Sacramento. Sergeant Manuel had a valid concern, which was that we not reveal any information on tactics that might endanger an officer. I assured him we were interested only in the mechanics of training and in how the CHP handles the problems of maintaining a high standard of training with an organization so spread out geographically.

Shortly after my talk with the sergeant, I received a call from the CHP academy commander, Captain Robert

Hayworth. After the captain was satisfied as to my intent, he set up a conference with the supervisor of weapons training. He did ask if I was any relation to a sergeant with the same name with whom he worked right after he graduated from the cadet academy.

Not wanting to be bound by anything I may have said or done some twenty-two years ago, I attempted to evade the question. It soon became apparent why he had made captain — he would not let go. I admitted that I had been a CHP sergeant during that time frame and in the location he named. He said, "Stop by my office when you visit the academy."

What could I have said or done? Damn! Now I had to get a haircut and figure out how to shine sneakers.

I met with Sergeant Ed Fincel, supervisor of the weapons training staff, and received an education as to how things have changed in the last fifteen years. Since it is impossible for Fincel and his staff to insure personally that the sworn members of the department comply with the shooting requirements, they are assisted by trained range officers in each command location. These range officers, if trained on every weapon the CHP uses, will have spent 240 hours undergoing formal training at the academy in Sacramento. During this period, they will have demonstrated not only proficiency with the firearm, but also in methods of instruction and correction of problems an officer may have in shooting.

Notice that shooting was mentioned rather than qualification. Members of the CHP must qualify two times a year, but they must shoot every month. The range officers

Sgt. Ed Fincel of the academy staff briefs the directors of other state police academies; liaison is maintained with law enforcement agencies throughout the state.

Most refresher training is carried out on the range in informal civilian attire. Although the handgun is the CHP officer's primary weapon, long guns aren't ignored.

also are trained to inspect the pistols carried by CHP officers. This inspection covers all of the standard safety checks including headspace and cylinder end-shake of revolvers. They do not perform any maintenance or repairs. The only people who perform other than routine maintenance are the academy gunsmiths.

One area in which range officers receive training is in development of shooting programs to hold the officer's interest and increase his or her proficiency. As long as these programs are safe and emphasize the correct practices, that is all that is required.

Sergeant Fincel's experience includes shooting on a Marine Corps pistol team and setting up a pistol team for a sheriff's office prior to becoming a member of the CHP.

It is quite obvious the sergeant was a Marine. His voice, combined with his stance, brooks no argument and with the trooper hat — which one could mistake for a drill instructor's cover — cocked over his eyes, one wishes he could do a hundred push-ups with ease.

Fincel's staff has over fifty years of law enforcement combined with over thirty years of military experience as regulars. The morning I arrived, Traffic Officer Jane Randall was conducting a firing exercise for cadets in which great stress is placed upon the trainee. After I listened to her for a short period, I was not surprised when Ed Fincel told me she had been a drill instructor in the Army.

Contrary to many police programs, the CHP starts cadets on a bulls-eye course at twenty-five yards. The trainees hold the pistol with both hands in one of the combat stances — their choice — and do all shooting double-action. Instructors do not insist any one stance is better than another. They allow the trainees to use whatever position is best for them. The feeling seems to be that if it's safe, whatever works is best.

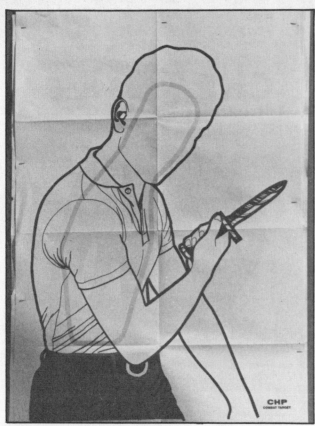

CHP has developed its own targets which can be used in shoot-don't-shoot situational training of the officers.

This course is meant to teach the necessity of sight alignment and trigger control. It also gives the trainee confidence that the pistol can hit a small target at a distance.

After the cadets have qualified on this course, they are moved to the outdoor combat range. This is a unique range in that it is enclosed on all four sides with a short road net that allows the use of vehicles in the training.

The combat course is set up in such a fashion that an instructor can turn any target as each position has a separate motor for turning the target. In addition, the targets turn 180 degrees rather than ninety degrees. This prevents the trainee from knowing if the target is a shoot or not shoot target — foe or friend.

On the combat course, training is conducted at all distances — from arm's length to fifty yards, all done double-action. After qualification on this course, the trainee is subjected to training on how to shoot when the stress is on. Included within this section is one wherein the officer must shoot and reload from the sitting position. Easy, you say? Try it! Magazine pouches and speed loader holders are not easy to get to when they are pushed up by this position. I know some people who couldn't find the pouches in the sitting position. Night practice is frequent, with flashlights used in some segments, only available light in others.

One of the stress simulations has the cadet run to a vehicle, strap in, start the patrol unit and drive, using emergency equipment, to a location selected by the instructor. Upon arrival, the instructor-passenger will designate targets,

One of the longarms with which California Highway Patrol officers train is the Mini-14 rifle produced by Ruger.

weapon and number of shots. All instruction is in a voice and fashion not designed to inspire calmness.

Reaction targets are used in some segments, but true to the staff's deep felt position that there is nothing that might not happen on the street, sometimes the reaction targets do not react. Trainees have been known to empty their pistols and stand there with a stricken look on their faces. They are told to expect anything — and never to be caught standing with an empty pistol! After this training, that is one lesson the student should not forget.

During the latter part of the program, the students are required to enact a foot chase. They are given a pistol which cannot fire and have to run a course which includes going over a barrier. They are watched closely, and if a finger should be on the trigger at the wrong time, it's push-up time. At the conclusion of the chase, there may be instructors from another discipline of training, and the students are required to perform other functions in which they have been trained. Classmates are used to add to the trainees' stress and discomfort, issuing comments during the entire exercise. They do this with great glee.

The outdoor range was designed to allow the staff to change the course of training almost at will. By the use of cutouts, barriers or items of cover, they can create a Hogan's Alley or any other situation that will test the student. Sergeant Fincel and his staff study police shooting incidents, and if it will benefit the students, recreate the situation. This versatility allows students to benefit from actual occurrences shortly after they happen.

Assigned to the range section are three gunsmiths who are responsible for the upkeep of all issued firearms. Having them in one location allows constant updating of problems which may arise with equipment purchased or selected by the CHP. Included within gunsmithing equipment is one of the latest electronic universal pressure guns. Com-

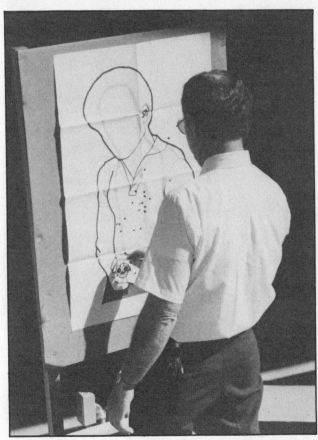

A plainclothes officer checks his target to determine how he did. Night firing is conducted with frequency.

California has not had enough water to present a problem in recent years, but academy range's targets are covered. The facility where highway patrolmen are trained is one of the better in the nation, surveys have determined.

CHP gunsmith checks new shotguns. After inspection, all will be test fired, cleaned, shipped to command units.

Sgt. Ed Fincel is in charge of training at the academy of the California Highway Patrol. Emphasis is on the practical side of combat shooting, not paper punching.

bined with a state-of-the-art chronograph, this allows the staff to insure that all ammunition purchased meets specifications.

In addition to training of cadets and range officers, the range and weapons section has the responsibility for regular in-service training of officers, special training with equipment such as hand-held automatic firearms, as well as testing and recommendations on the purchase of new equipment. In addition, they train all regional range officers. Allied police agencies from all over the world visit the CHP Academy to study methods of training; the range is one of the most visited spots.

This range facility is always busy. When CHP personnel are not using it, other police forces utilize it for training and testing. The staff recently completed a study of semi-automatics for issue to all personnel. Based on this study and a test program of the 10mm cartridge — and the pistols chambered for it — the CHP has adopted the Smith & Wesson Model 4006 chambered for the .40 S&W cartridge. This was an extensive testing progam which included a 5000-round firing test of each pistol submitted for consideration.

At present, the sidearm of issue is a revolver chambered for .38 Special or .357 magnum. Prior to the issue of the new semi-automatic pistol, each member will undergo at least twenty-four hours of instruction and fire 1000 rounds of service ammunition during this period. Sergeant Fincel feels this amount is necessary for two reasons: to acquaint the officer with a new firearms system, and to test each pistol issued.

After the new pistol is issued, all firing of that firearm will be done with factory service-type ammunition. It is the desire of the training staff that each officer will shoot and qualify with what he or she will carry on the street. The new pistol will have adjustable sights and the ammunition used should not require any sight adjustment after the pistol is sighted in.

The choice of adjustable sights for the issue sidearm reflects the vast knowledge of the weapons training staff. They know that it is almost impossible for everyone to

A sign marking the boundaries of the academy carries a reproduction of the lamp of learning and a book. This is to emphasize the importance of knowledge, training.

This news photo of an assailant firing at law enforcement officers is prominently displayed at the academy. It is meant to serve as a reminder of need for training.

have fixed sights shoot same point of impact. To adjust fixed sights so they will be correct for one officer would reduce the advantage of having a pool of spare pistols to issue when a sidearm is being repaired or inspected.

Members of Sergeant Fincel's staff are at the factory while the order for the new pistols is being filled. It is their desire that each pistol meet the specifications of the one submitted for test and they feel the best way to do this is to be present during the manufacturing process. This is in line with the way this group of officers handles everything, leaving little to chance.

The range has available almost every firearm that an officer might encounter during a tour of duty. These are used to demonstrate the effectiveness of such weaponry and to allow the trainee to learn how to safely handle such ordnance.

As duty location changes, so does the need for different firearms. Officers of the CHP have firearms other than the standard pistol and shotgun, depending upon their assignment. These may vary from a semi-automatic rifle to a submachine gun. You cannot tell from looking at the patrol unit what officers have with them.

When you combine this equipment with a first class, up-to-date training program staffed by true professionals, the California Highway Patrol takes a back seat to none in its firearms training program. It may have been a little slower than some other police forces in adopting a semi-automatic pistol, but when it did it was on the basis of testing not on rhetoric. Sergeant Fincel made it quite clear to me that he is only the supervisor of this unit. Without the backing of the academy commmander and the commissioner's office, he and his staff could accomplish nothing. It is apparent he has that backing.

Is a training program that takes as much time and money as this one worth it? The national average for effective shots fired during a time of hazard by police officers is about twenty percent. Records maintained by the CHP Academy indicates that the effective rate for CHP officers involved in shootings is a little better than forty percent. A hundred percent increase.

Today's Law Enforcement Training Comes From Networking And Information Exchange

Sergeant Bill Nelson lectured on task force that was used to develop advanced gunfight survival training for the San Diego Police Department. Effort was a success.

THE AMERICAN Society of Law Enforcement Trainers was formed at a meeting of top police instructors at the Ohio State Peace Officer Training Academy in January 1987. Its first seminar took place in New Orleans a year later, drawing 128 police instructors. The second international conference took place in Kansas City, drawing 308. The 1989 seminar in San Diego drew a record 368 police trainers from all over the United States and from nations ranging from Australia to the United Arab Emirates.

The firearms track contained seven topics, six with a single speaker and one "panel of experts." Two more firearms-related topics were included in the specialty training track. The "track" concept was developed by ASLET founder and executive director Ed Nowicki. At each seminar, seven programs are offered in areas of firearms, management supervision, motor skills such as unarmed

combat, arrest tactics and officer fitness, and specialized training. The last-listed curriculum for 1990 included countersniper training considerations, post-shooting trauma for the range officer, patrol survival considerations for instructors, the crisis in police pursuit driver training, liability of first responders, verbal/nonverbal communications, police recruit training in Sweden, contemporary terrorism, room-clearing techniques, advanced police firearms training strategies, military principles translated to tactical training, awareness of covert weapons and police psychology training tools.

The staff roster for the listed curriculum read like "Who's Who In Police Training." Instructors included Dr. Peter DiVasto, Seth Nadel, Kevin Gordon, Pat Gallagher, Barry Szymanski, Roland Ouellette, Tom Ackerman, Rod Chaney, Jennie May, Chuck Schroeder, Andy Casavant, Dennis Ramsey and Dr. Jim Chandler.

For many, the most important track was deceptively titled "General" and actually dealt with critical principles of adult education as applied to the peace officer. This program led off with a lecture/demonstration by Lieutenant Dave Smith, Arizona Department of Public Safety — and late of the street-survival seminars. Smith is best known among cops for his hilarious *Buck Savage* training videos, which use humor to bring home critical survival tactics. Bob "Coach" Lindsey gave his standard/nonstandard lecture on teaching complex psycho-motor skills. I say "standard/nonstandard" because it's his topic every year, yet each time he infuses new life into the subject with a different approach that only a gunfight veteran who has had

Panel of experts includes (from left) Captain John Cerar, NYPD Firearms & Tactics Unit commander; Seth Nadel, U.S. Customs Service; Sergeant Terry Campbell, the panel chairman; and New Hampshire chief, Russ Lary.

Chuck Taylor lectured on realities of special weapons use by police.

Gerry Smith represented the Smith & Wesson Academy, discussed police firearms training, legal problems.

Los Angeles PD Lieutenant R. Wemmer dissected recent police gunfights.

brother officers die in his arms can deliver from the heart. Other topics too numerous to mention were included in the curriculum and taught by some of the best of the nearly fifty staff instructors.

This publication, of course, is most concerned with the firearms track.

Lieutenant Rich Wemmer of the Los Angeles Police Department delivered numerous officer survival case histories. He has studied intensively the events leading up to the deaths of some 130 police officers. Of all the tragedies, Wemmer says he can count on his fingers the number that simply could not have been prevented.

Mental attitude is most important, he noted, citing the fact that the great majority of police gunfight survivors he'd interviewed attributed their survival to that factor. Wemmer enthusiastically endorsed the concept of backup guns, showing the videotaped re-enactment of a shooting in which a young reserve officer used a hideout S&W Model 36 Chief Special to shoot five times a hardened criminal who was trying to murder him with his own service revolver.

Wemmer is also an advocate of lots of ammo. He cited three recent cases in Southern California where officers emptied not only their issue .45 and 9mm autoloaders, but also every magazine on their duty belts before their gunfights were over. At least one fight resulted in the suspect escaping unscathed. Wemmer noted that the current trend in California is toward carrying four spare magazines on the Sam Browne belt, instead of the usual two, whether the gun is a high-capacity Wondernine or an old-fashioned .45. Rich Wemmer, himself, carries a high-capacity Beretta on duty and a thirteen-shot S&W Mini-Gun off duty. He called for more emphasis on accurate shot placement in training, but noted that range conditions don't replicate "the street."

Wemmer's commitment to learning what the Other Side was doing ran so deep that he arranged to be incarcerated with inmate population at San Quentin Penetentiary for a day. He observed cons training to kill cops. He noted that today's offender is more likely than ever to be wearing body armor, carrying a scanner — and armed with high-tech, high-fire-power weaponry. He noted that Los Angeles gangs also are aggressive, hunting down investigating police officers and even targeting the cops' families for revenge.

Chuck Taylor, former chief instructor at Jeff Cooper's Gunsite and now head of his own American Small Arms Academy, is famed for his expertise with submachine guns. At ASLET, he attempted to put that special-purpose gun into perspective with the police shotgun, the .223 "assault rifle," larger caliber battle rifles and the currently popular 9mm and .45 carbine.

"The police shotgun's great strength is also its great weakness: its short range," he told the class. Taylor feels the .223 semi-automatic rifle is more versatile for all but the most densely populated patrol areas and, like many others on the staff, personally disagrees strongly with "anti-assault rifle" legislation. He predicts that guns like the semi-auto Uzi and HK 94 in pistol calibers will be "the wave of the future" and feels the 10mm cartridge currently undergoing a flash of popularity in police pistol sales will serve better as a submachine gun or carbine cartridge.

Jim Cirillo, who was involved in numerous gun battles as a member of New York City's elite Stakeout Squad and killed several armed robbers in shootouts, retired after a distinguished career to become chief firearms instructor for the Customs Service in New York. He was transferred from there to the Federal Law Enforcement Training Center (FLETC) in Brunswick, Georgia. Cirillo's topic was the innovative man-against-man combat work that FLETC is using with laser-sensitive vests and handguns modified

Ron Flud (left) of Las Vegas coroner's office, and Massad Ayoob discuss wound ballistics. The latter presented a slide show on the subject for the assembled law agents.

Located on the Mexican border, San Diego has more than its share of armed violence and, even during the grim days when so many cops were dying, the department's members won more gunfights than they lost.

Gerry Smith represented the Smith & Wesson Academy at this training conference. An ex-cop with a background ranging from patrolman to tactical unit sniper to department instructor, Gerry emphasized the injection of reality into police weapons training. He called for added emphasis on close, fast shooting on multiple targets with decision-making factors thrown in. He noted that assault courses with a vast number of targets were unrealistic.

"When have any of you faced 17 bad guys by yourself," he asked the seasoned police audience, none of whom raised their hand. "If I were in that situation, I'd fall back and call for help. The training needs to be job-related."

Each point was underscored with actual incidents from Smith's encyclopedic knowledge of police liability case law. He noted that the S&W Academy is teaching use of the sights with the police handgun on any range beyond arm's length; this is based on the huge input from its police instructor trainees from all over the world.

"We also need to get away from shooting at nothing but 'center of mass,'" he emphasized. "More and more, today's suspect is smart enough to take cover. Train your officers to shoot for whatever part of the armed offender's body they can hit and not to wait for a center-X shot."

"Gunshot Wound Dynamics," as they relate to police shootings, was this writer's topic. More than three hundred slides, taken mostly in autopsy rooms, showed the effects of various smallarms fire (and knives and bludgeons) on the human body. Students learned the subtleties of identifying a shored or slit wound of exit and ramifications thereof that could convict or acquit a police officer wrongfully accused of a bad shooting in the wake of a self-defense incident. Photos also showed the effect doctors call "hyperextravasation" and ballisticians call "temporary wound cavity." This contradicted many experts who misquote that great trauma surgeon Martin Fackler and who erroneously assume no part of the body not actully touched by the bullet can be damaged enough to contribute to "stopping power." Evidence preservation at the shooting scene, in the emergency room and the medical examiner's office also were addressed, as were the graphically illustrated effects of certain types of ammunition.

Sergeant Terry Campbell of the Montgomery County, Ohio, Sheriff's Office chaired the panel of experts. In addition to the firearms track instructors, this panel included Seth Nadel of U.S. Customs, Captain John Cerar of the NYPD Firearms and Tactics Unit, Chief Russell Lary of the Grantham, New Hamphire, Police Department — also state director for Law Enforcement for Preservation of the Second Amendment — and Richard Garrison, a seasoned police weapons instructor from Georgia whose articles have appeared in numerous police professional journals.

Campbell is the embodiment of the kind of instructor ASLET is dedicated to creating: The cross-trained master teacher, equally functional all the way up and down the "escalation of force ladder." A nationally famous instructor in defensive tactics (the police term for unarmed com-

to shoot only laser beams. The students had the opportunity to duel with the laser equipment as they practiced Cirillo's concepts of advanced shooting from behind cover, "nose-pointing" without sights for faster close-range hits and engagement from awkward "downed officer" positions, such as flat on their backs and firing upside-down at an actual man coming in from behind them.

Sergeant Bill Nelson of the hosting department taught "Officer Survival: The San Diego Learning Experience." Some years ago, San Diego earned the dubious distinction of being the city with the highest number of police officer murders per capita. Then-Chief Bill Kollendar created an Officer Safety Task Force, which proposed nearly 130 changes in equipment, training and tactics, more than one hundred of which were accepted.

As a result of the study, high-capacity 9mm autoloaders were issued to new troops and made optional for in-service personnel. A strategy called "contact and cover" was conceived by Lieutenant John Morrison to give each officer more effective backup at any potential danger scene. Sergeant Nelson noted that complacency, after constant exposure to danger without being hurt, and lack of situational awareness were perhaps the biggest factors in the murders of law enforcement officers in his city. The new training has reduced the police death toll significantly.

Capstun incapacitant aerosol was demonstrated, as Tim Powers sprayed a big volunteer with mixture from a can.

Hit by spray, volunteer's head drops, knees begin to buckle. Moments later, subject was led away, helpless.

bat), he is also an internationally rated instructor with the PR-24 baton and has previously run an extremely dynamic live-fire shotgun course for ASLET.

Most of the 368 instructors in attendance participated in the panel's discussion. Their questions were fielded by the experts of their choice or the questions were directed to specific experts by Sergeant Campbell.

Among the most popular questions: "What's the story on the 10mm?" The panel unanimously agreed that the rush to the new caliber was premature, and several expressed cynicism over the testing by FBI on inanimate substances that led to their trend-setting adoption of a down-loaded 10mm cartridge. The coordinator of the firearms track took advantage of the presence of a Texas contingent to contact insiders in Houston for the lowdown on the first recorded gunfight usage of the 10mm; he passed on to the attendees the fact that a Hosuton cop had shot a gunman eight times with 10mm PMC hollow-points at close range, six times solidly in the torso. The bullets generally expanded well and pierced heart, aorta, lungs, liver and kidney. Still, the suspect was able to exit his vehicle and run thirty yards after taking these hits before he collapsed and died.

"What about Weaver versus isosceles shooting stances?" This question was directed to Taylor (Weaver) and Massad Ayoob (isosceles), with one arguing superior recoil control and the other citing compatibility of training to natural human reactions under life-threatening stress. Bruce Siddle, a famed police trainer, showed a film of an exercise in which police instructors trained in the Weaver stance and armed with guns that fired only cotton balls, instinctively "reverted" to isosceles and one-hand shooting stances when "attacked" by live role-players with similar weapons.

"Revolver versus autoloader?" The two strongest proponents of the revolver on the panel were Captain Cerar of NYPD and legendary modern gunfighter Jim Cirillo. Both noted that the auto takes longer to train a cop to use and that, with equal amounts of training time, the man with the auto will learn less about tactics. Cerar also cited the high

likelihood of accidental discharges with some autos among those rank and file cops who "aren't into guns." Most of the remainder favored the autoloader, with two — Taylor and Garrison — defending the cocked-and-locked Colt 1911-pattern .45 ACP.

"Safety catch or decock lever?" This question was directed toward Gerry Smith and Massad Ayoob, who are at opposite ends of an argument with cogent points on either side. Smith explained that the S&W Academy teaches the slide-mounted "safety" be used strickly as a decock lever with the gun carried immediately ready to fire with a pull of a trigger like a revolver, because (a) this ensured commonality of training and long-term experience with the revolver with which most in-service officers are much more familiar, and (b) the movement required to move a slide-mounted "safety" into the fire position is awkward, slow, and difficult to train into the student. The counter argument was that numerous documented cases exist of lives being saved with such pistols carried "on safe" when a suspect disarmed the officer and tried to shoot him but was unable to do so. No documented cases have been brought to light of an officer shot because he couldn't activate his manual safety and fire in self-defense in time.

The fourth annual ASLET international training seminar was held the second week of January, 1991, in West Palm Beach, Florida. The Palm Beach gathering emphasized live-fire training to the point that an ammo truck was assigned to the spacious range complex and attendees were ankle deep in brass!

Those who train police, be they cops themselves or civilians working for police in an instructional capacity, are eligible to join ASLET and attend the seminars. An all-star cadre of master instructors is planned for '91. Only members may attend the seminars. Police trainers interested in joining ASLET can write for applications to Massad Ayoob, P.O. Box 122, Concord, NH 03301. Police personnel will need to write on police letterhead or enclose a photocopy of their ID card; civilians who train police will need a letter from a police official confirming their status as such. The application will be sent by return mail.

IS YOUR DUTY GUN LAWYER PROOF?

A Tricked Up Custom Handgun Can Bring Courtroom Problems!

Fearsome weapons such as this, when issued, may deter a violent situation and have a psychological effect, but if you use a handgun — especially your own — that has been reworked to be visibly more efficient, it's trouble.

FOR A variety of reasons, most police officers carry the handgun issued to them by the department. Many times, they have no choice in the matter due to rules and regulations; this is especially true in the larger municipalities.

Personally, I find this somewhat restrictive, but there is a good reason for it. Given too much leeway, there always are a few in every department who will abuse the privilege and go off the deep end.

I recall a patrol sergeant who had a reputation for good marksmanship, if nothing else. He habitually carried a personally owned S&W K-22 revolver instead of the issued .38 Special. When questioned about this peculiarity, he always replied that he was such a good shot he needed only the .22 revolver. A few years later, I got the chance to revise the department's firearms policy and abolished this practice. Also outlawed were bolt-on "custom" items such as trigger shoes, thumb-rest target grips, et cetera, along

with any attempts at kitchen-table gunsmithing. If this isn't done, there always will be a certain percentage of officers who turn up with self-altered sidearms that may not work when needed.

Still, it's desirable to have the best handgun possible, and when an officer is interested in improvement, he should take the gun to a professional pistolsmith.

A good 'smith can tune the action for smoothness and reliability, but even here a lot of caution is required. One pistolsmith who had great local repute for competence always removed the hammer block from the S&W revolvers he tuned in order to get a better trigger pull. His trigger jobs were good, but he was wrong on two counts: It isn't necessary to remove this safety device to achieve an excellent double-action trigger pull. Also, the guns he worked on invariably fired if the hammer was struck or the gun took a fall. The man was a menace to public safety.

The best solution, as well as the most economical, is for

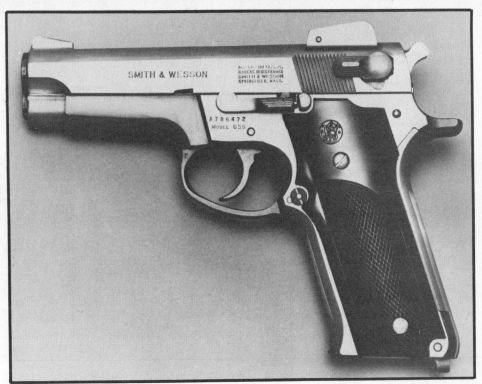

The Smith & Wesson M659 9mm has a 15-round magazine. It is law enforcement's effort to match crime's firepower.

the officer to take the gun to the departmental armorer. All major handgun manufacturers offer armorer's schools and a really good armorer will be a graduate. Some have attended several such gunsmithing classes and may be experts in the maintenance and repair of Colt, Smith & Wesson, Glock, SIG-Sauer or other handguns. Few armorers will attempt to do truly custom work, but all of them are capable of tuning the handgun to maximum performance, while staying inside factory specifications.

Issued handguns are seldom equal, and if most are satisfactory, there will always be a few which leave the factory in sub-standard condition. By smoothing the rough spots or eliminating defective parts, the armorer can transform the sidearm into the best example of the manufacturer's design.

Such a handgun can be so good no other work is necessary, but quality control during the manufacturing process can vary over the years. Smith & Wesson, for example, has had several owners over the last couple of decades, and gun quality dipped to an all-time low during the 1970s. Current S&W models, I'm happy to note, are outstandingly good.

In my personal battery is a .38 Special M12 Airweight revolver with a trigger pull so good I wouldn't change it for the world. How can you beat light, smooth and crisp? The newer S&W autos also have double-action trigger pulls that are excellent, with few needing any work at all. SIG-Sauer autos have had acceptable triggers from the beginning. In fact, the entire industry has cleaned up their trigger act tremendously in the last ten years.

Even so, there will be officers who want that extra edge, however slim it might be. Fortunately, we have many good pistolsmiths in this country, many of whom specialize in "street guns" or police sidearms.

It's a huge help if the pistolsmith is a former police officer or has some police experience. Unless you've been there, it's difficult to communicate the various situations in police work. Too often, in order to demonstrate his talent, a 'smith will lighten a double-action trigger pull too much, causing unreliable ignition of primers. Then, too, the single-action pull may be such a wish-off it endangers everyone in those common draw-and-cover situations or even in range practice.

I prefer a pistolsmith who knows police requirements over one who can achieve a light trigger pull. Cops are adaptable and can get by nicely with double-action pulls of about 7½ pounds. The single-action pull on autos or revolvers should never be less than 3½ pounds.

An excellent pistolsmith with a law enforcement background is Teddy Jacobson, who operates Actions By T in Sugar Land, Texas. Like any conscientious artisan, Jacobson will refuse to do work he considers dangerous in any way. He also won't turn out a gun he wouldn't carry himself on duty.

Typically, Jacobson will smooth and polish the sear and hammer notches to achieve the desired pull. On a revolver, he will time the cylinder to perfection and polish the bolt and rebound slide. On request, he will cut a new barrel crown of his own persuasion and throat the rear of the barrel to an optimum angle. Jacobson won't cut springs, but sometimes replaces them. A nice touch is the numbering of the charge ports with tiny numerals, making it easy to isolate the most accurate chamber in a revolver.

When you pick up a pistol or revolver Jacobson has worked over, it may be difficult at first glance to detect any major changes. In most cases there will be none, yet the gun is subtly better in every way.

This is just as well, for heavily customized handguns can and do draw legal fire in the courtroom.

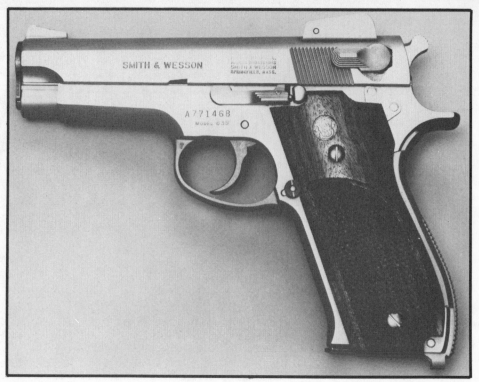

Tuning by a qualified gunsmith can make a Model 639 a more efficient law enforcement tool without being termed a "killing machine" by an attorney.

Badly informed or unscrupulous lawyers, even some judges, believe a slicked-up sidearm translates to a murderous character in the officer or citizen who carries it. If not, why would he go to such lengths to make shooting a felon easier?

There's a certain mentality which holds that all weapons are intrinsically evil — despite being inanimate objects — and never should be highly regarded or prized. No credit is given to a person who simply cherishes fine mechanical work or is conscientious about tools. Most officers and others who own custom guns have never shot anyone with them and, in fact, are no more murderous than the car owner who keeps his vehicle in top shape. Nevertheless, an obviously altered or improved handgun can give an opposing lawyer something to get his teeth into and perhaps put the officer on trial instead of the felon.

Teddy Jacobson will stand behind the work he performs on a customer's gun — in court or out. A skilled specialist in action jobs, he can tune a handgun to top performance with no visible, external indication the gun isn't factory standard. Unlike many pistolsmiths, Jacobson is familiar with all foreign handguns as well as domestic brands and often does action jobs on SIG-Sauer, Glock, Beretta and other autos of foreign manufacture. He's a top-notch police sidearm specialist.

Another good name to know in this business is that of Milton Morrison, a former California Highway Patrol armorer. Morrison now operates Qualite Pistol & Revolver (P.O. Box 550, Divide, Colorado 80814).

Like Jacobson, Morrison is an expert with all types of handguns and can perform just about any sort of work the shooter desires. However, his specialty is tuning police handguns in what has been termed a "lawyer-proof" manner. This means simply that, although the weapon is slicked over and made superior to a factory gun, none of the work is outside the tolerances and specifications laid down at the

factory. Since the same work could have been performed at the factory — given the same skilled hand labor — there isn't anything for a hostile attorney to attack. This is a novel approach, worth serious consideration by police officers or citizens with a need to carry a handgun for defense.

Pistolsmith Teddy Jacobson has a law enforcement past and knows the requirements for a policeman's sidearm. Author feels he is one of few qualified for such work.

The S&W Model 469 is still another handgun that can benefit from a tuning job to make it function better.

It should be emphasized that it isn't a crime to use a customized handgun in a defense shooting. However, it can be made into something socially reprehensible, if an attorney chooses to do so, thereby jeopardizing a case. The practice could be stopped cold by any forthright and honest judge. It should be made clear to an attorney that no such attacks or derisive comments will be allowed when the officer or citizen has otherwise acted properly and responsibly.

Even so, if no criticism is forthcoming, it's a mistake for a police officer to carry any sidearm which shows heavy external evidence of tuning or customizing. Handguns used in defense shootings, no matter how justifiably, are always seized as evidence by the court.

An especially fancy, attractive and cherished handgun will often "get lost" in the halls of justice and never find its way back to the owner. A cynic would say, "Why sink a

Teddy Jacobson has a reputation for his work and won't release a handgun unless he would carry it himself for a tour of duty in the streets; he is highly respected.

Jacobson checks the trigger pull on a revolver turned in to him for maintenance and repair by a police officer.

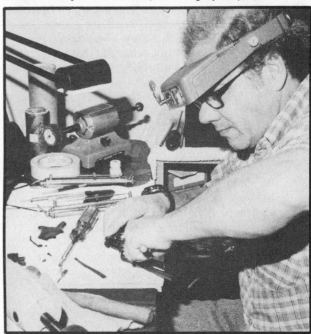

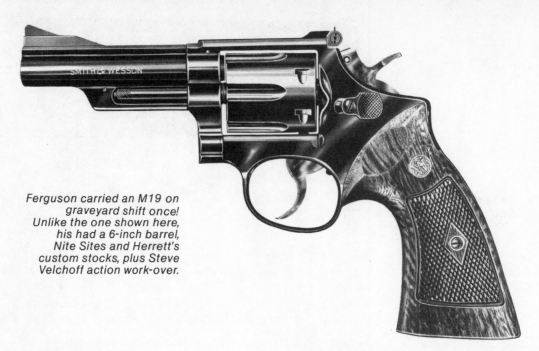

Ferguson carried an M19 on graveyard shift once! Unlike the one shown here, his had a 6-inch barrel, Nite Sites and Herrett's custom stocks, plus Steve Velchoff action work-over.

ton of money and effort in a handgun that will end up in some lawyer's pocket?"

For this reason, I almost never carried one of my prized custom revolvers on duty, even when it was permitted. Instead, I restricted customizing work to simple action jobs for a smooth double-action trigger pull and grips or stocks that fit my hand. I prefer fixed sights on a duty gun, so sights were never a problem.

The first sidearm issued to me was an S&W M10 heavy barrel .38 Special, which I carried for years with no modifications except for hand-filling stocks. These were necessary to help control recoil from the heavy .38 Special loads used and proved invaluable in drawing the gun quickly in emergencies.

Proper grips allow the hand, even when hurried, to get a shooting hold on the gun on the first attempt. The importance of this can't be overemphasizied, for in spite of scoffers and armchair critics, fast-draw situations do occur in police work. On at least three occasions that I remember, this gun, in combination with a high-rise holster, beat three of my opponents to the draw and was on them before they could align their own weapons. Fortunately, in each case the scofflaws realized I had them so cold no shooting was required. When so motivated, it doesn't take a felon long to surrender.

In 1974, my department bought four hundred Model 58 S&W .41 magnum revolvers, an initial shipment on the approved purchase of 1000. Sadly, no more ever arrived, for the M58 proved as unpopular with our department as it had with others. Smith & Wesson was then, I believe, under the control of Bangor Punta and the .41s we received showed terrible workmanship and lack of quality control. Of the four hundred revolvers, thirteen were rejected outright for major flaws, which included rear sights milled off-center and, in one case, a .44 magnum cylinder installed on a .41 M58 frame. The 387 remaining revolvers were hastily tuned and repaired by the departmental armorer and my crew of fellow firearms instructors.

To arm myself, I searched through at least fifty revolvers before finding an M58 I was willing to carry. These were the worst handguns I've ever seen from a U.S. manufacturer and did nothing to promote the adoption of the M58 .41, which in good examples is one of the finest police sidearms ever built.

Later, I had Ace Hindman do an action job on my M58, because it was my favorite uniform duty gun. The big N-

On request, Jacobson will fill the familiar three-dot combat sight system with luminous paint for night work.

In an emergency situation, Ferguson carried his own Model 29 on night duty. The sight of it in his hands caused felon's surrender.

frames take kindly to trigger jobs and this .41 has the best I've seen.

Hindman operates Ace Custom .45s (1880¼ Upper Turtle Creek, Kerrville, Texas 78028). He is a past master at tuning revolvers and virtually any make of autoloader.

For graveyard or dogwatch shift, as we called it, I carried a special S&W M19 .357 with a six-inch barrel. It was equipped with Juilo Santiago's glow-in-the-dark Nite Sites, custom Herrett stocks and had a superb action job by the now-deceased Steve Velchoff, a fine man and an excellent pistolsmith. The gun was always loaded with .38 Special mid-range target ammo (wadcutters). In combination with the six-inch barrel, these gave little muzzle flash. In spite of the relatively low-power ammunition, this was a most deadly after-dark sidearm.

Teddy Jacobson numbers each charge port of a revolver so the shooter can determine what chambers are accurate.

In the normal course of things, I preferred the .41 M58, but on occasion carried other sidearms. Policemen know that whenever you think no shooting will erupt, that's the exact time it will. Such situations always come up when you don't want them to.

Once I was in the process of altering a set of custom stocks for my city-issued .41 and left it at home. In its place I carried a much-prized M29 .44 magnum with a four-inch barrel to roll call. The big revolver had a nice action job by the late Harold Cline, an old-time exhibition shooter and contemporary of the famed Ad Topperwein. In addition to this sentimental value, the M29 was Mag-na-ported and otherwise tricked out in the best fashion.

It was much too fine a piece to be carrying on duty, but happened to be my only other N-frame revolver at the time.

Late that night, I had occasion to confront two armed robbery suspects just beginning an escape in their getaway car. The .44 was loaded with Remington 240-grain lead flat-tips. At 940 feet per second, they don't penetrate car metal that well.

In order to get a better shot through the suspects' windshield, I ran in front of the vehicle while it was still fifty feet away. Luckily, when the driver saw the big .44 leveled at him, he hit the brakes. Seconds later, the weapons of both came flying out the side windows and their hands went up. The thought of shooting them with my cherished .44 was nearly as frightening to me as it was to the robbers.

If the gun had been confiscated as evidence in the shooting, I'm quite certain I'd never have seen it again.

In the absence of an armorer or the pistolsmith's touch, most pistols and revolvers can be improved simply by dry firing. This practice not only smooths all rough spots and burrs off the hammer and sear, but also builds strength in the trigger finger. Many officers are under the impression dry firing breaks firing pins and other parts. In my experience, this isn't true, but the gun should be checked thoroughly before every tour of duty.

The bomb disposal unit built by Criminalistics of Miami, Florida, is used to transport explosives from the scene where they can be destroyed. Explosion's force is directed straight upward, as suggested in this photo.

CHAPTER FIFTEEN

BOMB SQUAD: HOW & WHY

If You Want An Expert Job Done, Get An Expert; Bomb Disposal Follows That Premise

EVERYONE KNOWS what it is and can recognize one instantly, but no one, not even scientists, can offer a good definition of an explosion.

The best I can come up with is that an explosion is a sudden, violent, noisy going away of something that was there before, not doing any harm. The matter assumes importance by degree. Naturally, exploding popcorn in your microwave causes little excitement, unless you're really hungry, but a dozen sticks of dynamite is a different proposition.

One of the most fascinating articles I ever read was published in a men's magazine during the 1950s. It was a photo-essay concerning a man who made his living by blowing himself up, usually with dynamite. He was a sort of Evel Kneivel with explosives and feared such objects no more than cops fear cartridges.

This guy would dress in a flamboyant costume, don a brightly colored football helmet and get down to business. Placing a small shield between himself and a dozen sticks of dynamite — while actually leaning on the stack! — he'd signal a helper to set it off. There was a flash and a big bang, then a rolling cloud of dust and smoke. The uproar tossed him a few feet, but he'd emerge from the cloud unscathed, though often a bit tattered.

Nobody in his right mind would attempt this, of course, yet the daredevil repeated the performance time after time without injury. When asked his secret, his reply went something like this: "To survive you must be as close as possible to the explosion. The flash and bang don't kill you, the wind does. Stand just a few feet away and the displaced air rushing outward will tear you to pieces."

This makes sense, as anyone who has seen large explosions can testify. I've stood four hundred yards from a length of detonating cord and felt the concussion on my face.

In this age of specialization, where we have an expert for every problem, it may seem strange that not so long ago, ordinary, untrained personnel were often called on to deal with explosives. The reason was simple: There were no experts available.

Things that disappear suddenly and violently have always frightened me, as they do most people, yet my bad luck has been to be closely associated with them for a long time.

As a young man, my first good job was with a major airline, loading baggage and cargo aboard the company aircraft. Bomb threats are a constant problem with any airline. An irate, disgruntled passenger may phone such a threat to the ticket counter, but those who plant real bombs aboard airliners seldom are good enough to call in a warning. As a youth, I didn't know that.

When a threat was received, the airplane was unloaded immediately and taken out of service until the mechanics — not bomb experts — checked it over thoroughly. Chances are, they didn't like this chore any better than I enjoyed unloading the plane, but there was no one else to do it.

It used to be that a significant part of a patrol officer's duty was to pick up and carry off exploding things that might hurt the public. Usually, these consisted of grenade and artillery simulators — big firecrackers — purloined from the Army, live or dummy grenades, live shells taken as souvenirs and sometimes commercial explosives such as dynamite.

We'd get the call and off we'd go to do a public service.

Bob Ellis, a longtime explosives handling expert, takes a look at a pair of hand grenades turned into his office by citizens who were reducing their wartime souvenirs!

her late husband had blown himself up, by any chance. Without humor, she replied that he had died of a heart attack. Trying not to have one myself, I eyed the dynamite carefully. It was indeed weathered, but although the paper wrappings were discolored, it wasn't growing "hair" — crystallized tendrils of exuded nitroglycerin.

Dynamite in that state should never be moved or even handled. If it can't be blown in place, a brave expert might de-sensitize it by carefully soaking it with gallons of acetone. This guarantees nothing, but if the explosive has to be moved, the try can be made.

My dynamite appeared much safer, but today I'd simply call the bomb squad. We had none then, so I decided to move it. With all the care in the world, I eased the torn cardboard box off the ground and — after sending the woman away — somehow got it to the back seat of my patrol car. Recalling the daredevil's admonition to stay close to the explosion, I put it right behind the driver's seat. Anyway, if the dynamite exploded in a sudden, violent manner, I didn't want time to think about it. Why I felt it was my duty to haul this stuff, I'll never know or be able to explain satisfactorily. Certainly, I'd refuse any such request today — but that was then.

By phone, I arranged to meet an Army demolitions expert at the gate of a distant Army base. On the way, I tried to avoid bumps in the road and, above all, an automobile accident. The dispatcher had forgotten he had sent me on the call and kept paging me over the radio. I refused to transmit and finally flicked the receiver off. Radio waves don't actually set off dynamite, I'm told. What they set off is dynamite detonators, the little tubes of fulminate that explode the stuff. In this case, I had no way of knowing a detonator was not lurking amidst the dynamite sticks. The little, thin detonators are powerful explosives themselves — when one explodes, the fragments fly at something better than 4000 feet per second. In other words, more than enough to put out an eye or take off a hand.

The Army demolitions man was there as promised, a capable-looking young guy in camouflage uniform. He kept his cool, until he looked in the back seat of the patrol car, then he gasped loudly. All the blood drained from his face as he took in the condition of the weathered dynamite.

"You hauled this stuff?" he asked incredulously.

"I'll tell you something funnier than that," I answered. "Now you're gonna haul it!"

And he did, however reluctantly. Fortunately, the Army disposal site was not far away; less than the distance I'd driven.

Wartime demolitions men have it much easier than cops or civilian bomb experts. In a war zone, the big problem is in finding and detecting the mines and booby traps. Once found, they simply attach a charge of C-4 and blow the stuff in place. In a war-torn landscape, who cares? It is by far the best way to deal with any hazardous explosives.

Cops can't do that and the dangers a bomb squad faces would take a book to describe. Why anyone makes a career of such danger is beyond me, but thankfully we have those who do. The reason most continue to live is because most felonious bomb-makers can construct only the most primitive devices. In a majority of cases, they are pipe bombs or other relatively unsophisticated contraptions. If highly educated felons ever decided to plant bombs, you'd see a

To prepare us for this tricky duty, we went through an abbreviated explosives school at a nearby Army base where we learned the characteristics of most common explosives. Most cops would be surprised to realize just how much of this stuff the citizens out there are harboring in their homes, usually as mementos of war.

One bright morning, I received a call for dangerous explosives and on arrival was led to a delapidated tool shed at the rear of a residence. In one corner, exposed to rain and sunshine, was a broken case of dynamite, containing perhaps two dozen weathered sticks. It had belonged to the owner of the house, now deceased, who once had a legitimate purpose for it. Now, his widow wanted it disposed of — and the disposer was me.

Trying to stay on the light side, I asked jokingly whether

Ellis heads up a five-man bomb squad that has seen a lot of potentially explosive situations over the years of service.

great reduction and huge casualty figures among the experts.

We had a taste of that in the 1960s, when disgruntled individuals from radical universities began constructing bombs. They were not ignoramuses when it came to bomb design. Most of their efforts were directed at the police, the hated symbols of the establishment.

Chemistry students discovered they could make a bomb or incendiary device from almost anything: hair oil, garden fertilizer, household cleaners, ad infinitum. Books were published on the subject and made available, some in university libraries. These dissidents could disguise a bomb or incendiary so it appeared to be an ordinary, innocent object. This information probably came from Vietnam and the Viet Cong.

There was a neat, little device consisting of powdered magnesium placed in a cigar box. The scumbag would hand it over to a police officer as if offering a gift. When the offender released his hold, the trigger ignited the magnesium, burning the officer's hands off.

Bomb work is dangerous because of human ingenuity. It is quite possible to construct a bomb that absolutely cannot be disarmed. It's also common for a talented bomb maker to attach a "Gotcha!" to his original device so that, even if you disarm the first, it arms and detonates a second bomb, a third one — or any number of extra Gotchas.

Watching Hollywood movies, we may tense up as the

bomb-squad hero disarms a particularly difficult bomb, thereby saving everyone's bacon. It is nonsense, of course. Any good bomb expert will back off from a highly sophisticated device and let it blow. Evacuations are as much a part of bomb work as disarming techniques, although the latter have become sophisticated, too.

Today's bomb teams are just that: teams of experts with proper schooling and the high-tech tools that can be used to disarm or neutralize all but the most intricate explosive devices. Robots with television "eyes" are much in evidence, along with Kevlar bomb suits for human officers. There are disarmers that fire high-velocity projectiles into complicated bombs to cut the wiring, X-ray cameras that provide a Polaroid picture of the interior and transporters to move the bomb to a safe location for disposal. When it comes down to the bottom line, nothing can replace the best tool of all — the skilled, trained human using a gifted pair of hands.

We need the high-tech equipment, of course, and it has saved many lives. Viewed realistically, however, it can't be considered cost-effective, and a cynic might say it takes a $50,000 robot to disarm a $40 pipe bomb. The truth is, these high-technology tools are most effective on relatively unsophisticated bombs constructed by equally unsophisticated makers. The inference here is that bombs are so dangerous when cleverly constructed, they shouldn't be messed with by anyone, let alone the ordinary patrol officer.

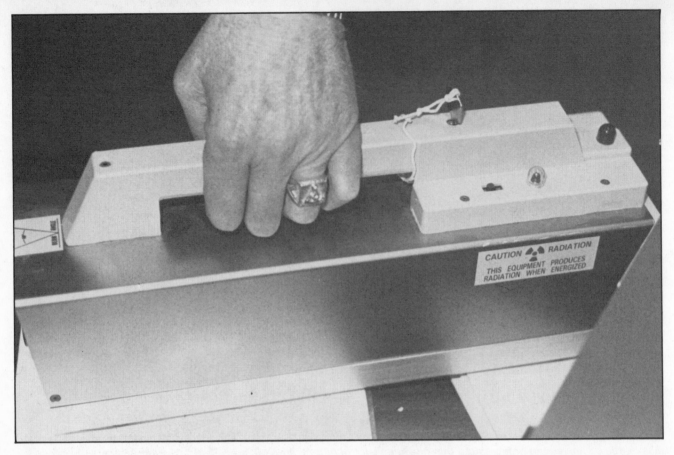

Ellis does not believe in a lot of exotic and expensive equipment, depending upon his hands and knowledge, but he admits that a small X-ray unit is a good piece of equipment to have along to look inside of packages.

All the anecdotal information supplied at the beginning of this chapter is just that: anecdotes more in the nature of what you shouldn't do, rather than information on how to deal with bombs. Leave them to the bomb squad.

Thankfully for the patrol officer, most bomb calls turn out to be hoaxes or some other form of false alarm, although this can't be counted on to be the case.

Police officers have the reputation of being a rough-and-ready bunch, most endowed with a sense of macabre if not gallows humor. It once was thought to be a good joke to display this frivolity on phony bomb calls.

I once received a call regarding an explosive device left on the doorstep of a residence. On investigation, I found the home shut tight and a brown leather satchel standing open on the front porch. It contained several large, dark bottles of a liquid vitamin and an instrument with a metered dial for taking blood pressure.

It had belonged to a door-to-door vitamin salesman whose ploy was to take the mark's blood pressure, announce it was terrible, then sell him the vitamins. In this instance, the unsuccessful salesperson had quit in disgust, leaving his satchel of goods on the doorstep. The resident thought it looked suspiciously like a bomb and called the police. Actually, it did resemble bottled nitro with an alarm clock attached.

While kneeling to peer into the satchel, I saw my cover officer arrive and dismount from his car. He happened to be an officer who tended toward unwarranted panic — and a good subject for practical jokes.

Cruelly, I allowed him to cover half the distance from the street to the porch, then jumped to my feet in mock terror. I shouted, "Run for your life! This damned thing really is a bomb!"

Side by side we ran for our lives a full block with our legs propelling us at our best speed, unmatched since cadet training. We lost our hats to the slipstream of wind and our holstered guns banged bruises on our hips. Exhausted, at last, we stopped for breath and I gave the joke away by bursting into laughter.

The gulled officer was furious, of course. After the angry scene that followed, I gave up such jokes forever.

When you want to know about dangerous things that go *boom*, it's best to get an expert opinion. With that thought in mind, I went directly to the Special Operations Unit where the office of Bob Ellis is located.

Ellis is an old friend who for many years has been the "bomb man" for the San Antonio Police Department. Currently he heads up a bomb squad composed of Officers Ronnie Welch, David Espinosa, Tom Shaw and Al Cavalier. All are veteran policemen with a lot of experience under their Sam Browne belts, most of it in dealing with dangerous or violent situations.

The only two pieces of exotic equipment used by Ellis' team are the X-ray unit and a device that fires a wedge-shaped slug for cutting wires and fuses. Most of the bombs dealt with in his jurisdiction are rather simple.

When first organized, the bomb squad responded to and was responsible for calls in a seventeen-county area around San Antonio, which insured a lot of knowledge gained fast. Technically their jurisdiction doesn't extend beyond the city limits of San Antonio, but if one has a bomb in his lap, who cares if help comes from eighty miles away? Later, the burden was eased when their territory was reduced to the confines of Bexar County, which surrounds San Antonio. Other than military units based at Fort Sam Houston, these are the only bomb experts in that area.

Bob Ellis sat at a functional, if cluttered, desk, surrounded by articles of death and destruction. The room is a cross between an armory and home workshop. On a three-tiered shelf, an array of deactivated hand grenades and souvenir land mines sat in rusted silence, all confiscated from the felonious owners or turned in by the public. There were such diverse objects as a Civil War rifled cannon shell, a Russian stick mine from Afghanistan and an assortment of 20mm cannon shells. A low table held cardboard boxes of aging smallarms ammunition: paper shotgun shells, .45 ACP ammo from 1943 and rifle cartridges of all calibers. Many citizens are uncomfortable around ordinary ammunition and hand it over to the bomb squad for disposal. In reality, it poses no particular hazard and is allowed to accumulate until space runs short.

On the far wall hung handtools that might be found in any garage or workshop — several types of hammers, saws and wrenches.

The only exotic or specialized tools were tucked away under shelves here and there: an X-ray machine to peer inside an explosive device and a sort of gun that fires a wedge-shaped slug for cutting wires and fuses. There were no bomb suits, remote control units or robotic TV cameras. Ellis is a straightforward sort of bomb technician and, as I later learned, believes a good pair of hands and a good brain can handle most situations. Not that he doesn't appreciate good equipment, but it must serve a real purpose. Bomb work is too delicate to tolerate gadgets.

Ellis, who I've known for twenty years, is not especially talkative. He's more a doer, and when the thought comes into his head, he simply does it. To me, this translates into self-confidence, which all bomb technicians must have in large amounts. When there is just you and the bomb, the bomb isn't going to help you and there's no one else to consult.

There is a popular concept that bomb men are daredevil brave, macho-defiant — or simply crazy. I don't get that impression at all. Instead, these are cool-headed, careful workmen who operate with all the skill — and about the same amount of bravado — as a watchmaker. They realize a mistake means failure and that failure can mean instant death. To men like Ellis, this simply means you have to do

With several military bases in the area, the San Antonio Police Department has been called upon to defuse many types of ammunition and grenades. These are some that have been retained for instructional and lecture uses.

everything right the first time, and he's careful to do that. It must be the perfectionist in his character.

Underlining the need for that trait was a series of graphic photos pinned to a wall. They showed the ragged remains of a citizen who made the mistake of using dynamite to perform some mundane chore, perhaps blowing tree stumps or quarrying in a gravel pit. Long accustomed to scenes of violence myself, I thought I was shudder-proof. Gunshot wounds and knife slashes pale in comparison, I found. I'd never seen a cross-section of the human torso before, in vivid color no less. Guns and knives are simple weapons used by angry human beings against one another. If you defeat the man, you defeat the gun or knife and avoid disaster. The fear generated by explosives is primal and more elemental, like a fear of thunder. Who can fight the thunder?

Ellis has been fighting the thunder for decades, but he fights it carefully. After his first tour of duty, this former Marine wanted to reenlist for a career as an ordnance expert, but the prospects seemed dim. After leaving the Marine Corps, he joined the San Antonio Police Department and, for a time, abandoned hope of pursuing a career as a demolitions man.

As luck would have it, the department was just beginning formation of a bomb unit and Ellis was the second person in the department to undergo training. He attended the

Army school at Redstone Arsenal, Alabama, and graduated at the head of his class. He is familiar with all ordinary explosives and quite a few exotic ones. He also has an advanced knowledge of smallarms — rifles, pistols, shotguns, grenades and launchers. His sidearm is a S&W Model 4506, because "there is nothing unknown or untested about the .45 ACP cartridge. It works." He carries round-nose ball ammo in the gun. In spite of Bob Ellis' chancey profession, my guess is there isn't much of the gambler in him.

Because the work is low-profile, some officers doubt the need for "bomb men" in the department. In response, Ellis looked in his log book briefly and stated his unit had made 244 calls this year — and it was only June. In addition, the bomb squad is responsible for dignitary protection, working closely with the Secret Service when political VIPs are visiting. The unit searches and secures all speaking areas and travels along in motorcades in the event an explosive device flies out of the crowd.

Most calls to Ellis' department are for the disposal of items turned in by the public. Patrol personnel have orders not to attempt to move any explosive or bomb. Other agencies don't seem to have the word, however, and occasionally this poses a problem. Only a short time before this interview, a deputy sheriff walked into the crowded lobby of the

At left are pipe bombs found by police officers. Note the taped spoon handle on the hand grenade. All are in a still-explosive state and bound for demolition range. Such items as the pipe bomb are crude but still dangerous.

police station, holding a live grenade and calling for the bomb squad. Not too bright, to say the least.

Ellis doesn't share my own contempt for crude pipe bombs. "If we're not there to deactivate them, they work as well as anything!" he said, relating how a fireman in another city built four such unsophisticated devices and planted them conspicuously. He planned to volunteer to defuse them himself, angling for a job as a bomb expert later.

Ellis and his crew picked up the bombs, then later exposed the plot and arrested the fireman.

"When we removed the bombs to a safe place for destruction, three of the four devices blew. He did a good job on them," Ellis added.

Ellis has survived several explosions in his long career, including one serious accident that damaged his hearing. It occurred as he was transporting dynamite for disposal. Luckily, the explosives were in the bomb trailer which guided the blast straight up.

The trailer has a large tank into which explosives are placed, and offers protection against most accidents. The tank walls are made of 1¼-inch armor plate. There are two walls, one drum placed inside the other. The space between is filled with a silica material as a buffer, similar to sand. The floor also carries padding of this material. The top is open to allow the blast to go upward in case of a

detonation. Jokingly, Ellis remarked that in this era of high rise glass skyscrapers, some closed sort of transport might be better.

As noted, Ellis is not an equipment freak. There are bomb suits on order at some $13,000 each, but Ellis states it often isn't possible to do bomb work while wearing them. The suits are heavy Kevlar with titanium-plate inserts and offer "about as much protection as you'll ever get!"

Naturally, the conversation got around to explicit case histories and I asked Ellis bluntly, "What is the worst you ever handled?" Ironically, it wasn't a bomb plot against the Pope or President, but a rather mundane case involving an irate husband and his ex-wife.

"The guy had an expert build the bomb for him, then wrapped it and sent it to his ex-wife through the mail. The woman had long fingernails and as she attempted to tear off the wrapping, she dragged a nail across the surface and felt wires. This made her suspicious immediately, for her husband had made several other attempts on her life. She phoned the police, and we responded.

"On arrival, I immediately X-rayed the package," Ellis recalled. "When I saw the inside of the thing, my heart began to go pitty-pat! This was one highly sophisticated device, containing six different triggers to blow the package when opened. Rather, it could be blown six different

Like a lot of law enforcement demolitions specialists, Bob Ellis gained his first experience with bomb disposal as a Marine. His early experience, like that of many Vietnam Marines, was in probing for land mines with his bayonet!

ways...we couldn't move it, that would certainly explode the bomb. So I had to disarm it. After several hours work, I managed to cut six copper wires intended to detonate the bomb and was about to declare it inert so we could move it. A final look showed a faint, blurry shadow on the X-ray and I felt for it gingerly. It was a final trip wire made of monofilament instead of copper...a clever Gotcha! trigger that almost worked!"

Ellis wiped his brow in remembrance, continuing. "To make things more difficult, the maker had built the bomb upside down. This was a nice trick, but proved to be his undoing. We later got a single thumbprint off the inside box lid and convicted him on it."

What makes disposal men tick and what makes them stick?

A psychiatrist might have a field day interviewing and interpreting them, advancing numerous theories. The odds are he'd be wrong in each instance.

I've know all these men for many years. We have an incomplete picture of Ellis: cool, reticent and competent. Then there is Ronnie Welch, who came straight from Vietnam to the police department twenty years ago: silent, quick and unshakable in emergencies. David Espinosa, likewise no gossiper, has self-confidence which allows him to tackle anything others might consider daring. Tom Shaw, expert rifleman and combat veteran of street and battlefield, spends words like they were money. Amiable Al Cavalier's experience includes a lifetime of work in virtually every bureau within the police department and an

The bomb transport unit from Criminalistics, Inc., is well built and glossy. Design is based upon a good deal of information from demolitions experts.

General design for bomb transport trailers is the same, but this one was built locally and simply.

inner toughness his friendliness conceals well. Now that I've listed them and listed my own evaluation, I see the only thing they have in common is a lack of wordiness and frivolous conversation.

But maybe not. New police officers often discover, for the first time, that there can be exhilaration in danger. It's a natural high that makes every cell in the body glad to be alive and smugly satisfied at a job well done. It comes with the first high-speed car chase, perhaps, or being the number one winner in an even-odds gunfight. The experience of most officers never goes beyond that point and they are content to leave it.

For others the pursuit takes the form of challenges in other areas, and to speak openly of it spoils the effect. This is speculation on my part, of course, and I could be as wrong as any rookie psychiatrist.

Whatever it is, my guess is that Ellis and his experts will continue being bomb men until it grows tiresome.

CHAPTER SIXTEEN

THE DOGS OF LAW

Today's Canine Enforcers Fulfill Many Tasks In Various Roles

THE SYMBIOTIC relationship between man and dogs goes back many thousands of years, to the first dim campfires of early human beings. Before *Homo sapiens* discovered fire, the wolf and wild dog were merely dangerous competitors in a savage world filled with enemies.

With fire, came the ability to cook raw meat and with the cooking came delicious odors that attracted the wolf. Content at first to scavenge man's abandoned campsites for bones and scraps, the intelligent animals soon became regular fireside companions, if not pets. They recognized the fire as a potential source of food and gradually lost their fear of man. There's no doubt the wolf was the first of man's domesticated animals, even if that domestication was only partial for centuries. The gradual transition of wolf into dog was a long time coming. The idea of the dog as a pet deserving real affection is a relatively modern concept.

Early man had no role models and little time for affection in a primitive world. Dogs were first used to help hunt and track game. When there was no game, early man ate the dogs. Later, he found other uses for the dog, which like the horse, played a significant part in the incessant warfare to which man seems addicted.

Some years ago, Hollywood released a movie entitled *The Dogs Of War,* an adventure tale of a mercenary's overthrow of an African government. No doubt the title mystified most viewers, who have no idea what "the dogs of war" really means. From ancient times through the medieval age — before the invention of firearms — dogs bred for size and ferocity were a vital part of many armies.

The huge English mastiff was a typical and horrifying example of the ancient war dog. Barrel chested and brave, almost as heavy as a man, they were unleashed by the hundreds on an opposing army. They didn't fight side by side with their masters. Sometimes partially armored and fitted with spiked collars, the dogs attacked alone. In a day when men fought with sword and spear, the dogs wore down an enemy quickly, exhausting sword arms and leaving the weary soldiers vulnerable to attack. Most of the dogs were killed of course, but their masters usually won the battle. To "loose the dogs of war" then is to open a particularly vicious, no-quarter battle.

Dogs never have disappeared from warfare. In both World Wars, they performed messenger, guard and attack duties with unfailing courage and loyalty. They had names, rank and, in many cases, won medals for outstanding acts of military duty.

A dog is just a dog and I'll make no attempt to present them as equals. Still, dogs have many of the virtues and qualities human beings prize in themselves — in the better examples at least. Dogs have pride and courage, along with a sense of shame and conscience. Trained dogs can seldom be frightened off or, even more rarely, bought off.

An intelligent dog will have a vocabulary of five hundred to six hundred words he actually understands. Sheepherders and cattlemen regularly train them to respond to dozens of hand signals. Small wonder then that dogs have endeared themselves to humans and have assumed a status above that of other animals.

To the list of virtues above, we must add the dog's natural talents — a keen sense of smell and hearing, excellent binocular eyesight and stamina and endurance in

These dogs, two Rottweilers and a German shepherd, are eager and ready for their next assignment. All commands begin with the dog on the left side of the handler.

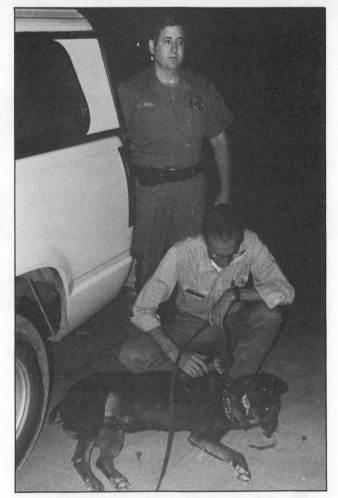

Joe Phillips' dog, Brutus, enjoys a friendly pat and some scratching. Despite training exercise ferocity, K-9s show their pet status when they are not on duty.

adverse conditions. All these things are employed in the service of human beings — and it's no exaggeration to say the canine race deserves better than it gets from mankind.

Dogs have been used in police work throughout American history and received undeserved bad press during the Civil Rights movement of the 1960s. Scenes of running marchers, protesters and rioters being set upon and harried by police dogs played to sympathetic viewers on American television screens. It was bad public relations, but it's well to remember it was the rioters who broke existing laws, not the dogs or police officers. Since that time, however, police dogs have been assigned to less aggressive duties and a low profile is maintained for them generally.

Like horses and some other animals, police dogs have intelligent, well defined personalities. I recall one dog named Duke that had not only a leather collar, but a badge as well, inletted into the top strap. When an arrest was made and Duke was involved, his name and badge number went on the booking slip, along with that of the arresting officer.

Duke's policeman owner lived in an apartment and because of the cramped quarters, he often freed the huge, beautiful German shepherd and let him roam at will. Duke was the king of the neighborhood. Other dogs feared him

too much to fight and Duke never bit nor molested human beings. Like any true king, Duke was noble and actually protective of small children. Duke's only problem was that, at times, he roamed too far and would find himself in unfamiliar territory. If that happened, he would stand in the road and stop the next passing patrol car — he knew one by sight, of course — and bum a ride home.

Probably I shouldn't tell this story on Duke, lest it diminish his reputation. On the other hand, it shows we all make mistakes and that makes me even fonder of this gallant old trooper.

Late one night, a burglar broke into a small business and several officers, including myself, responded to the alarm. The rear door had been smashed and the perpetrator apparently had fled with the loot. In spite of diligent human searching, no burglar was found. Duke and his owner happened to be nearby, so Duke gave the premises a thorough canine going-over. Eventually, he gave a dog shrug and walked out, as if to say, "No burglar!"

Five minutes later, a rookie officer looked behind an impossibly small water heater and found the impossibly small, but adult, male burglar in hiding. Duke apparently had missed his scent due to the many police officers crowded into the tiny room. The incident taught me that burglars are infinitely crafty and sometimes can conceal themselves even from dogs!

Then there was Sam, another German shepherd police dog of impeccable credentials but somewhat different in character. Sam never warmed up to me and seemed to not have a friendly bone in his body. Yet he performed faithfully for his owner and the police department.

As a cocky young police officer, I once boasted — because I was both larger and more intelligent than any dog — that I could strangle a dog like Sam with my bare hands. Wisely, his owner shook his head and replied, "You'd never do it!" Police dogs sometimes do become involved in violence and after seeing Sam in action, I lost no time in retracting my statement.

Coincidentally, Sam also was involved with a burglary suspect in a less pleasant way. Four burglars struck a business one night, setting off the alarm. Several officers responded and were quick enough to catch one suspect at the scene. The others fled in three directions and were chased, but not caught by officers on foot. The suspect in custody refused to reveal the identity of his fellow thieves, or even where they might be headed. In the confusion of the arrest and chase, the handcuffed suspect was mistakenly placed in the rear seat of Sam's patrol car, which he was occupying at the time.

For a while, the officers were too busy to notice the error. Then, almost simultaneously, they noticed the patrol car rocking from side to side and muffled noises issuing from the rear seat. On opening the rear door, the officers were surprised to see a ragged suspect emerge, swiftly pursued by an enraged Sam.

The big police dog had bitten the poor suspect in so many places that some of the fang marks had strikeovers. Naturally, the officers wanted to apologize for the mistake, but could hardly get a word in edgewise. The burglary suspect suddenly wanted to get everything off his conscience and insisted on talking about everyone and everything he knew. The man was a veritable crime encyclopedia on two legs.

Of course, that burglary — and several others — were cleared by four arrests, but only seldom does fortune favor the law in such a way.

I recently got an update in police dog training from Joe Phillips, a sixteen-year veteran of the K-9 Corps. Late one evening, we gathered "dog men" from four law enforcement agencies, including a railroad detective. The dogs were predominately German shepherds, with a couple of Rottweilers and a Belgian Malinois. Doberman's make excellent police dogs as well, but there were none present at this weekly exercise.

There is no agreement by dog handlers as to which makes the best, most intelligent police dog, but there is no discrimination either. The concensus is that all these breeds have excellent qualities for police work. Training takes about two months in most cases and the average age of the dogs is 4 years. The dogs can work until approximately 7 years old before retirement. Phillip's dog, Brutus, is a Rottweiler and well named, I might add. He looks like a boxcar with fangs and is over one hundred pounds in weight. Phillips prefers a dog of lesser weight, about ninety pounds, for ease in handling. Rottweilers do, however, come much heavier and can weigh in at 160 pounds or so.

Veteran dog handler Joe Phillips works with Brutus, a Rottweiler. This may have been the original war dog, as the breed is known to be one of the world's oldest.

Brutus was especially interesting to me, for as Phillips explained, the Rottweiler is perhaps the oldest breed in existence. One source states the dogs go back to ancient Egypt and the days of the Pharaohs. Another reference states the animals were the original dogs of war, used by Roman legions during their conquest of the then known world.

Rottweilers are big-boned, heavy animals with a generally terrifying appearance. Phillips says they are insensitive to pain and require a special "pinch collar" for control.

German shepherd in foreground and the big Rottweiler don't excite easily. Note pinch collars and the police department insignia on the latter's leather harness. They ignored the flashes from the camera at work.

The chain link collar is equipped with hooks on the inside which tighten to let the dog know who's in charge. The hooks are blunted, of course, and cause no injury, but perform the same function as the bit on a horse.

As a man who keeps a dog merely as a pet, I'm not qualified to pass judgment on training techniques used in law enforcement.

It did appear to me, however, that during exercise periods, the handling of the dogs was not especially gentle. The animals received their share of pats and praise, but at the slightest mistake they were made to know the error of their ways. This consisted mostly of harsh verbal reprimand, but occasionally the handler would jerk heavily on the leash or even throw the leash at the dog.

Oddly, the dogs seemed not to resent this and to my eye, even appeared grateful for correction. Trained for combat, they nonetheless are still dogs and want to please their owners. It's unreasonable to expect them to get the point by subtle reminder, as would a human being. The rough handling is not punishment. It's a direct way of letting the dog know he's made a mistake. The animal understands this communication.

Phillips told me police dogs of today are much more capable than those of the 1960s. Formerly, the canines were largely attack dogs, because it was thought they weren't intelligent enough to learn the full bag of tricks. Over the last couple of decades, trainers have discovered dogs can be taught almost anything, with the possible exception of algebra.

In gunfire situations, for example, dogs once were taught merely to go for the gun arm of the shooter — presumably the felon. Many times this resulted in the police officer finding a hundred pounds of mean dog hanging off his own gun arm. Now dogs are taught to distinguish friend from foe and will always pick the right person in a shootout. Likewise, if the handler is killed, wounded or disabled, the dog will protect his downed owner. He also is taught to distinguish between an enemy and a friendly officer or medical technician coming to help.

In hostile situations or armed combat, the dogs are commanded verbally in German, not English. There are a couple of reasons for this. Some of the dogs are indeed German by birth and understand the language. Any other language not commonly spoken in the region may be used.

Using this technique, a dog-wise felon — unless he speaks German — can't turn the dog around on his owner. For a great many years, German-trained dogs led the world in excellence. Phillips, however, feels today's American training now surpasses, by far, anything done in the rest of the world.

Dogs from a former day had vulnerable gaps in their educations, but these gaps have been closed. It may be enough to say I was thoroughly impressed by their professional performance in this exercise. The dogs obey hand signals. Anything they do by voice command, they do also at a gesture from the handler. They lie down, they sit, they chase, fetch and guard. The dogs "key" and attack on sight of a seemingly routine gesture. Two of the handlers showed this technique, one acting as a suspected felon and the other as the police officer. While frisking a suspect, the officer is vulnerable as he bends over to pat the ankles. If the felon lowers his hands or if the officer pats in a certain way, the dog will attack. I get the idea that every situation has been anticipated and it would be quite useless to resist arrest by a K-9 officer and his dog.

In another maneuver, the handlers put the dogs through an arm exercise. One handler donned a heavy arm pad and the dogs were sent to chase and grab the arm. Most of the biting is actually just holding by the dog's teeth, but they can distinguish between holding and actual savaging to kill.

Having been around dogs most of my life, I got the impression these canines considered this good fun, although the attack looked real enough. They didn't pull any punches, but somehow the effect was less than blood-chilling. In a real life situation, I doubt that impression would prevail and the sight of one hundred pounds of toothy dog would have a chilling effect, indeed.

One little female German Shepherd weighed only seventy pounds, but she captured my attention and heart by attacking more savagely than the others, as if to make up for her lack of weight. She hit hard and she meant it. Her owner was justifiably proud of her.

All the exercises begin with the dog at the left side of the handler and the methods are quite rigid and formal. These can be dangerous animals and it's important that no mistake in communication occurs. In constant contact with people and crowds, the dog cannot be allowed to make its own decisions. Every command must come from the handler and the animal must react to it.

To illustrate the safety factor, Phillips arranged the seven dogs in a circle of aggression. As they sat at the left side of their owners, Phillips played the part of a typical crowd member and taunted the dogs with threatening gestures. The older dogs with more training stood silently during the teasing. The younger dogs, with more to learn, barked and strained at the leash and were verbally reprimanded. The result of this training is a dog which is completely safe around crowds and bites no one — unless commanded by his owner.

Police canines now are so well trained they are used in many roles, including SWAT team work. They chase and attack in unarmed felon situations, but are not sent after a criminal carrying a firearm for obvious reasons. Criminals abound, but no one wants to lose a good dog to gunfire. The use of dogs in bomb threats and drug detection is well documented. For example, there is one legendary K-9 that has several different collars. When a certain collar is put on this dog, he is a sniffer-out of drugs. If another is put on, he becomes a bomb-sniffer, literally switching personalities. It can truly be said he wears many hats.

In the "arm exercise," the Rottweiler seizes supposed felon's arm. These dogs are huge and heavy and boast better natural armament with their teeth than any human.

Watching these dogs at work leaves one with a pleasant, quite unexplainable feeling of satisfaction. The rigidity of command amounts to no more than unmistakable communication between man and animal and doesn't detract from the personality of the dog, nor does it make him appear robotic. In fact, despite their sometimes fearsome displays of prowess, the dogs never quite lose or conceal the appearance of valued pets.

There is a distinct sense that the dogs know they are loved and they return this affection by becoming pathetically eager to please. The dogs display the same sort of pride a skilled workman has in his trade and are ashamed if they don't measure up. The human-to-human interface is always one of caution and sometimes outright distrust. No such feeling burdens the relationship of good dogs and men.

How would it be to have an accomplished, talented friend who *never* fails to do his duty?

Only the dog men know.

CHAPTER SEVENTEEN

AVIATION LAW ENFORCEMENT

The Airport Police Have Special Needs For A Special Mission

In many situations, airport police are responsible for private aircraft that are tied down at installation.

Seeing that valuable cargo or baggage is not stolen in the loading process is another airport police chore.

AVIATION LAW enforcement is a relatively new facet of professional law enforcement in the United States. It has been in existence, as we know it, only since 1973. Following a series of aircraft hijackings and bombings, the Congress of the United States mandated, through federal regulation, the presence of armed uniformed police officers in the major airports around the nation.

The airports come in several different categories and are owned by various entities. In some cases, the airport may be an independent authority and have a police unit operating under that authority. In other cases, the airport may be owned by a county or multiple counties or by a city and provide police service with municipal officers. Depending on the location and ownership of the airport, you can find city, county, state or airport authority uniforms on the officers engaged in aviation law enforcement. No matter what the uniform, the job is basically the same for all. Newcomers with years of experience in other aspects of law enforcement have described aviation law enforcement as "unlike anything I've ever done before."

Why so different? Several things make it this way. As a veteran police officer, I had become used to patrol and traffic enforcement, investigation of every kind of crime from A to Z, state law, city ordinances and all of the other things that every police officer has to do. After almost twenty years of doing and teaching others about street tactics and

law enforcement, I was surprised to find another world within my profession.

Airports are the equivalent of small cities in themselves. Not only do all of the above apply, but also many other duties. Enforcement of federal laws and regulations usually is reserved for federal officers. Not so at the airport! Airport police officers also have to be skilled in the application of laws and regulations that govern the airport under the direction of the Federal Aviation Administration.

Working a multiple accident on the freeway is one thing — but working an aircraft crash with hundreds of passengers is quite another. It's a bad situation any time an officer has to face a hostage situation in a business or residence. We all are familiar with the demands for transportation to the airport and an airplane to make the getaway. When that same situation happens on an airplane loaded with passengers, the whole picture changes drastically. Specially trained SWAT teams and officers get used to working together. But try getting used to working with city, state and federal SWAT teams all at the same time!

We all get used to answering questions about, "Where can I find..." or "How do I get to..." At the airport, those are constant requests. Confused travelers, seeing a police uniform, ask for everything from airline boarding gates to restrooms (and not necessarily in that order).

The high profile of the airport police officer keeps him under the constant watchful eye of the public. There aren't too many places to pull off on a side street and write a report! Try being professional with a drunk in front of six thousand people in a crowded terminal and see how many comments you can draw about the way you did it.

Then there is the businessman who forgot to take his gun out of his briefcase before coming to the airport. The case goes through the X-ray machine, the alarm goes off and here come the difficulties. Handling people in this situation is sticky at best.

Many casual observers believe that the job of airport police is simply to keep traffic moving at the terminal. As explained in this chapter, duties are much tougher.

We all have been schooled in the professional way to conduct ourselves when dealing with the public. At the airport, the federal government mandates that the officers be schooled even more in public relations. The two words that send airport officials into a panic are "tactics" and "weapons." Combine these two with public relations requirements and you have what amounts to "do what is necessary quickly, quietly, politely and get it out of the public view as soon as possible without complaints!" Impossible? Not with the proper training!

Aviation law enforcement, like other aspects of the profession, is not for everybody. It takes the right person, the right attitude and the right training to make it work.

A good example of "making it work" is the Airport Police Section of the Department of Aviation at the International Airport in San Antonio, Texas.

In 1973, the City of San Antonio complied with the new federal mandate and created the Airport Police Section of the city's Department of Aviation. What had been formerly known to the general public as Airport Security became the Airport Police.

Members of this newly formed unit were sent to the basic police academy and received the training necessary to be certified as police officers by the State of Texas. Over the eighteen years since this fledgling beginning, the San Antonio Airport Police have grown in both size and stature.

The entire direction of the San Antonio Airport Police Unit changed in 1989. After much discussion and study on how to improve police service for the airport, the city hired veteran police officer Maurice R. Rose to be the new chief of police for the airport.

The name Maurice "Reece" Rose is well known among law enforcement agencies around the state of Texas and beyond. After twenty-three years of service with the San Antonio Police Department, Rose retired as a detective in the Narcotics Division. He followed that colorful career with another five years of service as the chief investigator with the Bexar County Sheriff's Department in San Antonio.

Armed with a solid twenty-eight years of police experience, Rose set out to reshape the airport police into a functionally independent professional police agency. Under his direction, this police unit has become one of the more progressive units in aviation law enforcement.

Since San Antonio operates an international airport, these officers work closely with all of the federal agencies on a daily basis. United States customs and immigration officers are housed at the airport. The FBI and FAA have special agents assigned to an airport detail. The U.S. Marshal's Service, ATF, Border Patrol and others regularly work at the airport and depend on the airport police for support.

In the summer of 1989, another new detail was added to the San Antonio Airport Police operation. A joint federal narcotics task force was formed under the direction of the Drug Enforcement Agency and comprised of DEA agents, Texas Department of Public Safety narcotics officers and airport police officers.

In order to furnish the airport police officers with the necessary skills to accomplish the required tasks, as well as the new requirements, Chief Rose instituted another

If a passenger — or terrorist — attempts to board an aircraft with a firearm, the airport police usually move in and hold the suspect for federal authorities. Constant surveillance is carried out in this effort.

first for the airport. In October 1989, he formulated the Airport Police Training Section complete with classroom and practical training. Starting with one certified instructor and coordinating the classes through the San Antonio College Police Academy, the training began on a regular basis.

Groups of airport police officers were assigned to the training section to attend training classes as their duty assignment. Starting with the basics, classes continue on more than thirty different police subjects, all tailored for the airport operation.

One of the first classes conducted — because of the federal mandate — was on public relations. Most of the officers thought the class would be about smiling and shaking hands, avoiding arrest situations and how not to do police work. To their surprise, it consisted of such things as reading people and body language, how to use mental pressure instead of physical force, getting the job done under the worst circumstances without harsh language and maintaining a professional bearing while in view of the public.

This class was the basis for what was to follow. Combining two classes — mechanics of arrest and arrest, search and seizure — the entire department, from supervisors to patrolmen, went back to school.

Tactical training can be fun, but it also can be dangerous. A series of practical exercises was developed from actual airport police cases involving both armed and unarmed hostile individuals. In each case, officers were given the same type of minimal information they normally would receive over the radio. Using proper tactics and procedures taught in the classroom, they had to handle the situation as if on duty. We have all seen this done with family disturbances, bar situations, et cetera, but extra pressure is added with the proverbial "hot call" in an airport environment.

To make matters worse, three things added pressure to the officers attending the training. First, Chief Rose and the training instructor played the parts of the "bad guys." Secondly, quite a bit of interest was shown on the part of airport officials who happened to show up to observe the exercises. Lastly, off to the side was a video camera recording all of the happenings — good or bad!

Realism came into the training in the form of weapons. Most airports have a way of attracting strange and concealable weapons of all description. Officers have to be trained to deal with the usual guns, knives and clubs, but then come the hand grenades, explosives, karate-type weapons and numerous odds and ends of harm-causing objects brought to the airport by people every day.

Any kind of weapon in the airport environment is of great concern to officials and the public alike. Under the

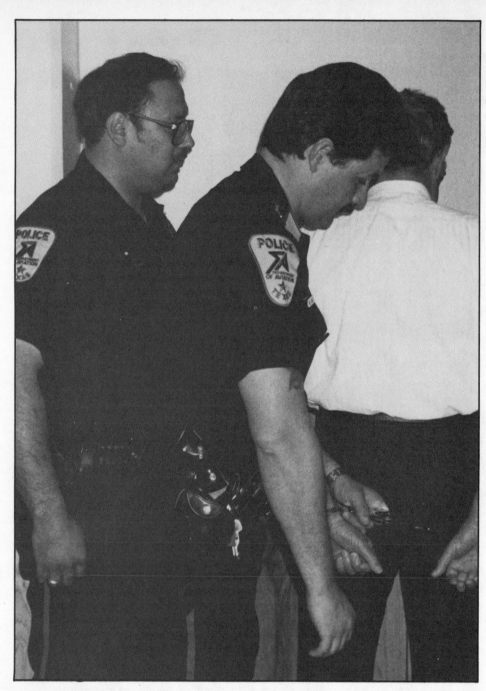

Airport police have authority to make arrests. Some airports have holding cells available to hold miscreants until they are transferred to large facility.

federal mandate, airport police officers must receive extensive training in the use of firearms. The department-issued weapon at the San Antonio Airport is the Smith & Wesson Model 66, .357 revolver. The issued ammunition is the .38 caliber 128-grain jacketed hollow-point. The airport opted to use the lighter-loaded .38 round because of the constant crowd situation encountered on most of the airport property. Training is concentrated on accuracy instead of power.

The San Antonio Police Department has a state-of-the-art training academy in south San Antonio and through the cooperation of that department, the airport police do all of their firearms training at that location.

The range is equipped with multiple bays that can accommodate up to ten shooters at a time. Targets are set up on a timer system that allows the range officer to "set and forget" the sequence for turning and firing time. This range

also is equipped with moving or running targets and, when necessary for special training, also can be set up into various configurations for working practical shooting problems.

Three airport police officers are trained and designated as the range officers. They conduct all department training and qualification on a semi-annual basis. Scores average in the mid to high nineties for most of the department, with a few exceptional members shooting perfect scores on a regular basis.

More so than in most police situations, aviation police officers must place more emphasis on knowing "when to" and "when not to" shoot, use physical force, know how to defuse potential conflict situations and use mental tactics rather than physical tactics.

In any airport, the officers never know who they will be

dealing with in any given situation. Every one from government officials, captains of industry, foreign dignitaries, and religious leaders to average every-day citizens use the airport facilities. Multiple language and customs situations are a daily routine problem. Extending the VIP courtesy to a traveler is a constant concern for the aviation law enforcement officer. This increases the paradox of the need for hesitation against the need for action.

Fortunately for the officers, the need for constant training and updates is recognized by the director of the airport and all of the officials that authorize funding, facilities, et cetera. Without their support, proper training would be a difficult task.

At San Antonio, all of the bases are covered — budget, equipment, facilities, manpower, support and time. Any training done at this location has been adapted to the aviation setting rather than general police work. The present training facilities will accommodate fifteen students at a time. Expansion is planned during the 1991/1992 cycle to increase the capacity to more than double that number. Every training class is certified by the Texas Commission on Law Enforcement Officers Standards and Education in Austin, sanctioned by and under the watchful eye of Brady Thompson, director of the San Antonio College Law Enforcement Academy and administered by the department's own training officer.

This kind of attention to detail has resulted in the Department of Aviation Airport Police in San Antonio carrying over eighty-two percent of its members with intermediate or advanced certification. Anyone familiar with Texas requirements would tell you that this is no small accomplishment. The department's manpower strength is, at present, in excess of fifty members, with plans to increase in the near future. Compared to other departments of that size, this has to be one of the best trained units in the business.

Within the area of responsibility of the aviation law enforcement officer is a world unlike any ever encountered by the average police officer. This is known as the air operations area. In simple terms, that area is anywhere on the airport that the aircraft operate.

After learning the names of all of the city streets, businesses and locations on the airport, the aviation law enforcement officer must learn about runways, taxiways and various odd-named items like jetways, fixed base operations, hold bars, lease lines and run-up areas, to name but a few. Most of them are referred to by letters instead of names, like AOA and FBO.

Operating an emergency vehicle in this kind of area can be a trick in itself. Most of us are used to having all traffic yield to emergency vehicles. Not so in the air operations area! Aircraft *always* have the right of way. One careless moment of inattention resulting in interference with the movement of an aircraft and what is known as an "incursion" happens. That nine letter word costs thousands of dollars in fines for the Department of Aviation by way of the Federal Government — and no excuses, please!

Then there is the "other" radio. Communications with the ground control operator in the tower is essential — except that the language and phonetic alphabet are totally different from the usual police jargon. (Things like "Roger" instead of "10-4"). Then there is the fact that the ground operator sits in the top of the tower and the air traffic controller sits in the basement of the tower!

One piece of advice given the first day out is, "If you hear what sounds like a lawn mower, it isn't! Look for the small plane!"

Instead of street signs, most everything is painted on the concrete or is on a funny looking lighted sign off in the grass somewhere. Red lines mean one thing, yellow lines stand for another, black for something else; then there are stripes, hash marks and, oh yes, that elusive "compass rose" we can't ever seem to find!

The only red and green light out there is up in the tower, operated by the controller in case the radio goes out. However, there are some interesting blue, red, white and even a few yellow lights stuck in the ground that can guide one to where one wants to go — maybe! At night, it can be hard to tell where you are if you don't pay attention all of the time. Reference points are few and far between at a casual glance.

There are federal requirements for both pedestrians and vehicles in the area, governing proper identification, markings, insurance requirements, where to walk and where not to, where to drive and where not to and more important do's and don'ts. Officers have to be well versed in all of these procedures. When is it a criminal trespass situation and when is it a federal security violation? Try detaining a federal agent for not having the proper identification sometime and see how much fun it can be. Worse yet, try not doing it because of the old "professional courtesy" and see how much trouble both of you can generate.

Most of us have had a problem trying to keep the various makes and models of cars and trucks straight. Now add to that the difference between a DC-10 and a 707. Then there are the aircraft with strange names that the officer has to locate on that vast expanse of concrete.

Most of this gets to be business-as-usual when all of a sudden someone like the President of the United States decides to drop in for a visit. Then things really get tight!

Anyone traveling during the recent hostilities in the Middle East is aware of how drastically security was tightened at all airports around the nation. When the shooting started over there, airports across our nation went into almost a total "lock down" situation. Pages of new rules were implemented and more restrictions enacted. There were different requirements for different size airports and for different types of air carriers. Again, more items for the officers to commit to memory and deal with on a daily basis.

Search and seizure laws became a daily concern as anything left unattended on airport property came under suspicion. Vehicles had to be towed away without notice and the confused public dealt with afterwards.

Procedures and tactics dealing with how to spot and how to handle potential or (heaven forbid) real terrorist activity had to be re-emphasised! In a place like San Antonio that contains five large military bases, the airport was considered the "soft target." Military personnel are constantly on the move through the airport, coming in and going out. Not only U.S. military, but military personnel from all over the world were coming in or leaving a conference or training assignment. Military personnel and civilians who have traveled in Europe are familiar with tight security at

The authority of the airport police ends on the ground. Once aloft, the captain or a sky marshal is the law.

the airports. The average U.S. citizen is not.

Job familiarization and knowledge, coupled with the intense public relations training and mental tactics, still play the most important roles in getting the job done. Though everybody voiced opinions on the restrictions, the professionalism of the officers kept the complaints to a minimum during the Desert Storm Crisis.

Under normal conditions, quite a few travelers seem to get confused around the airport. Officers have to keep on their toes in order not to react to some of the questions and complaints they get from the public. Questions like the one from the lady who approaches the officer in the baggage area of the terminal asking where she can pick up her luggage! Or the driver who pulls up to the officer directing traffic in front of the terminal and asks for directions to the airport!

Then there are the complaints about officers not knowing the flight schedules and flight numbers for the fifteen or twenty airlines operating out of the airport. Or the constant complaint that an officer would not let someone park in a No Parking zone. Self-control certainly becomes a must for the aviation law enforcement officer — and ten times more so when strict security measures are implemented.

Most police officers equate tactics with disarming a subject or with the proper way to control a hostile individual. Weapons training usually is equated with how to use a sidearm or shoulder weapon. For the aviation law enforcement officer, that is only the beginning. Learning proper tactics includes all of the proper physical movements and expands into the proper use of mental and psychological controls.

Weapons training starts with the usual shooting qualification and expands through a range of weapons and items that most officers only read about.

Crowd control is a specialized area that receives different levels of attention depending on the location and size of the law enforcement department. Aviation law enforcement officers have to be trained and skilled at handling large crowds on a moment's notice as part of their regular routine duties. Again, this is an area that requires more mental capability than physical tactics to get the job done.

Over the past thirty years, the police officer has developed a high degree of anonymity, with more and more officers using police cars instead of being "beat cops." At the airport, just the opposite is true. Although a lot of work is done out of a police unit around the airport, most of the officers are good ol' fashioned beat cops and do most of their work on foot. Their constant contact with and exposure to the public is a much closer parallel to our brethren of thirty years past than to the modern patrol officer. The majority of their duty assignments are accomplished with what they carry in their heads, instead of the sophisticated equipment used in so many other outfits.

However, with all of the training preparation to handle any situation that arises in the usual mass gathering, there are times when "somebody forgot to cover that one."

Every police officer I know has a wealth of stories they have collected over the time they are in the field.

Take, for example, the San Antonio airport police officer who received one of those "animal assistance" calls. After being asked to assist with a monkey that had gotten loose in the air cargo building, Officer Rodriguez thought to himself, "that's one they forgot to cover."

Like all police officers, he found when he got there that things weren't quite as described on the radio. As he approached the building, he noticed that everybody else was leaving in a hurry. Now what kind of trouble could a little monkey be? As he walked into the cargo area, all of a sudden he found himself facing a 4½-foot tall baboon! Everything was fine until, as he approached the animal, Officer Rodriguez put forth his best PR foot and smiled at the baboon. Nobody had told him that showing one's teeth to a

Like street cops, airport police must study and continue their training to remain sharp and to be able to meet any situation.

baboon is a challenge to fight — that's one you find out the hard way.

What does this have to do with police tactics? Armed with a borrowed tranquilizer gun and a pair of handcuffs, Officer Rodriguez managed to capture the animal. Recounting the event, he described it much as one would describe trying to arrest the rowdy drunk on a Saturday night. Quick thinking and adaptability to any situation become second nature at the airport.

Then there was the call about somebody tearing up the inside of an aircraft. The somebody turned out to be an angry Rhesus monkey who got loose from a shipping container in the cargo hold of an airliner. That's another of those "forgot to cover" items that requires a creative approach to handle.

The person who decided the word "routine" applies to police work evidently never worked at an airport. As stated earlier, aviation law enforcement is not for everybody. But, if you are looking to put to use all of the training you can get, this is definitely the place. The order of the day is: "Look sharp, be professional and polite — and get the job done — whatever it is!"

From The Pen Of A Pro...

I LEARNED a long time ago that if I want to know something about a specific subject, I should check with a professional in that particular field. With that reasoning, I asked Walt Myers to handle input for this particular chapter. The short rundown on his career that follows should explain my choice.

After three hitches in the United States Air Force, which included tours in Vietnam and Thailand and over 6000 hours of flight time in Air Rescue, the 1st Air Commando Wing and 20th Special Operations helicopter units, Walt Myers traded a military career for a police career in 1972.

Myers is also a combat veteran of the police service — injured in the line of duty — a skilled investigator and instructor. During off-duty hours, he does consulting work in investigation and drug abuse prevention, as well as writing for various professional publications.

Over the past almost twenty years, Myers has gone up through the ranks from reserve officer to chief of police. He has seen duty in three police departments, a sheriff's department, an organized crime unit and the latest, an aviation law enforcement unit.

Walt Myers holds a degree from Central Texas College, an advanced certification and an instructor's license from the Texas Commission of Law Enforcement Officers Standards and Education, a certification from the Texas Education Agency and has in excess of 2000 hours of training in advanced police courses. He is a staff instructor at the San Antonio College Law Enforcement Academy and has taught in several universities in the State of Texas.

Following the death of his wife in 1988, Myers resigned his position as chief of police in Boerne, Texas, and accepted the training position at the San Antonio International Airport with the intent of slowing down the pace of his career. Instead, he has put together a training section comprised of six instructors and six field training officers while also teaching more than thirty different classes in advanced law enforcement subjects.

He has received 178 awards, decorations and citations over the years, from national, state and local levels.

At age 48, Walt Myers has done anything but slow down. As he put it, "Only the Big Chief knows what the future holds for me!"

CHAPTER EIGHTEEN

GETTING THERE

Hooves, Hulls, Wheels, Wings And Tracks All Have Their Places in Police Transportation Today

Horses have long been a part of law enforcement whether used by the frontier posse to chase down the bad guys or, in modern times, to aid in crowd and riot control. It has been found a demonstrator will move away from a horse quickly!

Rugged bicycles built for use in the mountains are used by some departments to allow patrols more mobility in high-density areas. Such vacation spots as San Antonio, Texas, and Orange County, California, feature this type of patrol.

FROM WHAT was once the lawman on horse-back, the subject of law enforcement vehicles is now limited only by the imagination.

Every law enforcement officer, official and the people who control funding, all have their own personal preference as to make, model and manufacturer — or breed. Arguments about which is best have been around since time began and as each new item comes into use, will continue as long as there are people in the profession.

Although you will find some vehicles mentioned in the next few pages, they are only illustrations and not meant to be an endorsement for a particular brand or model. Choose for yourself — or as I have found, use what the boss tells you to use!

Walt Myers, in his lengthy military and law enforcement career, has had opportunity to use just about every mode of travel there is, so I asked him to offer an up-to-date rundown on what is available in the way of law enforcement vehicles. This is his report.

The faithful companion and normal means of transportation of yesterday's lawman, the horse, is still around throughout law enforcement agencies around the country and serves many needs that other forms of transportation will not. Crowd control, search and rescue and patrol duties are only a few of those needs. No matter what else shows up on the scene, the horse will continue to remain an integral part of law enforcement. Police departments, sheriff's departments, state and federal agencies from New York to California and between the Canadian and Mexican borders have horse units that are more than just "parade items." (I guess that would also qualify the horse trailer as a law enforcement vehicle, too!) Researching material for this subject took me from the lawman who carried all of his equipment in pockets and saddle bags to some real Buck Rogers-type of vehicles.

Asked to define a police vehicle, most officers come up with the "black and white" — the patrol car — as the answer. That's true, but it doesn't even scratch the surface of the total answer.

Take, for example, the downtown patrol unit that covers the famous River Walk of San Antonio, Texas. The area is confined and usually crowded. Cars can't get to it and

This bike carries a single instrument, which gives the speed of the bike, the distance traveled and the correct time!

horses don't really care for the stairs that lead up and down to the river. Foot patrolmen can only cover so much ground and only travel so fast. The answer? The San Antonio Police Department has trained and instituted a special squad of officers outfitted with mountain bikes! The first sighting of these officers is strange to say the least, but can you imagine the reaction of the first bad guy that was chased down by a cop in shorts, sneakers, a bike helmet and Sam Browne belt riding a bike? It only takes a few minutes of watching these officers get around in that area to realize that this special bicycle is the ideal vehicle for that kind of duty.

The "vehicle" is a twenty-one-speed mountain bike made by Miyata. According to Lieutenant Rudy Vernon, who is in charge of the Bike Patrol, these bikes are stripped down to the essentials with only a saddle bag to carry ticket books, extra handcuffs, et cetera.

These officers are a great deterrent to the fleet-footed shoplifters who prowl that area. The officers are able to maintain contact with the public that a foot patrol officer normally has, but with the mobility of the patrol car. The uniqueness of these vehicles has resulted in pictures taken of the officers and their "units" being sent all over the world, as well as a television special aired on CNN.

This, of course, is not the only community which has learned the advantages of pedal-powered transportation in certain environs. In California, for example, the Orange County Sheriff's Department has assigned officers to bicycle duty in the beach areas where there is heavy traffic of both a vehicular and pedestrian nature.

A number of California beach communities also use three-wheeled AVTs for patrolling the actual beaches,

while others utilize four-wheel-drive, open-top vehicles that can negotiate loose sand with a degree of ease.

Two-wheeled vehicles for law enforcement duty are by no means a new idea. The Texas Department of Public Safety has a 1930s vintage motorcycle on display at their training academy in Austin, so I'm sure they have been around at least a half century.

Police motorcycles come in many different sizes, shapes and configurations. From the full-dress police cycle complete with radio, lights and siren to the stripped down dirt bike for search and rescue work, motorcycles have been around almost as long as the horse.

Modern law enforcement motors come in the two-, three- and four-wheel variety. Ask any civilian what a police motorcycle looks like and it's a safe bet that they will describe those of CHIPS, the California Highway Patrol made famous via television. However, there is also the three-wheel model for working traffic and parking situations in some of the downtown metropolitan areas, the three- and four-wheel models used for such things as beach patrol by several of the coastal-based law enforcement units and the dirt bikes used in the mountains and rough country.

Next comes the patrol car. All of the Big Three auto manufacturers make a police package for various models of their cars. The basic vehicle starts out looking like any other showroom model and is beefed up with system changes. When ordering a new car, it can be ordered with the entire police package or parts of the package to custom-build the car to individual department's needs and budget constraints.

From stress reinforcements in the roof to special high-

Though certainly not rugged as a motorcycle helmet, the protective headgear worn by bike-mounted patrolmen is aimed at their protection. Note that the helmet is strapped on and is not likely to fall off if officer should take a spill.

speed tires, the options convert the showroom model into a high-speed pursuit vehicle. Engines are available in carbureted and fuel injection styles in both six- and eight-cylinder. The electrical systems are upgraded with heavy-duty alternators and a special wiring harness designed to handle all of the extra lights, radios, et cetera. Larger capacity cooling systems designed to take the extra stress of constant driving and extra equipment are part of the package, as well as special transmission cooling systems. And for those of you who have the ol' heavy foot, there is a first gear lock-out to keep you from tearing the wheels off the car if chasing speeders!

The suspension system can be upgraded all the way to what is normally found on race cars, utilizing swaybars, counterbalance weights, et cetera. Tires are available from standard street-type to special high-speed police tires. The only limitation on ordering a patrol vehicle is the amount of money you want to spend on the unit.

There are several companies that will even order your vehicle for you, equipped with overhead lights, radio, siren, cages, shotgun racks and all of the other needs law enforcement officers add to the basic unit. Some of these guys will even dress the unit out in your colors, stripes and decals if you want to pay for it.

The past decade has also seen the specially built sports car model of police pursuit vehicles. For example, the Texas Department of Public Safety purchased the Ford Mustang with five-speed manual transmission. "Where did he come from?" became a much used phrase by motorists on Texas highways! The need arose from the manufacture and sale of so many "hot" models of cars that the normal patrol car had trouble catching or staying with on the open roads.

I have had to justify the purchase of many a pursuit vehicle in my time to elected officials who had no concept of police tactics or procedures. These specially equipped vehicles — either sedan or sports models — are not intended to put law enforcement into the racing business. However, there are times that speed is necessary and, in that case, stability is a must.

Some law enforcement agencies have vans equipped for what might amount to complete investigative facilities. Such units are custom-built in most cases and can put a crimp in the budget, but they also pay off with the man-hours saved.

Just the fact that the exotic vehicle is present is sufficient to stop the majority of high-speed chases contemplated by drivers. A youngster in a hot new toy that daddy gave him for graduation can be tempted to pit his vehicle against a police car that looks and sounds like a well used family car that should have been traded in years ago. On the other hand, seeing a unit that both looks and sounds like it can get the job done has a sobering effect on that kind of judgment.

As a young officer, my mentor told me, "There is always a reason when they run!" It could be something as simple as the one listed above, or — it could be a felon determined not to get caught in the infamous routine traffic stop. Incidentally, in all these years, I have yet to find that "routine stop." Who came up with that term anyway?

Not only having the high-speed capability, but also the fact that a vehicle capable of doing 140 miles per hour is only using fifty percent of its power at seventy miles per hour while the one rated at eighty is already using ninety percent before the action really gets started. A stripped-down model will not last nearly as long as the police package. Taxi cabs that are used day after day, hour after hour, are equipped differently than your family car, so why not the police car? Want to save budget dollars? Order the car to do the job right and keep it in the fleet for three years instead of saving on the initial cost and trading it next year!

If you still are having trouble convincing your city coun-cilman to spend the money, try taking him for a ride in a stripped-down version while trying to catch a violator on a stretch of highway. Just be careful! Some of these guys scare easily!

The patrol cars described won't work for all applications of patrol work. Sometimes it is necessary to change from a sedan to something like a Blazer or Bronco with two- or four-wheel drive. There are numerous law enforcement units that need the four-wheel drive capability because of terrain. At many airports, for example, there are no sedans. Because of the vast amount of area to cover in all types of weather, in areas that are far from city street condition, the Airport Police in San Antonio use the Chevy S-10 Blazer with both two- and four-wheel drive. The high-speed chase is infrequent, but foul weather and rough terrain operation are constant concerns. Trying to respond to an aircraft crash across acres of grass, ditches, et cetera would be difficult indeed in a normal patrol car.

Then there are the rest of the law enforcement utility vehicles that range from vans to large trucks. Crime Scene units, specially equipped personnel and equipment vans for SWAT use, bomb squad vehicles and trailers, even RVs or busses converted for mobile command post duty; the possibilities are endless, limited only by funds and individual need. And these aren't even considered to be exotics!

The term exotic covers the all-terrain, armour-plated

Law enforcement units also can be charged with patrolling the waterways. Such facilities make the job a pleasure. Of course, lawmen can become involved in everything from drunk boating citations to major smuggling operations.

assault and personnel carriers. These are not converted military vehicles either, but special vehicles manufactured for law enforcement. There are several made in the United States and quite a few produced in Europe. Going through the list of equipment, you can find both gas and diesel engines, several different thicknesses of armor plating, water

cannons, surveillance equipment, machine guns, EOD and assault support equipment, wheeled and track designs.

A few years ago, I was sent a catalog on these types of vehicles. I even found a listing for an amphibious version. Applications for these units were listed for riot control, SWAT use, anti-terrorist, aircraft hijack configuartion —

Just as patrolling streets has a major effect in the law enforcement scheme, a patrol of waters can hold down aquatic crime levels.

For bigger game and deeper water, the U.S. Coast Guard has a fleet that can handle drug smuggling or piracy!

complete with ladders.

Like the military, law enforcement also has not only the ground troops, but airmen and sailors, too.

Starting with the smallest light helicopters up through the large troop transport models, rotary wing aircraft are as much a part of the law enforcement vehicle inventory as the patrol car. We find traffic patrol units and rescue units, as well as assault units available in many parts of the country. Just like the vehicle manufacturers, helicopter makers like Bell, Hughes and Sikorsky — to name a few — have models and equipment designed for virtually every conceivable law enforcement need. There are single-rotor and dual-rotor models, ranging from two-seaters to large capacity models. Some have fixed landing gear, others retractable landing gear; some tubular skids and even some with "bear paw" skids for landing in deep snow. Name it, manufacturers have it available.

Fixed-wing aircraft also have their place. Though maybe not quite as versatile as the helicopter, law enforcement units engaged in drug enforcement, state police and some other agencies all have a need for airplanes.

From simple passenger design to the exotic chase planes, there is some real mind boggling equipment available. One is a heat-sensing surveillance unit that can "see" how much fuel is left in the tanks of another airplane. Others have cameras designed to take identifiable photos from thousands of feet in the air at high speed.

Boats, too, have their place in law enforcement. Starting with the flat-bottom Jon boat that the game wardens use, right up through the big coastal gun boats used by the Coast Guard — like land and air vehicles — the list of styles, sizes and available equipment is extremely lengthy. Single hull or catamaran, flat or V hull, outboard, inboard, gas or diesel engine, the list goes on and on!

The only configuration that I cannot locate civilian information on is the submarine. That doesn't mean that some law enforcement unit doesn't have one, only that the information isn't as readily available.

As you can see, the subject of law enforcement vehicles is as diverse as the types of units and individual officers within the profession. The only proper definition of the law enforcement vehicle is "*any* vehicle used to support a specific law enforcement function!" The information in these pages is sparse indeed, but to do justice to each of the types of units and their associated equipment would take volumes on each. Even then, before the print was dry, something new would hit the market and make the publication obsolete. Even as these words hit this page, the future is here!

Computer-controlled robotics are now in the field and

There is a ready supply of helicopter pilots in many of today's police agencies, since many military veterans are choosing law enforcement careers. Some of the helicopters are obtained by police departments as war surplus.

being used in many places. They, too, fit the definition of the law enforcement vehicle. Applications of robotics are being used in surveillance and EOD work as you read this. Today, *Robo Cop* is a futuristic movie. By tonight, it could be a reality. As I've said before, the only limitation on what is available is money and imagination. We used to laugh at James Bond and some of his exotic vehicles that we saw in the movies. The hovercraft is a reality and now operates in places that water and soft terrain are a problem.

People laughed at Leonardo DeVinci centuries ago when he designed a helicopter. Back in the 1930s, the Doc Savage stories described vehicles and equipment that didn't even exist. Today, they are as common to law enforcement as the sidearm. Isn't it amazing what the human mind can come up with when the need arises? I don't know who coined the phrase, "necessity is the mother of invention!" But, as the criminal element we deal with becomes more sophisticated, we are going to be real busy!

Picture, if you will, a law enforcement officer in the year 2091, complaining to his supervisor, "Aw come on, Sarge! Not Mars patrol again! I've had it three times this year and you know how much I hate to drive those shuttlecraft!"

Police helicopters usually are unarmed and used for observation or search missions. They can go where the wheeled vehicles cannot, bringing another dimension.

Law Enforcement Can Be A Real Beach!

A radio that is tied into the law enforcement net and the local lifeguard service is a must for beach patrol.

Like any other law enforcement job, there are notes to be taken and reports to be made when on the beach shift.

A FEW DECADES back, there seemed to be enough open beachfront property in Southern California to satisfy the recreational needs of local residents forever.

Then came what has been described as the big, beaurocratic land grab. A century ago, pioneers were staking their claims on homestead lands. In more recent times, cities, counties — and even the State of California — have been working overtime to gain and control these oceanfront recreational properties. Orange County has been in the hub of all of this development — and has experienced the problems that go with such politically inspired expansion. The hard-line natives who have used the beaches and surf as their own for generations have come to resent the influx of visitors, the expansion for mass — and maximum — recreational use and the formal rules that go with this sort of thing.

In a twenty-mile stretch of Orange County shoreline, the past two decades have seen advances in use. Little Corona Beach used to be peopled year-round primarily by residents of Corona del Mar. Today, it has a parking lot and meters that cover much of the adjoining sand. The Irvine Coast, where locals once rode their horses into the surf, now is a

state park; no horses allowed, just a daily use charge at the gate.

Dana Point used to be a cove where residents dived for abalone. Today, the harbor has several thousand boats of all sizes, types and nomenclatures tied up side by side — and the resultant pollution has taken care of the shellfish crop.

Then there is Salt Creek.

This once was a beach that few knew about, other than the local residents. Today, it is a public recreation area with a huge, multi-million dollar hotel built on the privately owned bluffs overlooking the surf. There is the usual array of parking meters at the top of the cliff, then the long, paved accessway down to the sand and surf. The way down to the beach used to be a cow path. If one is a paying guest at the hotel, the climb is not as tough nor as long. In fact, there is a tram that hauls patrons up and down the steep hill. The natives walk.

This situation has created some difficulties. What once was simply another part of the county coastline now is a stretch of beach that has become highly populated during the summer months. The beach has been made a part of the recently incorporated City of Dana Point. This particular

An access road leads down to the Beach in Dana Point, California, but regular police cars cannot handle the sand.

city "rents" law enforcement personnel from the Orange County Sheriff's Department, and the assigned deputies are responsible for maintaining law and order along the beach.

In this instance, one man has the primary responsibility for maintaining that order along a two-mile stretch that cannot be reached by the standard police patrol unit.

Deputy Sheriff Russ Chilton is a native of Orange County and has been a deputy sheriff for six years. For the past three years, he has been assigned to duty in Dana Point — but now his patrols are being made on a Suzuki Model 185 all-terrain vehicle.

The all-terrain vehicle — or ATV, as it is termed in popular parlance — has been adapted from its role as a recreational vehicle and put to use in patrolling the sands. Even before this pilot program was initiated, the Orange County Sheriff's Department maintained eight of the ATVs at a substation near the Santa Ana Mountains. The little vehicles had been found useful in mountain rescue work, with the capability of getting into areas that a full-size, four-wheel-drive vehicle could not negotiate.

This piece of mobile equipment belongs to the sheriff's department, which is responsible for maintenance and repair, but it is assigned to Dana Point Police Services. This is the sheriff's contingent that handles law enforcement in the city on a contract basis.

"It is hard to say just who had the idea to do this," admits Lieutenant Dan Martini, the chief of police services for the city. "We were brainstorming on better ways of doing our job, when someone came up with the idea of using ATVs for our beach patrol."

The purpose of the experiment, of course, is to make patrolling the beaches an easier, more simple matter and, at the same time, build good will for the community. The patrol is conducted seven days a week in the period between Easter and Labor Day; that is when the recreational beaches carry their peak loads.

Salt Creek has had its problems, minor in most instances, but with one major incident. Two teenage surfers, carrying on what appeared to be a long-term vendetta, met on the beach in 1990 and one was slain with a handgun.

Lieutenant Martini is the first to admit it is highly difficult for sheriff's deputies in standard law enforcement vehicles to respond to calls on the hard-to-reach beach.

The Suzuki Model 185 ATV can travel at 15 miles per hour in the sand. A quality binocular is a must on this job.

From the metered parking lot at the top of the bluff, the sheriff's vehicle can drive down the access road to the sand, but once there, the car cannot be taken on the beach. The sand is too soft and too loose to support the vehicle or to provide traction. There are bicycle patrols in the area, but they are no good on sand, either. On occasion — before the ATV patrols — horses were used along the beach, but with ever-decreasing stabling facilities in the immediate area, this has presented logistical problems.

"The big difference between a horse and the ATV is that the machine doesn't have to eat when it's not being used," Deputy Russ Chilton is quick to point out. The horses used were the personal mounts of the deputies involved; this use presented liability problems that are not likely with the ATVs.

Whatever the approach, it became obvious to the police services unit that a visible presence was needed on the beach on a consistent basis during the summer and holiday periods when the beaches overflow.

The pilot program was introduced in June, 1991, the week that school ended for the summer in Southern California. The first few days were termed "educational" by

Deputy Russ Chilton maintains close liason with beach's lifeguards, since they often see trouble brewing first.

This surfer went into the rocks. When such accidents occur, the deputy sheriff works with beach lifeguards in first aid measures.

Sergeant Gus De La Torre, the traffic supervisor assigned to overseeing the ATV operation.

"We wanted to get the message across that we are not out to give people a bad time — just to make the beaches as safe as possible," the sergeant emphasizes. "Initially, we gave out a lot of warnings and talked to a lot of folks to let them know we would be there all summer."

Problems along the strip of beach had culminated in the September, 1990, shooting death, sparking research into a better means of patrolling the area.

"We had identified a small group that had taken control of the beach and was causing problems," Lieutenant Martini recalls. "We worked with the Enviornmental Management Agency and the lifeguards and decided we needed to be more aggressive in the beach patrol department.

"The beach draws a mixture of people, including families, surfers, bodyboarders and tourists," the lieutenant adds. "The problems are primarily juvenile-based and range from vandalism and graffiti to simple assaults between surfers and swimmers."

When the ATV patrol was approved as a pilot program, Deputy Russ Chilton was excited and volunteered. The fact that he had some experience with the ATV contributed to his being chosen as the primary beach patrolman. During summer periods, Chilton is on the beach five days a week, another deputy performing the duties on his days off.

When the deputy first took the ATV out on the sand for

It's a sandy job, but someone has to do it! A visible presence on the beach does much to reduce the problems.

Listening to complaints by tourists and handling any problems is part of the daily assignment on beach.

its first run, he found he was getting a lot of strange looks. It was not long, though, before Chilton and his vehicle became accepted as part of the beach scenery. The ATV can travel at about fifteen miles per hour in the sand, which makes it relatively simple to reach any problem area in minimum time.

Some beach communities outfit their officers in shorts during summer, but Deputy Chilton wears the standard forest green uniform of the Orange County Sheriff's Department — except for shoes. On his feet are black Reeboks instead of the standard prescribed, low-cut, leather shoes.

In addition to his department-approved Smith & Wesson Model 686 revolver, the beach patrolman also carries a hand-held radio that is tuned to the local law enforcement network. He also can pick up the radio channel for the lifeguard stations along the beach. Since the lifeguards, perched on their high towers, often can see a situation developing early, this communications link is important when it comes to defusing situations before they can get out of hand. A good set of binoculars is also a must.

As Deputy Sheriff Russ Chilton sees it, the beach patrol has affected his life in only two ways. Because of the blowing sand and salt spray, he has to clean his duty sidearm every evening to remove the accumulated grit.

The other problem deals with the the fact that the deputy is red-headed and fair-skinned.

"That means I have to buy sunblock by the gallon," he laments. "That's not an item the sheriff's department supplies!"

"Mission At Sundown" Sounds Like The Title Of A Western Film, But It Describes The Border Patrol's Horse-Mounted Unit

AS A UNIFORMED branch of the Immigration and Naturalization Service, the mission of the United States Border Patrol is to control the illegal entry of aliens across the nation's border. That's the mission which is much easier to identify than to fulfill.

The horse was involved in the beginnings of the U.S. Border Patrol. In the early 1900s, a force of sixty men was established along the U.S.-Mexican border. Called, simply, mounted guards at the time, this was a loosely organized and widely scattered force charged with capturing smugglers, cattle and horse rustlers and illegal aliens.

In 1924, a larger force was authorized by act of Con-

gress, with the number of officers increased to 450. These ranks were filled quickly by former border guards, deputy sheriffs, former soldiers and cowboys. Under the terms of the Congressionally authorized expansion, each of these individuals was issued a badge, a revolver and a Winchester rifle.

As with the original border guards, each of these officers still was required to furnish his own horse, saddle and tack. It wasn't until several years later that a uniform was authorized and the U.S. Border Patrol became a viable arm of the Department of Justice's Immigration and Naturalization Services.

During fiscal year 1990, 1,046,420 illegal aliens were

The border at Tijuana, Mexico, is the starting point for thousands of illegal entrants. The high fence is built of aircraft runaway matting used by the military, but it is penetrated each night by illegals entering the U.S.

apprehended along the U.S.-Mexican border. Forty-five percent of these — some 473,323 — were apprehended by Border Patrol agents in the San Diego Sector. This geographic block of Southern California real estate is only one of nine sectors located along the 2000-mile-long border between the United States and Mexico; it is one of the twenty-one Border Patrol Sectors nationwide. Historically, the San Diego Sector has been the most active area of Border Patrol operations.

"The severe depression of the economies in many developing countries, over-population and under-employment, combined with the lure of jobs and access to benefits in the United States, have precipitated a massive movement of persons to our back door," explains Gustavo De La Vina, chief patrol agent for the San Diego Sector.

Too, the mission of the Border Patrol has been expanded more by circumstance than by plan. "Smuggling of contraband across land boundaries continues to increase at an alarming rate," Chief De La Vina explains further. "During fiscal year 1990, San Diego Sector agents seized narcotics with an estimated street value in excess of $93,000,000." That's ninety-three million dollars!

The San Diego Border Sector encompasses more than 7000 square miles. It includes all of San Diego County and substantial portions of Orange and Riverside counties and shares sixty-six miles of international boundary with the Mexican state of Baja California. Flush against that boundary, flanked on its west side by the Pacific Ocean, is the city of Tijuana, with a population of 2,000.000. A smaller city, Tecate, with 50,000 residents, also borders the sector's area of responsibility.

Seven stations are located strategically throughout the sector to afford maximum enforcement efforts. Seventy percent of the sector's 991 authorized enforcement agents

U.S. BORDER PATROL

are deployed at four "line" stations and are engaged in immediate border responsibilities. In addition to autos, vans, buses and other support vehicles, the organization has four helicopters that are used to provide coordination and illumination for ground activities.

But headquartered at the Imperial Beach line station is perhaps the most unique unit of the sector — the horse patrol!

This enforcement entity is small. The unit has a current complement of eleven horses, with nine agents and two supervisors assigned to horseback duty.

Virtually from the time of its reestablishment in 1980, the San Diego Sector horse patrol has had woman riders assigned. At this writing, the woman agent is Agent Wendy Reach, a native of Calexico, California, a city located directly across the border from Mexicali, Mexico.

Brought up in the border environment, she speaks Spanish as well as any native. A blonde, blue-eyed law enforcer, Agent Reach has been with the border patrol for three years, but her involvement with horses dates back more than two decades. Her father, a veteran of seventeen years' service with the Border Patrol, operates a ranch along the

border, where the agent spent her teen years training.

When word went out that a volunteer was needed for the horseback unit, there were more than two dozen applicants for a job that starts at 5 p.m. and extends until 1 a.m., usually followed by a couple of hours of overtime duty in caring for the horses and filing reports.

History shows that the Border Patrol had used horses for many years before those patrols were replaced by automotive vehicles. It was not until 1980 that the horseback contingent was reestablished in the San Diego Sector for the purpose of patrolling areas that were virtually impossible to cover adequately by even four-wheel-drive vehicles.

Along the border at Tijuana, a ten-foot fence has been erected. It is composed of metal sections normally used in putting down military expeditionary landing fields for aircraft. And late every afternoon, hordes of illegals, seeking to escape their lives of poverty and oppression are lined up along the fence. Already on U.S. soil, they are simply waiting for the protective cloak of darkness.

In the area below the fence is an old stream bed that is laced with canyons, gullies and a creek that actually is sewage runoff from the Mexican city. The pollution of the creek can be smelled for thousands of yards. Trees and brush choke the stream bed and the adjoining sandy flood plain, but a network of well used trails display the routes favored by the illegals in the ever-continuing effort to get north to San Diego and Los Angeles, where they may be able to be absorbed by the population.

And while the illegals — not all of them Mexicans — wait for darkness, the horse patrol has saddled up and the animals have been trailered to the area where the agents suspect there will be the greatest activity.

On what is considered a "normal" night patrol, the mounted unit may capture up to two hundred line-crossers. When such captures have been made, the illegals are herded to an accessible roadway and a transport unit is called by radio to pick them up. They are transferred to buses and taken to the sector headquarters in San Ysidro for processing and return to Mexico, if they are citizens of that country.

If the illegal is found to be "OTM" — other than Mexican — this individual's consul is notified and he or she will

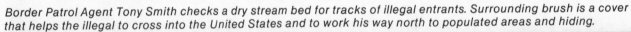

Border Patrol Agent Tony Smith checks a dry stream bed for tracks of illegal entrants. Surrounding brush is a cover that helps the illegal to cross into the United States and to work his way north to populated areas and hiding.

APPREHENSIONS
SAN DIEGO SECTOR

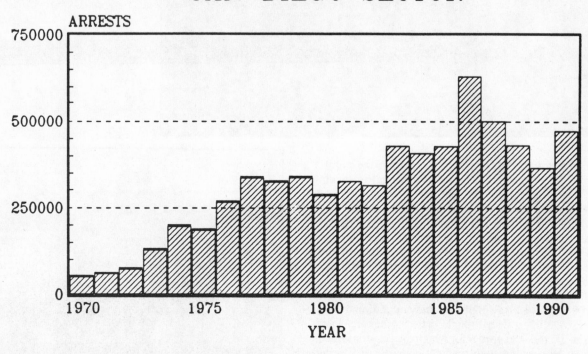

	FY 1985	FY 1986	FY 1987	FY 1988	FY 1989	FY 1990
OCT	24,125	37,179	50,361	26,884	26,685	35,097
NOV	20,557	33,028	32,412	25,655	21,475	27,396
DEC	22,446	29,056	23,931	24,004	13,973	26,447
JAN	37,406	53,868	47,523	53,711	27,662	41,717
FEB	33,348	53,320	42,248	54,527	22,670	40,335
MAR	45,613	64,475	43,307	52,328	29,146	44,863
APR	42,803	71,908	34,961	41,671	37,268	41,917
MAY	41,049	**73,360**	29,080	30,364	38,408	41,718
JUN	36,854	52,212	44,039	28,346	32,774	34,051
JUL	42,031	59,182	63,063	32,111	41,376	42,610
AUG	40,993	56,485	54,955	33,453	37,024	51,923
SEP	40,547	45,313	34,447	28,538	38,261	45,249
	427,772	629,656	500,327	431,592	366,757	473,323

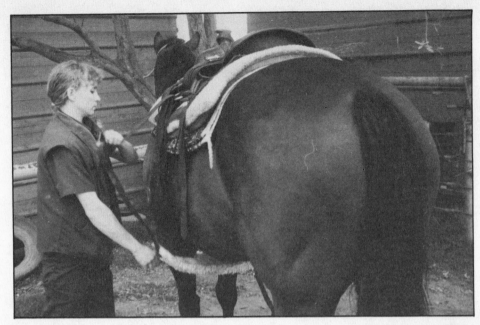

Agent Wendy Reach has a lengthy relationship with horses and her father was an agent for Border Patrol.

be turned over to that government for return to the country of origin. In instances wherein an individual is seeking asylum from his own government, investigations are handled by other branches of the U.S. government.

At the San Ysidro headquarters, each of the illegals is processed, interviewed and fingerprinted. If it is determined that one of the captives has criminal charges against him, he is turned over to the appropriate law enforcement agency.

If one doubts the mammoth proportions of the problem, look at the record. In a single three-day operation in July, 1991, extra officers were brought in from other areas and, along the 5½ miles of border for which the Imperial Beach line unit is responsible, more than 4500 illegals were apprehended. The horseback patrollers accounted for their share during this campaign.

Supervisory Border Patrol Agents Greg Terrones and Ken Foley share duties in heading up the mounted unit. Both feel the outfit requires a special type of person — and a special type of horse.

"When we need a replacement and start to interview volunteers, we usually are looking for someone who has had a good deal of experience with horses," Terrones says, "but that isn't an established requirement. We have our own training progam that covers about forty hours. We can watch a man ride and handle a horse for a few hours and pretty much know whether he is going to reach an acceptable level of proficiency at the end of those forty hours."

In 1980, when the mounted patrols were reestablished, there was little in the way of funding. The original horses were donated by local citizens. Today, one of those horses — a Morgan mare — still is on duty, but getting close to retirement. Of the eleven horses used by the contingent, seven are owned by the Border Patrol and four are leased from reliable livestock contractors.

Until now, the animals have been maintained at a commercial stable, but corrals, shelters and tackrooms are being built at the Imperial Beach station. When completed, the horses and equipment will be moved there.

"We tend to favor quarter horse breeding," Terrones

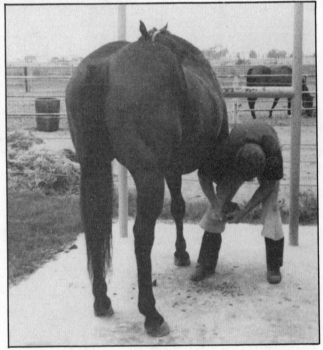

Agent Warren Templeton was an Arizona cowboy before he joined the Border Patrol. He acts as the unit farrier.

says, "because of their conformation and capabilities. The quarter horse gets along well out there in the bush.

"Our big problem is that we do not have the time, the personnel or the facilities for buying young horses, then training them our way. What we try to do is find a horse that is 5 to 9 years old and has been used to handling cattle. Preferably a gelding, the horse has to have a good rein on him and has to enjoy what he is doing." The thought occurs, of course, that cutting an illegal out of the bush may not be that much different from trying to isolate a crafty, old mossy-horned steer.

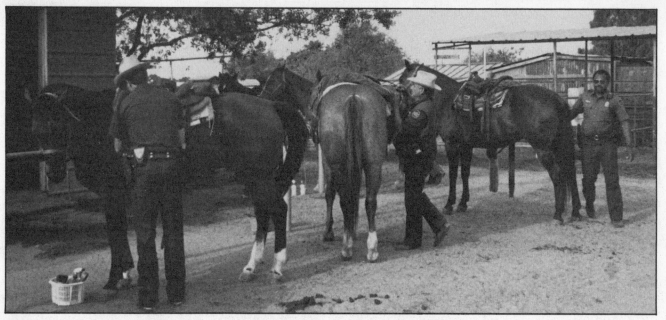

Each of the agents is assigned a horse when he begins the unit's forty hours of equine training. He or she will then continue to ride the same horse on duty throughout the length of the assignment; knowing the animal helps.

Average age of the horses now being used by the patrol is about 10. Terrones foresees retirement for one or two of the oldest in the near future and already is pondering the problem of finding proper replacement mounts.

Each Border Patrol agent is assigned an individual mount, and horse and rider work as a team from then on. "That makes the agent responsible for the horse and its welfare," Greg Terrones explains, "but it also establishes a familiarity between horse and rider that can become important when you are chasing someone through the bush at a gallop in the dark. We like to think our agent is going to know what his horse is likely to do in a specific situation — and that the horse knows what it can expect from its rider."

The saddles ridden by the patrol agents in the field are almost a decade old. They are heavy-duty Western-type balanced-ride or cutting horse saddles that have undergone a lot of hard use and are scheduled for replacement. These saddles are short on embellishment and decoration, except for the Border Patrol insignia that is carved into the fender on each side.

Replacement saddles, which have been ordered, will be built on saddle trees that are of wood and bound with rawhide for added strength. The saddles in current use all have trees of fiberglass and it has been found that these trees tend to spread with thousands of hours of hard use, combined with temperature changes.

Parade saddles have the same general specifications as those used in daily work along the border, but are in better shape because they have not been exposed to the rigors of the field. Bridle fittings are of brass that is polished to a high sheen for public viewing.

The appearance of the mounted Border Patrol unit in parades and at celebrations is done in the name of community relations; to impress upon the citizens that the mission of these agents is to serve. Such appearances, of course, are limited by requirements of the daily mission of the horses and their riders.

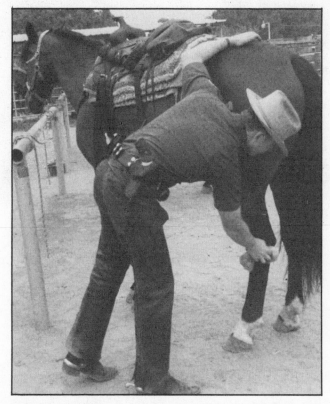

Agent Tony Smith checks out a small cut on the leg of his mount before beginning a night patrol assignment in bush. For any serious problems, a veterinarian may be called.

But there are instances in which the horse patrol's relationship with the public becomes more personal. For example, Agent Ruben Sais is known among Southern California law enforcement personnel as an outstanding tracker. On a number of occasions, Sais has been called upon to track

OTHER THAN MEXICAN ALIENS

COUNTRY	FY 89	FY 90	COUNTRY	FY 89	FY 90
Argentina	22	38	Italy	2	4
Australia	2	4	Ivory Coast	0	1
Bangladesh	2	0	Jamaica	37	15
Belgium	0	1	Japan	0	1
Belize	55	24	Jordan	3	2
Bolivia	37	14	Kenya	1	0
Brazil	245	49	Laos	0	2
Bulgaria	0	8	Lebanon	5	1
Canada	7	6	Morocco	1	0
Chile	4	7	Netherlands	1	0
China (PRC)	100	52	New Zealand	3	5
Colombia	138	56	Nicaragua	425	195
Costa Rica	54	9	Nigeria	4	8
Cuba	5	19	Pakistan	16	4
Dominican Republic	431	105	Panama	6	4
Ecuador	487	115	Paraguay	4	0
Egypt	12	9	Peru	212	83
England	1	8	Philippines	11	7
El Salvador	4304	3647	Poland	1	7
Ethiopia	0	1	Portugal	12	8
Finland	1	0	Romania	1	7
France	2	5	Senegal	0	1
Germany (F.R.)	0	4	South Africa	0	2
Ghana	0	1	South Korea	84	53
Greece	0	3	Spain	5	5
Guatemala	3765	2225	Sweden	1	0
Guyana	47	12	Switzerland	1	0
Holland	0	1	Syria	2	0
Honduras	875	596	Taiwan	1	0
Hungary	0	2	Tanzania	0	1
India	43	21	Trinidad	2	1
Indonesia	2	2	Turkey	3	0
Iran	9	4	United Kingdom	4	7
Iraq	2	1	Uruguay	46	17
Ireland	0	1	U.S.S.R.	0	1
Israel	1	2	Venezuela	16	32
			Yugoslavia	58	3
			Total	11,621	7,529

FY 1989 57 Nationalities
FY 1990 62 Nationalities

The San Diego Sector's mounted patrol takes part in a few parades in the immediate area each year, if duties allow.

missing children or hikers in the rugged Laguna Mountains east of San Diego. Other members of the mounted patrol unit act as searchers, since they can cover ground on the backs of their horses that cannot be negotiated by vehicle and only slowly on foot.

The unit's special equipment includes the chaps issued to each rider. These are considered organizational equipment and, like the saddle and bridle, are turned in at the time the agent is transferred to other non-equine duties. The chaps are of heavy leather with the smooth side out, allowing the rider to slide through the brush more easily. All of the chaps are dyed black, the same as the Border Patrol duty leather.

The Smith & Wesson Model 686 .357 magnum is the Border Patrol's official duty handgun, but officers now are allowed to carry personally purchased automatics, if they meet the organization's published criteria. Acceptable are the 9mm and .45 ACP models from SIG-Sauer, Glock and Heckler & Koch. In looking over the handguns carried by the equine patrol agents, I noted a preponderance of Glocks in 9mm.

Each of the mounted officers is required to undergo the same firearms training as other Border Patrol agents. This includes a quarterly qualification shoot, as well as one night qualification session per year.

Incidentally, if there is any doubt as to the seriousness of the mission and the dangers involved, each of the mounted agents is issued a Kevlar "bullet-proof" vest and urged to wear it in the field beneath the uniform shirt.

Once the horses have been hauled to the point of departure and unloaded from the big horse trailer, the patrol usually is split into three teams, according to Agent Ruben Sais, who often functions as the officer in charge.

"Three teams of three riders each is an ideal situation,"

Supervisory Border Patrol Agent Greg Terrones (left) is off-duty and in civilian clothes, but checks in with his riders before they saddle up for the hunt for illegals.

Sais explains. "Working together, they can back each other and, if they round up a good-size bunch, three riders can handle them better in getting them out of the bush and to a road where they can be picked up and moved out. Also, if there is some guy in the group that's going to cause trou-

These horsemen have been transported to this lonely road in the horse trailer in background. Usually, the riders operate in teams of three and four, providing a maneuver force as well as affording back-up for one in trouble.

The saddles used by the agents carry the Border Patrol logo, which is carved into heavy leather on the fender.

ble, it is easier for three agents to handle the problem than one or two who are trying to keep track of the other illegals they've captured."

Asked how a potential troublemaker might be treated, Ruben Sais explains, "The first thing an agent has to remember is the fact that the moment an illegal steps onto United States soil, he has the same civil rights as all the rest of us. Usually, just putting handcuffs on a guy will convince him he's not in much of a position to cause trouble."

Asked whether the Border Patrol agents ever get involved in shootouts there in the brush, Agent Sais offers an affirmative nod.

"It happens from time to time, but it's usually not the illegals who are the problem. It's the bandits!"

The canyons and gulleys the illegals use as routes for getting into the United States also hide these bandits who prey on the would-be immigrants. According to Border Patrol agents, the bandits invariably are Mexican nationals who cross the line, then hide in the bush, waiting for a "coyote" — or smuggler — to move his contraband, be it humans or drugs, northward.

The term, "coyote," has been popularized in the press and in fiction as the individual who contracts to guide illegals across the border and into a safe environment for a price. Border Patrol agents, however, tend to refer to this breed simply as smugglers.

"All too often, the smugglers are working directly with the bandits," Agent Sais reports. "The smugglers let the bandits know when and where they will be bringing a bunch of illegals through. The bandits wait for the illegals, then attack and rob them. When it's all over, the smugglers split the loot with the bandits!"

The veteran agent shakes his head. "There's no way these illegals can win, really, and it's their own people who are ripping them off."

Sais was an investigator for the Santa Barbara County

Horses are loaded into the horse trailers for hauling to the area where night's patrol effort will begin.

district attorney's office prior to joining the Border Patrol eight years ago. In his enforcement career, he has seen a good deal of violence. Some of what he has seen along the border, often from the back of a horse and deep in the bush, causes him to shake his head.

"Our horse patrols break up a lot of rapes and assaults," he says. "The agents will hear screams or sounds of a struggle out there in the bush and they ride in to investigate. But there are a lot of rapes we probably never know about that are never reported." Just riding through the bush is revealing. Quantities of female undergarments are strewn about, lending credence to the agent's voiced suspicions.

Once the horseback agents capture an illegal, he is taken to an accessible road or trail, and a vehicle is summoned via the portable radio each of the agents carries as part of the equipment. The rider stays with the illegal — or illegals — until transport arrives. At that time, the captives are questioned and a search for weapons is conducted.

"We seldom find an illegal with a firearm," Sais says, "but there are lots of knives, which we take away from them. If they are such illegal types as switch blades, butter-fly types or gravity knives, they are not returned when the aliens are turned over to the Mexican police at the border.

Not all of the illegals are Mexicans, as suggested earlier. Records for the San Diego Sector show that, during FY 1989, illegal aliens from fifty-seven other countries were detained. In fiscal year 1990 — October to October — illegal aliens from sixty-two countries were taken. While the vast majority are from other Latin American nations, there have been some real surprises.

For example, there have been captures of illegal entrants from the United Kingdom, Russia, Turkey, Yugoslavia, Iran and Iraq. Canada, England, Egypt and even Ireland and Israel have added their numbers to the statistics. New Zealand had three of its citizens apprehended in 1989, and five in 1990. In 1990, there were eight from Bulgaria.

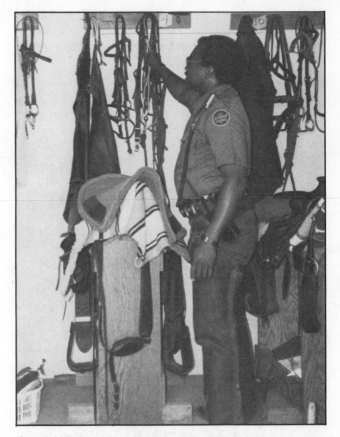

Agent M.E. Douglas checks out the tack that is assigned to him. Equipment is turned in when agent leaves unit. Douglas also is in charge of driver training for trailers.

Supervisory Border Patrol Agent Ken Foley queries cyclist at the edge of streambed. Mountains in the background are in Mexico. Patrolling the heavy brush in what seems a No-Man's Land is best accomplished with the horses.

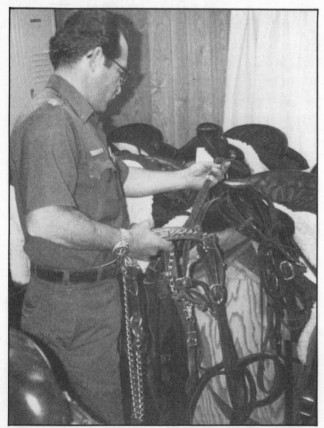

Greg Terrones checks on condition of the patrol's parade saddles and tack. Saddles are the same as those used in daily work, but are in better condition for appearances.

While the in-depth questioning is done by trained officers at the detention center, the patrol riders question their detainees after they have been searched for weapons. Part of this questioning is an effort to learn whether the captives are other than Mexican. By such questioning, the officers also may learn of other aliens and the routes they are taking.

The San Diego Sector equine unit isn't the only one in the U.S. Border Patrol. Today, mounted units of approximately the same size in manpower, number of horses and other resources are located at Douglas, Arizona; in that state's Organ Pipe National Momument; El Paso; and at Laredo, Texas.

The horse patrol was introduced in the Organ Pipe park several years ago, after a number of illegals from San Salvador were found dead of dehyration in the desert. It was — and is policy — of the park overseers not to allow wheeled vehicles to patrol the desert-like terrain.

The forty hours of on-horse training that each volunteer for the Southern California horse patrol must undergo is described by Ruben Sais as "five long days of sheer Hell!" He had, of course, been on horses before, but not for eight or more hours a day.

What might be considered a novel facet of the training lies in the fact that the new trainee will undergo all of his or her in-the-saddle schooling on the back of the same horse this agent will be riding in a duty status.

"There's no slack in those forty hours of training," explains Supervisory Border Patrol Agent Ken Foley, who conducts most of this instruction. Since vacancies in the unit are relatively rare, most of the training is one-on-one. "Even when a trainee breaks for lunch, he doesn't get

NARCOTIC SEIZURES

YEAR	TYPE	AMOUNT	VALUE
1987	Marijuana	12,133 lbs	$ 8,682,000
	Cocaine	1,106 lbs	13,458,000
	Heroin	3oz	31,000
	Amphetamine	33 oz	3,000
	Steroids	132,000 units	87,000
			$ 22,261,000
1988	Marijuana	12,558 lbs	$ 4,907,000
	Cocaine	668 lbs	6,474,000
	Heroin	2 oz	8,000
	Methamphetamine	256 lbs	5,953,000
	Steroids	203 units	50,000
	Other		32,000
			$ 17,424,000
1989	Marijuana	17,218 lbs *	$ 8,614,000
	Cocaine	2,290 lbs	29,293,000
	Heroin	7 oz	38,000
	Methamphetamine	36 lbs	301,000
	Steroids	4,588 oz	45,000
	Other		859,000
			$ 39,150,000
1990	Marijuana	48,160 lbs *	$ 24,252,000
	Cocaine	184 lbs	1,380,000
	Heroin	43 oz	136,000
	Other	422 lbs	1,386,000
			$ 27,054,000

* Includes the harvest of plants

Riders gather in dry stream bed for final briefing and instructions as the night's patrol is about to begin.

A new stable is being built on Border Patrol property. It was to be occupied in late 1991. In foreground are washracks for horses.

much peace. We continue to lecture right through that last sip of coffee before he or she gets back up in the saddle!" Foley declares. "And once this new rider comes out of the bullring and is put in the field on the back of his horse, he's still undergoing on-the-job training. It takes a while. For us, a finished rider is one who knows what his horse is going to do before it does it!"

In spite of the fact that each of the riders is equipped only with a powerful flashlight, it's not as though they are riding around in the dark, hoping to just stumble across an illegal. No, indeed. This is where the horse meets the age of electronic science!

Parked atop the highest hill in the immediate area is a Border Patrol van that is equipped with sophisticated infrared spotting scopes and associated equipment developed originally for military combat use.

The operator sweeps the entire area with his infra-red equipment and is able to pick up the forms of illegals, as well as those of the horses and riders. By this means, the spotter is able to direct the riders toward the illegals by radio. It is a highly effective system and explains why the

horse patrol can capture up to two hundred illegals a night.

There exists an air of teamwork and mutual consideration that one might not find in some other law enforcement unit. The Border Patrol agents come from varied backgrounds and experiences, but there still is a closeness that is difficult to explain.

"A lot of camaraderie is based upon the fact that most of us come from along the border and have grown up knowing about the Border Patrol and what it does. We usually have relatives or close friends who have served with it." That is the view of Warren Templeton.

"Get into middle America — the East, the Midwest and even parts of the South — and folks don't really understand what the Border Patrol is all about. They seem to think we are just a few guys wandering up and down the international boundary, trying to turn back the illegals. But those of use who live along the border know about the patrol and that's probably how we come to join up."

Templeton was an Arizona cowboy when he decided on a career in law enforcement. He found he was too young to

Above: A pair of illegals has been brought out of the brush by this three-rider team. They are made to sit so they will be less able to run or cause problems. (Right) Border Patrolman Ruben Sais searches one of the aliens for drugs, guns.

be taken seriously by most enforcement agencies, so he enlisted for a tour of duty with the U.S. Navy. He feels the experience and disciplines learned there helped him in passing the rigorous requirements of Border Patrol selection and training.

Agents Ruben Conde and Templeton attended the Border Patrol Academy in Georgia, graduating in the same class. They enjoy working together, because each seems to know what the other is thinking.

Some relationships are even closer. For example, Agent Don Cortez has a brother who also is a Border Patrol agent; his cousin is an agent — and his wife wears the same green uniform as the others of the family.

Sometime around 1 a.m., the three mounted teams get the word from the supervising agent that their day is done — sort of. They ride out of the bush and gather at the horse trailer. Their tired mounts are loaded and driven back to the commercial operation where they are stabled.

The horses are unloaded, unsaddled and looked over for lameness, cuts or other abrasions that might need treatment. The horses are brushed down, then stabled. After that, there probably is another hour of report writing and critique at the Pacific Beach line office.

As all of this is going on, busloads of Mexican illegals are leaving the detention center at San Ysidro. They will be driven back to the border and turned over to the Mexican police who will check them out to be certain they are not getting any OTMs — other than Mexicans — and that none of their countrymen are wanted by the law on the south side of the international boundary.

The riders, weary and perhaps a little saddle sore if it has been a tough shift, finally are ready for home and bed. But each of them knows that tomorrow night, the night after or perhaps the night after that, they probably will capture some of the same people taken during this night's patrol.

The problem has no end.

CHAPTER NINETEEN

THE PARA-LAWMEN

Trained Citizen Volunteers Are Making A Difference In Crime Prevention In Many Areas

Both male and female senior volunteers take part in the backup patrols conducted for the San Clemente police. This unpaid service saves the city countless overtime hours for regular officers...and the fines make money!

The patrol cars used by the Retired Senior Volunteer Program carry R.S.V.P. on the rear for proper identity. Volunteers are limited in the type of law enforcement duties they carry out and none of them carry firearms.

AS AN OFFICER, I came to learn that it is impossible to provide the American public with complete, positive, twenty-four-a-day protection from murder, rape and robbery. Unfortunately, in today's society, it cannot be guaranteed even by the President, himself. The lines of defense are simply too thin!

I didn't write those words. They were written fifteen years ago by the late Skeeter Skelton for *Shooting Times* magazine. However, as most of us probably realize, things haven't improved a bit. Truth is, if we stop to think about it, the conditions Skeeter described in April, 1976, had existed long before that. From my own standpoint as a police officer of the era, I am fully convinced that the bent toward violence began during the war in Vietnam, when demonstrators and mobs engaged in massive violence and property destruction, then stood behind the protective net of our Constitution to keep from paying the full price for their misdeeds.

This also became the era of the weak-kneed judges who sought votes by insisting they were more interested in reformation than in punishment. The collective answer for many of those wearing the black robes was to turn violent criminals back onto the streets where they could work on their reformation by committing more crimes. Incidentally, folks, if you think I'm not on a soap box, please take a hard look at where my feet are planted.

It should be pointed out, of course, that there are two schools of thought even among police officers. The more senior a policeman, the more rank he has in the department or agency, the more he tends to go along with the thinking of the judges and the political do-gooders. By the time an officer reaches the level of captain, all to often he has become a politician in his own right and is looking either at secure retirement or ultimate selection — by other politicians, incidentally — as chief of police or, perhaps, police commissioner. He has to adopt the party line.

On the other hand, talk to the street cop who is called upon to deal with violence every day and he will tell a different story — if he will talk about it at all. The average street cop is fully aware that the average citizen cannot be protected on the streets or in his home by the police.

While the high echelon police may talk about gun con-

Senior citizen volunteers frequently are called on to handle traffic during celebrations or emergency situations.

trol and getting guns out of the hands of the citizens, the street cop invariably is the one who is a member of the National Rifle Association, believes in the right of the people to have arms for their own protection and may even advocate it among his friends. However, this junior officer — the working street cop — can hardly get his own soap box, stand on a street corner in his uniform and tell people they ought to go buy a handgun, because he cannot protect them.

The Sarah Bradys, Handgun Control, Incorporated, and other activists involved in anti-gun efforts collect a batch of money from do-gooders; they pay excellent salaries to their staff workers; they work quite hard and with growing efficiency to disarm the honest citizen who, by the admission of his own law enforcement agencies, cannot be protected in the streets or even in his or her own home.

Yet Handgun Control, Mrs. Brady and the others don't really do anything about the crime problem. Their answer is to ban all handguns which is no answer at all. They insist that such a ban will help end crime. They don't accept the fact that any amateur mechanic can go into a junkyard and find the materials for building a handgun. He can assemble it in a matter of hours. In his own kitchen, he can come up with the materials for a propellant — gun powder, if you will — and if he wants to kill someone or use a handgun to commit a different type of crime, he's ready to hit the streets. Perhaps the organization should change its title to Handgun and Junkyard Control, Incorporated.

Such people are blind to the facts — or perhaps *by the fact* that it long ago was shown that there is plenty of money to be made by a few simply by being against something and organizing an effort to fight it with funds. Whatever their reasons, such believers and campaigners ignore the success of such events as the Kennesaw Story.

In 1982, the city fathers of Kennesaw, Georgia, passed a law that required all residents to own a gun, unless a person had a dissenting opinion due to religious beliefs. In the nine years since that law was passed, home burglaries have been reduced by eighty percent; there have been no murders; nor have there been any accidental shootings!

RSVP personnel are fully authorized to cite the owners of vehicles for a wide range of violations.

Portland, Oregon, officials recognized the day-to-day crime threat to the average citizen and decided these individuals should be allowed to carry guns. The city issued 2200 concealed-carry permits for handguns in a seven-month period. In that same seven months of 1990, homicides in the city dropped by thirty-three percent.

In February, 1991, Glamour magazine polled its readers — primarily women — and learned that eighty-three percent of those readers are more frightened of the crime problem than they were five years ago. More revealing, perhaps, is the fact that thirty-three percent of those polled now carry some type of weapon when out of the home.

Still, efforts are being made to combat the problem of lawlessness. Not unlike the vigilantes of old and the hard-riding sheriff's posses of a century ago, volunteers — serving without pay — are finding their services becoming important in a great number of communities.

Many police departments across the nation have had reserve officers on whom they call in time of need. This is not a new program. Similarly, there are teams of specially

qualified citizens who come to the fore when mountain or blizzard rescues are required; there are mounted posses drawn from the horse-owning citizenry who search deserts and canyons for anything from lost hikers to bodies. These might best be described as "special need troops."

But another type of volunteerism started in Ojai, California, about a decade ago, after the state's Proposition 13 was voted in by the heavily burdened populace. This vote vastly reduced the amount of monies available from property taxes. Those who filled the breach for the Ojai Police Department were the community's senior citizens!

This concept has spread to other California cities. One of the earliest to look at the idea and adopt it was San Clemente, a community of some 30,000 souls, situated along the shores of the Pacific.

The initial investigations of such a program were made for the City of San Clemente by one Robert McDonnell, then a lieutenant with the local police department. He now serves as chief of police in Woodland, California.

According to McDonnell's research, "Crime preven-

Sergeant Richard Corder (left) is the San Clemente PD liaison with the men and women of the volunteer patrol. Working with the RSVP, in addition to other duties, he has become a firm believer in the vaulue of the program.

tion in the United States, as we know it, started in the late 1960s, aided by federal grant monies and motivated by citizen outrage at rising crime rates.

"The basic concept was sound — anticipating crime risks and taking preventive action before the crime occurs. Crime prevention efforts spread rapidly across the nation among large and small police and sheriffs' departments. Almost everyone got into the act. Crime prevention began to encompass projects to prevent shoplifting, vandalism, cattle rustling, rape, robbery, arson, theft, assault and burglary. But the three most popular programs to emerge were operation identification, security surveys and Neighborhood Watch.

"Ironically," McDonnel recalls, "as public interest and commitment to crime prevention grew, federal funding began to diminish. In addition, public or local funding dwindled as economic conditions throughout the nation worsened. Yet, a survey taken in May, 1980, among crime prevention practitioners from twenty-seven states showed ninety percent were in strong agreement that in the next decade citizen interest in home security and crime preven-

tion would continue to increase."

In conducting his study, Lieutenant McDonnell found that a pressing question had to be addressed: How would police departments confront the rising citizen interest and demand for crime prevention programs when they were experiencing cutbacks in personnel due to budget shortages?

The answer began to materialize. Local law enforcement agencies began to recognize the services volunteers could provide to a community as an alternative to budget and personnel increases. It since has been shown that volunteers seem to have a special interest in working with law enforcement agencies. They are especially interested in crime prevention. After all, they live in the communities, they see themselves as potential victims of crime and usually are committed to bettering their homes and surroundings.

Subsequent experience has shown that volunteer programs can offer cities and law enforcement agencies many benefits — including closer cooperation between citizens and the police. Most important, perhaps, is the fact that

William J. Walsh, a retired high school principal, is an obvious choice when it comes to lecturing to any group of youngsters. He has coordinated the RSVP effort since shortly after retiring, moving to San Clemente.

such volunteer programs can utilize the valuable experience and knowledge of the senior citizens who are retired in the community.

As an illustration, the sheriff's department of Ventura County, California, initiated what has come to be known as the RSVP program. This has nothing to do with answering an invitation to a cocktail party, incidentally. Those four letters stand for Retired Senior Volunteer Program. That was in 1980.

Within a month, this program had been established in the town of Ojai which has a high retiree population. There were some fifty retired men and women in uniform driving a marked vehicle, volunteering their time to support local law enforcement. Activities for this original volunteer force ranged from preventive vehicle patrols, walking foot beats and registering bicycles to marking abandoned vehicles and conducting commercial and residential security checks.

With its proven success, the Ojai program was used as the model for the one established in San Clemente in 1984. As Lieutenant McDonnell recommended at the time, it has been designed to "utilize volunteers in all aspects of crime prevention, thus enabling citizens to assist the police department in effectively combating crime in the community."

Under the plan developed by Lieutenant McDonnell, there were five principal goals and objectives:

1. Provide a higher level of crime prevention programs to better serve the citizens of San Clemente.

2. Promote a high caliber police volunteer program which, through its efforts, would make the criminal element aware of its presence, thus reducing crime by reputation alone.

3. Promote community awareness and acceptance of the San Clemente Police Department Volunteer Program as a viable and important crime prevention tool.

4. Provide additional manpower to the San Clemente Police Department, thus enabling crime prevention programs to expand in the city without significant increases in cost to citizens.

5. By demonstrating the success of such a pilot program, pave the way for the use of volunteers in expanded functions throughout the police department — and perhaps the city.

William J. Walsh, a retired high school principal, coordinates the RSVP program at this time. He feels that "possibly the greatest value of our volunteers lies in their

The beach city has strict regulations as to what type of signs may be posted and for how long. Members of the patrol check these out and may even write citations. (Right) This is a copy of the monthly report submitted to the chief of police to show activities of the RSVP. Note the number of citations issued; serious business.

mere presence in San Clemente. The psychological effect is tremendous, presenting a united and cooperative crime prevention effort between citizens and the police department."

According to Bill Walsh, the city currently has twenty-five volunteers. Three of these are women whose duties are limited to administration at police headquarters. Of the remaining twenty-two, five are women who carry out the same patrolling and other duties as their male counterparts.

Volunteers are trained to conduct thorough security surveys of homes and businesses. In the past, these checks were assigned to sworn officers and police community service officers. The Neighborhood Watch program had outgrown the police department's ability to provide service by 1984 when there were only 2000 homes covered by the program. Today, in San Clemente, there are 343 Neighborhood Watches involving some 8000 homes and the program continues to grow.

With this growth, volunteers have been recruited and trained to give Neighborhood Watch presentations for the city's Crime Prevention Unit. In addition to home security, this program includes instruction in personal safety, senior citizens alert and fraud and swindle prevention.

San Clemente officers found that the Ventura County Sheriff's Department uses volunteers exclusively to perform all of their vacation home checks. It wasn't long before this duty was turned over to San Clemente's RSVP personnel. During 1990 alone, approximately 3200 vacation home checks were made by these volunteers, thus allowing sworn officers to devote that time to more pertinent duties.

San Clemente has no major malls, although there are several shopping centers as well as the main business district. Volunteers patrol these business centers, wearing distinctive uniforms that are compatible with those worn by the city's sworn police officers. It has been acknowledged that their mere presence has resulted in a reduction in shoplifting.

"The patrols have been found to be particularly impor-

	YEAR-TO-DATE LAST REPORT	CURRENT MONTH	YEAR TO DATE
NUMBER OF DUTY DAYS	284	25	309
HOURS TRAINING	337	40	377
HOURS MEETINGS	85	0	85
FIELD DUTY HOURS	4072	294	4366
CRIME PREVENTION UNIT HOURS	387	7	394
RECORDS SECTION HOURS	150	9	159
PERSONNEL DEPARTMENT HOURS	127	21	148
R.S.V.P. ADMINISTRATION HOURS	196	12	208
NUMBER OF UNATTENDED VEHICLE CHECKS	1830	235	2065
NUMBER OF VACANT HOME CHECKS	3012	183	3195
NUMBER OF FOOT PATROLS	13	2	15
NUMBER OF VISITS TO YANA PATROMS	550	36	586
NUMBER OF CITIZEN ASSISTS	218	14	232
NUMBER OF GRAFFITI REPORTS	16	7	23
CITATIONS ISSUED: 10.30 Fire Lane	124	12	136
11.2 Two-Hour Parking Limit	77	1	78
22507.8A Handicapped Zone	114	13	127
4000A No Current Vehicle Reg.	539	10	549
5200 Front/Rear Plate Required	408	46	454
5204 No Current License Tabs	1488	165	1653
LOCKOUTS	37	0	37
OTHER FIELD DUTIES PERFORMED (listed)			
15-40	13	2	15
15-41	158	19	177
15-59	25	3	28
SIGNS	625	84	709

The RSVP is involved in the city's Neighborhood Watch, a community program that has citizens covering for their neighbors and reporting any suspicious activity.

are primarily living alone or where one member of the family is bedridden and the mate is required to maintain the home. Each morning, these individuals receive a call from the police department to determine that all is well.

Volunteers have been used to expand this personalized service and even to visit YANAs in their homes. With such one-on-one service, the police department is able to identify any needs or special requirements that can be furnished in a more effective and timely manner.

"Often, those participating in the YANA program are shut-ins and their only contact with people is through the police department," Bill Walsh explains. "Personal visits by volunteers tend to enchance the quality of their lives."

Clerical duties are an important part of the RSVP program, also. With the expanded Neighborhood Watch and other citizen-oriented crime prevention efforts, correspondence, filing, issuance of press releases and notices have increased manyfold. The senior volunteers have filled this the gap.

The initial cost of recruiting, training and putting the first twenty volunteers on the street was less than $8000, according to city records. Today, it costs approximately $260 per volunteer to accomplish the same thing. But both the volunteers and the police department are convinced it is a good deal.

Sergeant Richard Corder is in charge of the RSVP program — among his other duties — and has been involved directly with the volunteers for the last four years.

"It may be that we sometimes tend to take the volunteers for granted," the sergeant admits, "until we start to record the money they save the city and, in some instances, the funds their efforts derive for the city treasury."

For example, San Clemente has several parades, surfing contests and other major celebrations per year. These events, frankly, are designed to generate tourist dollars for the city and its merchants and each draws thousands of outsiders to what normally is a small, residential beach community.

Handling traffic for such operations would mean bringing in off-duty officers from other communities — and paying them. The RSVP-trained volunteers now handle such problems, while the sworn officers devote their time to seeing that problems don't develop among the celebrants.

Members of the volunteer force also are empowered to issue citations for non-moving violations. Citations are written for such illegalities as parking in fire lanes or handicapped zones, exceeding a two-hour parking limit, having no current vehicle registration, missing license plates and not having current California license stickers.

In 1990, the total of such citations issued by RSVP personnel numbered 2997. The fine for such tickets ranges from $10 to $100; the net return to the city treasury speaks well for the initial cost of uniforming and training these volunteers!

The volunteers constitute an interesting cross-section of backgrounds. One is a retired U.S. Treasury agent, another was one of the top architects in Southern California before retirement. There also is a former airline executive, a retired college chancellor, a former airline pilot, a master carpenter and a woman chiropractor, not to mention an airline stewardess, several teachers and housewives whose children are long gone. There also is one husband-and-wife team.

tant during the holiday shopping season," Walsh reports. "Customers tell us they feel safer while shopping and there seems to be a marked improvement in rapport with the citizens as a result of volunteer foot patrol exposure."

The City of San Clemente requires that all bicycles in the city be registered. Prior to establishment of the RSVP program, compliance with the ordinance was poor, as evidenced by the number of bicycle thefts in the city. Lieutenant McDonnell's original plan was to approach the local school district and make it mandatory that every bike ridden to school in San Clemente be registered if it was to be on campus. Volunteers were called upon to aid in the mass registration program.

Another problem in the area was abandoned cars. Regular patrol officers were having difficulty in identifying and marking abandoned vehicles or those that had been parked in excess of seventy-two hours on a city street — violation of a local ordinance. The problem was time.

The retired volunteers took over this duty, marking the cars and reporting them. Towing decisions, however, are left to members of the police department. During 1990, more than two thousand such checks were made by volunteers.

San Clemente has a large retired population. At the time the RSVP program first was being considered, the city already had a program called YANA. The letters stand for "You Are Not Alone," a program designed to provide a measure of security and well-being for elderly people who

The Neighborhood Watch signs are posted at entrances to streets and residential communities. As evidenced by the wording, this is a no-nonsense program which has had a decided effect in reducing city crime statistics.

Whenever possible, according to Sergeant Corder, two volunteers are teamed in the specially marked patrol cars. That allows one person to concentrate on driving while the other member of the team watches for problems.

"Not long ago, two of our RSVP patrolmen were driving past an alley," the sergeant recounts, "where they saw a pair of Mexicans changing the license plates on a truck. They immediately notified the police dispatcher of what they had seen and one of our own units was sent to investigate.

"It turned out that the offenders were illegals, the truck was stolen and so were the extra license plates. Having those extra eyes out there on the streets is important to the success of our crime prevention work and it has paid off for the city and our citizens."

Arrest of the two illegals, incidentally, led San Clemente officers and Border Patrolmen to an apartment where eleven other illegal immigrants were holed up.

In recent months, the city staffs of Yuma, Arizona; Tampa, Florida; Anchorage, Alaska; and several in Washington State have called upon the San Clemente Police Department for information on the RSVP program.

Word of the effort's success is spreading and other communities see ways of making up in part, at least, for funds that are not available for their budgets.

One point was made both by Bill Walsh and Sergeant Corder. While most of the men assigned to patrols are service veterans and familiar with firearms, no type of weaponry is carried by RSVP personnel nor is it carried in their vehicles. One city in Florida does allow its RSVP people to carry handguns on duty.

Wiser minds, perhaps, have prevailed in San Clemente. In a city where a visiting ocean swimmer can collect more than a million dollars because he was stupid enough to dive into a wave without first checking the depth of the water, the word, "liability," has become an all too familiar term.

The swimmer did break his neck, incidentally. As for firearms, members of the Retired Senior Volunteer Patrol feel quite comfortable going about their duties unarmed.

"We're here to save the city money and hopefully improve the quality of life for our residents, not to make like we're a bunch of overage Wyatt Earps in the streets of Dodge City!"

Well put, I'd say.

Thomas H. Rynning captained the Arizona Rangers from 1902 until 1907. He was a former Army officer and an Indian fighter who had helped put down the Apaches. He introduced military tactics to his band of lawmen.

The Arizona Rangers: An Old Outfit With A New And Viable Mission

Burton C. Mossman was the first commanding officer of the Arizona Rangers and formed the first detachment. He served for only a year by his own choice, but was bringing in a captive outlaw after commisssion expired.

THE ARIZONA Rangers have been immortalized in song, legend and history books in spite of the fact that the tax-supported life of the organization was relatively short by law enforcement standards. The organization lives on today, but as an incorporated community service organization in support of law enforcement and youth activities while maintaining the traditions of the Old West.

Today's Arizona citizen who wears the badge of the Arizona Rangers seldom if ever gets on a horse in pursuit of his duties, and he may wear a Model 1911A1 or one of the newer 9mm autos on his gunbelt rather than the traditional .45 Colt Peacemaker. However, those who serve the organization are probably as dedicated in their aims as were the old timers at the turn of the century.

The Arizona Rangers actually date back to the Civil War, when the Army of the Confederacy developed plans to capture the southern portions of what now is Arizona and New Mexico. The purpose of this campaign was to insure that gold could be moved by the rebel sympathizers who had access to the California mines, transporting it safely to Texas and, ultimately, the Confederate treasury.

In August of 1861, a battalion of this campaign was organized in West Texas. These volunteers made up three companies: the Arizona Volunteers, the Arizona Guards — and the Arizona Rangers! These volunteers saw only limited action, since the Confederacy abandoned the area in mid-1862.

When Arizona was established as a separate territory in 1863, John N. Goodwin was appointed governor. For the next twenty-one years, succeeding legislatures passed some type of legislation aimed at the creation of a territorial ranger force to combat the Indians and to protect supply routes as well as communications and settlers. These forces were underfinanced — when financed at all — and all too often found themselves paying their own expenses.

Stanley A. Levin, a prominent Tucson physician who is a member of the modern day Rangers as well as a devout history buff, furnished a great deal of the material for this historical review. He recounts one incident that doesn't reflect too well on those early efforts at law enforcement. It seems that eleven members of a group called the Globe Rangers went in pursuit of an Apache raiding party. At a place called Hidden Valley, the leader called a halt for a siesta. While the Rangers were napping, the Apaches sneaked up and stole their horses. Not a shot was fired, but the pursuers had to walk all the way back to Globe!

In 1885, the Ranger companies — then considered militia — were disbanded and reorganized as the Arizona National Guard. However, later that year, the guardsmen who had been local Rangers were mustered out of the National Guard and reorganized as the Duncan Rangers. There appears to have been reason for this move. At that time, the National Guard unit could not operate beyond the borders of its own county. The Duncan Rangers could. The unit, however, was disbanded the following year due to lack of funding and non-payment of expenses.

Over the years, groups were formed in Prescott, Tubac, Tucson and other communities around the state. In virtually every case, the groups soon were disbanded. None ever received pay for their time and efforts. All of these groups, of course, were formed by authority of the legislature and were under the command and direction of the territorial governor; thus, all were known as "Arizona Rangers." During that era, they were assigned primarily to protecting settlers from Apache attacks.

It was not until 1901 that the Arizona Territorial Legislature finally passed an act authorizing the enlistment of a

This is the corporate insignia of modern day Arizona Rangers, a corporation that combines aid to enforcement agencies with charitable work, mostly with children.

company of Arizona Rangers. By ths time, hostile Apaches were mostly a thing of the past, but the state was loaded with outlaws, rustlers, thieves and killers; lawmakers finally had realized something had to be done.

Under the legislative charter, the company was to be composed of one captain who would be paid $120 per month; a sergeant to earn $75; and twelve privates at $55 per month. To sweeten the pie, each man would be allowed $1 per day for subsistence — and an additional fifty cents to feed his horse.

A well known cattleman, Burton C. Mossman, was commissioned as the first captain of the rangers. The cattleman, incidentally, had a formidable reputation as a result of his position as long-time foreman of the famed Hash Knife Ranch. When he had taken over that job, he had gone directly to the range from the train that had delivered him, observing with an experienced eye the ranch's cowboys and their actions. Shortly after, several of the hands were fired as suspected rustlers. According to legend, the foreman's suspicions proved to be right, as several later were arrested. Under Mossman's direction, the arms the Rangers would carry were specified; each had to furnish his own equipment — including his horse!

Another tested law enforcement agent and former soldier, Thomas H. Rynning, took over command of the company in September 1902. Several months later, the legislature authorized pay increases for the rangers — along with increased manpower. The company still rated one captain, upped in pay to $175 a month; the only lieutenant was

This photo of the early-day Arizona Rangers was taken at Morenci in 1903. At that time, there were twenty-six men and officers assigned to the organization, but there are only twenty-five rangers in this photograph.

added to the table of organization at $130; the number of sergeants was increased to four, each drawing $110, while the number of privates became twenty, each drawing $100 per month. In an era that found hard-working cowboys in their saddles six — even seven — days a week for $30 a month, the wages perhaps reflect some of the dangers associated with the Arizona Ranger badge.

However, the increase in pay might also be looked upon as a trade-off. Under the new pay regulations, each Ranger was required to furnish not only mounts and equipment, but he also had to pay subsistence for himself and his horses. The Rangers, however, were granted doctor and hospital bills for injuries suffered in the service of the Arizona Territory. If a Ranger had a horse killed in pursuit of his duties, he was paid for the loss. Incidentally, it was not until the early months of 1903 that the Rangers finally were issued badges. Today, only one such badge is known to exist.

Tom Rynning remained in command of the rangers until March 1907, when he was replaced by Harry C. Wheeler. Rynning was transferred to Yuma to serve as warden of the much-storied Territorial Prison. Incidentally, most of the films concerning the Arizona Rangers, as well as the television series of the Fifties, *Twenty-six Men,* have been constructed storywise around the Rynning era.

According to Dr. Levin, few official records concerning the rangers have been preserved. In February 1909, the Territorial Legislature passed a bill repealing the Rangers Act of 1903. Party politics obviously had raised its head and the opposition was accusing the governor of using the rangers as his personal police force. The governor vetoed the bill, but it was passed on a subsequent vote in the legislature and the ranger force was abandoned. The records of the company were stored in the basement of the State Capitol building and were lost in a series of floods.

A sidelight of the dissolution is the fact that it was done quickly and there was little publicity. With the poor communications of that era, it was not surprising that the legislators were able to accomplish this before the voters could protest what most of them considered shabby treatment of a fine force and a gallant group of men. As it was, a number of the rangers were out on assignments, tracking the territory's wrongdoers when they learned they actually had been out of a job for days — and in some cases, weeks.

"All of them could take pride in the fact that, over the years, they had done a great deal to make Arizona a safer place to live and had, in their way, helped to make the territory eligible for statehood in 1912," opines Dr. Levin.

As mentioned, in the early days, the Arizona Rangers didn't even have badges. Once these symbols of authority were issued, the officers invariably kept them out of sight, preferring to work undercover in a majority of situations. The badges usually were presented only when an arrest was being made. In those days, of course, matters were a great deal more simple than under our current, allegedly more civilized legal system. As Dr. Levin points out, there were no entrapment problems and no one ever had heard of the Miranda law. A number of the rangers, in fact, had operated on the other side of the law at one time or another. This might lead us to believe that Burt Mossman and Tom Rynning possibly subscribed to the theory that "it takes one to know one."

There also wasn't any official uniform. Most of the

This is no indication when this torn picture of the Arizona Rangers was taken or where, but it probably was before the early part of 1903, since none of them are wearing badges. Such badges weren't issued until 1903.

rangers wore the same clothing they would have worn had they been riding the range or carrying out similar frontier jobs. Each month, these rangers were called upon to ride about four hundred miles in performing their duties. It was recorded that one ranger rode 754 miles in a single thirty-day period.

The Arizona Rangers, under the dictates of their charter, could pursue a felon out of state or even into Mexico. If captured, however, this lawbreaker had to be turned over to a peace officer in the county where the crime had taken place.

Age did not seem to be a factor in picking rangers. Among the first fourteen to sign on for the initial one-year enlistment, the average age was 33; the youngest was 22, the oldest, 47.

It was not long before the citizens of the Arizona Territory could tell that their rangers were making a difference. A legend had begun and Burt Mossman added to it. An Apache-Mexican outlaw, one Augustine Chacon, had escaped from an Arizona prison only hours before he was scheduled to hang. Mossman made it his own assignment to bring in this renegade, who had fled south of the border to Sonora.

The ranger captain followed Chacon into Mexico, pos-

ing as a wanted Texas outlaw. In time, he captured the killer and returned him to Arizona for a rescheduled hanging. Oddly, Burt Mossman's commission as the commanding officer of the rangers had expired four days before he made the capture. He was declared a hero and urged to remain, but he turned over the command to Tom Rynning and took a train East for a visit.

Captain Rynning was better known as a soldier than as a lawman; he had campaigned against the Cheyennes and had ridden with General Crook in putting down Geronimo and the Apaches. He also had served with Teddy Roosevelt's Rough Riders in Cuba during the Spanish-American War. As might be expected, Rynning introduced a degree of military training and tactics into his command. As a result, in two years — 1903 and 1904 — the rangers brought in fourteen murderers, more than a hundred rustlers and ninety-three robbers. The captain paid his men a somewhat backhanded complement when he told a group of citizens, "All of my rangers quit school before they were taught the meaning of fear!"

On a somewhat less adventurous note, the rangers also returned four hundred goats to their proper owner; the animals had been found six hundred miles from their home pasture!

Dr. Stanley A. Levin (right), a prominent physician in Tucson, inspects a handgun to be certain it is not loaded during a local gun show. Dr. Levin's interest is in the history of the Arizona Rangers of the past.

As mentioned earlier, the Arizona Rangers were sacrificed on the altar of partisan politics; there were other contributing factors, including the jealousies of local sheriffs and town marshals, but the twenty-six men had made their mark. On the day the force was dissolved, one ranger captured a horsethief in the rugged Chiracahua Mountains. Another ranger captured a robber in the equally rough Dragoon range. Old records show that a ranger named Redwood still was chasing a band of rustlers five days after the legislative action had cancelled his commission.

During the years of service, 107 men wore the badge of the Arizona Rangers. Of this number, three were killed in service. The last of this band died in 1982 at the age of 97. A writer for *Harper's Weekly* declared in that magazine's pages, "To the Arizona Rangers, more than any other thing, we may trace the passing of the badman."

The spirit and traditions of the Arizona Rangers continue, however, even today. In 1957, the organization was rechartered as a volunteer organization. Today, companies of these volunteers are scattered in communities across the state; in keeping with tradition, each company can have a strength of no more than twenty-six men.

There also have been some changes in the table of organization; the state commander carries the rank of colonel. In addition to a headquarters company composed primarily of officers, companies are located in Chandler, Holbrook, Huachuca City, Show Low, Tucson, Queen Creek, Santa Cruz and Canoa. Under the organizational bylaws, the modern rangers have been organized to: "(1) render, when called upon by federal, state or local law enforcement authority, such law enforcement assistance as may be required and within the capabilities of the Arizona Rangers, but only under the direction and supervision of such authority; (2) to provide support to those youth organizations and activities which contribute to the development of youth in matters of good morals and good citizenship; (3) to support any activity, which, in the judgment of the voting membership of this corporation, is deemed to be of benefit to or in the best interest of the nation, the State of Arizona, the local community or this corporation; (4) to engage in activities which tend to keep alive the traditions of the Old West..."

Each of the modern ranger companies still is commanded by the traditional captain, except for the headquarters element. To form a company in a community, there must be at least five participants, but never more than the traditional "twenty-six men" — and now women! Several companies have disstaffers on their rolls.

Burt Mossman and Tom Rynning may be rolling restlessly in their repective graves, but women now are allowed in the modern-day Arizona Rangers as bona fide members. Some handle administration, others serve in the field.

Each enlistee must be willing to devote a minimum of eight hours per month to the organization's activities; such individuals are approved for membership only after a thorough police check has been made. Any individual with a felony record is not wanted, of course. Should a ranger be convicted of a felony in a court of law, he — or she — is dismissed automatically from the force.

Each new member serves a probationary period of ninety days and is required to undergo courses covering the laws of arrest, search and seizure; primary or advanced first aid; and a firearms safety instruction course. Each individual also is required to qualify with the handgun he or she will carry on duty. Qualifications usually are in keeping with those of local law enforcement agencies in the company's home community.

As with the original territorial rangers, the modern day

badge holders are charged with furnishing their own equipment. Unlike the originals, they serve in an authorized, prescribed uniform. For summer — in addition to Western-style boots — the outfit consists of black Western-type trousers, a black gunbelt with the approved handgun, white short-sleeve Western-cut shirt and a light-colored ten-gallon straw hat. The uniform for winter duties includes a black Western-style hat, a clip-on black gambler-style string tie, a long-sleeve Western-cut shirt and the black cowboy-style trousers.

Actually, a third uniform also is authorized specifically for some work details. Substituted are blue denim Levi shirts and trousers.

In the matter of sidearms, the manual of operations calls for a pistol or revolver of ".38 caliber or larger in good and safe condition; Western or standard law enforcement revolver. For Ranger duties only, a single-action revolver is accepted. For law enforcement duties, only double-action is accepted." Optional equipment for the individual officer — again, purchased out of his own pocket — may include a flashlight, night stick, handcuffs, a whistle and a white or clear plastic poncho. Specific styles of jackets are authorized for both winter and summer duty wear, with appropriate badges, shoulder patches, et al., worn in a prescribed manner.

All of this may sound like a group that is all dressed up with no place to go. It's not that way at all. In most instances, the Arizona Rangers receive more requests for help than they can fulfill. As an example, shortly after the first company was rechartered under Arizona law in 1957, the Pima County sheriff approached the group. He was exceedingly short of qualified law enforcement officers — probably due to budget restrictions — and he asked the rangers for help. The deal was that the rangers would receive police training necessary to carry out their duties. Other counties and communities over the years have enlisted ranger help on a limited basis. A number of local police agencies also have aided members of the organization with training, particularly with firearms.

Normal aid to a law enforcement agency is rather uncomplicated. Rangers often help with traffic and crowd control at rodeos, high school functions, parades and races. On occasion, however, companies have been called upon to lend assistance in emergency situations that have included floods, desert search and rescue operations and armed patrolling to prevent vandalism and looting. In most of these situations, the rangers are deputized and have standard law enforcement powers.

These volunteers also work in security capacities for private operations from time to time. For example, in Tucson there are periodic gun shows. Rangers are posted at all doorways to check any firearm that is being taken into the show area to ensure that it is not loaded.

The operators of such enterprises negotiate for the help of a specific number of Arizona Rangers and agree to pay the organization a specific amount. A minor percentage of such collected funds is used to cover operational overhead, but the bulk of the monies goes to support the Arizona Boys Ranch in Chandler, Arizona.

Each year, the Arizona Rangers sponsor a Christmas party for the less fortunate boys who live at the ranch. There are clothes, books and other presents for each of the young men, as well as whatever else the ranch may need.

The bylaws of the organization carry a section that concerns itself with "duties, responsibilities and general conduct." One passage states, "All Arizona Rangers, when working security and/or crowd control, shall be aware of their limitations of duty and then perform them accordingly." This passage also points out that "All Arizona Rangers will, when it becomes necessary to detain an individual, use just the minimum force required for the safety of all. Make sure that the action is necessary in the first place."

The volunteers are further advised, "All Arizona Rangers must never get the idea that they are law enforcement peace offiers. You have no powers of arrest other than citizen's arrest, unless you are sworn in by a certified law enforcement agency."

The modern rangers are equipped with radio and, if they choose, semi-automatic pistols. This ranger wears the winter uniform, which includes a black 10-gallon hat and a Western-cut white shirt with long sleeves.

In spite of these — and many other — limitations which may seem to reduce the effectiveness of this force, Arizona residents look upon their rangers with nostalgic favor and obvious respect. They constitute a link with the past and there is a felt reassurance when the Arizona Ranger badges are visible on the scene.

As for what seem the limited duties the modern Arizona Rangers perform in actual law enforcement situations, numerous county sheriffs and police chiefs across the state welcome their training and devoted efforts in handling chores that would take professional law enforcement agents away from the primary job of finding and jailing criminals.

Trained Volunteers Police Sun City, Arizona, Where The Average Age is 73!

Members of the Sun City Posse, an adjuct of the sheriff's department of Maricopa County, Arizona, are sworn deputies. As such, they carry the same handguns as regular deputies and undergo the same training with handguns and shotguns.

SUN CITY, Arizona, didn't just happen like a lot of Sun Belt communities that simply rose out of the desert sands, one structure at a time, without thought or plan. Sun City was planned right down to the last bright, white pebble in the desert landscaping by developer Del Webb, who has made a career out of creating retirement communities in the Southwest.

But, in retrospect, it would seem someone slipped up and didn't give much thought to law enforcement needs. Action was triggered when the Maricopa County sheriff made it plain he didn't have the resources to patrol the streets and furnish continuing protection to a city of more than 40,000 retired people. Then things began to happen. The retirees decided they could — and would — police and protect themselves, within established limits.

Thus, in 1973, residents of the new community founded the Sun City Sheriff's Posse. The organization was authorized by the Maricopa County sheriff to function on a continuing basis as a crime prevention posse.

Now let's face it, folks, there are sheriff's posses and there are sheriff's posses. Some do a great deal of good work as horse-mounted deputies in search and rescue work, crowd control at parades and civic events and in a host of other duties that aid an undermanned and often beleaguered sheriff's department.

There are other posses that are largely social organizations, carrying the county and state flags in parades. Some of these posses have become relatively famous, mounted on horses of the same color and breed, riding saddles of the same design, wearing matching Western-cut outfits and

Seventy-year-old Jack Sorenson, a retired Marine major, is the posse commander at this writing. The commander is elected by the posse and serves for a term of a year. He also is chairman of the board of governors for the period.

white ten-gallon hats. They may be of some help to their sheriff at election time. I don't know.

I do know that the Sun City Posse is unlike any other I have ever come across. These volunteer deputies, wearing the same uniforms as their professional counterparts, act as the eyes and ears of the sheriff's office and serve their community in a number of ways. In 1989, for example, this group of volunteers drove their patrol cars some 190,358 miles in performing an aggregate of 70,397 man-hours of service. This included patrolling the streets, making vacation watch checks on homes, directing traffic for various Sun City activities, participating in search and rescue missions, carrying out holiday season foot patrols, responding to emergency calls and handling other requests from the sheriff's office.

Unlike any other Southwestern sheriff's posse, a lot of these deputies have never been on a horse, so equine transportation plays no part in patrol duties. Each of the deputies is a volunteer who serves without pay. Authorized strength of the unit is 120, but at this writing, there are 158 men and women on the rolls, available for duty assignments. Many of the participants are retired law enforcement officers. Others are retired military; then there is a smattering of ladies who used to be housewives and mothers. Now they

are into law enforcement and are just as serious about it as they were in being homemakers!

The city of Sun City is not incorporated. However, the Sheriff's Posse of Sun City is. The organization has operated from the beginning of its existence with funds donated by residents of the community. Unexpectedly, perhaps, there have been years when not all of the funds collected were required for operations. There also has been money bequeathed to the organization in wills and memorials. Over the years, the posse's board of governors prudently invested this money with an eye to the future. Then, in 1987, when the posse headquarters was about to be bulldozed to make way for a widened thoroughfare, it was decided the posse should have its own headquarters, a structure to be owned by the corporation. The entire cost — some $1,600,000 — was paid without need to incure additional debt.

The present building has 12,400 square feet of floor space, plus additional land for a garage and covered parking. Incidentally, the posse also maintains a fleet of twelve patrol cars — exact duplicates of those driven by the Maricopa County Sheriff's Department. Since the posse is a recognized law enforcement adjunct, it has been possible for the Sun City group to simply tie onto the end of the sheriff's contract for new patrol units, realizing the fleet-

The posse's headquarters was built at a cost of some $1,600,000 and paid for with cash from donations by the residents of Sun City. Each year, a letter is sent out to residents, requesting contributions to maintain the posse.

buy savings. No public tax-derived funds are involved, of course.

"But such professional equipment is a requirement for the type of work we do," explains Jack Sorenson, commander of the posse at this writing. "This city covers twenty-six square miles. In the nearly 200,000 miles our patrols drove last year, there also have been such things as 21,921 vacation watch checks of homes and participation in six search and rescue operations." In that year, deputies

also did 630 man-hours of foot patrolling during the Christmas season and directed traffic for Sun City functions for 1083 man-hours.

Sun City, of course, is built in the Arizona desert. This means that there are real dangers to Alzheimer victims and others who may stray from the immediate home surroundings with which they are familiar. Most of the posse's search and rescue involvement is with such cases. A much rehearsed grid search can be initiated in minutes. Thus far,

The city of Sun City is not incorporated, but the posse is. This is largely for the purpose of any liability.

The Sun City sheriff's posse doesn't own a single horse, but does maintain a fleet of twelve fully equipped police units. These vehicles are owned by the posse, but they are purchased on the tail end of the county sheriff's order.

they have always found their man — or woman.

"Serving as the eyes and ears for the sheriff in our community, the posse saves thousands of dollars annually in added taxes that would be required for professional law enforcement officers to be recruited and placed on duty in the immediate area. There is no doubt our presence in the community serves as a major crime deterrent," the posse commander states.

Jack Sorenson, incidentally, is a retired Marine Corps major, a veteran of World War II and the Korean hostilities. Following his military service, he was a sales manager for a Southern California corporation. Retiring for the second time, he and his wife, Dusty, settled in Sun City. The post of posse commander also makes Sorenson chairman of the organization's board of governors.

As might be expected, age, illness and other factors create a continuing recruiting effort. "The posse is always in need of qualified men and women to become members of the organization," Sorenson states. "To become a posse member, no previous police experience is required, although a number of members have some background in law enforcement. All that is required is that the individual be reasonably healthy, be a permanent resident of Sun City, have an unrestricted driver's license and be of good moral character. We'll take care of the training."

Each posse member is required to pass a number of training courses. Some are taught by posse personnel, others are conducted by Maricopa County officers. Among these courses are: organization and mission of the unit; search and rescue operations; the aforementioned vaca-

tion watch; the posseperson and the law; uniform and dress; traffic control; communications; first aid; cardiopulmonary resusitation — more popularly termed C.P.R. — and defensive driving.

In addition, each recruit must complete a minimum of six training rides when the basic training courses have been completed.

Not all of the Sun City deputies carry firearms. In order to carry a firearm, additional training in weapons handling and firing is required.

The Sun City Posse perceived the problem of shrinking open land some years ago. Thinking ahead, the posse's board of governors purchased a stretch of open desert not far from the community — but distant enough not to cause complaints of the sounds of firing. Today, a modern firing range stands on the property. Oddly enough, the increase in land values and other pressures have resulted in several nearby law enforcement agencies having to close their own training ranges. As a result, these agencies now conduct their firearms training at the range owned by the Sun City Posse.

As might be expected, the posse has adequate certified range personnel to instruct and qualify its members to carry firearms. These instructors usually come from the ranks of the retired military and retired law enforcement agencies.

With construction of the new posse headquarters, the unit now has one of the finest radio networks in the area. Two base communications consoles allow immediate contact with the sheriff's office, the fire department and an

Members of the Sun City Posse undergo a rigid training program. Part of the course is taught by members of the posse, while professional lawmen teach other segments. It is imperative that possemen understand limits of power.

ambulance service, as well as police agencies in other towns surrounding the retirement community.

"The two radio scanners pick up all transmissions to the various listed departments and our dispatcher can send patrol units where it is deemed necessary," Sorenson explains. Posse patrols respond to all fire calls, all medical calls and all accidents in Sun City. In addition, five duty officers' patrol cars also are equipped with scanners and have direct contact with the sheriff's department. The posse also has a mobile communications unit that has proved useful in search and rescue and disaster operations. It has responded to numerous requests for aid in emergency missions in other localities.

There is a degree of fuzzy thinking even among old-time residents of Sun City as to the full extent of the posse member's powers. "Although we are a separate, non-profit organization, we operate under the direct authorization of the office of the sheriff of Maricopa County and are subject to call when needed to assist the sheriff's office — in or out of Sun City," Jack Sorenson explains.

When the recruit has passed his training course, he is issued a badge as a genuine deputy sheriff of Maricopa County. He has to pay for this badge at the time of issue,

but if he resigns or forfeits membership, he must return the badge and its cost is refunded. These badges are controlled by the sheriff under a strict accounting system. The reasons would seem obvious.

As suggested some pages back, it is not the mission of the deputies to go looking for trouble. "We don't really want any adventurers or frustrated soldiers of fortune," is the way Sorenson explains the mission. If there appears to be a serious problem that could prove dangerous to either the posseperson or other Sun City residents, the sheriff is notified immediately so his professionals can take care of the situation.

"After all, we're smart enough to know that a 75-year-old man on patrol isn't likely to have much success as a one-man SWAT team," Sorenson jokes...but he means what he says.

Yet each of the local duties the deputies carry out in Sun City come from techniques that have been given a lot of thought and planning over the years.

Take that vacation watch, for example. It goes beyond the normal door rattling associated with such checks.

If a home is to be unoccupied for an extended period of time, the resident can fill out a vacation watch card ten

Not all members of the Sun City Posse carry firearms, but a firing range now is owned by the organization for this type of training.

days prior to leaving and the posse will check the house periodically while the owner is away. The lack of burglary problems in the community proves the success of the program and residents are quick to utilize it.

Not all operations are a total success, however. Jack Sorenson tells of one incident wherein neighbors reported they had not seen an elderly resident for several days. Posse members checked out the home and found it locked up. There was no sign of life within. The woman resident had a history of illness and concern soon developed that she might be locked in the house, either too ill to answer the doorbell or possibly had died.

After due consideration, the deputies broke in the door only to find the house empty. It turned out later that the woman had gone to California to visit her daughter and had neglected to inform both the posse deputies and her neighbors.

"She later threatened to sue us for the cost of a new

Instructors and range personnel for the firing range are drawn from experienced posse personnel. The unit has a number of retired law enforcement and military people from which to draw. Law enforcement agencies use range, too.

The duty officer checks with a posseman before the latter starts his patrol. They serve as eyes and ears for the sheriff's department and call on that agency for help if they foresee a serious confrontation of any type ahead.

door," Sorenson recalls, "and she got it."

The posse, in conjunction with the sheriff's office, sets up neighborhood watch programs, too. What this means is that, basically, each neighbor watches the other's property. This type of program has been instituted in many cities and communities in one form or another and has been a great success in cutting down the number of burglaries across the nation. Neighbors, of course, are likely to be aware of strangers. The posse is called if a resident spots what might be a suspicious person in the immediate area.

Upon request of any Sun City resident, a trained posse team will visit the individual's home to check inside and out for security problems. Suggestions then are made to the resident as to how security of the property can be upgraded.

All of the commercial businesses and offices in Sun City have visible cards posted in their windows or doors, each carrying a coded number. Since most problems occur when the businesses are closed, this coded number enables the posse and the sheriff's office to locate the owner or his representative to help solve a problem.

As mentioned earlier, the Sun City posse receives no funding from the county, state or federal governments to aid in carrying out its programs. Instead, each October, a letter is sent to each Sun City homeowner asking them to support the posse with a contribution.

"Over the years, response to these requests has been most gratifying," says Jack Sorenson. "This generous support has allowed us to carry on our programs and to help maintain one of the lowest crime rates in the nation."

By now, readers probably are struggling with an obvious

question: If the Maricopa County sheriff offers support to this effort, what does he get in return? Can he expect support at the polls by the posse at election time?

No one can regulate the thinking and feelings of an individual member of the posse when it comes time to enter the voting booth, but the corporate bylaws governing the posse specifically ban any such activity as a body. The bylaws state:

This organization as such shall not attempt to influence legislation of the United States Congress, any State Legislature or any local council or similar governing body in any manner. Further, this organization shall not attempt to influence the public in any referendum, initiative, constitutional amendment or similar procedure.

This organization as such shall not participate or intervene directly or indirectly in any political campaign on behalf of or in opposition to any candidate for public office in any manner whatsoever.

Perhaps one posse member puts it more simply: "Sheriffs come and go, but we'll still be here. We're not interested in changing the world. We're just here to take care of the residents of Sun City, Arizona!"

All of this tends to bring us back to that firing range located on the outskirts of town.

The posse conducts what it calls a Second Man program. This means the volunteer is fully qualified to ride with a fulltime sheriff's deputy and take part in day-to-day law enforcement chores, furnishing backup.

It may well be that the marksmanship segment of this

Possemen make checks of the homes of vacationing people. More than 20,000 checks are made a year. (Below) Heart of the operation is this modern communication room.

If the posse member who holds a Second Man card fails to qualify, his card is pulled and he is scheduled for shooter improvement classes within three months. If the individual passes the shooter improvement class, he is slated for another qualification shoot.

If he fails the class, he has two options. He can be dismissed from the Second Man program or he can take the forty-hour weapons training program, again. If he still cannot qualify on the pistol and shotgun ranges, he will be dropped from the Second Man program. Actually, the posse's requirements go a bit beyond that. Any posseman who fails a firearms class is not allowed to carry a handgun until he — or she — qualifies with that handgun.

It should be pointed out, perhaps, that shotgun training is given only to those possemen who will be riding with regular deputies. No shotguns are carried in the posse's own vehicles.

In addition to the initial forty hours of weapons training, new Second Man candidates must undergo thirty-two hours of classroom instruction that ranges from mission of the sheriff's department and crime scene preservation to emergency first aid and traffic control.

A few years back, a great deal was being said about the Gray Panthers, that group of oldsters who still carried enough clout to be effective in elections. Sun City has a different type of Gray Panther. The residents may be retired, but that certainly does not mean they have given up any part of daily living. The average age of Sun City residents is reported to be 73, but most recognize that, if they keep busy doing something useful and productive, they'll add to their years.

Some of the Sun City posse members are more than 73 years of age. One woman deputy was driving a patrol car at 85. And while none of the posse members expect — or want — to be called for SWAT duty, they realize they are performing a needed service to their neighbors — and themselves.

training is the simplest part of the Second Man qualification course — and it's not easy! To qualify as a Second Man, the posse member must qualify annually with handgun and shotgun. A minimum handgun score of 210 points is required to qualify. In the case of shotguns, the candidate fires both buckshot and slugs and must come up with a passing score.

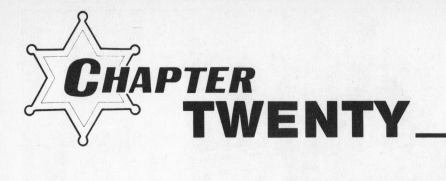

CHAPTER TWENTY

SPECIAL OPERATIONS UNITS

For Public Relations Purposes, They Go By Various Non-Violent Names, But The Purpose Doesn't Change!

SWAT teamers are taught that a good rifleman always uses a rest and that he should be able to improvise when a human life may well be at stake.

In the anti-sniper mode, Sergeant Jim Calvert is ready for business atop a building. This is what all the practice is about. The brass tacks reality is that his first shot with the rifle must be one of total accuracy.

THE FORMATION of special purpose tactical squads evolved from a simple premise: A team of highly motivated and well conditioned individuals especially equipped and trained to function as a tactical unit can be more effectively and safely employed in an enforcement confrontation than a larger group of people not so trained and equipped. It is believed that, in confronting a criminal or terrorist element with such a superior force, any inclination to use violent resistance will be discouraged.

This is a sound military tactic and simply calls for the concentration of overwhelming force when and where it is needed. The more powerful the application, the sooner the confrontation will be over and the potential for danger ended.

The general public doesn't understand this tactic; at least, not when used by police officers. For this reason, police departments often have different names for such groups which, if not benign, are at least innocuous: Special Employment Unit, Stakeout Squad, Quick Response Unit and others. My favorite semantical label is Emergency Rescue Squad, which leaves the impression the unit is involved in humane activity. Such names go down better with a sensitive public, and using them is a legitimate form of word-mandering.

Anyone should realize that the mission of a police department is to enforce the law, and a SWAT team is still a SWAT team by any other name.

My police experience pre-dates the advent of SWAT, which gives me a special appreciation for such units. As indicated in another chapter, I know how badly a situation can deteriorate and have been involved in several of them. In another publication, I once wrote I'd rather have a pocket full of quarters to phone the SWAT team than to have any amount of extra ammunition to deal with these hairy incidents on my own. When you need a specialist, call a specialist. It sounds like a flip remark, but I say it in earnest.

When a SWAT unit eventually was formed in my department, I didn't volunteer for a variety of reasons that seemed good to me at the time — and still do. In light of my lack of experience in this area, I asked Sergeant James Calvert, a former SWAT squad leader, to fill me in on the details of how such units are formed and what it is they do. Through Sergeant Calvert I learned just what a SWAT member goes through and what he must know to be effective in the

Instruction in the use of helicopters for getting into hard-to-reach places is part of special ops training.

most critical sort of police work.

A SWAT squad is formed as a tactical unit and the squad leader is an officer from the command level with as much operational experience as possible. The leader is present at all training sessions in order to learn the strengths and weaknesses of his men.

According to Calvert, the team leader, ideally, should have the authority to schedule working hours, training sessions and standby duty. He should recommend the acquisition of new equipment and be present at all training sessions and when any of the group is activated.

The chief of police usually is responsible for committing the SWAT team once negotiations have failed in a high-risk situation. This type of situation is defined as an act of violence in which a police officer is at a distinct disadvantage and subject to danger. These situations include — but are not limited to — sniper attacks or other ambushes, barricaded criminals, riots, demonstrations or civil disorders and terrorist activities.

The team's goal is the successful resolution of hostage situations, protection of bystanders, the apprehension of suspects and the restoration of normal community life with minimal property damage. SWAT is employed only in situations that exceed the capabilities of on-duty police personnel. Once the chief has committed the team to action, control switches to the SWAT leader. Naturally, his decisions, leadership abilities and judgment assume added importance during a high-risk scenario.

Few, if any, officers are assigned to SWAT work. Each team usually is made up of volunteers because of the personal danger they may encounter. The rigorous demands of the job require top physical condition, so flat bellies and hard muscles are the rule.

Every man has three to five years experience in law enforcement and is familiar with department policy and regulations. The ranks of the usual SWAT team are swelled disproportionately with combat veterans of the U.S. armed forces. Such people are used to working and relying on group effort and understand the value of discipline. All have been taught military movement, concealment and tactics and are familiar with weapons.

It may sound discriminatory, but identity of both hostages and target are so important that persons with eyeglasses or contact lenses are excluded, at least, in some special operations units. Glasses can be broken, or they may reflect light at a critical moment. Non-smokers are preferred, because smoke or light can give away a position, and many smokers become nervous or may cough at an inopportune time.

Lone wolves and Rambo heroes are not welcome. The SWAT member's ability to get along well with others in the group is an important consideration, since teamwork is necessary. Most departments insist on psychological testing of applicants.

Rappeling from a hovering helicopter requires special training, equipment not available to some departments.

members. In larger cities, there may be several such squads in order to provide round the clock availability.

Regardless of the number, at least two men always should work together for mutual protection and support. The squad should be a flexible entity with members cross-trained in most skills and the use of all weapons. Hostage or barricaded-felon situations receive most of the publicity, but a really flexible, well trained team can handle dangerous arrests, raids, stakeouts, sniper situations, VIP protection, rescue situations and bombings.

Before the SWAT team was implemented in my department, I handled many of these assignments myself, as an individual officer working alone. This is particularly true of raids, stakeouts and VIP protection. Speaking from experience, I know these duties are really more than a single officer can handle alone, and teamwork is better in that it's more effective. Raids always demand more than the single officer. Stakeouts can be managed alone, if necessary, but the check list in protecting important people is too extensive for one officer to handle.

In all SWAT units the "shooter," or rifleman, has the highest profile. His function is to give accurate, effective fire when called upon; consequentlyly he's the best marksman on the team. As a rule, he's equipped with a bolt-action rifle with telescopic sight and a sling.

The bolt-action configuration tends to stress fire control and reliance on the one-shot effort. There are a number of semi-automatic models, of which accuracy is outstanding, and they are well qualified for use as sniper rifles. But as pointed out elsewhere, they have the disadvantage of high cost without delivering superior tactical performance; purchase can't be justified in most departments.

Most SWAT units are using bolt guns with free-floating bull barrels, with the action bedded in fiberglass. With no intention of insinuation, the ordinary "varmint" version of popular rifles is ideal. SWAT work can be rugged, but in most cases the rifle is well protected in a padded storage case and need not be of indestructible military configuration. Typical SWAT rifles are based on the Model 700 Remington, Ruger Model 77 or Winchester Model 70 sporting rifles, and may be equipped with a barrel of varmint dimensions and a bipod.

Caliber selection is critical, and should be based on what *may be required,* as well as current requirements. An accurate, flat-shooting varminter may not be enough gun. Some SWAT units with which I am familiar have selected rifles for accuracy alone, and have come to regret that decision.

They were using the 6mm Remington cartridge in the belief it held a slight accuracy edge over other calibers. This may indeed be true, but the variety of ammo available for the 6mm is limited to JSP hunting rounds. In some SWAT situations, different bullet configurations may be required.

By contrast, the ammo for the .308 (or 7.62mm) cartridge comes in infinite variety, since it is a popular sporting cartridge as well as a former U.S. military round. The added recoil over any 6mm should not bother any seasoned rifleman, and the shooter has a choice ranging from match ammunition to tracer.

Ball ammo offers greater penetration and straight-line performance on thick window glass, automobile bodies and other materials often used as barricades. Long shots

Because the U.S. is a multi-cultured society with many ethnic groups, the SWAT team will benefit from having men of various racial and ethnic groups. At this time, I'm not aware of any female SWAT personnel, though the women are well represented in other areas of police work. No doubt this current exclusion will change as time goes by.

The size of a SWAT team depends upon a department's needs, the geographical location and population and whether the area is urban or rural.

Depending on the locale, crime rate and frequency of incidents, SWAT teams can range from three to eight

SWAT leader Jim Calvert sights in his Ruger M77 .308 from the bench, using every type of available ammo, then recording the zero for each type. The rifle has been glass-bedded for ultimate accuracy for sniper use.

are rare in SWAT work, with a majority falling in the fifty- to hundred-yard category. If a long shot is required, the .308 shoots flat enough for the purpose and offers excellent downrange performance.

The SWAT rifleman should be familiar with the ballistics and trajectory of any cartridge used, in the event a long shot is required. One-hole groups at fifty yards are not enough to qualify as a SWAT rifleman. He must be able to read the wind, mirage and temperature. In short, he must display all the skills necessary to a rifleman shooting for the highest stakes of all — a human life.

The cover rifleman has an equally important task, which is to provide cover fire for the team in the event of an opposing sniper or snipers. In the worst situations — riots or insurgency, for example — he can keep the unit from being overrun. He should be armed with a semi-automatic rifle with open sights for a quicker, if less precise, sight picture. For logistical reasons it should be the same caliber as the rifleman uses. If we're talking semi- or full-auto, this alone will limit choices to a few carbines or assault rifles.

To illustrate, there aren't many semi- or full-auto rifles in .22-250 caliber! The cover man's weapon likely will be a .308 (7.62mm) or .223 (5.56mm).

The squad defense man serves a similar purpose, being responsible for close range defense in the event of a sur-

prise assault by one or more opponents. He'll be equipped with a 12-gauge shotgun — pump or semi-auto — preferably with an extended magazine. He will have a good supply of buckshot and slugs for longer ranges.

The shotgunner serves a dual purpose when raids are conducted. Heavy, rifled slugs unlock doors better than a key when entry is desirable. They can disable a lock or take the hinges off most residential doors. Special slugs for this purpose usually are made of sintered (powdered) lead. On striking its heavy blow, the slug then breaks up into harmless dust which won't travel far. Many other special projectiles are offered in the 12-gauge hull. Flares, delayed fuse bombs and magnesium "fireball" rounds offer incredible versatility to the shotgun.

The grenadier or gas man forms the final element of the unit. His job is to deliver tear gas or other chemicals when needed. Smoke rounds can provide cover or create a diversion for team movement. He should be provided with a gas gun and an assortment of projectiles, as well as grenades carrying gas or smoke.

The circumstances of any given situation will dictate the manpower, equipment and weapons of the squad. It could be that a squad will be organized differently.

For example, if the squad is used as a cover team, it might consist of two riflemen, two cover riflemen and a

When possible, SWAT riflemen practice their trade at extreme ranges. Rifleman Cas Donnel fires at 1000 yards, using a concrete pit situated on a nearby military range. Most military bases tend to cooperate in such training.

defense man. If organized as an assault unit, the armament will run heavily to short shotguns, submachine guns and stun grenades.

A situation of this type offers probably the only legitimate use in law enforcement work for submachine gun or full-automatic fire. As a matter of practicality, few SWAT teams rely heavily on submachine guns; at least, those from municipal police departments. The submachine gun is difficult when it comes to training, and they eat up prodigious amounts of ammo. It's true that full-automatic fire will clean up a room full of terrorists in short order. Whether it does that better than a shotgun is a matter of opinion. For sheer "throw weight" and number of projectiles delivered on target in a given time frame, the shotgun wins, hands down.

SWAT handguns vary widely and may be carried in a shoulder rig or leg holster, depending on the SWAT member's job tasks and shoulder weapons. Departments that issue revolvers may insist their SWAT personnel use the issued handgun. In most cases, this will be a .357 magnum, either Colt or S&W.

I know of no SWAT unit carrying the .38 Special — but there probably are some. This particular caliber has recently received a shot in the arm with the introduction of superior factory loads and a few exotic rounds such as Glaser and MagSafe. They can be particularly useful in SWAT applications.

As an emergency and secondary reaction weapon, the revolver still is a viable choice in handguns. In compensation for the limited six-round capacity, it offers smoother, quicker handling than most autos and almost complete reliability.

However, not all police departments in which the revolver is general issue require SWAT personnel to use it. Realizing that SWAT members are more familiar with weapons than the average officer, administrators allow a

The Pepperfogger is a standard piece of SWAT equipment that can fill a building with smoke or tear gas in a matter of seconds. It also can be used outside, when there is the need to disperse a crowd that is unruly.

wide assortment of sidearms. The San Antonio SWAT personnel most often carry 9mm autos in place of the usual S&W M65 .357 revolver. Since there are many good-quality, high-capacity autos in that caliber, there is no standard brand. Some of the men wear Browning P-35 Hi-Powers; others have more modern guns such as the newer S&W double-action autos in 9mm.

The caliber was chosen for good reason — at the time, the 9mm was the only chambering available in high-capacity autos. Today, we have the .40 S&W autos with large magazine capacities and even a couple of .45s — the Glock and the Para-Ordnance each holding fourteen shots. As yet, none have been adopted, and the SAPD SWAT members cling to their 9mms. Is there any reason to change?

Only a few years ago, I'd have argued in the affirmative.

The reason for a SWAT pistol is close-range smashing power. Anyone knows the .45 ACP excels at this and is twice as effective as the 9mm. Even the .40 S&W beats the 9mm by a large margin. Today, though, the handgun power problem is no longer a one-way street leading to larger bores. It could be that new developments in ammunition make the 9mm an equally lethal proposition.

The new trends in 9mm ammo can be categorized into three classes: subsonic loads, +P loads and the exotic MagSafe loads. The subsonics made by several manufacturers have similar characteristics. All bullet weights hover around 147 grains and the muzzle velocity is about 950 feet per second.

Winchester developed the load for Navy SEAL teams who wanted a more accurate cartridge for their shoulder fired weapons such as submachine guns. The longer bear-

Gas masks are included in SWAT equipment and it becomes imperative that personnel train in proper employment.

ing surface of the heavy 9mm bullet contributes to outstanding accuracy, which is true of all brands of ammo using this bullet. Thanks to greater sectional density, penetration is increased over the usual 115-grain 9mm bullet. This is a bullet that will shoot through a lot of meat, if you need that.

After the 1986 FBI shootout in Miami in which two agents were killed and several wounded, the FBI temporarily adopted the Winchester 147-grain load in place of the 115-grain Silvertip. The story was that the Silvertip gave inadequate penetration. Actually, it performed about like it should, but the FBI condemnation set off a great outcry for more penetration.

Several police departments have adopted the heavy subsonic loads. They are mild to shoot, highly accurate and penetrate like crazy. Sadly, this hasn't translated into good street performance. What you have is a +P heavy bullet .38 Special; no great shakes as a manstopper.

The best of the subsonic 9mms probably is the Remington 140-grain scalloped-jacket revolver bullet with lots of exposed lead. This was designed originally as a practice load that would minimize damage to steel targets, and is labeled as such.

When introduced by Remington, this R9mm7 practice load carried the warning that it was not to be used as a com-

bat round, because the reduced velocity might inhibit expansion. Cops gave this the same attention they usually give to warnings, and used the round anyway.

As it turns out, the 9mm 140-grain practice bullet probably has a higher percentage of one-shot stops than any of the other subsonics. This performance still isn't up to what a really hot 115-grain JHP will produce.

The best SWAT application for the subsonics is exactly the same as used by Navy SEAL teams — greater accuracy in submachine guns and other shoulder weapons. The bullet will pick up a hundred feet per second or so in velocity, however, adding to the potential for expansion. This round offers compatability with 9mm sidearms and deserves consideration by SWAT units armed with 9mm long guns. Some optically sighted submachine guns are accurate enough for short-range sniper use. This ammo is a natural choice for those.

For years, the top velocities for the 9mm with 115-grain to 125-grain bullets were in the 1100 feet per second range. American ammo manufacturers were guided by SAAMI specs that called for a chamber pressure not exceeding 35,700 copper units of pressure. This limited velocity. The 9mm was stopped at the threshold of true performance, which begins to occur at about 1200 fps. The difference that a hundred feet per second can make is astonishing.

Typical SWAT rifles are bolt-actions fitted with the best of scopes and a bipod. In rough terrain, a bipod can lift the rifle above tall grass or rocks and steady aim of the rifleman. Bipods should have adjustable legs.

With bullets leaving at only 1100 fps, the 9mm is a barely adequate mid-level cartridge.

Given a muzzle velocity of 1250 feet per second, the bullets arrive on target with sufficient remaining velocity to expand violently and penetrate deeply. These velocities have been reached before, of course, but always with lighter-than-standard bullets in the 95-grain range. They offer violent expansion, but not always sufficient penetration.

Remington's R9mm6 load is a +P cartridge utilizing their excellent 115-grain JHP bullet at some 1250 fps in pistols. This is .38 Super performance, a cartridge long thought to be superior to the 9mm. Original .38 Supers carried a 130-grain FMJ bullet at 1275 fps, but in later years it has been watered down to a point almost equalling standard 9mm loadings at 1100 fps.

Owners of the 9mm pistols can switch to the Remington loads of +P rating and equal the on-target performance of many big-bore handguns. Expansion and penetration are there, along with the energy to dump an opponent fast. SWAT application is obvious: Here's a hot round well suited to pistol and submachine gun use.

With MagSafe rounds, all the older calibers that have endured abuse as weaklings finally have come into their own. It may be too much to say that MagSafes make bore diameter irrelevant, but that statement isn't far off the mark. The cartridges I'm thinking of are the .380 ACP, the 9mm Parabellum and the .38 Special. All have been cursed as "too little" in the past, but now are serious propositions, indeed.

MagSafes achieve their effectiveness through intelligent bullet design and extremely high handgun velocity. Speed alone is no killer, as several well known experimenters

have proven. When coupled with a properly designed bullet, however, it is the answer to handgun stopping power. Inventor Joe Zambone used twenty years of research to find the perfect design — and he may have achieved that goal. Development continues, however, and new designs with new configurations and ever-increasing velocities are emerging.

The MagSafe bullet is a copper jacket with the lead melted out. Lead is too heavy for what Zambone had in mind. A plastics and epoxy background told him such material could be made to perform well, while allowing much higher velocities. MagSafes could be produced more cheaply by using commercially available copper jackets. Zambone prefers to select a bullet with the proper nose configuration, then melt the lead out in an oven. This renders the copper dead-soft while getting rid of the heavy metal inside.

The lead then is replaced with a special epoxy of a gummy texture. Large birdshot pellets such as number 2 and number 4 are layered carefully inside this mass of plastic, which is capped with a fast-drying, hard epoxy of a different chemical nature. The result is a bullet that is quite light for the caliber and can be driven to high speeds with a large charge of fast burning powder. Zambone conducts on-going experiments with powders in an attempt to increase velocity and reduce muzzle flash.

Many MagSafe loads have little or no muzzle flash, which together with the light recoil from the mini-weight bullet makes a superb fighting cartridge.

Penetration? Always before, light bullets lacked sufficient penetration to be effective. Zambone didn't repeal any laws of physics; he just bent them to his advantage. Light bullets stop quickly in flesh, sometimes short of vital organs. All but the MagSafe lack killing power. This bullet impacts with terrific velocity, from 1400 to more than 2000 fps in ordinary pistol barrels.

The light copper jacket is slowed quickly, but before it does, it makes a huge permanent surface cavity. The drag of flesh slows it down rapidly, but the jacket is only a container for the mass of epoxy and birdshot pellets. As the jacket shreds to pieces, this cargo is hurled forward through the target, free of any drag — the jacket took most of that friction — and the epoxy and pellets drive onward without hindrance. They are, in fact, given added boost to drive deeply. This factor is what makes MagSafes deadly.

For sake of illustration, consider the shaped charge used in RPGs and anti-tank projectiles. Zambone has harnessed the shaped charge effect to a handgun bullet.

Because the bullet is light, MagSafe recoil is low in spite of high velocity, allowing fast follow-up shots. Muzzle flash ranges from negligible to non-existent. Penetration? Consider the .38 Special +P+ Agent load which drives a 56-grain bullet at more than 1910 fps in a two-inch Chiefs Special.

In a three-inch barrel it posts 2020 fps and even higher in four-inch service revolver barrels. This load defeats Level II-A soft armor, and will blow you out of your socks if wearing such a vest.

The .380 LTD uses a 52-grain bullet that gives 1720 fps in pistol barrels of the usual .380 length. I consider this tiny little round the equal of a .45 auto round — and it may be even more effective.

The news is equally good for 9mm users. MagSafe's 9mm #9KD load pushes a 52-grain frangible bullet to 2120 fps in the Glock M17, and over 2000 in the S&W M469. It penetrates Level II-A body armor and, after penetrating, drives to a depth of six inches in ordnance gelatin. This is only one of several destructive 9mm loads available to SWAT teams and other police officers.

Most centerfire rifle cartridges operate at speeds far in excess of 2000 feet per second and need no help in expanding. MagSafe offers these bullets in .308, however, due to their tendency to fragment into harmless particles when striking concrete. They are ricochet proof.

Accuracy in handguns and rifles alike is comparable to the best JHP bullets, because until it strikes the target, the shot-laden epoxy core is a solid mass bonded to the inner jacket walls. The jacket can't rotate around the core to cause wide fliers.

Zambone loads MagSafe bullets in all popular — and a few unpopular — handgun calibers. The jury is still out on the rifle-caliber MagSafes, but the handgun cartridges are unquestionably the most destructive available to SWAT teams.

Ironically, shooting gets most of the attention, but SWAT teams strive to end every situation without casualties on either side. According to Sergeant Calvert, doing nothing may be the best tactic of all, once the scene is isolated. Time is on the side of SWAT.

Barricaded suspects or hostage-takers are human, too, and time takes its toll on them. Hunger, thirst or just plain fatigue may cause them to surrender. Nobody rushes into action.

There is a time for action, however, usually in hostage situations. If a frustrated gunman begins taking innocent lives, an assault is launched quickly. It will come as a sur-

While there is an effort to market such submachine guns as the Heckler & Koch MP5 10mm to law enforcement for special operations use, many feel this is over-gunning.

prise, and is conducted with overwhelming force. Whenever possible, a negotiator will be present to deal with a hostage-taker by phone or other means of communication. When and if he fails, the SWAT leader makes the decision to attack. The negotiator is not notified, lest a change in voice inflection or other subconscious signal be revealed in his speech. The assault comes as a surprise to the negotiator as well as the felon.

Once a SWAT team is committed to an assault, it's usually over quickly. This is the only time in police work that gives the advantage to the officers involved. In the usual police shooting, it's the officer who must react to a shot fired at him or a pointed gun. He must come from behind timewise and his reaction time works against him. In the SWAT assault, the shoe is on the other foot, and the felon bears the burden of reaction time.

In any armed conflict such as the usual street gunfight, a person has a reasonable chance to win the fight if he reacts quickly. However, it is quite useless to resist overwhelming force, regardless of how fast one's reflexes are. A single felon has no more chance than a rat caught in the open by two rat terriers. Once the action begins it is incredibly swift and doesn't last long.

In SWAT work, only the objectives never change. Preventing loss of life on either side, protection of property, and lawful resolution of violence are the goals. To accomplish this, tactics and equipment are changing and evolving continually.

Just as there are no set scenarios, there is nothing written in stone for a SWAT team. A continual search for better tactics and weapons makes such SWAT teams more effective than ever before.

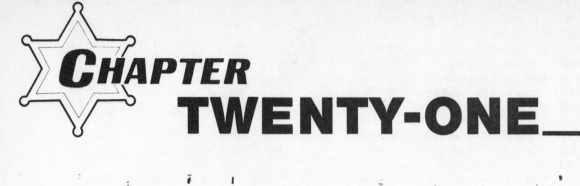

CHAPTER TWENTY-ONE

ONCE A COP, ALWAYS A COP

The Police Service Agent Doesn't Carry A Gun, But He Makes Life Easier For Those Who Do!

The main security desk at central police headquarters in San Antonio is staffed now by police service agents. The desk controls building access and handles security with the aid of remote control cameras, electric locks.

"**T**HE POLICE Service Agent Unit is an element of the Support Services Division of the police department. It operates through a systems framework that provides service and support for both law enforcement and the public. The unit is charged with the responsibility of performing desk duties at police substations (precincts). In fulfilling this responsibility, the Police Service Agent processes police reports, expedites certain categories of police reports, provides building and grounds security, provides information to the public, functions as a alternate information channel, provides courier service, and screens persons entering police facilities."

Persons with the job described above — taken directly from the manual — are the latest wrinkle in modern law enforcement. Their assignment is to take over routine paperwork and other duties that eat into the police officer's time. The effect is to put the officer back on the street where he can actively fight the rising tide of crime.

It has been estimated that only two percent of the average officer's duty hours are devoted to actual crime suppression. To perform the time-consuming administrative tasks, the service agent need not be a sworn police officer. In fact, the ranks are filled with retired officers, many of whom no longer are certified. A service agent must, however, have two years of experience as a law enforcement officer and

Patrick C. Sandeval is an able administrator and head of the Police Service Agent Program in San Antonio. The program orginated in this Texas city, but the concept spread to other local law enforcement agencies.

possess a working knowledge of the law and police procedure. The personnel roster includes both sexes. It also may include certified police officers from other states who are not currently with a police agency. This is a civilian position, but one best managed by those with law enforcement backgrounds. Usually the service agent is not a sworn officer, but is, nonetheless, tied subtly into the system.

Sometimes, the relationship is not so subtle. The duty can best be described as "Barney Miller at the front desk." Each substation or precinct headquarters is assigned a service agent who performs desk duties once reserved for the archetypical "desk sergeant."

He deals directly with the walk-in public, most of whom believe he is a police officer in mufti. The public-at-large is blissfully ignorant of distinctions between police personnel, and has enough trouble distinguishing between municipal officers and sheriff's deputies. Their problems range from petty civil matters to real trouble, all of which the service agent is expected to handle in an appropriate manner. It's by no means rare for a disturbance or fight to break out in the lobby. When it does, this requires the attention of uniformed personnel.

As an example, let's use a police department with which I am intimately familiar. The main headquarters is located

in downtown San Antonio, the substations situated in outlying residential areas. The old Report Message Center or RMC at central headquarters — once staffed by a single sergeant or uniformed detective — has been transformed into the "security desk." The new desk is larger, handles more duties and is staffed by at least two police service agents at all times. It contains the Telets machine for receiving and sending Telets messages, surveillance cameras and two computer terminals. The agents manning the desk control numerous door locks and have control of building access. When not providing information to the public, they deal with reports and screen persons entering the building. The municipal courts and other governmental agencies are in the same building, so the security desk is a busy place during daylight hours.

Substation duties are similar, but are handled by a single service agent. The subs are manned twenty-four hours a day by lone agents working A, B and C shifts. These correspond to, but are not exactly the same as the police shifts.

Service agents on A shift work mornings from seven o'clock to three o'clock in the afternoon. At three, the B shift takes over and the single agent works until eleven o'clock at night. He's relieved by the C-shift agent who

Remote television cameras guard police headquarters. Stan Lerma, a police service agent, activates controls, door locks, computer terminals, all within his reach. Many service agents are from retired police ranks.

remains until seven the next morning.

Substation desks run the length of the foyer, with a single locked door to permit or limit access from the front. The desk is equipped with a police radio, computer terminal, FAX machine and typewriter. The lobby is designed for public access, and the working machinery sits behind and below the counter.

Service agents will handle some types of walk-in complaints and write the reports. Although not sworn officers, they have badge numbers and are authorized to take police reports when a sworn officer is not required.

The service agent position is relatively new, and the majority of the public thinks of the agent as a police officer. This is a two-edged sword and doesn't always work to the agent's advantage. In the course of conducting business, the agent will communicate the fact that he is not a police officer, though he performs police functions and has a badge number. The agent assumes no police authority, and definitely does not attempt to deceive the public or impersonate a police officer. His is a civilian position. The agent has no power of arrest, and is not armed. The last not is a desirable situation, although it may seem so on the surface.

I retired from the San Antonio Police Department in 1980, and was a civilian for a decade. In April, 1991, I returned as a police service agent, having lost my state certification as a peace officer during the intervening years. I accepted the civilian position for a number of reasons, not the least of which is that I simply missed police work and the camaraderie of the organization of which I once was a part. As a police service agent, I'm again a part of that organization and do not feel diminished.

While I was a certified police officer, making the arrests and running the risks, I was nevertheless the first to realize that none of my derring-do and swaggering self-confidence would have been possible at all without the support personnel, who get no credit in the usual telling of police tales.

My life was saved on several occasions by police dispatchers, the unknown voice that sends a cop on his calls. They give you all the information they have, and try to get more before you arrive. There are no bad dispatchers, for bad ones don't last. By listening to events they become invovled, and are riding with you in spirit. When you are shot at, they flinch. When you are hurt, they feel the pain. When you are in trouble, they go into a mild panic, reading and anticipating your thoughts. If you are a rookie, they guide and direct you with no attempt to humiliate or belittle.

The dispatcher is a cop, and should have a badge num-

At a substation, Tom Ferguson contemplates a problem with a computer. Police service agents man the desks at all precinct stations in San Antonio. Many of them now are former street cops who are shouldering endless paperwork.

ber, too. He or she holds the power of life and death over a field officer through the dispensation of information. The dispatcher can send you on a call, and you must obey. Conscientiousness on the part of a dispatcher is assumed, but a bad one can send you to almost certain death, using nothing but a detached voice over a police radio. To their credit, they always choose life — for you, not themselves. A dispatcher can kill you with an address, but never does. It is a stressful job.

Dispatchers feel the tension, the pain and the terror of a policeman in trouble. When a policeman is killed, they go to the funeral. To quote an ancient poem: "They tearless stand at the graven stone, yet weep in the silence of night, alone."

For this, the dispatcher is paid civilian wages and treated no better than the man on the street who could care less about police officers or the important work he does — with the invaluable help of that dispatcher.

If you believe I approve of dispatchers, you are correct. If any officer thinks he can be such a hotshot without the dispatcher, he has another "think" coming and should examine his own character. If I had my way and wrote the checks, the dispatchers pay would be equal to that of the certified police officer.

The mechanic in vehicle maintenance would receive similar pay. I remember the time I had two high-speed car chases inside the city limits in a two-week period. The chases were long and dangerous, requiring every last bit of courage and staying power on my part. Yet none of my tires blew out, none of my emergency equipment failed and my car didn't let me down. My engine was tuned to perfection, and couldn't be heard idling from ten feet away. I had a

Substations — or precinct stations — have permanently assigned personnel who work out of that facility and seldom visit the downtown headquarters. Police service agents in such substations work closely with officers.

brake-light switch that killed the lights when I was sneaking around catching burglars.

After the last chase, I went to my police mechanic and thanked him from the bottom of my heart. He could have done a lesser job, but he didn't choose to do so. Any officer worth his badge will go to his garage mechanic and thank him with hat in hand. I have seen vehicles fail at high speed, and I don't want to see that again.

In some police agencies, the armorers are civilians. They fix the guns, order the best equipment their judgment and experience will allow — and have the safety of the officer uppermost in their minds at all times. To get the best for their men — the cops — they take on police chiefs, city council members and even the mayor in bitter budget battles no police officer could, or would hope to win. They usually are more experienced than police officers, and with

no obligation to do so, often advise and direct them in a proper fashion. Armorers often are retired police officers themselves — and wear the look. If you think I respect police armorers, I do.

Support personnel are as much a part of a police department as any hotshot officer who makes a hundred felony arrests per month.

One of my treasures is the fact that I grew up in a sort of Golden Age in police work. When I joined, professionalism was replacing corruption, and all the bad characters were leaving the department through age, retirement, death or dismissal. The men (no female officers then) I worked with, knew and trusted were of the highest types. It was a definite privilege to be associated with them, and to be one of them.

Even today, I'm occasionally approached by old-timers.

These days, Tom Ferguson serves in mufti instead of a uniform. On his service desk are a police radio, FAX machine, telephone and computer, as well as television screens used in conjunction with the remote cameras.

We shake hands and recall the old times. My department was among the last in the United States to accept federal funds. Our chief, Emil E. Petes, knew well that, when you accept federal money, you dance to the federal tune.

We had female officers and minority officers. The men and women who were police officers were not unblemished, but they were not washouts from society, either. We represented the community of San Antonio and we lacked much: Our vehicles were worn and old, our pay scale was low. We didn't even have enough shotguns to equip all the patrol cars. The list of what we did not have was long. The city tax base simply couldn't provide the things we needed. What we did have was character, pride and a code of honor.

Because the officers possessed this code, the department had respect. We rode alone, but never failed the code, regardless of circumstance. Rule number one was never to use any more force than necessary to effect the arrest. Rule number two was, once a prisoner was in handcuffs, he was

as safe as he would be in a church. No officer ever hit or abused a handcuffed prisoner. Rule three was never to stack charges to increase bail, or accuse a prisoner of an offense he did not commit. There were more rules; unwritten, but seldom violated.

Did we think we were some sort of glorious knights in white armor, defending society? You're damned right we did. What's wrong with being a white knight riding to the rescue? What is wrong with honorable behavior, except that most people don't practice it and we were in the minority?

The pistol never was our weapon; honor and respect were. Almost everyone knows it when they see it, and will submit to it. I put down two riots by myself, with command presence and dignity that no one dared violate. I have walked through hostile mobs whose members were so fearful of offending me their faces turned pale if they accidentally brushed my sleeve. Such was our reputation for handling the bad and defending the good.

No such situation exists today. Were we better men? Not by any means. I have come back to the police department after a ten year absence. A new generation is doing the job I used to do. Let me say with no reservation that they are far better police officers than I ever was — or any of my old comrades ever were. These officers are better educated in some ways, physically more capable and possessed of a higher I.Q and learning capacity.

The bad old days of affirmative action, when persons with felony records were hired, seems to be over. They were weeded out, and those who remain deserve the job. They include men and women of black, white, Hispanic and virtually any other race that makes up America. Individually, I respect them as police officers. To a person, they are better officers than I ever was.

But they are being betrayed in their efforts to be police officers and the lack is glaring. Not long ago, I read a report from one of these sincere young officers who had arrested a driver for operating a motor vehicle while his license was suspended.

This is not a penitentiary offense, yet the officer's report was *nine* pages of required detailed information. It must have taken several hours to complete. Officers object to the paperwork but take it in stride. Small wonder they have only two percent of their time for fighting street crime!

Today's officers face something officers of my time never did. Since 1960, the courts and lawyers have been diminishing the police officer's discretion and authority, garnering all power to themselves. The current crime holocaust is an accurate reflection of the police officer's lack of authority.

In the 1970s, legislators thought this feasible, especially when they eliminated requirements and used the police departments as a dumping ground and for job placement of incompetents. The result was inevitable, when you have dummies for cops.

Tactics quickly switched, but the jails filled up too quickly. Now they are overflowing, and no one knows what to do. The criminal justice system — by stealing authority from the police — has created chaos. Today's officer all too often is merely a report-taker and social worker.

Young men and women who are police officers today want to do a good job, but often are not permitted to do so. In my day, it was considered suicidal for a criminal to attempt to grab a police officer's gun. Now, it is an accepted event, and officers are forced to wear snatch-resistant holsters as a matter of course. They also endure verbal abuse when none should be tolerated. We were not better police officers in my day, but we were different. We had police brass who would back us up, as would the criminal justice system.

The problem started with such public relations ploys as the Los Angeles Police Department used in the 1950s. Their slogan became "To Protect and Serve." The police officer's job is not to protect and serve, it is to enforce the law. That's why we are called law enforcement officers.

On my first night as a police service officer, I took a phone call from an elderly black woman who complained she was under constant harassment by a group of illegal Mexican aliens living nearby.

She stated they often played loud music, paraded in the streets at late hours, broke her windows by hurling rocks, and cursed her when she appeared in the front yard of her residence. They also threatened her with bodily harm if she came in sight, even on her own property.

I gave the old woman a pep talk. I advised her that she didn't have to tolerate this harassment, especially by people who were in this country illegally. I advised her to stick up for her rights as an American citizen, and call the Immigration Service to have them deported.

A young police sergeant overheard my conversation and wanted to show his superior compassion and humanity.

"I suppose you would burn them out or lynch them!" he charged.

I replied in a way he didn't expect, and it startled him. "I am an American citizen and will take no harassment from people who don't even have a right to be in this country!"

The young sergeant looked at me as if I were a neanderthal. This man was a supervisor of police, but in his personal philosophy, would rather defend the transgressions of an illegal alien over the rights of an American citizen.

To cap off this sergeant's story, he was involved in a shooting shortly after our conversation and was hit by a man firing a shotgun. He wasn't seriously injured, but he didn't even fire back. Another, less humane cop had to do the dirty work for him, killing his assailant!

The idea for police service agents was originated by Police Chief William O. Gibson, of the San Antonio Police Department. In 1987, Gibson realized the great need to put certified officers back on the street to fight crime. He initiated this program and since that time it has been adopted by other cities nation wide.

Bill Gibson is a patrolmen's chief. I've known him since he was sergeant many years ago, and there is no man of my acquaintance better fitted to head the department. He has the welfare of the law abiding public at heart.

The Police Service Agent Program is new and there are many flaws. Police officers are jealous of their authority, and resent civilians taking over police duties. This applies even to retired officers. The thing about any police department is that, if you're in, you are in; if you are out, you're out. Young officers give short shift to old folks and past deeds — like youngsters anywhere.

In the Texas of today, only active peace officers may be armed. This is a state constitutional change made in 1974, when the state constitution was rewritten.

A police service agent is not authorized to carry a handgun. This is a tragedy in the making, and it's only a matter of time until an agent is killed. There is no provision in state law to arm them. It is a tremendous, culpable mistake to assign personnel to police duties, confronting a hostile public, without legally allowing them the means to defend themselves. It is no use designating the job as a "civilian" position. The police service agent deals directly with the public. The public believes he is a cop.

On duty in the substation, the service agent is a mother hen to the patrol officers. The station belongs to the agent, who is always present, but there is dual authority. A police sergeant or lieutenant is on duty, too. They work closely, and the agent is not subservient to the police officer. At the desk, I perform a lot of chores the officers would have to do themselves otherwise.

I get respect and I give advice. I'm still in the police biz in a big way!

A LOOK AT THE FUTURE

Law Enforcement Has Long Been Seeking The Ultimate Handgun Caliber. The .40 S&W Just May Be It!

This .40 S&W pistol has been developed at the Smith & Wesson Performance Center. It is a hand-fitted pistol along the lines of the Model 4006, but is equipped with a five-inch slide and barrel. It's a one-of-a-kind gun.

This is the standard Model 4006 from Smith & Wesson produced in .40 S&W.

SIG-Sauer has gotten into the act with the P229. Chambered for .40 S&W, it is a double-action-only model and is available in blued or stainless steel.

THE FORMULA for a popular, successful defense gun is easy. It should be reliable, light in weight for ease in carrying and have adequate — if not smashing — stopping power on human adversaries.

Almost a hundred years ago, the firm of Smith & Wesson thought they had that when they introduced the .38 Special Military & Police model, now known as the Model 10. The gun appeared just before the turn of the present century, and it reigned supreme in police holsters for the next six decades.

However, few experts would recommend the Model 10 today as the last word in sidearms for policemen, which brings up the question as to why it's no longer acceptable. If the .38 Special served so well for so long, why is a better gun/cartridge combination necessary?

The .38 Special — housed in a six-shot revolver — was enough gun in normal times for normal people. That era ended in the 1960s, and abnormality became the rule rather than the exception. Once rare, police shootings became commonplace. There was a golden time when police officers fired their sidearms to enforce the law. Today, more often than not, they fire them in self-defense rather than in the public interest. Police weaponry makes an interesting social commentary.

The .40 S&W — both gun and cartridge — met with instant acceptance, because it's what the shooting public and police officers wanted all along. In this chapter, Chuck Karwan discusses the development of the .40 S&W cartridge and the guns we now have to shoot it.

The .40 S&W and the Model 4006 pistol chambered for it were introduced by Smith & Wesson in January 1990. No other handgun cartridge in memory has ever created such a massive reaction in the firearms industry in such a short time as this cartridge. Within days, several other manufacturers promised handguns chambered in .40 S&W. The rush was on and it still hasn't abated.

Before we go into the many models of .40 S&W handguns on the market — or soon to be on the market — it might be a good idea to look into how this new cartridge fits into the Big Picture. Back in the Sixties, Jeff Cooper noted in print the excellence of the Browning Hi-Power 9mm pis-

The folks at Glock have been on top of the trend and were quick to introduce their Model 22 in .40 S&W. This is a double-action; the maker calls it the Safe Action.

tol — except for its punny round. He stated his wish for a Browning chambered for a "man-size cartridge." I believe it was also Cooper who suggested that a compromise cartridge half way between the 9mm and the .45 ACP might be the ultimate answer.

By the early Seventies, a ballistic genius, Whit Collins, had developed a wildcat cartridge called the .40 G&A. Made from a cut-off .30 Remington rifle case loaded with 180-grain, .401-inch, .38-40 bullets, the .40 G&A was loaded to velocities up to 1100 feet per second. Cooper declared the .40 G&A cartridge and reworked Browning Hi-Power pistol combination to be "the first feasible successor to the .45 auto." It combined a truly powerful cartridge with a large magazine capacity in a handgun of moderate size.

Nothing much happened with this promising cartridge until the Eighties, when Dornaus & Dixon developed what they hoped would be the ultimate combat handgun, the Bren Ten. This pistol was based on the design of the excellent Czech CZ-75 9mm pistol. It was to be the first to combine high power, large magazine capacity and a double-action trigger, all in one normal-size handgun. In the developmental stage, Dornaus & Dixon reportedly approached Jeff Cooper to ask whether the new pistol should be chambered for a cartridge like the .40 G&A that approximated the power of the .45 ACP or go for something even more powerful. Reportedly, Cooper opted for the more powerful choice and development proceeded in that direction. Thus, with the help of Norma, the 10mm Auto cartridge was born.

This was fortunate for fans of the 10mm Auto cartridge like myself, but it probably wasn't the best decision from a commercial standpoint for Dornaus & Dixon. They could not copy the CZ-75 and its magazine directly. Instead, they had to totally re-engineer the design for a longer, more powerful cartridge. Dornaus & Dixon went under and the Bren Ten pistol saw an early demise.

Fortunately, the excellent 10mm cartridge survived, largely thanks to the fact that Colt chambered it in a version of its Government Model, calling it the Delta Elite. As outlined in another chapter, the Federal Bureau of Investigation became interested in the 10mm — but only in a downloaded version — to fire a 180-grain bullet at only 950 fps. Smith & Wesson was one of the primary manufacturers competing for the FBI contract. Some of the R&D folks at S&W were aware of Whit Collins' original .40 G&A, as well as other development work along the same lines such as the wildcat Centimeter cartridge made from a cut-down 10mm case. They also were aware of the .41 Action Express cartridge that achieved major ballistics in a short cartridge that would function in many 9mm-formatted pistols.

As a result, S&W approached Winchester to do the final development work and production of a .40 (10mm) cartridge that would duplicate ballistics of the 10mm load desired by the FBI, but be short enough to fit into a 9mm staggered-magazine format. The result was the .40 S&W cartridge as we know it today.

Ironically, the FBI was not interested in this cartridge, even though it gave them everything they wanted ballistically — as well as larger magazine capacity than S&W

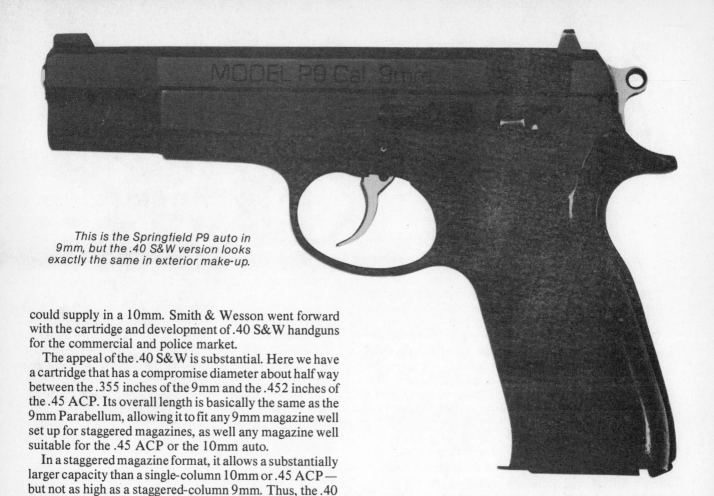

This is the Springfield P9 auto in 9mm, but the .40 S&W version looks exactly the same in exterior make-up.

could supply in a 10mm. Smith & Wesson went forward with the cartridge and development of .40 S&W handguns for the commercial and police market.

The appeal of the .40 S&W is substantial. Here we have a cartridge that has a compromise diameter about half way between the .355 inches of the 9mm and the .452 inches of the .45 ACP. Its overall length is basically the same as the 9mm Parabellum, allowing it to fit any 9mm magazine well set up for staggered magazines, as well any magazine well suitable for the .45 ACP or the 10mm auto.

In a staggered magazine format, it allows a substantially larger capacity than a single-column 10mm or .45 ACP — but not as high as a staggered-column 9mm. Thus, the .40 S&W is a compromise in regard to magazine capacity, as well.

Heckler & Koch didn't want to be left out of the .40 caliber sweepstakes. Their entry is called the P7M10.

Springfield Armory's Omega Match model has either a five- or six-inch barrel and now is available in the popular .40 S&W chambering.

Ballistically, the cartridge has energy, momentum, bullet weight and velocities close to those of the .45 ACP with a 180-grain bullet traveling at about 975 fps.

When selecting an auto pistol for use as a weapon, the choice often is between the power of a .45 ACP or the large capacity of a 9mm. In the .40 S&W, one gets nearly the power of the .45 and nearly the magazine capacity of a 9mm. Incidentally, ballistics, bullet weight and bullet diameter of the .40 S&W are nearly identical to that of the 1874 vintage .38-40 cartridge.

There is no question that the .40 S&W cartridge is a touch of genius from a marketing aspect. When applied to a staggered magazine pistol of the "wonder nine" variety, it offers a workable option to the seemingly endless debate over which is better — the large capacity 9mm or the .45 ACP? Fans of the .40 S&W will say neither and answer that a moderately large capacity .40 S&W is better than either.

The anti-9mm folks are saying here, at last, is a cartridge-handgun combination that finally will lay the "puny" 9mm to rest. The pro-9mm folks are saying the best high-performance 9mm loads already perform just as effectively as the best .45 ACP loads, so the .40 S&W is unnecessary. Worse yet, it holds less rounds than a comparable 9mm and recoils more. Only time will tell who is right. Enough people think it's a good idea, and the .40 S&W is here to stay.

The S&W Model 4006 was the first .40 S&W pistol to be announced, but it was followed quickly by the Glock Models 22 and 23. Ironically, the first .40 to reach the market seems to have been the AMT/IAI Skipper. As this is written, I know of no less than thirty-four different semi-automatic pistol models either in production or scheduled for production in the near future, all in .40 S&W chambering. The American Derringer Corporation also is offering its over-and-under Derringer in .40 S&W.

To no one's surprise, Smith & Wesson has embraced the .40 S&W cartridge to a greater extent than anyone else — with no less than nine different models.

The first, the Model 4006, basically is an all-stainless steel, heavy-duty version of the S&W 5900 series 9mm. As such, it is extremely comfortable in most hands, well balanced albeit somewhat heavy and features a slide-mounted hammer-dropping safety. Magazine capacity is eleven rounds.

This excellent pistol already has been adopted as standard by the California Highway Patrol and other police agencies. Keeping with S&W's policy of making their models to suit every taste, the same basic gun is available with a frame-mounted decocking lever as the Model 4026 and a double-action-only as the Model 4046.

Smith & Wesson also makes .40s in compact, lightweight versions. The model with a slide-mounted, hammer-dropping safety is the 4013. It features an aluminum alloy frame with other parts made from stainless steel. Magazine capacity is eight rounds. This light, flat little pistol is similar in size and concept to the familiar 3913 9mm or the 4516 .45 compacts. A double-action-only version is available as the Model 4053. There also is a blued carbon steel Model 4014 and a blued double-action-only Model 4054.

If all these weren't enough, the Smith & Wesson Performance Center also is making a couple of interesting .40s, including a version with a five-inch barrel and a longer slide to match, plus a competition model complete with muzzle brake. I am told that these are incredibly accurate guns, with beautiful triggers and tight tolerances.

Obviously S&W is committed to the success of this new cartridge.

Other handgun manufacturers also have lined up .40 S&W models of their own. In alphabetical order: Auto-Ordnance is offering their M1911A1 clone in .40 S&W. This modestly priced pistol makes for a cost-effective way to try out the .40, as well as a good basic gun for rebuilding into a competition gun.

Such guns as Springfield Armory's Trophy Master Competition model are available from company's custom shop in .40 S&W chambering, if desired.

So far, Colt is only offering its Double Eagle Officer's ACP in .40 S&W. However, a Colt spokesman told me the much-anticipated Model 2000 9mm also will be offered in .40 S&W, once it gets into production. The Double Eagle .40 is just like its .45 ACP brother, except it holds one more round in the magazine.

The Model 2000 is a completely new double-action-only auto with a staggered magazine and a polymer frame. The prototypes I handled had an extremely comfortable grip and looked to me like a splendid home for the .40. The 9mm version is expected to be available by the time you read this — with the .40 S&W following shortly after.

The folks at Glock thought so much of the .40 S&W cartridge idea that they put their 10mm auto and .45 ACP pistol on the back burner until they could field pistols in .40. Glock has two guns in .40 — the Models 22 and 23. Externally, they are identical to their Models 17 and 19 respectively, except for the caliber markings.

Besides the unique Glock trigger action and polymer frame, these .40s hold several other distinctions. Holding fifteen rounds in its plastic magazine, the Model 22 has the largest magazine capacity of all the .40s on the market, actually exceeding or equaling that of most high-capacity 9mms. The Model 23 is no slouch either, since it holds thirteen rounds and has the distinction of being the lightest .40 on the market at only 22.43 ounces, empty.

I have fired them both and found the recoil was notably heavier than their respective 9mm brothers, but still not harsh or uncomfortable in any way. The Glock .40s actually hit the market at about the same time as the S&Ws. As with the S&Ws, interest from law enforcement agencies has been high with the South Carolina Law Enforcement Division and the Missouri Highway Patrol, among others, adopting Glock .40s.

Heckler & Koch has announced the addition of the .40 S&W P7M10 to their line. Except for chambering, it appears nearly identical to the 9mm P7M13, using the same unique squeeze-cocking mechanism. As the model number would indicate, it has a magazine capacity of ten rounds. An insider at H&K indicated a possibility that the P7M10 never will see light of day, because they are working on an entirely new double-action pistol that could be chambered in .40. Time will tell.

While IAI, the old AMT folks, was the first to get a .40 on the market in their Skipper, they also were the first to introduce an entirely new pistol design in .40 S&W, the IAI On-Duty. This is a new staggered-magazine pistol featuring a double-action-only trigger that is remarkably smooth and light. The general mechanism of the pistol is of the Browning type with an external appearance somewhat reminiscent of the SIG-Sauer. IAI also offers their Hardballer in .40 S&W, giving this small but progressive company three .40s in their line.

The .40 S&W may totally kill the .41 Action Express cartridge. The only pistol now on the market in .41 AE is the KBI Jericho; now even that pistol will be available in .40 S&W. The Jericho is an Israeli-made gun that has the general design of the Czech CZ-75, except for a slide-mounted safety. I would be willing to bet good money the .40 will out-sell the .41 AE, though the latter has the advantage of being easily convertible to 9mm by changing only the barrel, magazine and recoil spring.

The Llama pistols imported by Stoeger will include no less than three .40 S&W models in the near future. One will be in Llama's series of M1911 clones that are currently available in 9mm, .38 Super and .45 ACP. Another will be built on the same frame as the excellent Llama M85 pistol. The last is reportedly a compensated competition gun also based on the M85.

Although the Bren Ten is long gone, as is its manufacturer, in a real sense, it is back again as the Falcon made by Peregrine Industries. Peregrine is making an absolute dead ringer of the old Bren Ten, except for a number of internal design improvements. The Falcon will be available in the original 10mm Auto, .45 ACP and .40 S&W. In spite of the rather substantial size of the Falcon, the magazine capacity in 10mm and .40 is only ten rounds.

It should come as no surprise that Ruger has added a .40 variation of its well-established P85, called the P91. It is so similar to the P85 that you have to look at the markings to tell the difference. Different from the standard P85 is a decocking lever in place of the safety on the P91. Pushing the lever down safely drops the pistol's hammer, but when pressure is taken off the lever, it springs back up, instead of staying in a safe position. There appears to be a trend toward this system, and it would not surprise me to see it become standard on all Ruger double-action autos.

Another company that has gone for the .40 in a big way is Springfield Armory. If your preference is single-action autos, Springfield offers their "Linkless" series in .40 S&W as well as 10mm. This is a clever spin-off of their M1911A1 clones of the ancient and honorable Government Model .45.

Externally identical to their standard M1911A1, the Linkless uses a solid cam for locking and unlocking the slide and barrel instead of a swinging link. The advantage of this system is that it allows the slide and barrel to remain fully locked together a bit longer in the firing cycle. It is a strong, durable system that renders excellent accuracy.

This same system also is used in Springfield's new Omega Match model, available in .40 S&W in both five- and six-inch lengths. The Omega Match is an upgraded version of the standard Omega that features a heavier slide assembly designed and manufactured in Germany by Peters. This would be an excellent selection for a wide variety of target-shooting games.

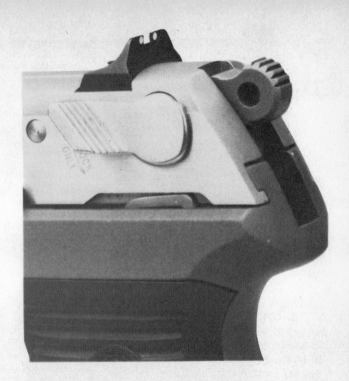

Ruger has introduced the P91DC model, which is the .40 S&W in a stainless steel decocker pistol. The decocking lever enables the shooter to uncock this cocked pistol without pulling the trigger. Capacity is twelve rounds.

A recently introduced Federal round for the .40 S&W has a 180-grain jacketed hollow-point bullet for efficiency.

If your taste runs to high-capacity, double-action autos, Springfield Armory also offers the P9 .40 S&W. The P9 is a clone of the CZ-75. In this case, the clone actually is better than the original, when it comes to fit and finish, as well as accuracy. A unique feature of the P9 is that it allows the user to carry the pistol either with the hammer down for a double-action first shot or cocked-and-locked (safety on) for a single-action first shot. In effect, one can treat it as either a single-action auto or a double-action.

Springfield Armory also has a custom shop that can supply either of the above guns in a wide range of variations for self-defense or target shooting, be it IPSC, bullseye, bowling pins, Bianchi Cup, Steel Challenge or what have you. The options and potential variations are nearly infinite.

SIG-Sauer has long been a major player in the defensive handgun and law enforcement market. Consequently, it is not surprising to find a .40 added to that line. Called the P229, the new SIG-Sauer .40 S&W is a dead ringer for the P228 9mm. However, there are a number of internal changes, foremost of which is a slide made from one piece of metal instead of being fabricated from a composite of stampings and milled inserts. The slide is somewhat heavier than that of the P228, as is the whole pistol. Otherwise, the P229 operates precisely like its 9mm brother.

There also will be a P229 double-action-only, as well as a model that combines an anodized aluminum alloy frame with stainless steel for the rest of the parts. As an indicator of how important the .40 S&W cartridge is considered by the SIG-Sauer folks, the P229 will be made in a new plant in New Hampshire.

The Spanish company, Star, has embraced the .40 S&W, as well. They have the distinction of offering the smallest semi-auto .40 on the market in their remarkable little Firestar M40. Externally, it is identical to their 9mm Firestar which is smaller than many .380 pistols. To pack so much power into such a small package is quite an accomplishment.

The Firestar M40 .40 S&W is made entirely from steel, so it is not the lightest .40. That distinction goes to the Glock 23. However, the Star M40 is the most compact. Besides, the weight comes in handy to help control the significant recoil of the .40 S&W cartridge.

Going against the current trend toward double-action autos, the M40 is strictly single-action in design. As such, it must be carried cocked-and-locked to be ready for action.

Star is about to offer the .40 S&W in their excellent M31 double-action staggered-magazine pistol; previously it was available only in 9mm. This under-appreciated pistol has some of the best engineering extant in its design. Manufacture and materials are excellent. The only negative is that the gun is a bit large for some people with small hands or short fingers. The Star M31 is a sleeper that deserves far more attention than it has received to date. The Star line is imported by Interarms.

Brazilian-based Taurus is known for offering some of the best dollar values in handguns. Their basic Model PT-92 9mm pistol has been fitted with a heavier, stronger slide, heavier recoil springs and other appropriate changes to make the new PT-100 .40 S&W pistol. This pistol also will have Taurus' new safety that includes a decocking function. This safety allows the pistol to be carried cocked-

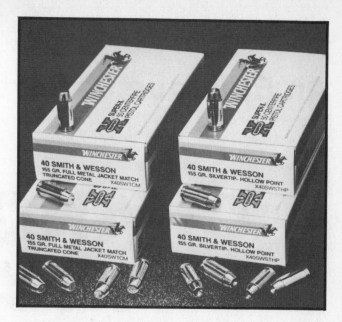

Winchester has two new loads for the .40 S&W. The first of the two new rounds is loaded with 155-grain Silvertip hollow-point bullets. The other round is loaded with the maker's 155-grain full metal jacket truncated cone bullet.

and-locked or it will decock the pistol without touching the trigger so that it may be carried hammer down, with the safety either on or off.

Along with the PT-100, a version with low-mounted adjustable sights will be introduced as the PT-101. Taurus currently is tooling up to manufacture the new pistol in their plant in Florida. As with the other Taurus handguns, I suspect these new .40s will offer top performance at moderate prices.

The TD Arms CZ-40 is a .40 version of the 9mm CZ-99 pistol that has been on the U.S. market for the last year or so. Made in Yugoslavia by the 133-year-old Zastava Arms Works, the CZ-40 is a heavy-duty pistol designed from the outset for long-term ruggedness and durability. In general layout and function, it is quite similar to the SIG-Sauer P226, but is a copy of that gun by no means. It features an aluminum frame, chrome-lined barrel and tritium glow-in-the-dark sights as standard equipment.

The CZ-40 uses a frame-mounted decocking lever like several other current autos. However, this same lever also serves as the slide hold-open and slide release — a clever setup. A couple of my friends own CZ-99 9mms and wax ecstatic over the performance and features. I suspect the CZ-40 will be more of the same.

It is amazing that there should be so many .40 S&W handguns introduced in just over a year's time. No other handgun cartridge in history — including such greats as the 9mm Parabellum, the .45 ACP and the .357 — has created such a stir in so short a time.

The .40 S&W story is not over, either. Beretta, Browning, Walther, Astra and Brno have not announced .40 S&W pistols for their companies, but it is virtually certain some will produce a .40 S&W in the near future.

An Epilogue Of Sorts...

CHANGES OF HEART

After Years Of Experience Where Angels Fear To Tread, The Author Would Do Some Cop Chores Differently!

As a young, hard-charging street cop, Tom Ferguson was convinced that surviving high-speed chases and going through windshields were all just part of the job.

MARK TWAIN, the famed author and humorist of the last century, said it best.

As a young man, he related he was convinced his father was almost certainly the most ignorant man alive. Later in life, after he, himself, had matured, Twain expressed surprise at how much the old man had learned during the intervening years.

Virtually all of Mark Twain's observations owe their popular appeal to the fact that we've all felt that way ourselves at one time or another.

Usually, the articles I write deal with a single topic — a gun or associated piece of police equipment. Since I began writing in 1977, there's been no real continuity; just whatever seemed urgent or appropriate at the moment. The single consistency has been to direct the column toward the young, inexperienced police officer; the one slandered throughout police history as "The Rookie."

All beginning police officers are rookies, and it takes about five years of hard duty to escape that quasi-derogatory classification. No ten-year veteran is apt to seek wisdom in these pages and the goal has been to speak to those who lack such experience.

I started to title this final chapter, *Things I No Longer Believe* and that still would be accurate. Naturally, when I list these things, there can be no continuity and it will emerge mostly as a list of rather negative "Don'ts!"

Probably these thoughts and advice were prompted by the recent deaths of several officers in my area, all in the line of duty; some of them were personal friends of long standing.

Without going into factual detail, I can say these deaths all were preventable, which makes the tragedies much worse.

I went through such a period once before, in the early 1970s. Shortly after the U.S. Supreme Court declared the death penalty unconstitutional, my department lost thirteen officers in thirteen months to gunfire.

The criminal revelry continued until the court reversed the opinion — and I learned something right then and there. Hardly more than a rookie myself, I came out of this period still on my feet, if not completely unscathed. With the stroke of an overeducated pen, the Supreme Court justices had cost our police department more casualties in a year than we'd suffered in the previous twenty-five! But that is politics. In the matter of street survival, there are a great many things an officer can do — or refuse to do — which will enable him to grow smarter as the years go by: Entry-Level Survival, if you will.

As a rookie cop, I not only walked where angels feared to tread, but I actively sought out places where trouble abounded. Young men are invulnerable, you know. For example, there is nothing so fine as a brand-new, well tuned police cruiser. It's almost a pleasure to chase a fleeing felon through city streets at one hundred-plus miles per hour, feeling the engine's power surging like a good horse at the touch of a spurred heel.

It is, in fact, exhilarating. We have the right to chase; we have the duty to chase; and, by God, we chase! It is far the most dangerous thing a cop ever does — guns, gangs and Uzis not excluded.

After wrecking three patrol cars and going through two windshields, I had a change of heart. Today, I still would chase — but only a little bit. After all, if you have a fatal accident, you'll never catch up.

My injuries had less effect on me than the accident I saw when a local doctor's big Lincoln, carrying six passengers, missed avoiding a bridge abutment. Now I have the memory of that scrambed-egg interior and a couple of scars on my right cheek to remind me. The lesson is — keep in sight the taillights of people you chase. Nothing more will be required of you and, sooner or later, your fleeing fugitive will crash himself. Nobody — felon or pursuing cop — can sustain high-speed driving indefinitely.

As a rookie, I did not envision myself as a gunman of any sort and I slung my service revolver in a crossdraw holster over my left kidney, where it would be out of the way while I performed my blue-shirt social work. The majesty of my badge would be sufficient, I knew, and I snorted at the idea of a snatch-resistant holster. Besides, I had two well proven fists.

Within short weeks of this decision, I was beaten thoroughly into a dazed condition by a stronger man and my gun was taken from me.

It took six of my comrades — rushing to my aid at the risk of their own lives — to rescue me. I think you could say I learned something right there, too. Were I assigned to the pavement today, I'd be wearing a snatch-resistant holster and brushing up on my boxing skills.

On no other occasion did I risk the lives of others to bail my foolish self out of a lethal situation. Remember, they have wives, families and better things to do. But the police fraternity is a strong one, bonded by danger, and officers must come if you call. Just make certain you give them a valid reason to come.

Let's suppose that somehow a people-hating, mis-anthropic dictator suddenly became a chief of police. If so, he could hardly devise a more debilitating, burdensome regimen than the average patrolman endures. Forget the work. The big problem is rotating shifts of ten or twelve hour days, followed by weeks of night watch, then more months of mid-watch.

No human body could adjust to such sleep patterns, and soon the poor cop is a hollow-eyed, stumbling ghost of his normal self. The intellectuals who know call it a disturbance of cycloid (or something like that) rhythms. It's more than discomfort; it is deadly, a form of endless jet lag that travelers suffer. No sick body can sustain an alert mind, and the reflexes and general health suffer. The organs deteriorate, the mind makes bad decisions. To a cop dealing with the public, a missed gesture of voice inflection can mean it is too late.

Combat veterans of World War II, Korea and Vietnam will tell you the same thing, regardless of age. "I was always so tired!", they say. It's the one impression they never lose — and some never get over it.

Staying alert is hard enough with a young, tough physique. Fortunately, police departments are beginning to realize the problem and many now offer permanent, non-rotating shifts. In addition, most have liberal vacation or time-off options that should be taken advantage of to the full extent.

Once, there was a great tendency to regard a police officer as just another civil servant — and to treat him accordingly. The truth is we never were delivering mail or reading water meters, even in less violent times. The extra stress imposed upon working cops is too incredible today to ignore any longer.

I used to be a tough guy, too, but I've had a change of heart. Today, I'd use my vacation time to relax and think things over rather than make a bad personal decision on duty.

Now in an administrative capacity with the police, he limits his handgunning to target practice, plus the evaluations of guns and ammo for gun magazines.

Acknowledgements

When I agreed to do this second edition of Law Enforcement Weapons & Tactics, I was full of confidence and had definite ideas on what the book shouldn't be. It wouldn't be a catalog of police equipment, and definitely not a manual on how to be a police officer. Such books are, at best, silly. When I began to ponder just what the book ought to contain, I realized rather quickly the scope was beyond the capability of any single individual. Police subjects are enormously complex. Law enforcement is more social work than anything else, and changes quickly. What can be written today may be obsolete by tomorrow.

I decided to touch only on those subjects most familiar to me, and enlist the aid of experts for the rest. That's the reason you'll find commentary by such men as Jim Andrews, a twenty-eight year veteran of the California Highway Patrol who has an encyclopedic knowledge of police subjects. Similarly, there are subjects covered by Walt Myers, a former chief of police and narcotics officer who has an astonishing career on which to base his comments. Chuck Karwan is an arms expert whose memory banks are accurate and unfailing. I often consult Chuck on police and weapons matters, and believe me, I'm not given to consulting anyone for anything! Dean Grennell supplied many of the photos here, which accounts for their excellence. As a former cop himself, Dean knows where I'm coming from. There are others who made this book possible, and to them I offer my heartfelt thanks. I hope that, together, we have compiled a book police officers will read. If we have done that, our goal is accomplished.

Most of all, editor Jack Lewis quite literally hammered this book together. When I lost patience, direction and tenacity, Lewis gently supplied it. Whether this book is a success or failure in the reader's judgment is a responsibility I'll be glad to assume. But in the writing of it, I came to be a wiser, better person than I was before, and I owe that to Jack Lewis.

Lastly, I want to thank the police officers of America who are exercising every available option in the fight against crime. Only the police officer realizes how thin is the veneer of civilization, how little it takes for society to descend into anarchy. If the lights ever go out in our country, though, the last gleam will be the reflection of a police officer's badge. The secret of a winner is to endure, and thanks to the uniformly good character of America's police officers, they can do that. Endurance is the one thing in police work that remains inflexible and never will change.